R00007 50435

D0672430

2/13

Style and Substance
Reading and Writing Prose

Style and Substance
Reading and Writing Prose

TRAVIS R. MERRITT

Massachusetts Institute of Technology

Harcourt, Brace & World, Inc.

New York / Chicago / San Francisco / Atlanta

© 1969 BY HARCOURT, BRACE & WORLD, INC.

All rights reserved. No part of this publication
may be reproduced or transmitted in any form
or by any means, electronic or mechanical,
including photocopy, recording, or any information storage and retrieval system, without
permission in writing from the publisher.

Library of Congress Catalog Card Number:
69–17153

Printed in the United States of America

Preface

The aim of *Style and Substance* is to challenge the student to think extensively about such matters as the nature and capacity of language, the relation between ideas and their expression, the significance of defining the audience, the meaning of "imagination." Writing and reading are presented as correlative acts, stressing the working relationship between the arts of composition and literary appreciation.

The chapters take up in turn the several kinds of practical analysis illuminating rhetoric and structure. Chapters One through Six move from the essayist's situation and purpose to the most concrete and localized features of his performance, culminating in two chapters on the difficult question of style. A chapter on value then draws upon all preceding chapters, suggesting the terms in which a student may judge performance, including his own. A final chapter in Part One gives experience in some depth of a single important essayist of diverse interest and talent: Aldous Huxley, chosen for his intelligence, his verbal power, the wholeness and consistency of his collective effort, the relevance of his writings to his time and our own.

The volume concludes with Further Readings, which can be profitably compared with those encountered in the earlier chapters. A special feature here is a cluster of writings centered on Stephen Crane's story "The Open Boat"; by studying this group of selections, the reader can discover useful relationships between narrative and other kinds of prose. These selections also provide an occasion for further critical writing within a regulated context.

Generally, the essays in this volume have been selected as much for a persistent quality of living argument and insight as for their uniform excellence. Although a number were written before 1900, the strongest representation is of the twentieth century, and particularly the decade just past. The interest is, in the main, rather specifically American. And because the editorial design is literary, the book contains many essays that deal directly with language and literature, a feature that should prove helpful to students learning to write critically.

120726

The questions and exercises are meant only as suggestions. If they have a special method or pedagogical claim, it is that they recurrently demand of the student-as-reader an honest critical examination of his own responses, and of the student-as-writer a written analysis of his own performance. This "reflexive" technique has value in leading students to that kind of self-consciousness in which speculation on the larger ends and means of literature is fused with a directed effort to master the art of writing well.

Too many persons have helped in this book either directly or indirectly to make it practical to list them here. Special thanks, however, go to Richard Ohmann, Wesleyan University; Laurence Perrine, Southern Methodist University; Edward P. J. Corbett, Ohio State University; Scott Elledge, Cornell University; and Owen Jenkins, Carleton College, for having provided especially helpful criticism and tactful encouragement.

Travis Merritt

Contents

A Narrative and Critical Response   392

Part One

The Elements of the Essay

CHAPTER ONE

Reading and Writing the Essay

The idea that "real" literature comprises poems, plays, and stories and that all other forms are secondary, or somehow less "real," is perhaps the most thoughtless of all the easy assumptions that too often affect our thinking about literature. According to this attitude, the lyric, dramatic, and fictive uses of language require an intensity of art and skill that one rarely finds in an essay, a historical account, a political commentary, or a biography. Students may be especially apt to accept this idea for the essay, since they are continually required to write about assigned poems, plays, and stories. The work of acknowledged masters is offered, seemingly, as an occasion for the students' own secondary, less expert and less original, efforts. Were it not for the one, the other would not need to exist.

To dispel the illusion that the essay is a second-rank literary form, we need only remember what it does. Like all literature, the essay records a reaction to experience, the persistent human attempt to organize and interpret what is seen, thought, and felt. In this shared enterprise, skill and imagination serve the essayist as necessarily as they serve the novelist, the playwright, or the poet. Even the critical essay, which takes as its subject some other literary work, must be given full status as literary art. The reading of a novel is, after all, no less an experience than a day at the racetrack or a moment of secluded meditation or any other matter that an essayist might choose to discuss. Seen in this way, the maker of an essay—whether his subject is a written document or something else—is engaged in a form of commentary on life that is very distinctly first-hand, especially since his language is unequivocally his own, written in his own person and resembling good conversation. The very directness of the essay, in fact, makes its study immensely valuable for anyone who cares to improve his own writing. For it is in written prose, more than in any of his other uses for words, that a person finds his own voice as a serious member of the intellectual community.

1

Much can be learned about effective method and procedure in writing simply through consideration of the more important qualities by which nearly all good essays control the reader's response. Such consideration tells us, for one thing, that it is always dangerous to think of form and content as if they were separable elements, for such thinking leads eventually to the notion that content, once it has been isolated and freed from the language structures that express it, may be packaged neatly as a set of ideas for the memory to hold. Paraphrasing an essay—putting its substance into your own language in order to improve your understanding and retention of it—is risky because it is almost always reductive. That is, it reduces the substance of the essay to an artificial simplicity in its effort to emphasize and accentuate what is most important. And this is as true of mental paraphrase as it is true of written. The content is not effectively translated; it is altered, and usually for the worse.

If, for example, we read William Faulkner's "An Innocent at Rinkside" (pp. 18–20) for the purpose of extracting essential nuggets of meaning from it, we are quickly in trouble. Suppose we decide that the essay makes two major and related points: that sport in America is becoming too exclusively an amusement for passive spectators, and that Americans show off their patriotic allegiance so regularly and so often because they have forgotten what is supposed to command that allegiance. These, surely, are not difficult formulations to remember; nor are they inaccurate, as far as they go. But no one in his right mind would suppose that such reductions successfully capture what Faulkner says in this essay. We have missed the sense of perplexity and momentary delight, the acknowledged display of sheer professional competence, the purely physical sensations, the author's way of qualifying and requalifying his point of view so as not to present the experience dishonestly. And this is only a fragment of what has been left out. To understand the full grossness of the distortion, we have only to read the essay again.

This process of boiling literature down to rudimentary summarized content is in the long run more damaging to the boiler than to the boiled object. The point is not that we never will or never should have occasion to think of Faulkner's essay in some handily reduced form. No doubt there may even be times when we need remember no more of Keats's "Ode on a Grecian Urn" than that the urn comes to represent a fusion of beauty and truth. The difficulty, rather, is in the habit we may develop, as we read, of anticipating the simplified formula, looking for it always, paying attention not so much to what the essay is as to what uses we may find for it if we can just get it wrapped, labeled, and filed away. We ought to read an essay with full attention to the whole statement that it makes, perceiving the complexity of meanings, finding fully those patterns and structures that the essay itself seems to put forward for recognition, not merely those that provide an easy but false "grasp."

In writing good prose there is, of course, a necessary correlative to all this: One should write meanings that are complicated, qualified, and adjusted as much as they need to be, recognizing that the complication *is* the meaning, not some odd and devious process that "happens to" the meaning. To say something well is to say it *continuously*, never to interrupt saying it for the momentary sake of embroidery, never consciously to fill out or "pad" some bony outline of one's intention. In addition, certainly, one must know when not to stop; too many essays stop before they are finished.

A good test is this: If you find yourself asking, "What more can I say about this?" or "Can I say this over again, in a different form?" or "What manoeuvres shall I go through before I get to the point?", then you are probably working from an initial frame of ideas that you have made leaner than it should be. The usual cause of this failing is the desire to be clear, forceful, and even tidy in making statements, and it brings with it a reluctance to face fully the complication of meanings that a full and true expression almost always involves. So that your essay will not look simple-minded, you would do well to aim at an ambitiously complex statement from the beginning. Otherwise, you may find yourself sheepishly adding on complications afterward. This advice may seem to contradict what you have always been told about good composition: that the first aim is to be economical, clear, and concise. But remember that economy, clarity, and concision are qualities of the language as it is used; they are not reasons for reducing your intention, your proposed idea, to the simplest possible form. If, of course, you are interested only in avoiding mechanical errors, in keeping your prose safe from faults in grammar, syntax, and idiom, then you should take care to attempt saying only what is very simple indeed. The result may be rather dull, but it will be "clean." Expression of the complex and the difficult always puts much greater stress and strain on the language used, and the chances of mechanical trouble are increased accordingly. But so are the chances of producing a worthwhile essay.

This leads to a further piece of advice—one that is far easier to give than to take. Many essays require more than a single reading, and they make their fullest effect if read at something less than top reading pace. There are two reasons for this. First, language is made up of a sequence of sounds and can in itself give pleasure, like a well-modulated voice in conversation. That pleasure can be cancelled by the sort of quick reading that does not at all recognize the sound-content of clause, phrase, and word, or the rhythms formed in the progression of sentences. Of course it would be foolish to pretend that all, or even most, essays require reading aloud to "savor each syllable on the tongue." Not many essays would get read in a lifetime at that rate. But equally misleading is the idea that the sense of pleasing sound can be had only from an oral reading; after all, we can "hear" language even when reading silently. And, of course, it is wrong to assume that pleasing sound sequences are to be found only in prose poems, gorgeous prose, and "purple" passages.

The second and more important reason for using a deliberate reading pace is that if the piece is a valuable one, its author has probably made an argument or presentation of some subtlety, not a mere résumé of facts. Even a leisurely reading is likely to catch only part of the total coloration of meaning; a quick rush through the text will catch almost none of it. There is no use denying that our present culture and society, including our academic habits, place a high premium on rapidity of performance and instant comprehension. It will not always be possible to read a given essay, slowly, two or three times. But it is important to understand the need for such reading of certain essays, if only because we should feel entitled to expect the same treatment for our own writing. Anyone who has tried to write out cogently a long, difficult argument or a fully honest rendition of some experience knows how essential it is to realize that readers will go over the account carefully and more than once. Unless the writing is for a newspaper that may be thrown away tomorrow, there is really no reason to think that it must be perfectly easy to understand, *totally* clear, the first time through. With some reasonable expectation of the time and energy a reader will give you, you will find it easier to follow faithfully the complete richness of your thought, rather than to compromise by writing a highly readable essay that is a bit vacuous.

Finally, even a limited experience with essays shows that the exciting writer is the writer who commits himself, takes a position, argues a case or an interpretation of facts. We are very much mistaken if we expect Faulkner to make a fair statement of the counter-argument in favor of indoor professional ice hockey. Generally it is the mark of a good essay that its author's values and prejudices show through in a personally identifying way. He is offering a view, after all, not the whole truth and nothing but the truth. When a writer becomes too continuously aware that there is much to be said on both sides, intellectual and verbal paralysis is likely to result. The reader will be nonplussed when he should be enthusiastic or angry or amused. What this idea implies for the writing of student essays should be clear, and it can be put briefly: If you have something to say, you may as well try to generate some heat, as well as accuracy and honesty, in saying it.

2

What, then, should an essay be? There is no convenient answer, no prescription to be filled. The best we can do, for a beginning, is to fall back on the root meaning of the term itself. As a verb, "to essay" means "to try"; an essay is therefore a trial or an attempt of some kind. So, built into the term is a suggestion of venture, of experiment, maybe even of risk, as opposed to the cut-and-dried, the pat, and the easy. An essayist tries to say something about something. The specific nature of his attempt depends entirely on himself and on the varying circumstances in which he works. To prescribe in advance what characteristics an essay should have is only to limit falsely the versatile openness of the form. One sad result of such prescription is the rather limp view, held often enough by students, that the essay is a sort of innocuous writing exercise practiced chiefly by nice old ladies who have nothing better to do with their time (and practiced too, unwillingly, by students), an exercise in which a great deal of verbiage is used in playing with some rather vague idea or flowery sentiment.

Still, even the most open-minded reader thinks he knows an essay when he sees one; clearly, there are practical criteria. One reasonably sound method of discovering these criteria is simply to find out what actual essays have been like in the past. This method requires a great deal of reading, and no quick descriptive survey here could be a useful substitute for first-hand experience. For our purposes, it will be enough to note that since the sixteenth century, when Montaigne published his volume of *essais* and Francis Bacon his collection of essays, the brief topical composition in prose has evolved along both formal and informal lines. The model established by Montaigne was witty, intimate, and casual; Bacon's short philosophical discourses showed precision, rigor, and clarity in exposition of ideas. As the rise of magazines and newspapers made essay-writing an increasingly popular business, there was a general trend in favor of the less formal manner, particularly during the early 1800's when the "familiar" essay achieved great eminence. But formal argumentation has never passed entirely out of fashion among essayists, and sometimes the two elements have been successfully combined in a single piece.

Whether its prime impulse is formal or informal, the essay has been distinguished traditionally by the sense that it gives of the individual human intelligence at work, the special quality of a personal expression of views. That quality often involves others. We expect the essayist to perform simply as an intelligent and interested man, rather than as a specialist or professional expert in a certain field. We expect his performance to be readable at a single sitting, as if it were part of a natural conversation we might hold with him. We expect him to write in prose, because prose is the language of everyday discourse. But these expectations cannot be (and are not) very firm, for they are violated again and again. We know that some essays (Pope's *Essay on Man,* for instance) are written in verse, and that some essays require more than the span of an hour for comfortable reading. Above all, we know that the essayist often does bring special information and knowledgeability to his job, as well as special interest. Thus, although one *can* set up distinctions among the sermon, the tract, the manifesto, the dissertation, the editorial, the meditation, the treatise, the preface, the review, the dialogue, the commentary, the report, the biographical sketch, and the public oration, and then in turn distinguish each of these from the essay as narrowly defined, it is far more helpful to see how persistently these categories overlap and interpenetrate in practice. The prose pieces included in this volume, though all safely identifiable as essays, represent in some measure the vast range of available possibilities.

REAL WOMEN

Robert Graves

The most important historical study of all, utterly dwarfing all economic and political ones, is for me the changing relationship between men and women down the centuries—from prehistoric times to the present moral chaos in which both sexes have become equally confused about their roles. But I am a poet by calling, and have lived outside ordinary civilization for so many years that anything I write about real women must read oddly. Except perhaps to real woman themselves, and the occasional man whom some accident of birth or experience tempts to agree with me.

A real woman, by my definition, neither despises nor worships

REAL WOMEN: Reprinted by permission of Collins-Knowlton-Wing. Copyright © 1963 by International Authors, N.V., from *Mammon and the Black Goddess,* published by Doubleday & Company, Inc.

men, but is proud not to have been born a man, does everything she can to avoid thinking or acting like one, knows the full extent of her powers, and feels free to reject all arbitrary man-made obligations. She is her own oracle of right and wrong, firmly believing in her five sound senses and intuitive sixth. Once a real woman has been warned by her nose that those apples are tasteless, or assured by her fingertips that this material is shoddy, no salesman in the world can persuade her to the contrary. Nor, once she has met some personage in private, and summed him up with a single keen glance as weak, vain or crooked, will his mounting public reputation convince her otherwise. She takes pleasure in the company of simple, happy, undemanding women; but seldom or never finds a friend worthy of her full confidence. Since she never settles for the second best in love, what most troubles her is the rareness of real men. Wherever she goes, her singularity will arouse strong feelings: adulation, jealousy, resentment, but never pity for her loneliness. Real women are royal women; the words once had the same meaning. Democracy has no welcome for queens.

It would be wrong to identify the real woman with the typical wild one who, after a difficult childhood, has left home early to live by her wits at the expense of men. The wild woman is incapable either of friendship for other women, whom she cannot fail to regard as rivals, or of love for a man, her declared enemy. But at least she keeps her eyes open and ridicules the view that women must enthusiastically accept this glorious modern world of plenty bestowed on them by their hard-working menfolk, and that they enjoy being passionately swept off their feet and afterwards treated with amused indulgence. There was never, of course, any truth in the comic-strip legend of a primitive he-man who would grab his woman by the hair, threaten her with a knobbed club if she refused his advances, and haul her off panting ecstatically to his cave. In ancient Majorca, the island which I have made my home for more than thirty years, the woman, not the man, owned their cave; and, according to the Roman historian Strabo, if he took things too much for granted, she would merely say, "Begone, and take your possessions with you," and out he had to go—the children were hers in any case.

To reach some understanding of real women, one must think back to a primitive age, when men invariably treated women as the holier sex, since they alone perpetuated the race. Women were the sole agriculturists, guardians of springs, fruit trees, and the sacred hearth fire, and lived unaffected by any notions of progress. Tribal queens never thought in terms of historical time, but only of seasons; judged each case on its own merits, not by a legal code, as real women still do; and showed little regard for trade or mechanical invention. Chance discoveries or new techniques in arts and crafts were welcome, so long as these neither upset tribal economy nor enhanced the importance of individuals. It was the queen's task to restrain men from letting their ambition or intellectual curiosity override practical common sense, as it is still the woman's task to ask her husband: "Must you kill yourself making money? Haven't we enough for the next five years at least, even if you stopped working altogether? Surely you don't enjoy your martyrdom?" But even if he cares to listen, social pressures compel him to provide for his family until he drops dead.

History begins with the emergence of men from female rule. They had at last discovered that a woman cannot conceive without male assistance—and brooded over the implications of this surprising fact. After long whispered conferences it was agreed that men ought to claim their freedom. They asked, "Why should descent be reckoned in the female line, not the male? Why should a man when he marries go to the woman's home, not contrariwise? Why should a woman, not a man, sow the seed corn? Why should women control the tribe? Surely men are the true creators, sowers of seed, and therefore the holier sex, as well as being physically stronger?" Thus the male habit of reasoning from irrelevant facts, rather than relying on woman's practical wisdom, began the war between the sexes that has been raging ever since.

Men gradually usurped women's prerogatives in farming, magic, handicrafts, war—the Amazons are no mere figment—and government. The story is epitomized in a classical Greek myth: how the goddess Hera pitied a poor, bedraggled cuckoo and warmed him at her breast. This cuckoo was her brother Zeus in disguise, who ravished and humiliated her by seizing throne and sceptre. Later, when Hera and her kinfolk rebelled against Zeus, he hung her from the vault of heaven, with an anvil tied to each foot. . . .

Men consolidated their victory. They reckoned descent in the male line, brought wives to their own homes, invented historical annals, legal codes, weights and measures, standing armies, engineering, logic and philosophy. On the excuse of protecting the weaker sex, they placed woman under male tutelage: henceforward she must serve her father's or husband's domestic needs as though not only spiritually but mentally inferior to him.

Greek myths record an occasional dramatic protest against this state of affairs: how the fifty Danaids stabbed their husbands, the sons of Aegyptus, on their common wedding night, and were punished in hell for this crime; how the Lemnian women murdered theirs for importing concubines from Thrace; how Amazons attacked Athens. . . . Yet, as a rule, the sex war has been fought sporadically in the home between father and daughter, husband and wife, mother-in-law and son-in-law. Only isolated regions, such as Galicia, Majorca and Pictish Scotland, kept their matriarchal traditions.

It seems puzzling that the real women of those days let all this happen to them. The sole reason I can suggest is that they thought far ahead. Since man had a certain undeveloped intellectual capacity, of which it would have been wrong to deny him full use, the real women sat back patiently, prepared to give him a free hand for some hundreds of thousands of years. Only a long series of disastrous experiments could make him realize the error of his headstrong ways. Eventually he must return to them in willing and chastened dependence.

Priests of the new male gods even modified the ancient myth of a sole goddess who had created the world, giving her a male assistant; and in *Genesis*—a comparatively late book—Jehovah creates the world entirely by Himself; and models Eve, the first woman, from man's rib! It is added that this woman's disobedience to God caused man to stumble and sin. In fact, the story is based on a Hebrew pun: the same word means both "rib" and "make to stumble." According to Hesiod's contemporary Greek myth, an inquisitive woman named Pandora opened a divine jar entrusted to her and let loose on mankind all the evils that now plague us. Yet "Eve" was originally a title of the sole creatrix; as was also "Pandora."

Financial pressures of men's own making brought about the recent so-called emancipation of women. Grown daughters could no longer stay idling at home, a burden to their parents and to themselves until married off. Industry was booming and, with appropriate moral safeguards, they might fill the widening gaps in man-power. Women, who can now earn and keep their own money, even when wives, and have been granted the franchise—"franchise" originally meant "freedom from being a serf"—need show men no gratitude for this liberality. Their freedom is still limited. They remain citizens of the second degree, auxiliary male personnel barred from all the highest offices; and would never have got where they are so quickly had it not been for two world wars and such loveless male inventions as machine guns, submarines, bombing planes and universal conscription.

Strangely enough, it is easier to be a real woman in backwaters of Christianity or Islam or Hinduism, where codes of behaviour have not changed for centuries, than in urbanized Europe or America.

There she knows what part she must play, and can guard her inborn dignity. Although the husband, as head of the family, makes all decisions, he will never dare overrule even her unspoken protests. Among Majorcan peasants who live beyond the tourist range, no man would ever think of buying or selling so much as a hen without his wife's approval. She is always referred to as *la madonna*, titular guardian of the home.

What is home? In ancient days it meant a clan settlement, a camp or kraal, ruled by elders, where men had comrades and women their gossips, and children ran about in packs; and where a happy man-woman relationship could exist in some small corner away from the communal bustle.

Among us Westerners, because of man's jealous insistence on marital privacy, *home* has shrunk from settlement to farmhouse, thence to the cottage, thence to the 10-roomed apartment, thence to three rooms and a kitchenette with the usual labour-saving devices, in a huge residential block full of utter strangers. The housewife has her washing machine, telephone, television, refrigerator, electric cooker, car and door keys, to pay for which a husband must be out working all the week. She cannot regret (because she never knew) the easy companionship of her great-grandmother's day: quilting bees and husking bees, taking the cousins to do a week's washing down at the creek, lending a hand with the shearing and harvest, making jams and pickles, getting up round dances, singing and playing practical jokes. But no real woman can ever accept the present situation.

Man's logic has defeated itself. Boredom often drives the married woman back to a job as soon as she can leave her children at a nursery school; or to infidelity; or to an analyst. Home is home for only two days of the week. Which is why some paternally-minded industrialists take advice from professors of sociology and plant their employees all together in a wholesome suburban neighbourhood, where the company's standards of taste and respectability must rule their lives. Husband obeys boss; wife obeys husband, and preserves amicable relations with her fellow company wives, or else. . . . Spouses are thus shackled by a well-paid job to which the husband need no longer commute, by house, garden and swimming pool, by children, by hope of advancement and the prospect of a pension. Any sign of non-compliance is scored against both. No real woman can ever accept this situation either.

Attempts to liven things up socially are all too often masked under the dubious name of charity. It is characteristic of a real woman never to support public charities—on the ground that she neither knows the persons to whom her money goes nor has any assurance that it will be properly distributed. She gives only to those whose needs are familiar to her, and then from friendship, not pity. She will not be found at bridge clubs or at cocktail parties. Bridge, which is, after all, a money contest between individual players, cannot be a substitute for the good humour of a communal wash-day; nor can a cocktail party supply the intimate gossip of a quilting bee.

Wild women take advantage of this artificial state of affairs by exploiting the dormant dissatisfactions of husbands. One of them told me the other day, "Yes, you may call me a mean, greedy, undependable, lazy, treacherous, spendthrift bitch. That's true enough a good part of the time; but it isn't the whole story. In fact, I've given myself to myself, and to no one else. My beauty is my own, and I take good care of it. If I choose a lover, I grant the lucky fellow no rights over me; and if he has sense, he won't claim any. As for breaking up a home, nobody can do that unless it's already cracked!"

A real woman likes beautiful things of her own choosing. She prefers a handleless cup, a backless chair, a mattress on the floor and a packing-case for the table to good taste conferred on her wholesale by interior decorators. There is an eighteenth-century English song, *Sally in Our Alley:*

> Her father, he sells cabbage nets
>   And through the streets doth cry 'em.
> Her mother, she sells laces long
>   To such as care to buy 'em—
> Who'd think such rascals could beget
>   So sweet a girl as Sally?
> She is the darling of my heart
>   And lives in our alley. . . .

The lover was a square: an honest, idealistic London apprentice, intent on becoming a journeyman, a master-craftsman and eventually a rich merchant—perhaps even Lord Mayor:

> When Eastertide comes round again,
>   Oh, then I'll have some money—
> I'll save it up, and box and all
>   I'll give it to my honey. . . .
> And when my seven years' time is o'er
>   Oh, then I'll marry Sally,
> Ay, then we'll wed, and then we'll bed—
>   But not in our alley!

Their broken-down, foul-smelling alley was a settlement, a home, the denizens of which were bound together by common poverty, shiftlessness, pugnacity, humour and a hatred of landlords and police. Yet no well-planned housing estate can ever compete with its spirit, which a Sally was always found to keep alive. From 1940 to '43 the German blitz levelled what remained of these alleys, and their sites are now occupied by large all-glass office blocks. The last of the Sallies found herself in a suburban life-box—one of hundreds built to the same design and set down in parallel rows—longing for a return to poverty, vice, dirt and even flying bombs.

Marriage, like money, is still with us; and, like money, progressively devalued. The ties between these two male inventions get closer and closer. Originally marriage meant the sale of a woman by one man to another; now most women sell themselves, though they may have no intention of delivering the goods listed in the bill of sale. Not only is the wife, on an average, five years younger than her husband, but she lives statistically longer. So money power passes progressively into the hands of women. Also, divorce legislation (forced on guilt-ridden legislators by nagging spouses) grossly favours the wife. A youthful rival figures in most divorce suits, and though she and the wife seldom act collusively, they share an old-fashioned insistence on the honourable state of marriage, which enriches both. Wild women will commit matrimony when things go hard for them, without the least thought of keeping their obligations. The entranced husbands never know what has hit them, nor do they profit by the experience.

The United States, though often described as a matriarchy in all but name, remains patriarchal. Matriarchy, to be effective, needs real women. When women organize themselves intellectually on masculine lines, they merely stimulate the feminization of men, who, for terror of husband-hunting viragoes, are apt to seek refuge in the cul-de-sac of homosexuality.

Though men are more conventional than women and fear to infringe the Mosaic law (*Deuteronomy* xxii. 5) which forbids their wearing of women's clothes, women have no scruples about flouting the companion law: "The woman shall not wear that which pertaineth unto a man . . . for all that do so are abomination unto the Lord. . . ." Even matrons now unblushingly wear blue jeans zipped in front.

The pseudo-patriarchal trend encourages women to respect legality, which they had hitherto found distasteful. A real woman, giving evidence in a court of law, scorns factual truth. Should her sense of equity run counter to the formal demands of justice, she will perjure herself in replies of cool and convincing honesty. When obliged to exercise a vote, she scorns the male axiom that the majority is always right.

A few real women survive in the old royal sense among West African queens, who rule with a silver knot-of-wisdom sceptre and claim the moon-goddess Ngame as their remote ancestress. A "knot of wisdom"—known in English as "the true lover's knot"—is the sort that tightens more securely the harder you tug at either end. Symbolically it means, "My command can never be disobeyed!"

In civilized society royal women have neither thrones nor territorial queendoms, but the moon inspires them still, and they can wield formidable powers in times of emergency. Yet, since they avoid becoming public figures—the personality cult is another male invention—their names pass into history far more seldom than those of notorious wild women. A remarkable exception was Elizabeth I of England, whom her poets addressed as Cynthia—"The Moon"— and whose cynical disparagement of herself as "but a weak woman" concealed an unshaken faith in her royal wisdom. Elizabeth ruled through awe and love, was on playful terms with her ladies-in-waiting, inspired her male subjects to feats of heroism and flights of poetry never known before or since among the English, always said "No" to a doubtful petition and then slept on it.

A real woman's main concern is her beauty, which she cultivates for her own pleasure—not to ensnare men. Though she despises fashion as a male financial business, she will not make herself conspicuous by a defiance of conventions. The materials, colours and cut of her clothes, her hair style and her jewels are all chosen to match a sense of personal uniqueness. She can dress in advance of fashion, yet seem to lead it; and to any irregular features she may have, she lends a lovely ugliness denied to common beauty queens. Perfect detachment from the artificial or second-hand keeps her face unclouded. She has no small talk on current topics, and will suddenly vanish from a party, however grand, as soon as it grows boring.

If she plays games, it will be for fun, not competition; and if up against a win-at-all-costs opponent in tennis or golf, she will take care to lose handsomely—as one who competes only against herself. If she drinks, it will be because she likes the taste; and if she smokes, it will be for the same reason, not to steady her nerve.

She misses real men—men who would recognize her potentiality and agree that our world, despite its appearance of rational organization, is a wholly haphazard one, clanking on noisily to its fate along a random course once defined as "progress." And that a calamitous collapse must come before a new start can be made—from the point where the sex war was first declared and woman's conservative instinct as the guiding force of humankind repudiated. Because womanhood remains incomplete without a child, most real women marry—preferring simple, affectionate husbands who cannot understand them. This is not a renunciation of real love, since they agree with the thirteenth-century Countess of Narbonne: "Conjugal affection has absolutely nothing in common with love. We say 'absolutely,' and with all consideration, that love cannot exist between husband and wife."

Man's biological function is to do; woman's is to be. This difference is not a contrast of mere activity with mere passivity. "To be" is indeed a full-time occupation. A real woman has no leisure in the modern economic sense—leisure as a consumer's relaxed insistence on commercial entertainment—but is always thinking, taking stock of herself, setting a stage on which actors can perform. If she paints or writes, this will be for her own private amusement, not to satisfy ambition; and if forced to earn her livelihood in this way, she repudiates the public personage forced on her by dealers and critics.

A real woman is content to dress with a difference, to make her home unmistakably her own, to illuminate any company she enters, to cook by instinct, not by the cookery book. This is her evidence of being, the proof of which lies in her sense of certitude. She is no feminist; feminism, like all "isms," implies an intellectual approach to a subject; and reality can be understood only by transcending the intellect.

Mental institutions on both sides of the Atlantic house hundreds of young, beautiful, silently brooding girls, victims of the sex war—defeated before they could come to terms with life. Their tragedy has been brilliantly described in *The Ha-Ha*, a novel by Jennifer Dawson, whose heroine is almost a real woman, because: "she never just plays a game with herself or other people, and refuses to learn the rules of society—meaning the worthy, useful, ordinary women who are so busy finding husbands and houses and good income brackets that they just haven't time to be conscious of themselves, and who see the world as an inventory, a container of so many things, and other people as so many tin-openers to undo it for them."

The friendly and intelligent staff of the mental institution cannot persuade her that she should realign herself with the orderly outside male world. Being not quite real enough to escape defeat by pretending conformity, she loses all pride in her appearance, ceases to concentrate on any self-imposed task; and when at last she desperately breaks out, the police, we foresee, cannot fail to fetch her back for sedation and still closer surveillance.

A real woman somehow avoids suicide, or virtual suicide, or the mental institution; but is always painfully aware of having been born out of her true epoch; considered as either the past, or as the long-distant future. A sense of humour saves her from defeat. "This is not worthy of me," she will remind herself ten times a day, "but to preserve my inner self I must once more act an alien part."

None of her women neighbours, idly content with money and what it will buy, feel any need for drastic change in the man-woman relationship; she treats them politely, and has patience. If she ever comes across a real man, the thin thread of human hope that eventually the world will make practical sense again—cannot yet have snapped.

QUESTIONS AND EXERCISES

1. Does it seem to you that the content of this essay can be summed up in a sentence or two? Try it. Suppose that, having tried to do this in two short sentences, you are now permitted to expand your summary into a paragraph of about 75 words. Does this make the job easier or more vexing? Why?

2. Without looking back, can you reconstruct Graves's account of the rise of male dominance? Does it follow a step-by-step progressive sequence? What changes would you make if you wanted to render this account easier to remember?

3. More specifically—and, again, do not look back at the text—what does Graves have to say about the condition of the modern home? Does it seem reasonable to you that under a matriarchy the nature of the home would be radically changed? If so, why do you suppose Graves does not explicitly develop the idea of such potential change?

4. After another careful reading of the essay, try questions 2 and 3 again.

5. As the author discusses women as his immediate subject, how much does he manage to say, or distinctly imply, about his companion idea of "real men"? Might the priorities be reversed—that is, would it work as well to define real women indirectly through a definition of real men? Would you guess that this essay was originally intended for a predominantly male audience?

6. Write a 500-word essay entitled "Real Women Really," in which you disagree specifically with what Graves has said.

7. Write a short essay that you suspect your instructor will disapprove of for the wrong reasons, and append a short paragraph explaining why.

8. Do you think it true that a "real woman" cultivates beauty for her

own pleasure, and not to attract men? Write as long an essay on this
as you find necessary to express your view adequately. Then write
a two-page commentary on your own essay, indicating as closely as
possible what you think makes your statement hard to paraphrase or
to summarize reductively.

AN INNOCENT AT RINKSIDE

William Faulkner

The vacant ice looked tired, though it shouldn't have. They told
him it had been put down only ten minutes ago following a basket-
ball game, and ten minutes after the hockey match it would be
taken up again to make room for something else. But it looked not
expectant but resigned, like the mirror simulating ice in the Xmas
store window, not before the miniature fir trees and reindeer and
cosy lamplit cottage were arranged upon it, but after they had been
dismantled and cleared away.

Then it was filled with motion, speed. To the innocent, who had
never seen it before, it seemed discorded and inconsequent, bizarre
and paradoxical like the frantic darting of the weightless bugs which
run on the surface of stagnant pools. Then it would break, coalesce
through a kind of kaleidoscopic whirl like a child's toy, into a pattern, a design almost beautiful, as if an inspired choreographer had
drilled a willing and patient and hard-working troupe of dancers—a
pattern, design which was trying to tell him something, say something to him urgent and important and true in that second before,
already bulging with the motion and the speed, it began to disinte-
grate and dissolve.

Then he learned to find the puck and follow it. Then the individual players would emerge. They would not emerge like the sweating
barehanded behemoths from the troglodyte mass of football, but
instead as fluid and fast and effortless as rapier-thrusts or lightning—
Richard with something of the passionate glittering fatal alien quality
of snakes, Geoffrion like an agile ruthless precocious boy who maybe
couldn't do anything else but then he didn't need to; and others—
the veteran Laprade, still with the know-how and the grace. But he

---

AN INNOCENT AT RINKSIDE: © Copyright 1955 by Estelle Faulkner and Jill Faulkner Summers. Reprinted from *Essays, Speeches, and Public Letters* by William
Faulkner, edited by James B. Meriwether, by permisison of Random House, Inc.

had time too now, or rather time had him, and what remained was no longer expendable that recklessly, heedlessly, successfully; not enough of it left now to buy fresh passion and fresh triumph with.

Excitement: men in rapid hard close physical conflict, not just with bare hands, but armed with the knife-blades of skates and the hard fast deft sticks which could break bones when used right. He had noticed how many women were among the spectators, and for just a moment he thought that perhaps this was why—that here actual male blood could flow, not from the crude impact of a heavier fist but from the rapid and delicate stroke of weapons, which like the European rapier or the Frontier pistol, reduced mere size and brawn to its proper perspective to the passion and the will. But only for a moment because he, the innocent, didn't like that idea either. It was the excitement of speed and grace, with the puck for catalyst, to give it reason, meaning.

He watched it—the figure-darted glare of ice, the concentric tiers rising in sections stipulated by the hand-lettered names of the individual fan-club idols, vanishing upward into the pall of tobacco smoke trapped by the roof—the roof which stopped and trapped all that intent and tense watching, and concentrated it downward upon the glare of ice frantic and frenetic with motion; until the by-product of the speed and the motion—their violence—had no chance to exhaust itself upward into space and so leave on the ice only the swift glittering changing pattern. And he thought how perhaps something is happening to sport in America (assuming that by definition sport is something you do yourself, in solitude or not, because it is fun), and that something is the roof we are putting over it and them. Skating, basket-ball, tennis, track meets and even steeple-chasing have moved indoors; football and baseball function beneath covers or arc lights and in time will be rain- and cold-proofed too. There still remain the proper working of a fly over trout water or the taking of a rise of birds in front of a dog or the right placing of a bullet in a deer or even a bigger animal which will hurt you if you don't. But not for long: in time that will be indoors too beneath lights and the trapped pall of spectator tobacco, the concentric sections bearing the name and device of the lion or the fish as well as that of the Richard or Geoffrion of the scoped rifle or 4-ounce rod.

But (to repeat) not for long, because the innocent did not quite believe that either. We—Americans—like to watch; we like the adrenalic discharge of vicarious excitement or triumph or success. But we like to do also: the discharge of the personal excitement of the triumph and the fear to be had from actually setting the horse at the stone wall or pointing the over-canvassed sloop or finding by actual test if you can line up two sights and one buffalo in time. There must have been little boys in that throng too, frantic with the slow excruciating passage of time, panting for the hour when they would be Richard or Geoffrion or Laprade—the same little Negro boys whom the innocent has seen shadow-boxing in front of a photograph of Joe Louis in his own Mississippi town—the same little Norwegian boys he watched staring up the snowless slope of the Holmenkollen jump one July day in the hills above Oslo.

Only he (the innocent) did wonder just what a professional hockey-match, whose purpose is to make a decent and reasonable profit for its owners, had to do with our National Anthem. What are we afraid of? Is it our national character of which we are so in doubt, so fearful that it might not hold up in the clutch, that we not only dare not open a professional athletic contest or a beauty-pageant or a real-estate auction, but we must even use a Chamber of Commerce race for Miss Sewage Disposal or a wildcat land-sale, to remind us that liberty gained without honor and sacrifice and held without constant vigilance and undiminished honor and complete willingness to sacrifice again at need, was not worth having to begin with? Or, by blaring or chanting it at ourselves every time ten or twelve or eighteen or twenty-two young men engage formally for the possession of a puck or a ball, or just one young woman walks across a lighted platform in a bathing-suit, do we hope to so dull and eviscerate the words and tune with repetition, that when we do hear it we will not be disturbed from that dream-like state in which "honor" is a break and "truth" an angle?

QUESTIONS AND EXERCISES

1. In the first three paragraphs Faulkner seems interested only in conveying first impressions of the spectacle of professional ice hockey. In view of the essay's eventual statement, would a description of some other type of athletic contest (such as football, baseball, basketball) do as well at the beginning, or can you see ways in which ice hockey (as Faulkner renders it) is particularly apt? Explain.

2. Twice at the close of paragraph 1 Faulkner takes the trouble to negate one thing as he is asserting another ("not expectant but resigned," "not before . . . but after . . ."). Where else in the essay do you find this technique used? Taking up several particular cases one by one, comment on the effect achieved. Would it have been more economical and concise simply to make the affirmation without the accompanying denial? More memorable?

3. Explain how paragraph 4 makes a transition between what precedes and what follows it.

4. Comment on the relevance of the concluding paragraph to the rest of the essay. As you read the essay a second or third time, how does your advance knowledge of what that paragraph says affect your response to the whole piece?

5. Faulkner identifies himself throughout in the third person—"the innocent." Besides reminding you that this is his first experience of a hockey match, what effect is gained through the use of this label? Does it seriously impair the personal flavor of the described experience and the resulting thought?

6. Imitating Faulkner's technique in paragraph 2, write a short account of some first experience of your own (it need not be an athletic event, but something involving action will lend itself well to your purposes); try as much as possible to convey the sense of partial bewilderment and confusion that you felt. Add to this a paragraph of commentary, explaining what specific problems you had to surmount in order to capture the desired effect.

7. Write a page of agreement with or dissent from Faulkner's position.

CHAPTER TWO

Subject, Thesis, Substance

In this chapter we shall try to clarify certain relationships among the parts of the literary process. A reader who is to do justice to the essay in front of him needs to be conscious of the several distinctive operations at work, of the more or less constant tension between the stuff of subject and the shaping impulse of thesis, and of the emerging configuration of the resulting substance. Although we shall work from several points of view for the sake of full understanding, one basic concept will stand at the center of the discussion: The essayist's prime responsibility is to make forcefully clear the *purpose* of his effort. In order to understand this concept in practical detail, we need a definition of terms.

1

Subject: The subject of any literary discourse is the area of experience and knowledge to which the discourse refers. If you say, "My essay deals with air transport during the 1960's" or "I am writing about my emotional response to movies," you are talking about subject. It may be helpful—though it is not entirely accurate—to think of subject as the "raw material" or "stuff" that the writer uses, the unshaped aggregate of all things that might possibly be relevant to his purpose. The chief flaw in this way of regarding subject is that it may lead us to think that subject is necessarily something physical or factual, part of the reality "out there." Actually, of course, a writer's subject may encompass far more than physical objects and scientifically provable facts. Human feelings, values, dreams, illusions, and speculations may all be parts of the material. The only reasonable limitations of subject are the limitations of the writer's own range of experience.

Thesis: Strictly speaking, a thesis is a proposition advanced through argument. In an essay whose subject is air transport in the 1960's, the thesis might be that the increasing popularity of air travel causes us to lose our sense of landscape, or that smaller jet aircraft are needed to provide more frequent service between small cities, or that high-speed flight helps the cause of world brotherhood by shrinking the world. For any one of these theses it would be possible to build a formally structured argument of the sort that a lawyer or logician might like. But the same ideas might be put forward without any of the logical moves that we normally associate with formal argument; and general experience tells that many essays do their asserting, their saying of what they have to say, as much by implication as by explicit argumentation. For present purposes, the term *thesis* will be used because it has a convenient force and clearness of meaning, but we must understand that it covers a great number of possible strategies of presentation.

The essayist's thesis, then, is what he has to say or show about his subject; it is the aim, the purpose, the point of his discourse. Whether the main activity of the essay is description, analysis, appreciation, questioning, invective, narration, presentation, or dispute, it must have within it the organizing impulse of an intended *act*, a particular end to be achieved. A strong thesis is not necessarily one that can be expressed clearly in a propositional sentence or two. Often the leading idea of an essay, its very reason for being, cannot be formulated accurately in few words. Besides, the relative strength or obtrusiveness of the thesis matters far less than its *consistent* presence in the essay.

Substance: Substance is the full realization of the thesis in the subject. If subject is the matter treated, and thesis the intention of the treatment, then substance is the successful fusion of the two as the total statement or effect that the essay makes. In a first-rate essay the substance *is* the essay itself. In most performances, of course, the fusion is less than perfect, with patches of incompletely controlled (and maybe irrelevant) subject matter, as well as patches where the thesis runs irresponsibly away from the subject, becoming mere arbitrary assertion. But the substantialness of the discourse, far more than the inherent interest of the subject or the appeal of the thesis, is what affects the reader, and for good reason: A subject, after all, can exist independent of the writer himself. Even a thesis is something he may inherit, take over ready-made from someone else. Substance, the essay itself as a personal act, is his own achievement.

2

The determination of the thesis is the first step in the process of writing an essay. Failure to understand this point can put both reader and writer at a serious disadvantage. Most students have been taught, at one time or another, that the best beginning is to select an interesting subject, which should then be narrowed down, made particular enough to be manageable, and finally made into an essay by the use of appropriate expression. The result, more often than not, is a shapeless sort of idea-salad, a purposeless inventory of information and opinion. Common sense should show that this method of beginning is a badly confused one. Can any reader of "An Innocent at Rinkside" suppose that Faulkner started off by thinking to himself, "Let me see—I guess I'll write an essay on the subject of American spectator sports"? Indeed not. He had something to say about an experience, a specific view to be expressed, and his essay evolved from that beginning. For an essay-writer, the thesis defines the subject area, not vice versa.

But is it not true, someone may ask, that as a broad subject is narrowed down to workable proportions the purpose of the essay will automatically come into being? Again, no. Subject matter is, by itself, inert stuff. Subdividing it does not change its basic nature. If I start with rabbits as my subject, and then decide more practically to write about female snowshoe rabbits in Akron, Ohio, I have done nothing whatever to supply purpose to my essay. True, there are things that might be said about rabbits in the particular category that would not hold true for rabbits in general. But other theses might be applied to all rabbits. The point is that mere shrinking or subdividing of the subject only leaves a smaller subject, not a thesis. Before the essayist starts to write, he must have something to say, not just something to talk about.

How, then, does a thesis arise? Certainly it does not in most cases spring fully articulated into the writer's mind in the form of a complete proposition. More likely it starts with a somewhat vague impulse: an awareness, perhaps, of something not noticed before; the sense of an injustice that needs to be set right; the urge to exclaim over pleasure; the recognition of a discrepancy that wants resolving; suspicions about the cause of some well-known effect. Here begins the process of narrowing the focus, refining the intent. Thesis, not subject, is being sharpened into effectiveness. As the writer's view of his purpose grows clearer, he can begin to trace out the basic shape that his essay will have; at the same time he will need to make decisions about which elements of available subject matter he should use. But throughout the acts of planning and composition, the thesis —whether its function is to demonstrate a truth or simply to reveal a quality of experience—remains the controlling force. Where its control is skillfully maintained, the resulting substance of the essay will be solid and forceful at the same time.

The above discussion is not meant to suggest that subject matter is unimportant. No author's intention can exist in a vacuum, and the reader's attention cannot exist there either. In algebra, proofs are established within a self-contained system of symbolic language. It is not necessary to know what a, b, c, and x stand for, and in fact it is better to assume that they represent nothing but themselves. Verbal discourse differs. Any statement that is made—except for pure gibberish—*refers* to a reality beyond itself, and as a result its accuracy and appropriateness can be judged by any listener or reader who has some knowledge of the reality referred to. Thus the successful writer must know as much as he can about any subject in which his thesis may be involved. In Chapter One the essayist was partly defined as a commentator who works chiefly in his capacity as a generally intelligent man rather than as a specialist. This role should not be used as an excuse for being scornful of information, data, and an assured command of one's subject. Without a certain amount of authoritative reference, even the most ingeniously dazzling thesis will break up under the stress of serious thought. But how can a writer determine when to stop learning about his subject, short of becoming a full-fledged specialist? The answer is that he should get whatever information the thesis itself requires for effective presentation. More important, he should be sure to let the reader know, in some way, what are his qualifications and what his limitations.

For a critical reader of essays, the discovery of the thesis does not occur in such predictable steps. In some cases, the author's intention is carefully spelled out in the first paragraph or two, so that the sense of thesis-controlled substance is present throughout. More often, a reader will find himself first in the presence of a certain subject without knowing for a while what is going to be done with it. Occasionally, the essay's objective is concealed or withheld until very near the end, so that its revelation dawns suddenly and throws what has gone before into new perspective. Effects like this do not necessarily mean that the writer's craftsmanship has failed or that he has done a bad job of converting subject matter to substance. In fact, it may be a particularly rare skill that enables him to lead the reader to the point where the essay's entire substance, the purpose and function of everything it has said, becomes apparent at once.

LEVANA AND OUR LADIES OF SORROW

Thomas De Quincey

Oftentimes at Oxford I saw Levana in my dreams. I knew her by her Roman symbols. Who is Levana? Reader, that do not pretend to have leisure for very much scholarship, you will not be angry with me for telling you. Levana was the Roman goddess that performed for the new-born infant the earliest office of ennobling kindness—typical, by its mode, of that grandeur which belongs to man everywhere, and of that benignity in powers invisible which even in Pagan worlds sometimes descends to sustain it. At the very moment of birth, just as the infant tasted for the first time the atmosphere of our troubled planet, it was laid on the ground. *That* might bear different interpretations. But immediately, lest so grand a creature should grovel there for more than one instant, either the paternal hand, as proxy for the goddess Levana, or some near kinsman, as proxy for the father, raised it upright, bade it look erect as the king of all this world, and presented its forehead to the stars, saying, perhaps, in his heart, "Behold what is greater than yourselves!" This symbolic act represented the function of Levana. And that mysterious lady, who never revealed her face (except to me in dreams), but always acted by delegation, had her name from the Latin verb (as still it is the Italian verb) *levare*, to raise aloft.

This is the explanation of Levana. And hence it has arisen that some people have understood by Levana the tutelary power that controls the education of the nursery. She, that would not suffer at his birth even a prefigurative or mimic degradation for her awful ward, far less could be supposed to suffer the real degradation attaching to the non-development of his powers. She therefore watches over human education. Now, the word *edŭco*, with the penultimate short, was derived (by a process often exemplified in the crystallization of languages) from the word *edūco*, with the penultimate long. Whatsoever *educes*, or develops, *educates*. By the education of Levana, therefore, is meant, not the poor machinery that moves by spelling-books and grammars, but by that mighty system of central forces hidden in the deep bosom of human life, which by passion, by strife, by temptation, by the energies of resistance, works for ever upon children, resting not day or night, any more than the mighty wheel of day and night themselves, whose moments, like restless spokes, are glimmering [1] for ever as they revolve.

If, then, *these* are the ministries by which Levana works, how profoundly must she reverence the agencies of grief! But you, reader, think that children generally are not liable to grief such as mine. There are two senses in the word *generally*—the sense of Euclid, where it means *universally* (or in the whole extent of the *genus*), and a foolish sense of this world, where it means *usually*. Now, I am far from saying that children universally are capable of grief like mine. But there are more than you ever heard of who die of grief in this island of ours. I will tell you a common case. The rules of Eton require that a boy on the *foundation* should be there twelve years: he is superannuated at eighteen; consequently he must come at six. Children torn away from mothers and sisters at that age not unfrequently die. I speak of what I know. The complaint is not entered by the registrar as grief; but *that* it is. Grief of that sort, and at that age, has killed more than ever have been counted amongst its martyrs.

Therefore it is that Levana often communes with the powers that shake man's heart; therefore it is that she dotes upon grief. "These ladies," said I softly to myself, on seeing the ministers with whom Levana was conversing, "these are the Sorrows; and they are three in number: as the *Graces* are three, who dress man's life with beauty; the *Parcæ* are three, who weave the dark arras of man's life in their mysterious loom always with colours sad in part, sometimes angry with tragic crimson and black; the *Furies* are three, who visit with retributions called from the other side of the grave offences that walk upon this; and once even the *Muses* were but three, who fit the harp, the trumpet, or the lute, to the great burdens of man's impassioned creations. These are the Sorrows; all three of whom I know." The last words I say now; but in Oxford I said, "one of whom I know, and the others too surely I *shall* know." For already, in my fervent

---

[1] As I have never allowed myself to covet any man's ox nor his ass, nor anything that is his, still less would it become a philosopher to covet other people's images or metaphors. Here, therefore, I restore to Mr. Wordsworth this fine image of the revolving wheel and the glimmering spokes, as applied by him to the flying successions of day and night. I borrowed it for one moment in order to point my own sentence; which being done, the reader is witness that I now pay it back instantly by a note made for that sole purpose. On the same principle I often borrow their seals from young ladies, when closing my letters, because there is sure to be some tender sentiment upon them about "memory," or "hope," or "roses," or "reunion," and my correspondent must be a sad brute who is not touched by the eloquence of the seal, even if his taste is so bad that he remains deaf to mine.

youth, I saw (dimly relieved upon the dark background of my dreams) the imperfect lineaments of the awful Sisters.

These Sisters—by what name shall we call them? If I say simply "The Sorrows," there will be a chance of mistaking the term; it might be understood of individual sorrow—separate cases of sorrow —whereas I want a term expressing the mighty abstractions that incarnate themselves in all individual sufferings of man's heart, and I wish to have these abstractions presented as impersonations, that is, as clothed with human attributes of life, and with functions pointing to flesh. Let us call them, therefore, *Our Ladies of Sorrow*.

I know them thoroughly, and have walked in all their kingdoms. Three sisters they are, of one mysterious household; and their paths are wide apart; but of their dominion there is no end. Them I saw often conversing with Levana, and sometimes about myself. Do they talk, then? O no! Mighty phantoms like these disdain the infirmities of language. They may utter voices through the organs of man when they dwell in human hearts, but amongst themselves is no voice nor sound; eternal silence reigns in *their* kingdoms. They spoke not as they talked with Levana; they whispered not; they sang not; though oftentimes methought they *might* have sung: for I upon earth had heard their mysteries oftentimes deciphered by harp and timbrel, by dulcimer and organ. Like God, whose servants they are, they utter their pleasure not by sounds that perish, or by words that go astray, but by signs in heaven, by changes on earth, by pulses in secret rivers, heraldries painted on darkness, and hieroglyphics written on the tablets of the brain. *They* wheeled in mazes; *I* spelled the steps. *They* telegraphed from afar; *I* read the signals. *They* conspired together; and on the mirrors of darkness *my* eye traced the plots. *Theirs* were the symbols; *mine* are the words.

What is it the Sisters are? What is it that they do? Let me describe their form and their presence, if form it were that still fluctuated in its outline, or presence it were that for ever advanced to the front or for ever receded amongst shades.

The eldest of the three is named *Mater Lachrymarum*, Our Lady of Tears. She it is that night and day raves and moans, calling for vanished faces. She stood in Rama, where a voice was heard of lamentation—Rachel weeping for her children, and refusing to be comforted. She it was that stood in Bethlehem on the night when Herod's sword swept its nurseries of Innocents, and the little feet were stiffened for ever which, heard at times as they trotted along floors overhead, woke pulses of love in household hearts that were not unmarked in heaven. Her eyes are sweet and subtle, wild and sleepy, by turns; oftentimes rising to the clouds, oftentimes challenging the heavens. She wears a diadem round her head. And I knew by childish memories that she could go abroad upon the winds, when she heard the sobbing of litanies, or the thundering of organs, and when she beheld the mustering of summer clouds. This Sister, the elder, it is that carries keys more than papal at her girdle, which open every cottage and every palace. She, to my knowledge, sat all last summer by the bedside of the blind beggar, him that so often and so gladly I talked with, whose pious daughter, eight years old, with the sunny countenance, resisted the temptations of play and village mirth, to travel all day long on dusty roads with her afflicted father. For this did God send her a great reward. In the spring time of the year, and whilst yet her own spring was budding, He recalled her to himself. But her blind father mourns for ever over *her:* still he dreams at midnight that the little guiding hand is locked within his own; and still he wakens to a darkness that is *now* within a second and a deeper darkness. This *Mater Lachrymarum* also has been sitting all this winter of 1844–5 within the bedchamber of the Czar, bringing before his eyes a daughter (not less pious) that vanished to God not less suddenly, and left behind her a darkness not less profound. By the power of the keys it is that Our Lady of Tears glides, a ghostly intruder, into the chambers of sleepless men, sleepless women, sleepless children, from Ganges to the Nile, from Nile to Mississippi. And her, because she is the first-born of her house, and has the widest empire, let us honour with the title of "Madonna."

The second Sister is called *Mater Suspiriorum*, Our Lady of Sighs. She never scales the clouds, nor walks abroad upon the winds. She wears no diadem. And her eyes, if they were ever seen, would be neither sweet nor subtle; no man could read their story; they would be found filled with perishing dreams, and with wrecks of forgotten delirium. But she raises not her eyes; her head, on which sits a dilapidated turban, droops for ever, for ever fastens on the dust. She weeps not. She groans not. But she sighs inaudibly at intervals. Her sister, Madonna, is oftentimes stormy and frantic, raging in the highest against heaven, and demanding back her darlings. But Our Lady of Sighs never clamours, never defies, dreams not of rebellious aspirations. She is humble to abjectness. Hers is the meekness that belongs to the hopeless. Murmur she may, but it is in her sleep. Whisper she may, but it is to herself in the twilight. Mutter she does at times, but it is in solitary places that are desolate as she is desolate, in ruined cities, and when the sun has gone down to his rest. This Sister is the visitor of the Pariah, of the Jew, of the bondsman to the oar in the Mediterranean galleys; of the English criminal in Norfolk Island, blotted out from the books of remembrance in sweet far-off England; of the baffled penitent reverting his eyes for ever upon a solitary grave, which to him seems the altar overthrown of some past and bloody sacrifice, on which altar no oblations can now be availing, whether towards pardon that he might implore, or towards reparation that he might attempt. Every slave that at noonday looks up to the tropical sun with timid reproach, as he points with one hand to the earth, our general mother, but for *him* a stepmother, as he points with the other hand to the Bible, our general teacher, but against *him* sealed and sequestered;[2] every woman sitting in darkness, without love to shelter her head, or hope to illumine her solitude, because the heaven-born instincts kindling in her nature germs of holy affections, which God implanted in her womanly bosom, having been stifled by social necessities, now burn sullenly to waste, like sepulchral lamps amongst the ancients; every nun defrauded of her unreturning May-time by wicked kinsman, whom God will judge; every captive in every dungeon; all that are betrayed, and all that are rejected; outcasts by traditionary law, and children of *hereditary* disgrace: all these walk with Our Lady of Sighs. She also carries a key; but she needs it little. For her kingdom is chiefly amongst the tents of Shem, and the houseless vagrant of every clime. Yet in the very highest ranks of man she finds chapels of her own; and even in glorious England there are some that, to the world, carry their heads as proudly as the reindeer, who yet secretly have received her mark upon their foreheads.

But the third Sister, who is also the youngest——! Hush! whisper whilst we talk of *her!* Her kingdom is not large, or else no flesh should live; but within that kingdom all power is hers. Her head, turreted like that of Cybele, rises almost beyond the reach of sight. She droops not; and her eyes, rising so high, *might* be hidden by distance. But, being what they are, they cannot be hidden: through the treble veil of crape which she wears the fierce light of a blazing misery, that rests not for matins or for vespers, for noon of day or noon of night, for ebbing or for flowing tide, may be read from the very ground. She is the defier of God. She also is the mother of lunacies, and the suggestress of suicides. Deep lie the roots of her power; but narrow is the nation that she rules. For she can approach only those in whom a profound nature has been upheaved by central convulsions; in whom the heart trembles and the brain rocks under

[2] This, the reader will be aware, applies chiefly to the cotton and tobacco States of North America; but not to them only: on which account I have not scrupled to figure the sun which looks down upon slavery as *tropical*—no matter if strictly within the tropics, or simply so near to them as to produce a similar climate.

conspiracies of tempest from without and tempest from within. Madonna moves with uncertain steps, fast or slow, but still with tragic grace. Our Lady of Sighs creeps timidly and stealthily. But this youngest Sister moves with incalculable motions, bounding, and with tiger's leaps. She carries no key; for, though coming rarely amongst men, she storms all doors at which she is permitted to enter at all. And *her* name is *Mater Tenebrarum*—Our Lady of Darkness.

These were the *Semnai Theai* or Sublime Goddesses,[3] these were the *Eumenides* or Gracious Ladies (so called by antiquity in shuddering propitiation), of my Oxford dreams. Madonna spoke. She spoke by her mysterious hand. Touching my head, she beckoned to Our Lady of Sighs; and *what* she spoke, translated out of the signs which (except in dreams) no man reads, was this:

"Lo! here is he whom in childhood I dedicated to my altars. This is he that once I made my darling. Him I led astray, him I beguiled; and from heaven I stole away his young heart to mine. Through me did he become idolatrous; and through me it was, by languishing desires, that he worshipped the worm, and prayed to the wormy grave. Holy was the grave to him; lovely was its darkness; saintly its corruption. Him, this young idolater, I have seasoned for thee, dear gentle Sister of Sighs! Do thou take him now to *thy* heart, and season him for our dreadful sister. And thou," turning to the *Mater Tenebrarum*, she said, "wicked sister, that temptest and hatest, do thou take him from *her*. See that thy sceptre lie heavy on his head. Suffer not woman and her tenderness to sit near him in his darkness. Banish the frailties of hope; wither the relenting of love; scorch the fountains of tears; curse him as only *thou* canst curse. So shall he be accomplished in the furnace; so shall he see the things that ought *not* to be seen, sights that are abominable, and secrets that are unutterable. So shall he read elder truths, sad truths, grand truths, fearful truths. So shall he rise again *before* he dies. And so shall our commission be accomplished which from God we had—to plague his heart until we had unfolded the capacities of his spirit."

[3] *"Sublime Goddesses"*: The word σεμνος is really rendered *venerable* in dictionaries—not a very flattering epithet for females. But I am disposed to think that it comes nearest to our idea of the *sublime*—as near as a Greek word *could* come.

QUESTIONS AND EXERCISES

1. Distinguish this essay's subject from its thesis. At what point in your reading of the essay did the thesis become clear? Before you

reached that point, did you suppose that some other thesis was being developed? Specify where and why.

2. Logical argument is not DeQuincey's chief means of supporting his thesis. How would you describe his method? *Could* the point have been made through argument?

3. In the opening paragraph, what does De Quincey assume about the audience's knowledge of Levana? What does he assume, later, about its knowledge of the three Sisters? Would it be accurate to say that the audience knows about De Quincey's subject only as much as it knows about Levana and the Sisters? Explain.

4. By referring specifically to different parts of the essay, show where and how De Quincey tries to display his authority, his command of the subject. Is this effort successful in contributing to the essay's substance?

5. Paragraph 3 makes the point that grief is a potent force—even a killing force—in the lives of young children. Here the author asserts his authority flatly ("I speak of what I know"). Why, in terms of the essay's thesis, does this point require such emphatic authority?

6. In describing the three "Ladies of Sorrow," De Quincey shows that each of them rules a special province of suffering. One is described as being the eldest and as having "the widest empire." Another presides over a smaller kingdom, but her form of suffering is probably the most anguished of the three. Specify as categorically as you can what the three different Sisters represent, and then explain how this differentiation is important to the advancement of the thesis and the final effect of the substance.

7. The personal experiences that De Quincey recounts here are dream experiences. How does he describe the visible appearance of the Sisters without losing the effect of dream-like awareness?

8. Write a long paragraph in which you try to capture some visual effect from a dream you have had. Add another paragraph explaining exactly what methods you have used in the first.

9. Levana and the three Sisters are symbolic personifications. Write an essay whose thesis is approximately the same as De Quincey's, but leave these ladies out of it entirely.

10. De Quincey tells us that Levana's function must be closely connected with "agencies of grief"—that is, the Sisters. Using the device of personification, write an essay that shows a different set of "agencies" helpful to Levana.

THE DECLINE OF THE MACHINE

John Kenneth Galbraith

Those who guide our worries on large issues regularly ask us to ponder man's losing competition with the machine. On the assembly lines he is being replaced by automatic machinery which is regulated and instructed by electronic controls. If the resulting product is a consumer item it has almost certainly been designed to minimize both the effort and intelligence required of its user. Not even the question of whether people will want it has been left entirely to judgment. This has been ascertained by market surveys and insured by advertising and both, perhaps, were analyzed with the aid of an electronic computer, sometimes too ambitiously called an electronic brain.

The tendency to dispense with men and intelligence is held to go far beyond the consumer gadgets. The unmanned missile is about to replace the old-fashioned hand-operated bomber. In the near future, according to enthusiasts, unmanned missiles will take flight to intercept other unmanned missiles which will prevent these from intercepting other automated missiles. The operation will be handled under contract by IBM. If the globe were larger or the explosions smaller the prospect would be not unattractive. The machines having taken over, men would all be noncombatants. The charm of war has always been greatest for those whose role was to guide it from a certain distance.

These visions of the triumph of the machine can be multiplied endlessly. We do not take them quite seriously for we do not really believe that we are being replaced, and our instinct is sound. If there is a competition between man and machine, man is winning it—not for at least two centuries has his position been so strong as compared with the apparatus with which he works.

And the fact that this is the age of ascendant man, not triumphant machine, has practical consequences. If machines are the decisive thing, then the social arrangements by which we increase our physical plant and equipment will be of first importance. But if it is men that count, then our first concern must be with arrangements for conserving and developing personal talents. It will be these on which

THE DECLINE OF THE MACHINE: From *The Liberal Hour* (1960), by John K. Galbraith. Reprinted by permission of the publisher, Houghton Mifflin Company.

progress will depend. Should it happen, moreover, that for reasons of antiquated design our society does well in supplying itself with machines and badly in providing itself with highly improved man-power, there would be cause for concern. There is such cause, for that, precisely, is our situation.

But first, what is the evidence that men have been gaining on machines—that skill and intelligence have become more important in what we call economic progress than capital plant and equipment?

2

The change is most prominently reflected in the changed position of the owner or supplier of physical capital. For a half century he has been a man of steadily declining prestige and importance. Once it was taken for granted that ownership of an industrial enterprise—the ownership of the capital assets or a substantial share of them—gave a man a decisive voice in its direction. So it was with Ford, Carnegie, the elder Rockefeller, Commodore Vanderbilt, and John Jacob Astor. And to be a source of capital, as in the case of the elder Morgan, insured an almost equal power over the enterprise. It also insured a considerable position in the community. Indeed, it was because the provision of capital conveyed such power that the system was called capitalism.

Now the ownership of capital, or the capacity to supply it, accords no such power. Few large corporations are now run by their owners; those like Du Pont where, for many generations, a talented family has had a decisive influence on the enterprise it owns, are becoming a rarity. Typically the power lies with the professional managers. These make elaborate obeisance to the stockholders. But they select the Board of Directors, which the stockholders then dutifully elect, and in equally solemn ritual the Board then selects the management that selected it. In some cases, for example the Standard Oil Company of New Jersey, once dominated by the first Rockefeller, the Board consists exclusively of managers selected by the managers who were selected by the Board.

There are a number of reasons for the rise of the professional manager, but by far the most important is that ownership of capital has come to count for much less than ownership of ability, knowledge, and brains. The man of ability could get the capital; the man who had capital and was devoid of other qualification had become pretty much a hopeless case. (Even to give away his money would eventually require the services of a professional.) The relatively impecunious but better-trained, more intelligent, more determined, or politically more adept managers have almost everywhere taken over. Once in office it is only rarely that the owners of capital can dislodge them.

Nor is this a misfortune for the companies in question. Some of the worst cases of corporate misfortune in recent times have been those in which the owners of the capital have managed to use their power to keep the professionals out. In the thirties and early forties the elder Henry Ford used his power as the sole owner of the Ford Motor Company to remain in command. It is now freely acknowledged that the company suffered severely as a result. Following his death the management was professionalized and much improved. The great merchandising house of Montgomery Ward under Sewell Avery provided a parallel example. Control and direction of a large company by a capitalist has become, indeed, a rather risky affair. He may try to do what can only be done well by a professionally qualified group of diverse and specialized talent.

3

But though it is most visible at the top, the shift in the comparative importance of men and capital is perceptible throughout the modern industrial enterprise. The procedures by which the large and successful enterprise raises funds for new plant and equipment are orderly and predictable. And, depending on circumstances, there is a considerable range of choice—earnings can be withheld, there can be resort to banks, or securities can be sold. A great deal of pompous ritual attends this process, but for the large and successful firm this signifies neither uncertainty nor difficulty but only that we have considerable respect for money and expect large sums to be handled with decent ceremony.

There is no similar certainty in the procedures by which even the most successful concern supplies itself with talent. It must send its emissaries to participate in the annual talent hunt, and if the most imposing men still go to the money markets, the most eloquent go to the colleges. The bag is always uncertain and frequently inadequate. If a successful firm is contemplating a considerable expansion it will almost certainly worry more about where to find the men than where to get the money.

And the change is reflected in the fears and apprehensions of the community at large. We wonder whether we are investing as much as we should in physical capital; we hear that the Soviets, who in our time have largely replaced conscience as the stern small voice of duty, are doing much more. But there is more everyday concern about the state of our schools and colleges. Are they doing properly by our children? Where can we find the resources to enable them to do better? Increasingly we are wondering about the adequacy of our output of highly trained and educated people.

This shows itself in a very practical way. Every family knows that the automobile industry is equipped to supply it with a new car almost on a moment's notice. Such is the admirable condition of our physical plant. But it cannot be at all sure there will be a place for all the children in a good college. Even the automobile executive may wonder where he can get his boy in. Such is the contrasting state of our facilities for human development.

4

The forces back of the change in the relative position of man as compared with capital are not new. Some of them, curiously enough, are those which, at first glance, seem to suggest the ascendancy of the machine.

The classical trinity of productive factors were land (including natural resources), labor (broadly defined to include both physical and intellectual effort), and capital. All production was seen as resulting from the combination of these factors in one form or another and in one proportion or another. Some economists have questioned whether there was much difference between land and capital goods—both support man's efforts to produce things, and many economists have insisted on adding as a fourth factor of production entrepreneurship or the human effort which was devoted to organizing and managing the other three factors. Subject to these modifications and a few quibbles, the classical delineation of productive agents is still accepted and, indeed, is deeply imbedded in economic thought.

All production requires all three (or all four) factors and in this sense all are equally vital. But the importance attached to the different factors has changed remarkably in the last hundred and fifty years. At the beginning of the last century—the formative years of modern economics—land seemed peculiarly important. Population was growing. Europe and Asia seemed very crowded. The vast fertile spaces of the Americas, Australia, and Africa were but slightly appreciated. The effect of modern agricultural techniques on production per acre was, of course, beyond view. Both Ricardo and Malthus, two of the towering figures in the history of economic ideas, concluded that, in different ways, man's fate would be largely decided by the relentless pressure of population on limited land. Labor being abundant, perhaps excessively so, it seemed far less important than land. Capital, though important, also lacked the life-and-death significance of the land supply. Land was the factor of greatest prestige.

As the nineteenth century passed, capital gained rapidly to a position of dominance in the trinity. The new world added enormously to the supply of land. The decisive question was its development and for this ports, steamships, roads, railroads, farmsteads, and farm equipment were needed. The land was there; the labor came almost automatically; but the more capital the greater the pace of progress.

This emphasis on capital was reinforced by the nature of industrial advance during the last century. It consisted not of the invention of a great number of new techniques but the spread of a relatively small number of spectacularly important ones. Thus, textile manufacture became a factory industry. Steam power was applied to manufacturing, transport, and mining to replace power from men, animals, falling water, or wind. Iron and steel became plentiful and cheap and thus available for many new uses.

These inventions resulted, so far as anyone could tell, from a combination of accident, inspiration, and genius. Men like James Watt, Benjamin Franklin, and Eli Whitney could not be cultivated, and while they might under some circumstances be protected by the patent office, that was about all that could be done to foster technological progress.

But if little could be done to stimulate inventions, much could be done about putting them to use. Savings could be stimulated by exhortations to thrift—and even more by a system of ethics and religion which assured the diligent, abstemious, and self-denying man esteem in this world and salvation in the next. Investment could be encouraged by stable government and laws which assured investors that profits would be theirs to enjoy. Looking rationally at the thing that was subject to wise policy, economists came to measure progress by the proportion of the nation's income that, each year, was saved and invested.

5

Investment in physical capital is still a prime measure of progress but it is an obsolescent one. More and more progress is coming to depend on the quality rather than the quantity of the capital equipment in use and on the intelligence and skill of those who use it.

There are reasonably good figures to go on. Between the early seventies of the last century and the decade 1944–53, according to calculations made under the auspices of the National Bureau of Economic Research, the net output of the American economy increased by an average of 3.5 per cent a year. Less than half of this (1.7 per cent) is explained by increases in the supply of capital and labor.[1] The rest was the result of improvements in capital equipment—technological advance—and improvements in the working force, including, of course, its leadership and direction. The *share* in the advance attributable to technological improvement and to the improved skill and ability of workers, technicians, and managers has been increasing.

But both technological advance and improved skills and abilities are the product of personal development. Machines do not improve themselves; this is still the work of highly improved men. And most technological advance is now the result not of the accident of inspiration or genius but of highly purposeful effort. Once we had to wait for the accidental appearance of Edisons and Wrights. Now through education and organized effort in a laboratory or experimental shop we get something approaching the same results from much more common clay.

So it comes to this. We now get the larger part of our industrial growth not from more capital investment but from improvements in men and improvements brought about by highly improved men. And this process of technological advance has become fairly predictable. We get from men pretty much what we invest in them. So now in its turn, after land and after capital, labor—highly improved labor to be sure—has come to the center of the stage. Investment in personal development is therefore at least as useful as an index of progress as investment in physical capital. It could be more valuable. This is the kind of change which solemn men of self-confessed soundness of judgment will continue to resist; the familiar is always defended with much more moral fervor just before it becomes foolish.

What then of our practical accommodation to this new urgency of investment in personal development?

6

At first glance our position would seem to be quite good. We have been reaping large gains from the application of trained intelligence

[1] These figures have been most thoughtfully interpreted by Professor Theodore Schultz to whom all who discuss these matters are in debt. See his "Investment in Man: An Economist's View," *Social Service Review*, Vol. XXXIII, No. 2 (June, 1959).

to our economic life. This is the fruit of one of the world's pioneer experiments in public education. Surely our advantage will continue.

We cannot be so optimistic. Until the last century learning and even literacy were the badges of privilege. They had always been reserved to the favored few. Accordingly learning was a symbol of equality—a symbol that our grandparents, determined to establish their claim to full equality, were not disposed to overlook. Hence the free elementary schools, high schools, the Land Grant College system, and the remarkable number and variety of other institutions of higher (and not excessively high) learning.

This system was adequate, even admirable, so long as education was a socially provided service designed to insure (though it had other purposes too) rough equality of opportunity. It has ceased to be sufficient as education has become a form of investment.

The test of what a community should spend on a social service is what it can afford—what it believes it can spare from other forms of consumption. The test of investment, by contrast, is what will pay for itself. We apply the investment test as a matter of course to physical capital and even the commonplace terminology reflects the different attitudes; while we "invest" in physical capital, we "spend" for education.

The investment test is far the more generous of the two—that is to say, it sanctions much larger outlays. It implies an aggressive canvass of all possible uses of funds to see what will pay off at a profit. To find new ways of investing at a profit is to prove one's enterprise. One of the most familiar theorems of accepted economics is that, subject to some lags and irregularities, investment in physical capital will occur whenever marginal return exceeds the marginal cost; that is, whenever the return to additional investment is sufficient to cover the added cost including interest and some allowance for risk.

The test of what can be afforded, by contrast, invokes far more frugal attitudes. The outlay, even if it is for education, is vaguely self-indulgent. If we wish it—if we wish our children to have the prestige and satisfactions and opportunities from learning—we must measure the cost against other important alternatives. Virtue resides not in finding ways of investing more but in finding ways of spending less. The community honors the man who is identified with economy. These attitudes remain even though, as we have seen, the outlays economized may yield as large a return (perhaps larger) as those for physical capital.

Investment in personal development is also handicapped by the lack of a close relationship of outlay with the resulting benefit. A chemical company invests in a new plant because it knows it will get the higher earnings. If it invests in the education of a young chemist it has no similar assurance that it will get a return from its outlay. The fellow may decide to become an artist or a farmer, or he may go faithlessly to work for a competitor.

One can see by a simple illustration what the kind of firm relationship of cost to benefit that exists for physical capital would do for investment in personal development if it existed there. Imagine an arrangement by which promising youngsters, when halfway through high school, were indentured for life to a corporation. The corporation would then be responsible for all further education and would be assured of their services for life. Performance of the companies tomorrow, it would soon be evident, would depend on the quality of the postulant executives, scientists, and other specialists being selected and trained today. The quality of this group would become a matter of major concern. It would be under the eye of accomplished educators. Money would start flowing into it. Investment fund managers would send scouts to seek information on its quality. If one of the larger oil companies found that the schools and colleges available for training its oncoming geologists and engineers were inadequate, it would obviously have to take steps to remedy the situation—perhaps by establishing its own. Otherwise, in a few years, it would be outclassed by the companies with better talent. One can easily imagine bond issues by backward companies to develop stronger technical echelons. The result would be a substantial and possibly an astronomical increase in outlays for personal development—all justified by the resulting profit. All this would be the result of giving the corporation a firm lien on the individual's services and thus on the return on the money it spends on him. It has such a lien on a machine; the example only makes human beings as privileged, for purposes of investment, as are machines.

The final reason for thinking that our arrangements for investing in personal development are deficient is that the Soviets have, technically speaking, superior ones. They begin with all resources under public control; hence, there is no problem in transferring those to be devoted to personal development from private to public use. And outlays for physical capital and those for personal development are items in the same huge budget. The returns from one type of investment can be measured against the returns from the other. There is no inherent reason why physical capital should have a preference as in our case. The result is that the U.S.S.R., by our standards still a comparatively poor country, treats its schools, research and training institutes, universities, and adult and worker education with a generosity which impresses all Western visitors. These outlays, needless to say, not old-fashioned expansion of physical capital, were decisive for launching the Sputniks and for landing their successor on the moon.

7

We cannot solve the problem of personal investment by indenturing our youngsters at a tender age to a corporation. And we should not expect the kindly corporation to rise to the rescue with large voluntary grants for education. Time has already been wasted on this notion. The problem is far too serious to be left to the conscience of those with a particular willingness to spend the stockholder's money.

Most likely we will solve the problem by making fuller and better use of the familiar instruments of public finance. We must see spending for personal development not as a cost but as an opportunity. Then we must make sure that we are taxing ourselves sufficiently to exploit this opportunity. That the Federal Government must play a role is elementary. It has access to fiscal resources that are inherently far greater than those of states and localities; now that education has become an investment rather than a social service, these resources are indispensable. It is also the unit of government with responsibility for national development and growth. There is at least a likelihood that investment in personal development is a better guarantee of national power than some of our military expenditures.[2]

We need also to review our attitudes toward state and local taxation. In a poor country there are sound reasons for reluctance in taxing objects of everyday consumption in order to have more public services and amenities. But we are not a poor country and personal development has become not a service but an investment. So states and localities should no longer hesitate to use sales and excise taxes (as an addition to and not as a substitute for others) to pay for schools and universities. And liberals, in particular, should not be too indignant when this is proposed.

There is another way of putting provision for personal development on a par with capital development that we should consider. We assume that a corporation, either by withholding from earnings or by resort to the capital market, will take responsibility for improving and expanding its own physical plant. The pressure for voluntary contributions by corporations to education reflects, no

[2] We must see too that waste, including that of the athletic circuses, is brought under control. It is not only indefensible in itself, it brings investment in human development into disrepute.

doubt, a feeling that there is a similar responsibility for personal development. Corporations are the largest employers of trained talent. They reap the rewards from employing such people. Why shouldn't they pay a part of the cost of training this talent?

Perhaps they should. Voluntary contributions will always be inequitable as well as inadequate. Conscience can readily be assuaged by a small contribution and the levy falls only on those with a social view of the corporation. But a special tax for education and training would encounter no similar objection. Levied as a percentage of total payroll—executive, scientific, skilled and unskilled—it would be roughly proportioned to the quantity and quality of the people employed. Thus it would be related to benefit from past investment in personal development; and it would mean that the company was assuming its rough share of the cost of replacing with improved talent the skilled workers, technicians, scientists, and executives that it employs. Initially the tax would presumably be borne in the form of higher prices by the consumers of the product. Ultimately the better talent would bring better methods, improved efficiency, and hence lower prices. It would be self-liquidating for it supports a profitable investment.

Corporations are now at great pains to explain that their prices must include provision for earnings sufficient to replace and expand their physical capital. This, they regularly assure their public, means that production will continue and be more efficient in the future. But, as the National Bureau figures show, we have more to gain from improving the quality of people. So a levy for this purpose would be an even better bargain.

Maybe there are other ways of augmenting the flow of resources into personal development. In a society that is changing we dare not assume that we have thought the last thoughts on any such subject. For man has not retreated before the machine; rather the machine has become desperately dependent on the improvement of man. And our economy is still arranged to supply machines rather than to improve men.

QUESTIONS AND EXERCISES

1. Distinguish between the subject and the thesis of this essay. At what point do we get our earliest indication of Galbraith's main purpose?

2. In his second paragraph, the author introduces the concept of totally automated warfare. Explain how he uses this idea to prepare the reader for the direction of his argument.

3. The writer comes close to contradicting himself in order to make his argument seem plausible. In what sense can men be called ascendant over machines, if men themselves do not recognize and take advantage of such ascendancy? Is the contradiction a real one or only apparent? Can you account for its usefulness here in terms of the kind of subject matter under discussion? Would such a device be as successful if the author were discussing, say, the need for recognizing the ascendancy of air travel over rail travel in America?

4. Has Galbraith argued that big business wholly neglects personal talent because it is so concerned with capital and material assets, or rather that it has neglected one very important aspect of the talent problem, while recognizing clearly other aspects of the problem?

5. Aside from the argument that it makes, how *informative* is the essay? That is, how much factual data does it supply that, taken alone, simply describes the subject rather than inherently supports the writer's position or argument? How, in these particular cases, does Galbraith convert such information to serve his specific purpose?

6. Describe how the writer uses the idea that genius is the means by which technological advance was achieved in the past.

7. At the end of the essay, where Galbraith uses his emphatic distinction between spending and investment, is he adding something new to the thesis of his essay or merely approaching the same argument through another form? Explain.

8. Write a paragraph (on any subject) that you regard as purely descriptive or informative, and that involves no argument, commentary, or interpretation of things, but just reveals part of a subject. Next, write another paragraph explaining why you have failed in the first, why it was impossible absolutely to exclude opinion and judgment from your description. Finally, write a third paragraph in which the same data are deliberately made part of a forcefully directed argument.

9. Does Galbraith's argument imply (or assume) that business-owners and suppliers of capital tend to be relatively dull-witted and uninventive? Write about 400 words on this question, making very particular reference to the text of the essay.

10. Think of another argument that the author might have used in presenting his case, and demonstrate in a couple of paragraphs how it could have been incorporated in the essay.

11. In 300 words draw your own distinction between investment and spending.

CHAPTER THREE

Relationships

The nature of the literary process, and especially the difference between information and argument, may be understood in another way by considering the essay itself, the finished product, in the context of its relationships to the world about which it speaks, the author who makes it, and the audience to whom it is addressed. The following diagram should help to illustrate these relationships:

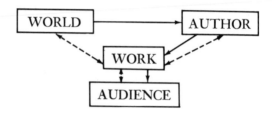

The solid arrows in the diagram represent the consecutive train of relationships by which an essay (or any literary work) is produced: The world (or some element in the author's experience of the world) affects the author in a certain way, and he embodies his reaction in a work that in turn impresses itself on the awareness of an audience. It is easy to see, once the work is finished, that in judging its value and understanding its art, the relationships shown by the dotted arrows in the diagram must be taken into account. A work can be assessed by its correspondence to the reality of the world, by its truthfulness in showing the inward condition of the author, and by its suitability to the audience. Most works tend, even on a first reading, to show which kind of judgment might appropriately be made. An essay with a strong imitative (or *mimetic*) intention compels us to notice the amount of fidelity with which it mirrors the subject. Another piece, more emotionally lyrical than descriptive, requires attention to its *expressive* capability. A third, unmistakably designed to move its readers to think or act in a particular way, will be viewed in terms of its success in manipulating the audience.

Of course none of these categories is airtight. A work is never purely mimetic or expressive or rhetorical. The three-way division gives only a rough guide to the business of asking useful critical questions. Remember, while asking them, that as a critic one does not cease to be a member of the reading audience. However, to judge the mimetic success of a work, a critic needs an exceptionally wide and penetrating knowledge of the world; to judge its expressive power, he needs a knowledge of the author's own state of awareness, which is very hard to come by; to judge its rhetorical effectiveness, he needs some knowledge of the audience for whom the work was intended, and perhaps some honest self-knowledge as well.

From experience we know that the essayist is almost never content to write a piece that can be judged by narrowly mimetic criteria, by how well it simply holds a mirror up to the world. On the one hand, he tends to speak with a special and personal voice of his own, rather than in the aloof and impersonal anonymity of clinical description. On the other, he is nearly always bent on urging, expostulating, arguing his audience into an altered position, whether he means them to act, to hold new opinions, or only to recognize what they have not recognized before. If we say that most essays contain either something of sermon or something of song, or both, we have oversimplified the matter but not grossly falsified it. And, of course, any practicing writer must recognize the difference between the expressive and rhetorical functions, so that he may carefully control the mingling of the two.

In this context, let us consider the question of the author's involvement or self-expression. In some cases this is unmistakable; the author verbally re-creates, in effect, his own most intimate and subjective feelings. He may be recalling what it is like to fall in love or to attend a child's funeral. But it is in the less obvious cases that his personal intrusion works most interestingly. An essay on the decline of vegetarianism may pretend to a perfectly maintained cool objectivity, yet so reveal in almost every sentence the author's eccentric views on the subject that those views supplant vegetarianism itself as the center of our interest. This can happen, of course, even when the first-person pronoun "I" does not appear at all and even when the language itself carries all the superficial signs of scientific objectivity. But we also occasionally read an essay in which this state of affairs is reversed, where what at first seems to have the personally revelatory or confessional note turns out in the end to be a highly rational and scrupulously objective inquiry after truth. The relative obtrusiveness or unobtrusiveness of the author, the degree to which he makes himself an active and particularized presence in the reader's awareness, is controlled by a great number of variable elements in the work itself, and these range from the most localized forms of verbal style (to be discussed in Chapter Five) to the overall shape and strategy that the argument follows. It will be helpful to note briefly some of the special issues involved.

For one thing, consider the proposition that whenever an author constructs an argument he automatically becomes personal, that arguing necessitates personal involvement as, say, laboratory description does not. But we need a distinction. One may work hard to convince an audience of something without giving away much of one's own *personality*. I can argue hotly and long for abolition of capital punishment without letting my readers know whether I am a naturally quiet man or a wild-eyed extrovert, or whether I prefer personal comfort to public usefulness. So in one sense I am involved in the piece, in another sense I am not involved much at all.

Then too, we are told that the more specialized the knowledge that an author uses to conduct his argument and the more he depends upon unusual or little-known information to say what he has to say, the more individual his essay becomes, since the peculiarity of his personal knowledge must flavor his total performance. There is truth in the statement. Yet we need a distinction between what I *have* (which may include money, books, wives, and bakery goods as well as information) and what I *am*. After all, anyone who reads academic journals knows perfectly well that the special interest of a scholarly article does not ensure the revelation of its author's personal self.

Still, it is true that the more a writer tinkers with received experience, selects or edits from it, rearranges parts, analyzes it to discover submerged patterns and structures, the greater the chance that he will reveal not only his intellectual habits but his personality as well. When he is content to describe passively, to make a record of passing events, then the opportunity for him to display his own being and idiosyncrasy will not come so often.

Naturally, much of what has just been said is affected in turn by the author's knowledge of his audience and the assumptions, if any, that he makes about that audience. Even when he seems to have taken no particular notice of the kind of people who will probably read his work, it is usually clear that a writer understands something or other about their capacities. The tabloid journalist may work toward the lowest common denominator, careful never to write anything that will tax the minds of the witless, willing at the same time to use any sensational means of catching and holding a feeble attention, but the serious essayist works under different circumstances. Being a man of literate intelligence and a certain amount of sophistication, he may either assume wrongly that all who read him have similar talent, or, even worse, that they are so far beneath him that he must write down to them. In fact the chief danger is that an author will generalize the imagined character of the audience too much, thus oversimplifying the tactics for dealing with it. The best policy, and that of most reputable essayists most of the time, is to assume that the readers are moderately well informed and intelligent, though not necessarily versed in special areas of information and terminology.

But even the writer who works from such a judicious assumption as this is not free from difficulties. He must still decide whether his subject and substance require that he inform his readers of certain facts that are not common knowledge. Then he must determine how much of this information he can give without (1) alienating the audience by making it feel embarrassingly ill informed or (2) obscuring the main direction of the essay's statement. Prescriptions do no good here. Probably the best way for the practicing essayist to learn how to relate to his audience is by trial and error. But perhaps if we go through an illustrative essay looking for both the authorial intrusions and the recognition of audience, we will be in a better position, at least as critics, to approach the pieces that follow.

THE INTELLECTUAL AND THE MASS MEDIA

Leo Rosten

In 1958, the editors of Daedalus *(published by the American Academy of Arts and Sciences) and the director of the Tamiment Institute conspired to hold a three-day conference on "Mass Culture" in the smoky blue Poconos. They invited a group of exceptionally cerebral scholars to this symposium, among them Hannah Arendt, Daniel Bell, Ernest van den Haag, Sidney Hook, Paul Lazarsfeld, Arthur Schlesinger, Jr., Edward Shils. To off-set the academicians, the sponsors invited James Baldwin, Stanley Edgar Hyman, Randall Jarrell; and to introduce the hard note of professional experience in debasing our culture, I suppose, they invited Frank Stanton, President of Columbia Broadcasting System, and me.*

THE INTELLECTUAL AND THE MASS MEDIA: Reprinted with permission of *Daedalus*, Journal of the American Academy of Arts and Sciences, Boston, Mass. Spring 1960, "Mass Culture and Mass Media."

The Tamiment Conference was about as good as any I ever attended. The papers presented there were published in a book called Culture for the Millions? *and sub-titled* Mass Media in Modern Society. *It is, I think, an excellent symposium—even though the flap of the jacket begins: "In this lively and entertaining book. . . ." How the pure of mind have fallen—into the very vocabulary of the hucksters they correctly castigate for spurious excitation!* Culture for the Millions? *is often provocative and sometimes profound, but it is not, by even the most charitable verdict, either "lively" or "entertaining." This is what happens when scientists, like paperback publishers or fountain-pen salesman, try to lure customers into buying their wares.*

I made myself miserable during a week on the beach in Florida, brooding over the paper I was to present in the Poconos. I was, after all, tarnished by concourse with "mass circulation" on Madison Avenue. In the end, I simply composed a list of the charges commonly leveled against television, movies, and magazines—and responded to them as best I could. An introduction and a coda *rounded out the essay you may read below. I hope you will.*

Most intellectuals do not understand the inherent nature of the mass media. They do not understand the process by which a newspaper or magazine, movie or television show, is created. They project their own tastes, yearnings, and values upon the masses—who do not, unfortunately, share them. They attribute over-simplified motivations to those who own or operate the mass media. They assume that changes in ownership or control would necessarily improve the product. They presume the existence of a vast reservoir of talent, competence, and material which does not in fact exist.

A great deal of what appears in the mass media is dreadful tripe and treacle: inane in content, banal in style, muddy in reasoning, mawkish in sentiment, vulgar, naïve, and offensive to men of learning or refinement. I am both depressed and distressed by the bombardment of our eyes, our ears, and our brains by meretricious material designed for a populace whose paramount preferences involve "fun."

Why is this so? Are the media operated by cynical men motivated solely by profit? Are they controlled by debasers of culture—by ignorant, vulgar, irresponsible men?

Many intellectuals think so and say so. They think so and say so in the face of evidence they either do not examine or cannot bring themselves to accept: that when the public is free to choose among various products, it chooses—again and again and again—the frivolous as against the serious, "escape" as against reality, the lurid as against the tragic, the trivial as against the serious, fiction as against fact, the diverting as against the significant. To conclude otherwise is to deny the data: circulation figures for the press, box-office receipts for the movies and the theater, audience measurement for radio and television programs.

The sad truth seems to be this: that relatively few people in any society, not excluding Periclean Athens, have reasonably good taste or care deeply about ideas. Fewer still seem equipped—by temperament and capacity, rather than education—to handle ideas with both skill and pleasure.

The deficiencies of mass media are a function, in part at least, of the deficiencies of the masses. Is it unfair to ask that responsibility for mental laziness and deplorable taste be distributed—to include the schools, the churches, the parents, the social institutions which produce those masses who persist in preferring pin-ball games to anything remotely resembling philosophy?

Intellectuals seem unable to reconcile themselves to the fact that their hunger for more news, better plays, more serious debate, deeper involvement in ideas, is not a hunger characteristic of many. They cannot believe that the subjects dear to their hearts bore or repel or overtax the capacities of their fellow citizens. Why this is so I shall try to explore later. At this point, let me remark that the intellectual, who examines his society with unyielding and antiseptic detachment, must liberate himself from the myths (or, in Plato's term, the royal lie) by which any social system operates. It is ironic that intellectuals often destroy old myths to erect and reverence special myths of their own. A striking example is found in the clichés with which they both characterize and indict the mass media. Let us consider the principal particulars in that indictment.[1]

"The mass media lack originality."

They certainly do. Most of what appears in print, or on film, or on the air, lacks originality. But is there any area of human endeavor of which this is not true? Is not the original as rare in science or philosophy or painting as it is in magazines? Is not the original "original" precisely because it is rare? Is it not self-evident that the more that is produced of anything, the smaller the proportion of

[1] For the best general summary, and critical comment, see Chapter XV in *The Fabric of Society*, by Ralph Ross and Ernest van den Haag (Harcourt, Brace & World, 1957), a work of remarkable lucidity and good sense.

originality is likely to be? But is the absolute number of novel creative products thereby reduced? Are we dealing with Gresham's Law—or with imperfect observation?

The mass media are not characterized by endless inventiveness and variation. But they are considerably more varied and inventive, given their built-in limitations, than we give them credit for. Consider these limitations: neither life nor truth nor fiction offers infinite choices: there is only a limited number of plots or stories or themes; there is only a limited number of ways of communicating the limited body of material; audiences develop a cumulative awareness of resemblances and an augmented resistance to the stylized and the predictable; and even the freshest departures from routine soon become familiar and routine. Besides, originality is often achieved at the price of "balance" or proportion: the most arresting features in, say, *The New Yorker* or *Time* often incur the displeasure of scholars precisely because these journals prefer vitality to a judicious ordering of "all the facts."

The artist, of course, wrests freshness and new insight from the most familiar material; but true artists, in any field at any given time, are so rare that their singularity requires a special word—"genius."

The mass media are cursed by four deadly requirements: a gargantuan amount of space (in magazines and newspapers) and time (in television and radio) *has* to be filled; talent—on every level, in every technique—is scarce; the public votes, i.e., is free to decide what it prefers (and it is the deplorable results of this voting that intellectuals might spend more time confronting); and a magazine, paper, television or radio program is committed to periodic and unalterable publication. Content would be markedly improved if publications or programs appeared only when superior material was available. This applies to academic journals no less than to publications or programs with massive audiences.

"*The mass media do not use the best brains or freshest talents.*"

Surely the burden of proof is on those who make this assertion. The evidence is quite clear that talent in the popular arts is searched for and courted in ways that do not apply in other fields: seniority is ignored, tenure is virtually nonexistent, youth is prized. In few areas is failure so swiftly and ruthlessly punished, or success so swiftly and extravagantly rewarded.

And still—talent is scarce. It is a woeful fact that despite several generations of free education, our land has produced relatively few first-rate minds; and of those with first-rate brains, fewer have imagination; of those with brains and imagination, fewer still possess judgment. If we ask, in addition, for the special skills and experience involved in the art of communicating, the total amount of talent available to the media is not impressive.

"The best brains" in the land do not gravitate to the media—if by brains we mean skill in analyzing complexities, or sustaining abstract propositions for prolonged intellectual operations. But the best brains would not necessarily make the best editors, or writers, or producers, or publishers—at least they would not long survive in a competitive market.

The media are enterprises, not IQ tests. They feed on inventiveness, not analytic discipline. They require creative skills and nonstandardized competences. Their content has, thus far at least, resisted the standardized and accumulative statement of propositions of a Euclid or an Adam Smith.

"*The mass media do not print or broadcast the best material that is submitted to them.*"

To edit is to judge; to judge is, inevitably, to reward some and disappoint others. One man's "best" is another's bane.

The assumption that a vast flow of material pours into the editorial offices of the media—from which publishers or producers simply select the worst—is simply incorrect. A huge proportion of what finally appears in magazines, radio, and television was "dreamed up" inside the media offices, and ordered from the staff or from freelance writers. And as often as not, even when the best talent is employed at the highest prices and given complete freedom, the results disappoint expectations. Excellence is not necessarily achieved because it is sought.[2]

"*The mass media cannot afford to step on anyone's toes.*"

The following recent articles in popular magazines most conspicuously stepped on quite powerful toes: "What Protestants Fear About Catholics"; "Cigarettes and Lung Cancer"; "Birth Control"; "The Disgrace of Our Hospitals"; "Fee-Splitting by Doctors"; "Agnosticism"; "Financial Shenanigans and Stock Manipulations"; "A Mercy Killing"; "The Murder of Negroes in the South."

[2] Yet consider that the mass media have recently presented to the public such indubitable highbrows as, say, Jacques Maritain, Reinhold Niebuhr, Robert Oppenheimer, Edith Hamilton, Aldous Huxley, Warren Weaver, Edith Sitwell, Jacques Barzun, James Bryant Conant, and Julian Huxley.

The movies and television recently offered all but the deaf and blind these scarcely soporific themes: miscegenation; adultery; dope addiction; white-Negro tensions; the venality of television; the vulgarity of movie executives; the cowardice of a minister, a banker; hypocrisy in business and advertising; big business and call girls; the degeneracy of Southern whites.

It was long assumed that the most sacred of sacred cows in a capitalist society is the Businessman or Big Business as an institution. But in recent years we have been exposed to a striking number of revelations about Business. Advertising men and methods, presumably too "powerful" to expose, much less deride, have been raked with coals of fire—in media which depend upon advertisers and advertising. *The Man in the Grey Flannel Suit* became a symbol of conformity to the masses, no less than the intellectual, through the mass media.

It is worth noticing that the sheer size of an audience crucially influences the content of what is communicated to it. Taboos, in movies or television, are not simply the fruit of cowardice among producers (though their anxiety is often disproportionate, and their candor unnecessarily hampered by pessimistic assumptions of what public reaction will be). Taboos are often functions of audience size, age-range, and heterogeneity. Things can be communicated to the few which cannot be communicated (at least not in the same way) to the many.

Books, magazines, and newspapers can discuss sex, homosexuality, masturbation, venereal disease, abortion, dope addiction, in ways not so easily undertaken on television or film. The reader reads alone— and this is a fact of great importance to those who write for him.

"The mass media do not give the public enough or adequate information about the serious problems of our time."

Never in history has the public been offered so much, so often, in such detail, for so little. I do not mean that Americans know as much as intellectuals think they ought to know, or wish they did know, about the problems which confront us. I do mean that the media already offer the public far more news, facts, information, and interpretations than the public takes the trouble to digest. I find it impossible to escape the conclusion that, apart from periods of acute crisis, most people do not want to be *involved* in precisely those areas which the intellectual finds most absorbing and meaningful.

Consider these recent authors and subjects in popular journalism: Winston Churchill on the war; Harry S. Truman on the presidency;

Geoffrey Crowther on United States-British relations; William O. Douglas on Russia; Dean Acheson on Berlin; Joseph Alsop on Suez; George Kennan on Europe; Henry Kissinger on nuclear weapons; Adlai Stevenson on nine different countries and their problems; Nehru on India and the West; Ben-Gurion on the Middle East.

I wonder how many academic journals have been more relevant or edifying.

Do intellectuals find it unnoteworthy that, year after year, four to five times as many citizens in New York City choose the *Daily News* as against the New York *Times* or *Herald Tribune?* Or that for decades the citizens of Chicago have preferred the Chicago *Tribune* to competitors closer to the intellectuals' heart? Or that for decades the people of Los Angeles have voted in favor of the Los Angeles *Times*, at the expense of less parochial competitors?

"The aesthetic level of the mass media is appalling: truth is sacrificed to the happy ending, escapism is exalted, romance, violence, melodrama prevail."

The mass media do not attempt to please intellectuals, on either the aesthetic or the conceptual plane. Some commentators believe that if the media offered the public less trivia, the taste of the public would perforce be improved. But if the media give the public too little of what they want, and too much of what they don't want (too soon), they would simply cease to be mass media—and would be replaced by either "massier" competitors or would drive the public to increased expenditures of time on sports, parlor games, gambling, and other familiar methods of protecting the self from the ardors of thought or the terrors of solitude.

The question of proportion (how much "light stuff" or staple insipidity to include as against how much heavy or "uplifting" material) is one of the more perplexing problems any editor faces. It is far from uncommon to hear an editor remark that he will run a feature which he knows will be read by "less than 5 per cent of our readers."

I suspect that intellectuals tend to judge the highbrow by its peaks and the nonhighbrow by its average. If we look at the peaks in both cases, how much do the mass media suffer by comparison? American movies, for instance, caught in staggering costs (and, therefore, risks), have produced, in a short span of time, such films as *The Bridge on the River Kwai, Marty, The African Queen, Twelve Angry Men, The Defiant Ones, High Noon, The Sheepman, Seven Brides for Seven Brothers,* etc.

Television, beset by the problem of a heterogeneous audience, and submitting to the disgraceful practice of advertisers permitted to exercise editorial censorship, has produced some extraordinary news and documentary programs, and such dramas as: *Middle of the Night, Patterns, Little Moon of Alban, Days of Wine and Roses, The Bridge of San Luis Rey, The Winslow Boy, Requiem for a Heavyweight.* CBS's "Camera Three" recently presented, with both skill and taste, three programs dramatizing Dostoevski's *Notes from the Underground, A File for Fathers* (scenes from Lord Chesterfield, Lewis Carroll, Oscar Wilde), *Père Goriot,* Chekhov's *The Proposal.*

In my opinion, some of the more insightful work of our time can be found in the mass media, for example, the comic strip *Peanuts,* which throws an original and enchanting light on children; the comic strip *Li'l Abner,* which is often both as illuminating and as savage as social satire should be; the movies of, say, William Wyler, George Stevens, Jules Dassin, John Huston, David Lean, Delbert Mann.

Intellectuals generally discover "artists" in the popular arts long after the public, with less rarefied aesthetic categories, has discovered them. Perhaps there is rooted in the character structure of intellectuals an aversion, or an inability, to participate in certain sectors of life; they do seem blind to the fact that the popular can be meritorious. This changes with time (e.g., consider the reputations of Twain, Dickens, Dumas, Balzac, Lardner). And a Jack Benny or Phil Silvers may yet achieve the classic dimension now permitted the Marx Brothers, who—once despised as broad vaudevillians—have become the eggheads' delight.

> *"The mass media corrupt and debase public taste; they create the kind of audience that enjoys cheap and trivial entertainment."*

This implies that demand (public taste or preference) has become a spurious function of manipulated supply. Here the evidence from Great Britain is illuminating: for years the government-owned BBC and the admirable Third Program offered the British public superior fare: excellent music, learned talks, literate discussions. For years, the noncommercial radio defended the bastions of culture. Yet when the British public was offered choices on television, it dismayed Anglophiles by taking to its heart the same silly quiz shows, panel shows, Western, melodramas, and "situation comedies" which the critics of daily newspapers deplore both in London and New York.

Or consider what happened in March, 1959, when the Granada TV network, a British commercial chain, presented *The Skin of Our*

Teeth with no less a star than Vivien Leigh—and in her first appearance on television. The noncommercial BBC ran, opposite the Wilder play and Lady Vivien, a twenty-five-year-old American movie, *Follow the Fleet*, with Ginger Rogers and Fred Astaire. The English critics sang rare hosannahs for Thornton Wilder's play, its glamorous star, the script, the direction, the production. But for every seventeen homes in London that chose the Pulitzer Prize play, sixty-six preferred the twenty-five-year-old musical. Outside of London, the ratio was even more depressing. Viewers by the millions, reported Reuters, switched their dials away from Wilder and Leigh to Fred and Ginger. The head of the Granada network even castigated the BBC in the press, urging that it be "ashamed of itself" for seducing a public that might have adored Art by offering it Entertainment. (A similar *contretemps* occurred on American television when the magnificent production of *Green Pastures* lost viewers by the millions to the ghastly *Mike Todd Party* in Madison Square Garden.) The final and crushing irony lies in the fact that *Follow the Fleet* put a BBC program among the first ten, in popularity, for the first time in the year.

Doubtless the mass media can do more, much more, to elevate what the public reads, sees, and hears. But the media cannot do this as easily or as rapidly as is often assumed. Indeed, they cannot get too far in front of their audiences without suffering the fate of predecessors who tried just that. There is considerable evidence to support the deflating view that the media, on the whole, are considerably *ahead* of the masses—in intelligence, in taste, in values; e.g., the vocabulary in almost any popular journal, not excluding fan magazines, is often too "highbrow" for its readers.

It seems to me a fair question to ask whether the intelligence or taste of the public is really worse today than it was before the mass media came along.

"The mass media are what they are because they are operated solely as money-making enterprises."

Publishers and producers are undoubtedly motivated by a desire for profits. But this is not *all* that motivates them. Publishers and producers are no less responsive than intellectuals to "ego values"; they are no less eager to win respect and respectability from their peers; they respond to both internalized and external "reference groups"; they seek esteem—from the self and from others.

Besides, producers know that a significant percentage of what they present in the mass media will not be as popular as what might be substituted—but it is presented nonetheless. Why? Partly because of nonpecuniary values, and partly because of what critics of the crass profit-motive seem blind to: the fact that part of the competitive process involves a continuous search for products which can win favor with audiences not attracted to, or satisfied by, the prevailing output. New and minority audiences are constantly courted by the media, e.g., the strictly "egghead" programs on television, the new magazines which arise, and flourish, because they fill a need, as *Scientific American, American Heritage.*

Whenever profits, used as either a carrot or a stick, are criticized, it is tacitly assumed that reliance on other human impulses would serve man better. Is this so? Do virtue, probity, self-sacrifice guarantee excellence? It seems to me that most of the horrors of human history have been the work not of skeptical or cynical or realistic men, but of those persuaded of their superior virtue.

To replace publication for profit by publication via subsidy would of course be to exchange one set of imperfections for another.[3] The postal system offers scant support to those who assume that non-profit enterprise is necessarily better than private competition (I hasten to add that in some fields, e.g., public health, it clearly is).

It should be noted, parenthetically, that anyone who enters the magazine or newspaper field in the expectation of high profits is either singularly naïve, extremely optimistic, or poorly informed: few areas of American business show so high a mortality rate, are plagued by such unpredictabilities, promise so many headaches, and return so low a net profit. Successful magazines earn as modest a profit as three percent on invested capital. To the purely profit-minded, business has long offered innumerable opportunities outside of publishing which far surpass it in profitability, security, or potential.

"The mass media are dominated—or too much influenced—by advertisers."

The influence of advertising is often too great—even if that influence is one-tenth as potent as many assume it to be. The editorial function should be as free of non-editorial influences as possible.

---

[3] It is unthinkable, for instance, that any open competitive system would have barred from the air someone like Winston Churchill—who was not given access to BBC, for his then-maverick opinions, from 1934 to 1939. Nor is it likely that a government-controlled network would be able to withstand the furor that followed CBS's initial interview with Nikita Khrushchev. Nor would a governmentally supervised program dare to present a show such as *The Plot to Kill Stalin.*

But publishers, producers, and editors would respond to power or influence *even if all advertising were abolished*. It is an inescapable fact of human organization that men adjust to power (that, indeed, is one of power's attributes); that men consider, or try to anticipate, the effect of their acts on those who hold most of whatever is most prized in a society.

There is a reverse and paradoxical angle to advertising: when a newspaper or magazine, a radio or television station becomes successful, the advertiser needs it as much as the other way around. Revenues from many advertisers increase the capacity to resist pressure from individual advertisers. Organs which can be "bought" nearly always decline in prosperity and influence.

Purely professional calculations often override vested interest. Some news or stories are so significant that it is impossible to prevent their publication.

The instance of the cigarette industry, mentioned above, is worth notice. Tobacco companies represent one of the largest and most consistent sources of national advertising revenue. Yet within an hour after medical reports appeared linking cigarette smoking to lung cancer, they were fully and dramatically presented to the public—not only on the front pages of newspapers but in radio and television reporting as well. The news was simply too big, too 'newsworthy" to be suppressed (even though several discussion programs shied away from the subject). The deficiencies of automobiles, where safety is concerned, have been analyzed in magazines which receive huge advertising revenues from automobile companies.

This is not to say that all truths which threaten power—in business, in the arts, even in the groves of academe—always gain as swift and public an airing as they deserve. They often do not. They do not because men, even men in power, are often timid, or weak, or frightened, or avaricious, or opportunistic, or unwise, or shortsighted. Some media operators, like some politicians, some clergymen, some labor leaders, some economists, are overly sensitive to the side on which their bread is buttered.

There is another and telling body of evidence about advertising on which no one, so far as I know, has commented: motion pictures accept no advertisements, never did, never depended on it, and were never "at the mercy of advertisers." [4] Yet of all the mass media, it is the movies which have been most parochial and timorous. Is it because movies do depend entirely on box-office receipts, and have no advertising revenues to subsidize independence?

[4] Some movie theaters show advertisements on their screens before and after a feature, but advertising is not to be found *in* movies.

Advertisers seem to me to exercise their most pernicious influence in television. For in television, advertisers are permitted to decide what shall or shall not appear in the programs they sponsor. This seems to me insupportable. An advertiser in a newspaper or magazine buys a piece of space in which to advertise his product. He does not buy a voice on the news desk or at the editorial table. But the television advertiser buys time both for his commercials and for *the time between commercials;* he becomes a producer and publisher himself. I am convinced that this is bad for the public, bad for television, and (ultimately) bad for the sponsors.[5]

"The mass media do not provide an adequate forum for minority views—the dissident and unorthodox."

Producers and publishers give more space and time to minority views (which include the *avant-garde*) than numerical proportions require. They feel that it is the function of specialized journals to carry specialized content. The popular media carry far more material of this kind than anyone would have predicted two decades ago. They hunger for the *interesting*.

The democratic society must insure a viable public forum for the dissenter—in politics, morals, arts. That forum will never be as large as the dissenters themselves want. But I know of no perfect way to determine who shall have what access to how many—at the expense of whom else—except to keep pressing for as free a market as we can achieve.

It may seem to some readers that I have substituted an indictment of the masses for an indictment of the mass media; that I have assigned the role of villain to the masses in a social drama in which human welfare and public enlightenment are hamstrung by the mediocrity, laziness, and indifference of the populace. I hope that detachment will not be mistaken for cynicism.

I should be the first to stress the immensity of the social gains which public education and literacy alone have made possible. The rising public appreciation of music, painting, ballet; the growth of libraries; the fantastic sales of paperback books (however much they are skewed by *Peyton Place* or the works of Mickey Spillane), the striking diffusion of "cultural activities" in communities throughout

[5] When I wrote a similar criticism in *Harper's Magazine* in 1958, certain television executives hotly denied this. That was eighteen months before the recent and sensational revelations of advertiser-control over quiz shows.

the land, the momentous fact that popular magazines *can* offer the public the ruminations of such nonpopular minds as Paul Tillich or Sir George Thomson—the dimensions of these changes are a tribute to the achievements of that society which has removed from men the chains of caste and class that hampered human achievement through the centuries. I, for one, do not lament the passing of epochs in which "high culture" flourished while the majority of mankind lived in ignorance and indignity.

What I have been emphasizing here is the inevitable gap between the common and the superior. More particularly, I have been embroidering the theme of the intellectual's curious reluctance to accept evidence. Modern intellectuals seem *guilty* about reaching conclusions that were once the *a priori* convictions of the aristocrat. It is understandable that twentieth-century intellectuals should dread snobbery, at one end of the social scale, as much as they shun mob favor at the other. But the intellectuals' snobbery is of another order, and involves a tantalizing paradox: a contempt for what *hoi polloi* enjoy, and a kind of proletarian ethos that tacitly denies inequalities of talent and taste.

The recognition of facts has little bearing on motivations and should surely not impute preferences. The validity of an idea has nothing to do with who propounds it—or whom it outrages. The author is aware that he is inviting charges of Brahminism, misanthropy, a reactionary "unconscious," or heaven knows what else. But is it really heresy to the democratic credo for intellectuals to admit, if only in the privacy of professional confessionals, that they are, in fact, more literate and more skillful—in diagnosis, induction, and generalization, if in nothing else—than their fellow-passengers on the ship of state?

Perhaps the intellectual's guilt, when he senses incipient snobbery within himself, stems from his uneasiness at being part of an elite, moreover, a new elite which is not shored up by ancient and historic sanctions. For intellectualism has been divorced from its traditional *cachet* and from the majesty with which earlier societies invested their elites: a classical education, Latin or Greek (in any case, a language not comprehensible to the untutored), a carefully cultivated accent, the inflection of the well born, the well bred, or the priestly. One of the painful experiences spared intellectuals in the past was hearing Ideas discussed—with profundity or insight—in accents which attest to birth on "the other side of the tracks."

It may be difficult for shopkeepers' sons to admit their manifest superiority over the world they left: parents, siblings, comrades. But the intellectual who struggles with a sinful sense of superiority, and who feels admirable sentiments of loyalty to his non-U origins, must still explain why it was that his playmates and classmates did not join him in the noble dedication to learning and the hallowed pursuit of truth. The triumph of mass education is to be found not simply in the increment of those who can read, write, add, and subtract. It is to be found in a much more profound and enduring revolution: the provision of opportunities to express the self, and pursue the self's values, opportunities not limited to the children of a leisure class, or an aristocracy, or a landed gentry, or a well-heeled bourgeoisie. The true miracle of public education is that no elite can decide where the next intellectual will come from.

Each generation creates its own devils, and meets its own Waterloo on the heartless field of reality. The Christian Fathers blamed the Prince of Darkness for preventing perfectible man from reaching Paradise. Anarchists blamed the state. Marxists blame the class system. Pacifists blame the militarists. And our latter-day intellectuals seem to blame the mass media for the lamentable failure of more people to attain the bliss of intellectual grace. This is a rank disservice to intellectuals themselves, for it dismisses those attributes of character and ability—discipline, curiosity, persistence, the renunciation of worldly rewards—which make intellectuals possible at all. The compulsive egalitarianism of eggheads even seems to lure them into a conspicuous disinterest in the possible determinism of heredity.

Responsibility increases with capacity, and should be demanded of those in positions of power. Just as I hold the intellectual more responsible than others for the rigorous exploration of phenomena and the courageous enunciation of truths, so, too, do I ask for better and still better performance from those who have the awesome power to shape men's minds.

.   .   .

It would be preposterous to claim that Leo Rosten's chief purpose here has been to "express himself," if we take that phrase at its usual value. He is bent not on self-revelation but on argument, and there is in his argument little evidence to suggest that he offers his view as something singularly his own, the sort of thing that only he might say, given his distinctive personality. This is partly because the essay has virtually no autobiographical content—Rosten does not describe, for instance, his own subjective response to some particular television program or magazine article, or a face-to-face interview with an executive of one of the mass media—and partly because, in the very manner of its arrangement, there is an unmistakable air of a step-by-step, no-nonsense method that does not invite mere personality to get in the way. And, after all, this is a situation where personality would not be very helpful, since the essay's announced intention to dispel myths must be accomplished mostly by adducing facts.

Yet "The Intellectual and the Mass Media" does not have the tone of a legal document. In some respects, Rosten does allow us to have a sense of himself as something more than a mechanical mouthpiece. In the first place, he does not exclusively avoid "I" and "me," though they appear only sparingly. The effect of these pronouns is always surprisingly strong, however infrequently they appear, and sometimes the very infrequency adds to the effect. Rosten uses the first person at the outset in a peculiarly emphatic way, so that no matter what his argument may suggest there will be no mistaking his own dissatisfaction with the phenomenon he may later appear to defend: "I am both depressed and distressed by the bombardment of our eyes, our ears, and our brains by meretricious material. . . ." Usually the references to himself are less personally revealing, since they indicate only his presence within the activity of the essay itself rather than in the prior experience on which the essay is based. Thus we find a sprinkling of "I shall try to explore," "I do not mean," "I do mean," "I find it impossible to escape the conclusion that," "I wonder," "I suspect," and "it seems to me." These phrases tend to appear in small clusters, as if to remind the audience, at suitable intervals, of the author's personal presence without unduly and continuously stressing it. They are particularly noticeable in the concluding eight paragraphs, where the author has finished his central arguments and is summing up.

Beyond such outward signs as these, what do we know about Rosten when we have completed a reading of his essay? Not much. We know where he stands on a specific issue in criticism of contemporary society, but this is something we might have known if he had written in the exaggeratedly detached manner of a laboratory report. What about the way his mind works, the way he argues? Look at a short segment of the argument—his response to the third cliché—"The mass media do not print or broadcast the best material that is submitted to them." He begins by citing the necessity for judgment in editing and notes in the next moment that this judgment is bound to be subjective. However, the next paragraph appears to follow a different tack, simply denying the cliché itself as factually incorrect. But notice that in order to make such a denial, Rosten has had to reduce the cliché to absurdity: "that a vast flow of material pours into the editorial offices of the media—from which publishers or producers simply select the worst. . . ." The original formula could not be ridiculed so easily, as the author knows well enough. Further, what is the intellectual link between the two pieces of argument that he uses here? There seems to be none whatever, although each in its own right carries a certain amount of weight and has partial relevance to Rosten's position. If he argues that the definition of "best" is open to dispute on grounds of personal taste, he is not logically in a sound position to offer next an argument that removes the opportunity to make any judgment. Apparently, Rosten has not tried to reason in a logically consistent way. He is more interested in an accumulation of persuasive effects than in the internal order and consistency of his case. This isolated instance may or may not be a clue to the more permanent aspects of his character as a writer and as a man—we would need to read a great deal of Rosten's work in order to venture an assessment along those lines— but it is bound to color our view of the Rosten who enters our awareness here and to this extent. Our judgment depends mostly on our expectations about the seriousness of the case a writer is trying to make. Will variety and liveliness replace intellectual rigor? Rosten's method here may tell us at least that he is somewhat more relaxed and informal (though certainly not folksy or chummy) than a formal logician.

This brings us close to the question that the essay must in some way answer if it is to be successful, a question that concerns relationships among three or four different points of view within the society: Who is Rosten himself? Where does he stand? With the intellectuals, the masses, or the men who control and operate the media? The most obvious answer would be that he tries to avoid a clear association with any one of these groups, lest his impartiality be tainted. The intellectuals are not "we" but "they." Clearly Rosten is not himself a television producer or movie director; just as clearly, he regards his own taste as better than that of the masses. But the matter cannot be dropped so quickly. If we pay full attention to what is going on, we will see that Rosten, if he does not care to identify himself forthrightly as an intellectual, nevertheless makes it clear that he has spent a lot of time among the intellectuals and understands their position uncommonly well. He quotes directly the "higher" clichés he has heard them speak. For instance, in his reference to the Marx brothers he shows that he knows the intellectuals' tastes and enthusiasms. Above all, he unabashedly admits to sharing the intellectual community's general distaste for the productions of the mass media, if not for exactly their reasons. Hence he tends to project himself as the kind of intellectual who is yet a whole man, an honestly forthright assessor of his cultural surroundings, not one to be easily misled by democratic sentiment into a false representation of the way things are. We have no reason to imagine that all this is in any way false, a mere pose. And our confidence is made possible mainly because, instead of putting himself forward as a vaguely defined version of the well-rounded intellectual, Rosten has made plain the precise means by which he transcends the limitations of the standard intellectual viewpoint: through knowledge of the business mind and business methods. He makes perfectly clear, in each case, what he claims the academicians do not understand.

Lastly, what assumptions does Rosten make regarding his audience, and how do these assumptions bear upon his performance in the essay? If we read the italicized foreword, in which the circumstances of the essay's origin are explained, we can picture a man who looks the way a Leo Rosten should look, sitting at a conference table and reading his paper to a group of distinguished persons, some of them more unmistakably intellectual than others, but most of them surely intellectuals and not representatives of the masses. Although this picture shows the essay's actual relation to its first audience, much more can be said about Rosten's performance as rhetorically affective writing. The essay is designed to improve the intellectuals' understanding without questioning their basic judgment of the media, and to gratify the sensibilities and defend the motives of the businessmen who control the media. In fact, it is exactly this joining together of the two angles of insight that gives this essay its wide appeal. Only the masses themselves appear to be shut out. But Rosten seems to speak as if with the understanding that no one of *us* is actually a member of the mass audience whose low taste and lack of intellectual ambition he condemns.

Beyond this, there are no special qualifications that the audience is assumed to possess. Rosten does not use sophisticated methods of reference here; there are no arcane allusions to ideas and events that only a scholar would know. What is needed is a little day-to-day acquaintance with the mass media themselves and a fair amount of ordinary intelligence. When the author tells us something new—presents us, that is, with a new piece of information or interpretation of appearances—his tone is that of someone who casually reminds us of something we already know, rather than that of someone who archly informs us of something we do not know. If the style and vocabulary, or indeed the entire idiom of thought, are somewhat more sophisticated than the average reader would expect to find in a popular magazine, that is just as well. It is not the author's intention to lure into a reading of his essay those who will only feel insulted by it. He is after the readers who can be helped to understand the problem.

In the three essays that follow, you will have a chance to trace the various interactions of author, audience, and the world of experience as they impinge upon the quality of the finished literary statement.

RECALLED TO LIFE, *OR*,
CHARLES DICKENS AT THE BAR

Mary McCarthy

March 1953

In the eighty-odd years since his death, Charles Dickens has been summoned again and again from the tomb to face the verdict of history. The latest qualified expert to view the body and announce his findings is Edgar Johnson, a professor at City College, the author of an eleven-hundred-page biography that reads like the report of some officially constituted commission that hands in its verdict as follows: the deceased is cleared of the charge of sentimentality (finding: healthy emotion), chidden for his domestic conduct, and awarded a place among the world's great authors, in recognition of his social vision.

Dickens hated officials, but his critics and biographers, almost inevitably, feel called upon to assume an official air when dealing with his "case." Each critic clears his throat with a vast administrative harumph and scans the expectant courtroom before imparting his conclusions. Attorneys for the defense scribble while listening to the prosecution's summation; on the bench a hanging judge peers over the bar to anathematize the quivering defendant; alienists and character witnesses succeed each other on the stand. Advocates of Dickens like Mr. Johnson have the anxious note of apologists, now glossing over and extenuating, now reprobating stoutly, lest they be charged with undue partiality. His assailants, on the other hand, present themselves as inquisitors, text in hand,

---

RECALLED TO LIFE, *or* CHARLES DICKENS AT THE BAR: Reprinted with the permission of Farrar, Straus & Giroux, Inc. from *On the Contrary* by Mary McCarthy. Copyright © 1953, 1961 by Mary McCarthy.

eager to convict poor Dickens out of his own mouth of crimes of bad writing, crudity, unreality, unfriendliness to the proletariat, to business, to the Jews, to foreigners; "he could not paint a gentleman," and it is "questionable" whether he regarded the poor as equals.

Here, as in most inquisitions, the metonymic principle is at work— the part is substituted for the whole, and a single "incriminating" utterance is produced in court to lay bare the man in his totality. This desire to criminate has singled Dickens out uniquely among great writers; Dostoevsky sometimes wrote badly; he was virulently anti-Semitic, anti-Polish, anti-Catholic; but nobody seeks to indict him for it. And Dickens' defenders accept the criminative method when they produce a good Jew, Riah, to offset the bad Fagin, sympathetic aristocrats and proletarians to offset their opposite numbers; in their eagerness to give Dickens a clean bill of health, they are willing to strip him down to a few inoffensive platitudes.

Perhaps this zeal, however, merely testifies to the fact that Dickens is still alive—a burning issue. Certainly, the performance of Anthony West in *The New Yorker* recently suggests that it is a living man who is being collared and haled before justice. Reviewing Mr. Johnson's biography becomes, for Mr. West, an occasion for a violent attack on Dickens—the most violent attack, to my knowledge, in all Dickens literature.

He was *not* a great writer, proclaims Mr. West, but a mere entertainer, an artist who sold his birthright for popular applause. Furthermore, he was a pious fraud and a hypocrite, a veritable Pecksniff. He was not really interested in industrial reforms, but jumped on the band wagon when he saw that Mrs. Gaskell and others were making a good thing of the cause. When he attacked social abuses, he was merely following in the wake of his audience, which was way ahead of him in its clamor for social change. Far from being a critic of imperialism, he was guilty of being an imperialist of the lesser-breeds-without-the-law order; his "real" feelings about this subject are embodied not in his novels but in a private letter to a philanthropic lady written at the time of the Indian Mutiny. ". . . the attack on heartless economic theory," as embodied in Scrooge, was "a safety play that can be relied upon to ruffle nobody." Another attack on heartless economic theory, *Hard Times*, is "dubious social criticism . . . childish in its ignorance of what businessmen are like or were like as it is in its conception of industrial problems."

"Dickens's imagination, in matters of finance, never got beyond petty cash. None of his rich men are really wealthy, and none of them are engaged in credible affairs. *Hard Times* is, however, whole-

hearted in its attack on two things—education and Parliament—
that were the really effective instruments of social reform. . . ."

What is bewildering in this violence is first of all the fact that it
seems to issue from an almost insensate ignorance of Dickens' writing
and life—is it education that Dickens is attacking in *Hard Times* or
"education"? Compare the dates of Mrs. Gaskell's *Mary Barton*
(1848) and *The Old Curiosity Shop* (1841), where Dickens first
assailed the factory system—who was following whom? "Petty
cash"—Mr. Merdle's transactions? Dombey not wealthy, or Jarn-
dyce of *Bleak House* or Mr. Boffin, the golden dustman? And if
Dickens was cut off "from easy intercourse with his intellectual
equals all through his life" and surrounded himself "with an en-
tourage of second-raters," is this meant to be a judgment on
Thackeray, the Carlyles, Mrs. Gaskell, Lord John Russell, George
Eliot and George Henry Lewes, Tennyson, Landor, Mazzini,
Lamartine, and Victor Hugo—Dickens' friends and intimates? If
Dickens was following in the wake of his audience, how did that
audience make its views felt? Not in legislation, certainly, which
lagged far behind Dickens. Was it Parliament or Dickens that was
the really effective instrument of social reform?

It has been argued that Dickens the social reformer and pamphleteer swamped Dickens the artist. Edward Sackville-West put this
case at its strongest when he declared that Dickens' bathos was required to awaken pity in the hardened Victorian heart. But if this
was a sin, it was a generous sin, as most of Dickens' critics have
conceded. Mr. West is the first, so far as I know, to pretend that
Dickens' art was a calculated untruth aimed to swell the volume of
sales.

Yet a child (to take Dickens' own favorite touchstone of truth
and purity of response) has only to read a single chapter of *Oliver
Twist*, say, to perceive that here is both a heated critic of society
and a ready sentimentalist. We do not need a biographer to tell us
that Dickens wrote his "affecting" passages with tears in his eyes;
that is precisely what makes us wish to turn our own dry eyes away
from the moist spectacle of the author. George Eliot also underwent
a hysterical transformation as she wrote her climactic pages, the very
pages we cannot read today without mortification for that gaunt,
moralistic dame.

And the highbrow reader of the era was attuned to these vibrations. Daniel O'Connell, the Irish political leader, was so affected by
the death of Little Nell that he burst into sobs and threw the book
out the window of the railway carriage he was traveling in, groan-
ing, "He should not have killed her." Walter Savage Landor, Mac-

ready the actor, Carlyle, and Jeffrey the critic were all overcome by the chapter; in Jeffrey's case, a visitor, perceiving his condition, feared she was intruding on a real bereavement. I do not agree with Mr. Johnson that this was healthy emotion; rather it has the eerie quality of a mass phenomenon, like the possession of the nuns of Loudun.

In any case, it was genuine enough, of its kind. The excessive suggestibility of the Victorians probably had something to do with "alienation," with the transformations being wrought in man and countryside by the process of mechanization. Already, in the eighteenth century, in the early stages of the Industrial Revolution, there appeared that taste for prodigies, for the august and the sublime, that the Victorians brought to fulfillment in their passion for mountain-climbing, for gorges and precipices, for the abysmal vertigo of crime and innocence, horror and bathos. Feeling, shrinking before the industrial vistas, sought to accommodate itself to the new scale of things by developing its own kinetics. Popular authors like Dickens and George Eliot differed from the ordinary public in that they possessed an internal self-starter of emotion.

Yet if Dickens was the prosperous owner of such a gadget or patent, he was also, of all his contemporaries, the man who looked upon the new mechanized human being with the greatest sense of fear and astonishment. For this is what many of his famous "characters" are: wind-up toys, large or small, that move in jerks and starts, whose machinery whirs toilsomely before they begin to speak. How a man can become a monster or a mechanical marvel is the question that preoccupies Dickens throughout the whole of his work. And these mechanical marvels he shows us are not travesties of men invented by a satirical author; they are appallingly true to life. Mr. Dorrit, Pecksniff, Uriah Heep—these are the travesties man has made of himself.

Leaving aside the heroes and heroines, Dickens' world is divided into two kingdoms: the kingdom of metal, which is dominated by the hunchback Quilp, that malignant Vulcan, armored and carapaced, who eats hard-boiled eggshells and prawns with their heads and tails on and cools his brazen throat by drinking boiling grog straight from the saucepan; and the kingdom of vegetables, presided over by Mr. Dick, Mr. Wemmick, and the Aged P.

The vegetable kingdom is more amiable; its inhabitants have lapsed into nature and present themselves as botanical curiosities—harmless on the whole, except for an occasional flycatcher plant. But they too have lost their humanity, which stirs in them only as a rum memory. They have obdurately become things, like the men of brass and iron, and they differ from the latter principally in that they do not treat other men as things but are content to soliloquize mystifyingly, in their own patch of ground. This obduracy is typical of all true Dickens creations: a true Dickens character never listens to the protests of reality; he inflexibly orates. In short, he has officialized himself, like Mr. Dorrit, the Father of the Marshalsea, receiving his testimonials; or Mr. Bounderby, who has invented his own authorized biography; or Mrs. Gamp, who has invented her own reference, the imaginary Mrs. Harris. All these people live in shatterproof hierarchical structures.

The thingification of man, to use Kant's term, is Dickens' inexhaustible subject and the source of his power and fascination. To treat another man as a thing, you must first become a very large thing yourself—an impervious thing. This was Dickens' discovery about character, and he remains the only writer (outside of Gogol, whom in many ways he resembles) to have this dreadful insight, not as an abstract theorem but as a concrete apprehension of a process, like the processes of manufacturing that were being developed with such rapidity in his day. "There's a young man hid with me, in comparison with which young man I am a Angel," says the convict Magwitch, impressively, to frighten the boy Pip in the churchyard. This passage has been criticized on the ground that Magwitch, realistically, would not look upon himself as a horrid apparition. But this casual self-knowledge, precisely, is what transfixes not only the boy Pip but the reader: the man Magwitch—how is it possible?—sees what he has become and uses himself as a bogy to terrify a child in a graveyard; and the fact of the frank perception prepares for Magwitch's redemption, the change of heart on which Dickens places so many hopes. Otherwise, the accents are those of Marlowe's Mephistophilis: "Why this is hell, nor am I out of it."

When Dickens tries to create virtue or manliness, he often fails (though he is very good at a kind of boyish manliness—Nicholas Nickleby, Martin Chuzzlewit, David Copperfield—with a blush still on its cheek). And yet this quality is not absent from his work, for it is present in wonderful abundance in the author himself. *This was a man*—again and again one is halted in the midst of a page to make this wondering observation, as though Dickens himself, and not his characters, were the marvel.

The author does not mean to display his manliness, as he displays, say, the virtue of Little Dorrit or Nell; it takes the reader unawares. He did not mean to display it in his life, but time and again the reader of any Dickens biography is halted by the blaze of energy, the bravery, the spontaneous anger, the magnanimity, the quick assumption of responsibility.

Can it be that this is what is amiss? Are today's critics and biographers sincerely disturbed to find a *man* entombed in the Westminster Abbey grave? A *man* entombed in the novel— the last place, apparently, they would expect to find one today? Is this why even the best of Dickens' recent critics approach him in such a gingerly fashion, as if they feared to be held accountable for any slip of the pen concerning him?

In a certain sense, of course, they are right to take these precautions, to keep their distance from Dickens and display him as a specimen that has come under official notice. Mr. West's outburst in *The New Yorker* is evidence that there exists a profound hostility to Dickens that may break out anywhere without warning, though not, as one might think, in highbrow circles, where the charge "mere entertainer" might have some appropriateness, but in commercial journalism: Orville Prescott in the New York *Times* promptly echoed Mr. West's judgment, and *Time* magazine found a citation from Lenin to prove that Dickens was not "a social revolutionary." Like the mysterious utterances of Mr. F.'s aunt, this animus of Mr. West's spouts up from arcane caverns that perhaps underlie the whole of modern "humanistic" culture.

QUESTIONS AND EXERCISES

1. An assumption regarding the (captive) audience of *Style and Substance* has been made in selecting this review-essay for inclusion. The assumption is that the reader will have had *some* experience with Dickens so that he may judge, at least partly, the views of Mary McCarthy, as well as those she reports—those of Anthony West and Edgar Johnson. Do you think a person who had had no direct contact with Dickens would find reading this essay worthwhile? Would you say, incidentally, that the main purpose of the essay is to review a book? Or is it something else? If so, what else?

2. What does Mary McCarthy assume about her reader's knowledge of Dickens and of Dickens scholarship? Can you find specific parts of her essay—paragraphs, sentences, even single phrases—that seem designed to provide necessary information for the reader who does not know as much as he should about these matters? In this connection, what is the function of paragraph 7?

3. In developing her idea about Dickens' preoccupation with the "thing-ification" of man, the author distinguishes between the kingdom of metal and the kingdom of vegetables. As this duality is introduced,

which of the two kingdoms is the reader naturally inclined to admire more? Why? Does the author at all upset these expectations? Do you think she provides enough information—e.g., about Quilp, Mr. Wemmick, and so forth—to make the duality meaningful even for a reader with no experience of Dickens' work? If you have read several of Dickens' novels, you may want to comment on the accuracy of Mary McCarthy's analysis.

4. As she works out her disagreement with Johnson and West, does Mary McCarthy depend more on the amassing of factual evidence or on subjectively personal response? In paragraph 9, do you think that it was good strategy to use the first person plural rather than the singular ("We do not need a biographer to tell us . . . what makes us wish to turn our own dry eyes away from the moist spectacle of the author")? Again, in paragraph 16 she uses "one" where she might have said "I" ("again and again one is halted in the midst of a page to make this wondering observation"). Is the effect of the "one" more personal than that of the "we" in the earlier instance?

5. At what points in the essay do you get distinct impressions of the author's temperament and personality? Taken together, do these impressions add up to a coherent image of her? And is that image, whether complete or not, particularly useful to the reader in understanding the full significance of the essay?

6. Since Mary McCarthy has seized the occasion of a book review to write an essay that says relatively little about the book, considerably more about a magazine piece, and still more about her own view of Dickens, try to do her one better: Write a "review" of her essay (about 600 words long) in which you concentrate mainly on the other works to which she refers, including those by Dickens himself.

7. Write a 300–400-word essay very obviously subjective in content, in which you are at least as important as your ostensible subject. Then rewrite it so as to preserve as much of the original content as possible, but get rid of all immediately personal effects in your language ("I" becomes "one," for example; and "I saw" may be converted to "it was observed that"). But do not let it become too hopelessly wooden.

8. Write a single well-developed paragraph in which you work out a relational idea similar to Mary McCarthy's metal-versus-vegetable dualism. After reading over what you have produced, write another paragraph in commentary on the first, identifying if you can any personal quirks or habits of your mind (or speech) that you find there. If the sense of personal identification is strong, do you regard this as appropriate to your subject or not? Explain these things carefully and exactly.

CONCLUSION

Walter Pater

Δέγει που ʻΗράκλειτος ὅτι πάντα χωρεῖ καὶ οὐδὲν μένει

To regard all things and principles of things as inconstant modes or fashions has more and more become the tendency of modern thought. Let us begin with that which is without—our physical life. Fix upon it in one of its more exquisite intervals, the moment, for instance, of delicious recoil from the flood of water in summer heat. What is the whole physical life in that moment but a combination of natural elements to which science gives their names? But those elements, phosphorus and lime and delicate fibres, are present not in the human body alone: we detect them in places most remote from it. Our physical life is a perpetual motion of them—the passage of the blood, the waste and repairing of the lenses of the eye, the modification of the tissues of the brain under every ray of light and sound—processes which science reduces to simpler and more elementary forces. Like the elements of which we are composed, the action of these forces extends beyond us: it rusts iron and ripens corn. Far out on every side of us those elements are broadcast, driven in many currents; and birth and gesture and death and the springing of violets from the grave are but a few out of ten thousand resultant combinations. That clear, perpetual outline of face and limb is but an image of ours, under which we group them—a design in a web, the actual threads of which pass out beyond it. This at least of flame-like our life has, that it is but the concurrence, renewed from moment to moment, of forces parting sooner or later on their ways.

Or, if we begin with the inward world of thought and feeling, the whirlpool is still more rapid, the flame more eager and devouring. There it is no longer the gradual darkening of the eye, the gradual fading of colour from the wall—movements of the shore-side, where the water flows down indeed, though in apparent rest—but the race of the mid-stream, a drift of momentary acts of sight and

CONCLUSION: This "Conclusion" is the final chapter of Walter Pater's *Studies in the History of the Renaissance*, first published in 1873. The text printed here comes from a later edition of the work and contains some revisions by the author.

passion and thought. At first sight experience seems to bury us under a flood of external objects, pressing upon us with a sharp and importunate reality, calling us out of ourselves in a thousand forms of action. But when reflexion begins to play upon those objects they are dissipated under its influence; the cohesive force seems suspended like some trick of magic; each object is loosed into a group of impressions—colour, odour, texture—in the mind of the observer. And if we continue to dwell in thought on this world, not of objects in the solidity with which language invests them, but of impressions, unstable, flickering, inconsistent, which burn and are extinguished with our consciousness of them, it contracts still further: the whole scope of observation is dwarfed into the narrow chamber of the individual mind. Experience, already reduced to a group of impressions, is ringed round for each one of us by that thick wall of personality through which no real voice has ever pierced on its way to us, or from us to that which we can only conjecture to be without. Every one of those impressions is the impression of the individual in his isolation, each mind keeping as a solitary prisoner its own dream of a world. Analysis goes a step farther still, and assures us that those impressions of the individual mind to which, for each one of us, experience dwindles down, are in perpetual flight; that each of them is limited by time, and that as time is infinitely divisible, each of them is infinitely divisible also; all that is actual in it being a single moment, gone while we try to apprehend it, of which it may ever be more truly said that it has ceased to be than that it is. To such a tremulous wisp constantly re-forming itself on the stream, to a single sharp impression, with a sense in it, a relic more or less fleeting, of such moments gone by, what is real in our life fines itself down. It is with this movement, with the passage and dissolution of impressions, images, sensations, that analysis leaves off—that continual vanishing away, that strange, perpetual weaving and unweaving of ourselves.

Philosophiren, says Novalis, *ist dephlegmatisiren, vivificiren*. The service of philosophy, of speculative culture, towards the human spirit, is to rouse, to startle it to a life of constant and eager observation. Every moment some form grows perfect in hand or face; some tone on the hills or the sea is choicer than the rest; some mood of passion or insight or intellectual excitement is irresistibly real and attractive to us—for that moment only. Not the fruit of experience, but experience itself, is the end. A counted number of pulses only is given to us of a variegated, dramatic life. How may we see in them all that is to be seen in them by the finest senses? How shall we pass most swiftly from point to point, and be present always at the focus where the greatest number of vital forces unite in their purest energy?

To burn always with this hard, gemlike flame, to maintain this ecstasy, is success in life. In a sense it might even be said that our failure is to form habits: for, after all, habit is relative to a stereotyped world, and meantime it is only the roughness of the eye that makes any two persons, things, situations, seem alike. While all melts under our feet, we may well grasp at any exquisite passion, or any contribution to knowledge that seems by a lifted horizon to set the spirit free for a moment, or any stirring of the senses, strange dyes, strange colours, and curious odours, or work of the artist's hands, or the face of one's friend. Not to discriminate every moment some passionate attitude in those about us, and in the very brilliancy of their gifts some tragic dividing of forces on their ways, is, on this short day of frost and sun, to sleep before evening. With this sense of the splendour of our experience and of its awful brevity, gathering all we are into one desperate effort to see and touch, we shall hardly have time to make theories about the things we see and touch. What we have to do is to be for ever curiously testing new opinions and courting new impressions, never acquiescing in a facile orthodoxy of Comte, or of Hegel, or of our own. Philosophical theories or ideas, as points of view, instruments of criticism, may help us to gather up what might otherwise pass unregarded by us. "Philosophy is the microscope of thought." The theory or idea or system which requires of us the sacrifice of any part of this experience, in consideration of some interest into which we cannot enter, or some abstract theory we have not identified with ourselves, or of what is only conventional, has no real claim upon us.

One of the most beautiful passages of Rousseau is that in the sixth book of the *Confessions*, where he decribes the awakening in him of the literary sense. An undefinable taint of death had clung always about him, and now in early manhood he believed himself smitten by mortal disease. He asked himself how he might make as much as possible of the interval that remained; and he was not biassed by anything in his previous life when he decided that it must be by intellectual excitement, which he found just then in the clear, fresh writings of Voltaire. Well! we are all *condamnés* as Victor Hugo says: we are all under sentence of death but with a sort of indefinite reprieve—*les hommes sont tous condamnés à mort avec des sursis indéfinis:* we have an interval, and then our place knows us no more. Some spend this interval in listlessness, some in high passions, the wisest, at least among "the children of this world," in art and song. For our one chance lies in expanding that interval, in getting as many pulsations as possible into the given time. Great passions may give us this quickened sense of life, ecstasy and sorrow of love, the various forms of enthusiastic activity, disinterested or otherwise, which come naturally to many of us. Only be sure it is passion—that it does yield you this fruit of a quickened, multiplied consciousness. Of such wisdom, the poetic passion, the desire of beauty, the love of art for its own sake, has most. For art comes to you proposing frankly to give nothing but the highest quality to your moments as they pass, and simply for those moments' sake.

QUESTIONS AND EXERCISES

1. Is the content of this essay highly personal, intimate? Does the author refer specifically to his own private experiences, or express directly his most personal sensations and emotions? In short, does Pater's own personality become perhaps even more important than what he is talking about, so that we are less concerned with what he says than with the revealing manner in which he says it? Are there, for instance, any moments in which the image-making power of his language forces you to visualize the author himself in this situation or that?

2. How can you reconcile your answers to question 1 with the fact that Pater is talking about the necessarily subjective and transitory nature of all human experience? If the essay fails to describe much of the author's own particular experience—the sort of experience, indeed, that only he could know well—by what means does he convince his audience that he knows what he is talking about? Considering the nature of his subject, would you say that his language tends to be remarkably more concrete than abstract?

3. Pater says that we should try always to realize "Not the fruit of experience, but experience itself. . . ." What connection is there between this statement and his attack on *theorizing*? Does he mean that all philosophical speculation is useless? Cite evidence.

4. Does Pater seem to be addressing himself to an audience that he assumes will be sympathetic to his views, or hostile? Of what part of that audience does he seem to be most particularly aware, and what are the signs of this special recognition?

5. Soon after its first publication, Pater came to regard this essay as potentially dangerous and misleading for young readers, so much so that he was reluctant to let it appear in print again. Can you see any cause for such concern? What do you suppose would be the moral assumptions and presuppositions of an audience that might regard the piece as dangerous or shocking?

6. In making a substantive statement here, Pater obviously edits and selects from experience in order to make his point with the greatest

possible force. In paragraph 3 he makes a brief representative catalogue of those experiences in which exquisitely intense beauty is to
be found. Do you notice the omission, whether deliberate or not, of
any particular area of experience?

7. Write a 750-word analysis of the various means by which Pater
conveys the quality of constant change and flux in life.

8. Explain in about 300 words what the author means when he speaks
of burning with a "hard, gemlike flame."

9. Write a serious (though not solemn) essay of 500 words persuading
a hostile audience that it should live life with more attention to
physical beauty. Add to this an analytic paragraph explaining how
your essay has tried to recognize and deal specially with the anticipated hostility of your readers.

HUB FANS BID KID ADIEU

John Updike

Fenway Park, in Boston, is a lyric little bandbox of a ballpark.
Everything is painted green and seems in curiously sharp focus, like
the inside of an old-fashioned peeping-type Easter egg. It was built
in 1912 and rebuilt in 1934, and offers, as do most Boston artifacts, a
compromise between Man's Euclidean determinations and Nature's
beguiling irregularities. Its right field is one of the deepest in the
American League, while its left field is the shortest; the high left-
field wall, three hundred and fifteen feet from home plate along the
foul line, virtually thrusts its surface at right-handed hitters. On the
afternoon of Wednesday, September 28th, 1960, as I took a seat
behind third base, a uniformed groundkeeper was treading the top
of this wall, picking batting-practice home runs out of the screen,
like a mushroom gatherer seen in Wordsworthian perspective on the
verge of a cliff. The day was overcast, chill, and uninspirational.
The Boston team was the worst in twenty-seven seasons. A jangling
medley of incompetent youth and aging competence, the Red Sox
were finishing in seventh place only because the Kansas City Ath-
letics had locked them out of the cellar. They were scheduled to
play the Baltimore Orioles, a much nimbler blend of May and

HUB FANS BID KID ADIEU: © Copyright 1960 by John Updike. Reprinted from
Assorted Prose by John Updike, by permission of Alfred A. Knopf, Inc.
Originally appeared in *The New Yorker*.

December, who had been dumped from pennant contention a week before by the insatiable Yankees. I, and 10,453 others, had shown up primarily because this was the Red Sox's last home game of the season, and therefore the last time in all eternity that their regular left fielder, known to the headlines as TED, KID, SPLINTER, THUMPER, TW, and, most cloyingly, MISTER WONDERFUL, would play in Boston. "WHAT WILL WE DO WITHOUT TED? HUB FANS ASK" ran the headline on a newspaper being read by a bulb-nosed cigar smoker a few rows away. Williams' retirement had been announced, doubted (he had been threatening retirement for years), confirmed by Tom Yawkey, the Red Sox owner, and at last widely accepted as the sad but probable truth. He was forty-two and had redeemed his abysmal season of 1959 with a—considering his advanced age—fine one. He had been giving away his gloves and bats and had grudgingly consented to a sentimental ceremony today. This was not necessarily his last game; the Red Sox were scheduled to travel to New York and wind up the season with three games there.

I arrived early. The Orioles were hitting fungos on the field. The day before, they had spitefully smothered the Red Sox, 17–4, and neither their faces nor their drab gray visiting-team uniforms seemed very gracious. I wondered who had invited them to the party. Between our heads and the lowering clouds a frenzied organ was thundering through, with an appositeness perhaps accidental, "You *maaaade* me love you, I didn't wanna do it, I didn't wanna do it. . . ."

The affair between Boston and Ted Williams was no mere summer romance; it was a marriage composed of spats, mutual disappointments, and, toward the end, a mellowing hoard of shared memories. It fell into three stages, which may be termed Youth, Maturity, and Age; or Thesis, Antithesis, and Synthesis; or Jason, Achilles, and Nestor.

First, there was the by now legendary epoch [1] when the young

[1] This piece was written with no research materials save an outdated record book and the Boston newspapers of the day; and Williams' early career preceded the dawning of my *Schlagballewusstsein* (Baseball-consciousness). Also for reasons of perspective was my account of his beginnings skimped. Williams first attracted the notice of a major-league scout—Bill Essick of the Yankees— when he was a fifteen-year-old pitcher with the San Diego American Legion Post team. As a pitcher-outfielder for San Diego's Herbert Hoover High School, Williams recorded averages of .586 and .403. Essick balked at signing Williams for the $1,000 his mother asked; he was signed instead, for $150 a month, by the local Pacific Coast League franchise, the newly created San Diego Padres. In his two seasons with this team, Williams hit merely .271 and .291, but his style and slugging (23 home runs the second year) caught the eye of, among others,

bridegroom came out of the West and announced "All I want out of life is that when I walk down the street folks will say 'There goes the greatest hitter who ever lived.'" The dowagers of local journalism attempted to give elementary deportment lessons to this child who spake as a god, and to their horror were themselves rebuked. Thus began the long exchange of backbiting, bat-flipping, booing, and spitting that has distinguished Williams' public relations.[2] The spitting incidents of 1957 and 1958 and the similar dockside cour-

---

Casey Stengel, then with the Boston Braves, and Eddie Collins, the Red Sox general manager. Collins bought him for the Padres for $25,000 in cash and $25,000 in players. Williams was then nineteen. Collins' fond confidence in the boy's potential matched Williams' own. Williams reported to the Red Sox training camp in Sarasota in 1938 and, after showing more volubility than skill, was shipped down to the Minneapolis Millers, the top Sox farm team. It should be said, perhaps, that the parent club was equipped with an excellent, if mature, outfield, mostly purchased from Connie Mack's dismantled A's. Upon leaving Sarasota, Williams is supposed to have told the regular outfield of Joe Vosmik, Doc Cramer, and Ben Chapman that he would be back and would make more money than the three of them put together. At Minneapolis he hit .366, batted in 142 runs, scored 130, and hit 43 home runs. He also loafed in the field, jabbered at the fans, and smashed a water cooler with his fist. In 1939 he came north with the Red Sox. On the way, in Atlanta, he dropped a foul fly, accidentally kicked it away in trying to pick it up, picked it up, and threw it out of the park. It would be nice if, his first time up in Fenway Park, he had hit a home run. Actually, in his first Massachusetts appearance, the first inning of an exhibition game against Holy Cross at Worcester, he *did* hit a home run, a grand slam. The Red Sox season opened in Yankee Stadium. Facing Red Ruffing, Williams struck out and, the next time up, doubled for his first major-league hit. In the Fenway Park opener, against Philadelphia, he had a single in five trips. His first home run came on April 23, in that same series with the A's. Williams was then twenty, and played *right* field. In his rookie season he hit .327; in 1940, .344.

[2] See *Ted Williams*, by Ed Linn (Sport Magazine Library), Chapter 6, "Williams vs. the Press." It is Linn's suggestion that Williams walked into a circulation war among the seven Boston newspapers, who in their competitive zeal headlined incidents that the New York papers, say, would have minimized, just as they minimized the less genial side of the moody and aloof DiMaggio and smoothed Babe Ruth into a folk hero. It is also Linn's thought, and an interesting one, that Williams thrived on even adverse publicity, and needed a hostile press to elicit, contrariwise, his defiant best. The statistics (especially of the 1958 season, when he snapped a slump by spitting in all directions, and inadvertently conked an elderly female fan with a tossed bat) seem to corroborate this. Certainly Williams could have had a truce for the asking, and his industrious perpetuation of the war, down to his last day in uniform, implies its usefulness to him. The actual and intimate anatomy of the matter resides in locker rooms and hotel corridors fading from memory. When my admiring account was printed, I received a letter from a sports reporter who hated Williams with a bitter and explicit immediacy. And even Linn's hagiology permits some glimpses of Williams' locker-room manners that are not pleasant.

tesies that Williams has now and then extended to the grandstand should be judged against this background: the left-field stands at Fenway for twenty years have held a large number of customers who have bought their way in primarily for the privilege of showering abuse on Williams. Greatness necessarily attracts debunkers, but in Williams' case the hostility has been systematic and unappeasable. His basic offense against the fans has been to wish that they weren't there. Seeking a perfectionist's vacuum, he has quixotically desired to sever the game from the ground of paid spectatorship and publicity that supports it. Hence his refusal to tip his cap [3] to the crowd or turn the other cheek to newsmen. It has been a costly theory—it has probably cost him, among other evidences of good will, two Most Valuable Player awards, which are voted by reporters [4]—but he has held to it. While his critics, oral and literary, remained beyond the reach of his discipline, the opposing pitchers were accessible, and he spanked them to the tune of .406 in 1941.[5] He slumped to .356 in 1942 and went off to war.

In 1946, Williams returned from three years as a Marine pilot to the second of his baseball avatars, that of Achilles, the hero of incomparable prowess and beauty who nevertheless was to be found sulking in his tent while the Trojans (mostly Yankees) fought through to the ships. Yawkey, a timber and mining maharajah, had

[3] But he did tip his cap, high off his head, in at least his first season, as cartoons from that period verify. He also was extravagantly cordial to taxi-drivers and stray children. See Linn, Chapter 4, "The Kid Comes to Boston": "There has never been a ballplayer—anywhere, anytime— more popular than Ted Williams in his first season in Boston." To this epoch belong Williams' prankish use of the Fenway scoreboard lights for rifle practice, his celebrated expressed preference for the life of a fireman, and his determined designation of himself as "The Kid."

[4] In 1947 Joe DiMaggio and in 1957 Mickey Mantle, with seasons inferior to Williams', won the MVP award because sportswriters, who vote on ballots with ten places, had vengefully placed Williams ninth, tenth, or nowhere at all. The 1941 award to Joe DiMaggio, even though this was Williams' .406 year, is more understandable, since this was also *annus miraculorum* when DiMaggio hit safely in 56 consecutive games.

[5] The sweet saga of this beautiful decimal must be sung once more. Williams, after hitting above .400 all season, had cooled to .39955 with one doubleheader left to play, in Philadelphia. Joe Cronin, then managing the Red Sox, offered to bench him to safeguard his average, which was exactly .400 when rounded to the third decimal place. Williams said (I forget where I read this) that he did not want to become the .400 hitter with just his toenails over the line. He played the first game and singled, homered, singled, and singled. With less to gain than to lose, he elected to play the second game and got two more hits, including a double that dented a loudspeaker horn on the top of the right-field wall, giving him six-for-eight on the day and a season's average that, in the forty years between Rogers Hornsby's .403 (1925) and the present, stands as unique.

surrounded his central jewel with many gems of slightly lesser water, such as Bobby Doerr, Dom DiMaggio, Rudy York, Birdie Tebbetts, and Johnny Pesky. Throughout the late forties, the Red Sox were the best paper team in baseball, yet they had little three-dimensional to show for it, and if this was a tragedy, Williams was Hamlet. A succinct review of the indictment—and a fair sample of appreciative sports-page prose—appeared the very day of Williams' valedictory, in a column by Huck Finnegan in the Boston *American* (no sentimentalist, Huck):

> Williams' career, in contrast [to Babe Ruth's], has been a series of failures except for his averages. He flopped in the only World Series he ever played in (1946) when he batted only .200. He flopped in the playoff game with Cleveland in 1948. He flopped in the final game of the 1949 season with the pennant hinging on the outcome (Yanks 5, Sox 3). He flopped in 1950 when he returned to the lineup after a two-month absence and ruined the morale of a club that seemed pennant-bound under Steve O'Neill. It has always been Williams' records first, the team second, and the Sox non-winning record is proof enough of that.

There are answers to all this, of course. The fatal weakness of the great Sox slugging teams was not-quite-good-enough pitching rather than Williams' failure to hit a home run every time he came to bat. Again, Williams' depressing effect on his teammates has never been proved. Despite ample coaching to the contrary, most insisted that they *liked* him. He has been generous with advice to any player who asked for it. In an increasingly combative baseball atmosphere, he continued to duck beanballs docilely. With umpires he was gracious to a fault. This courtesy itself annoyed his critics, whom there was no pleasing. And against the ten crucial games (the seven World Series games with the St. Louis Cardinals, the 1948 playoff with the Cleveland Indians, and the two-game series with the Yankees at the end of the 1949 season, when one victory would have given the Red Sox the pennant) that make up the Achilles' heel of Williams' record, a mass of statistics can be set showing that day in and day out he was no slouch in the clutch.[6] The correspondence columns of the Boston papers now and then suffer a sharp flurry of arithmetic on this score; indeed, for Williams to have distributed all his hits so they did nobody else any good would constitute a feat of placement unparalleled in the annals of selfishness.

[6] For example: In 1948, the Sox came from behind to tie the Indians by winning three straight; in those games Williams went two for two, two for two; and two for four. In 1949, the Sox overtook the Yankees by winning nine in a row; in that streak, Williams won four games with home runs.

Whatever residue of truth remains of the Finnegan charge those of us who love Williams must transmute as best we can, in our own personal crucibles. My personal memories of Williams began when I was a boy in Pennsylvania, with two last-place teams in Philadelphia to keep me company. For me, "W'ms, lf" was a figment of the box scores who always seemed to be going 3-for-5. He radiated, from afar, the hard blue glow of high purpose. I remember listening over the radio to the All-Star Game of 1946, in which Williams hit two singles and two home runs, the second one off a Rip Sewell "blooper" pitch; it was like hitting a balloon out of the park. I remember watching one of his home runs from the bleachers of Shibe Park; it went over the first baseman's head and rose methodically along a straight line and was still rising when it cleared the fence. The trajectory seemed qualitatively different from anything anyone else might hit. For me, Williams is the classic ballplayer of the game on a hot August weekday, before a small crowd, when the only thing at stake is the tissue-thin difference between a thing done well and a thing done ill. Baseball is a game of the long season, of relentless and gradual averaging-out. Irrelevance—since the reference point of most individual contests is remote and statistical—always threatens its interest, which can be maintained not by the occasional heroics that sportswriters feed upon but by players who always *care;* who care, that is to say, about themselves and their art. Insofar as the clutch hitter is not a sportswriter's myth, he is a vulgarity, like a writer who writes only for money. It may be that, compared to such managers' dreams as the manifestly classy Joe DiMaggio and the always helpful Stan Musial, Williams was an icy star. But of all team sports, baseball, with its graceful intermittences of action, its immense and tranquil field sparsely settled with poised men in white, its dispassionate mathematics, seems to me best suited to accommodate, and be ornamented by, a loner. It is an essentially lonely game. No other player visible to my generation concentrated within himself so much of the sport's poignance, so assiduously refined his natural skills, so constantly brought to the plate that intensity of competence that crowds the throat with joy.

By the time I went to college, near Boston, the lesser stars Yawkey had assembled around Williams had faded, and his rigorous pride of craftsmanship had become itself a kind of heroism. This brittle and temperamental player developed an unexpected quality of persistence. He was always coming back—back from Korea, back from a broken collarbone, a shattered elbow, a bruised heel, back from drastic bouts of flu and ptomaine poisoning. Hardly a season went by without some enfeebling mishap, yet he always came back, and always looked like himself. The delicate mechanism of timing and power seemed sealed, shockproof, in some case deep within his frame.[7] In addition to injuries, there was a heavily publicized divorce, and the usual storms with the press, and the Williams Shift—the maneuver, custom-built by Lou Boudreau of the Cleveland Indians, whereby three infielders were concentrated on the right side of the infield.[8] Williams could easily have learned to punch singles through the vacancy on his left and fattened his average hugely. This was what Ty Cobb, the Einstein of average, told him to do. But the game had changed since Cobb; Williams believed that his value to the club and to the league was as a slugger, so he went on pulling the ball, trying to blast it through three men, and paid the price of perhaps fifteen points of lifetime average. Like Ruth before him, he bought the occasional home run at the cost of many directed singles —a calculated sacrifice certainly not, in the case of a hitter as average-minded as Williams, entirely selfish.

After a prime so harassed and hobbled, Williams was granted by the relenting fates a golden twilight. He became at the end of his career perhaps the best *old* hitter of the century. The dividing line falls between the 1956 and the 1957 seasons. In September of the first year, he and Mickey Mantle were contending for the batting championship. Both were hitting around .350, and there was no one else near them. The season ended with a three-game series between the Yankees and the Sox, and, living in New York then, I went up to the Stadium. Williams was slightly shy of the four hundred at-bats needed to qualify; the fear was expressed that the Yankee pitchers would walk him to protect Mantle. Instead, they pitched to him. It

[7] Two reasons for his durability may be adduced. A non-smoker, non-drinker, habitual walker, and year-round outdoorsman, Williams spared his body the vicissitudes of the seasonal athlete. And his hitting was in large part a mental process; the amount of cerebration he devoted to such details as pitchers' patterns, prevailing winds, and the muscular mechanics of swinging a bat would seem ridiculous, if it had not paid off. His intellectuality, as it were, perhaps explains the quickness with which he adjusted, after the war, to the changed conditions—the night games, the addition of the slider to the standard pitching repertoire, the new cry for the long ball. His reaction to the Williams Shift, then, cannot be dismissed as unconsidered.

[8] Invented, or perpetrated (as a joke?) by Boudreau on July 14, 1946, between games of a doubleheader. In the first game of the doubleheader, Williams had hit three homers and batted in eight runs. The shift was not used when men were on base and, had Williams bunted or hit late against it immediately, it might not have spread, in all its variations, throughout the league. The Cardinals used it in the lamented World Series of that year. Toward the end, in 1959 and 1960, rather sadly, it had faded from use, or degenerated to the mere clockwise twitching of the infield customary against pull hitters.

was wise. He looked terrible at the plate, tired and discouraged and unconvincing. He never looked very good to me in the Stadium.[9] The final outcome in 1956 was Mantle .353, Williams .345.

The next year, I moved from New York to New England, and it made all the difference. For in September of 1957, in the same situation, the story was reversed. Mantle finally hit .365; it was the best season of his career. But Williams, though sick and old, had run away from him. A bout of flu had laid him low in September. He emerged from his cave in the Hotel Somerset haggard but irresistible; he hit four successive pinch-hit home runs. "I feel terrible," he confessed, "but every time I take a swing at the ball it goes out of the park." He ended the season with thirty-eight home runs and an average of .388, the highest in either league since his own .406, and, coming from a decrepit man of thirty-nine, an even more supernal figure. With eight or so of the "leg hits" that a younger man would have beaten out, it would have been .400. And the next year, Williams, who in 1949 and 1953 had lost batting championships by decimal whiskers to George Kell and Mickey Vernon, sneaked in behind his teammate Pete Runnels and filched his sixth title, a bargain at .328.

In 1959, it seemed all over. The dinosaur thrashed around in the .200 swamp for the first half of the season, and was even benched ("rested," Manager Mike Higgins tactfully said). Old foes like the late Bill Cunningham began to offer batting tips. Cunningham thought Williams was jiggling his elbows; [10] in truth, Williams' neck was so stiff he could hardly turn his head to look at the pitcher. When he swung, it looked like a Calder mobile with one thread cut; it reminded you that since 1954 Williams' shoulders had been wired together. A solicitous pall settled over the sports pages. In the two decades since Williams had come to Boston, his status had imperceptibly shifted from that of a naughty prodigy to that of a munici-

---

[9] Shortly after his retirement, Williams, in *Life*, wrote gloomily of the Stadium, "There's the bigness of it. There are those high stands and all those people smoking—and, of course, the shadows. . . . It takes at least one series to get accustomed to the Stadium and even then you're not sure." Yet his lifetime batting average there is .340, only four points under his median average.

[10] It was Cunningham who, when Williams first appeared in a Red Sox uniform at the 1938 spring training camp, wrote with melodious prescience: "The Sox seem to think Williams is just cocky enough and gabby enough to make a great and colorful outfielder, possibly the Babe Herman type. Me? I don't like the way he stands at the plate. He bends his front knee inward and moves his foot just before he takes a swing. That's exactly what I do just before I drive a golf ball and knowing what happens to the golf balls I drive, I don't believe this kid will ever hit half a singer midget's weight in a bathing suit."

pal monument. As his shadow in the record books lengthened, the Red Sox teams around him declined, and the entire American League seemed to be losing life and color to the National. The inconsistency of the new super-stars—Mantle, Colavito, and Kaline—served to make Williams appear all the more singular. And off the field, his private philanthropy—in particular, his zealous chairmanship of the Jimmy Fund, a charity for children with cancer—gave him a civic presence matched only by that of Richard Cardinal Cushing. In religion, Williams appears to be a humanist, and a selective one at that, but he and the abrasive-voiced Cardinal, when their good works intersect and they appear in the public eye together, make a handsome pair of seraphim.

Humiliated by his '59 season, Williams determined, once more, to come back. I, as a specimen Williams partisan, was both glad and fearful. All baseball fans believe in miracles; the question is, how *many* do you believe in? He looked liked a ghost in spring training. Manager Jurges warned us ahead of time that if Williams didn't come through he would be benched, just like anybody else. As it turned out, it was Jurges who was benched. Williams entered the 1960 season needing eight home runs to have a lifetime total of 500; after one time at bat in Washington, he needed seven. For a stretch, he was hitting a home run every second game that he played. He passed Lou Gehrig's lifetime total, and finished with 521, thirteen behind Jimmy Foxx, who alone stands between Williams and Babe Ruth's unapproachable 714. The summer was a statistician's picnic. His two-thousandth walk came and went, his eighteen-hundredth run batted in, his sixteenth All-Star Game. At one point, he hit a home run off a pitcher, Don Lee, off whose father, Thornton Lee, he had hit a home run a generation before. The only comparable season for a forty-two-year-old man was Ty Cobb's in 1928. Cobb batted .323 and hit one homer. Williams batted .316 but hit twenty-nine homers.

In sum, though generally conceded to be the greatest hitter of his era, he did not establish himself as "the greatest hitter who ever lived." Cobb, for average, and Ruth, for power, remain supreme. Cobb, Rogers Hornsby, Joe Jackson, and Lefty O'Doul, among players since 1900, have higher lifetime averages than Williams' .344. Unlike Foxx, Gehrig, Hack Wilson, Hank Greenberg, and Ralph Kiner, Williams never came close to matching Babe Ruth's season home-run total of sixty.[11] In the list of major-league batting records, not one is held by Williams. He is second in walks drawn, third in

[11] Written before Roger Maris's fluky, phenomenal sixty-one.

home runs, fifth in lifetime average, sixth in runs batted in, eighth in runs scored and in total bases, fourteenth in doubles, and thirtieth in hits.[12] But if we allow him merely average seasons for the four-plus seasons he lost to two wars, and add another season for the months he lost to injuries, we get a man who in all the power totals would be second, and not a very distant second, to Ruth. And if we further allow that these years would have been not merely average but prime years, if we allow for all the months when Williams was playing in sub-par condition, if we permit his early and later years in baseball to be some sort of index of what the middle years could have been, if we give him a right-field fence that is not, like Fenway's, one of the most distant in the league, and if—the least excusable "if"—we imagine him condescending to outsmart the Williams Shift, we can defensibly assemble, like a colossus induced from the sizable fragments that do remain, a statistical figure not incommensurate with his grandiose ambition. From the statistics that are on the books, a good case can be made that in the *combination* of power and average Williams is first; nobody else ranks so high in both categories. Finally, there is the witness of the eyes; men whose memories go back to Shoeless Joe Jackson—another unlucky natural—rank him and Williams together as the best-looking hitters they have seen. It was for our last look that ten thousand of us had come.

Two girls, one of them with pert buckteeth and eyes as black as vest buttons, the other with white skin and flesh-colored hair, like an underdeveloped photograph of a redhead, came and sat on my right. On my other side was one of those frowning chestless young-old men who can frequently be seen, often wearing sailor hats, attending ball games alone. He did not once open his program but instead tapped it, rolled up, on his knee as he gave the game his disconsolate attention. A young lady, with freckles and a depressed, dainty nose that by an optical illusion seemed to thrust her lips forward for a kiss, sauntered down into the box seat right behind the roof of the Oriole dugout. She wore a blue coat with a Northeastern University emblem sewed to it. The girls beside me took it into their heads that this was Williams' daughter. She looked too old to me, and why would she be sitting behind the visitors' dugout? On the other hand, from the way she sat there, staring at the sky and French-inhaling, she clearly was *somebody*. Other fans came and eclipsed her from view. The crowd looked less like a weekday ball-park crowd than like the folks you might find in Yellowstone Na-

[12] Again, as of 1960. Since then, Musial may have surpassed him in some statistical areas.

tional Park, or emerging from automobiles at the top of scenic Mount Mansfield. There were a lot of competitively well-dressed couples of tourist age, and not a few babes in arms. A row of five seats in front of me was abruptly filled with a woman and four children, the youngest of them two years old, if that. Someday, presumably, he could tell his grandchildren that he saw Williams play. Along with these tots and second-honeymooners, there were Harvard freshmen, giving off that peculiar nervous glow created when a sufficient quantity of insouciance is saturated with enough insecurity; thick-necked Army officers with brass on their shoulders and steel in their stares; pepperings of priests; perfumed bouquets of Roxbury Fabian fans; shiny salesmen from Albany and Fall River; and those gray, hoarse men—taxi drivers, slaughterers, and bartenders—who will continue to click through the turnstiles long after everyone else has deserted to television and tramporamas. Behind me, two young male voices blossomed, cracking a joke about God's five proofs that Thomas Aquinas exists—typical Boston College levity.

The batting cage was trundled away. The Orioles fluttered to the sidelines. Diagonally across the field, by the Red Sox dugout, a cluster of men in overcoats were festering like maggots. I could see a splinter of white uniform, and Williams' head, held at a self-deprecating and evasive tilt. Williams' conversational stance is that of a six-foot-three-inch man under a six-foot ceiling. He moved away to the patter of flash bulbs, and began playing catch with a young Negro outfielder named Willie Tasby. His arm, never very powerful, had grown lax with the years, and his throwing motion was a kind of muscular drawl. To catch the ball, he flicked his glove hand onto his left shoulder (he batted left but threw right, as every schoolboy ought to know) and let the ball plop into it comically. This catch session with Tasby was the only time all afternoon I saw him grin.

A tight little flock of human sparrows who, from the lambent and pampered pink of their faces, could only have been Boston politicians moved toward the plate. The loudspeakers mammothly coughed as someone huffed on the microphone. The ceremonies began. Curt Gowdy, the Red Sox radio and television announcer, who sounds like everybody's brother-in-law, delivered a brief sermon, taking the two words "pride" and "champion" as his text. It began. "Twenty-one years ago, a skinny kid from San Diego, California . . ." and ended, "I don't think we'll ever see another like him." Robert Tibolt, chairman of the board of the Greater Boston Chamber of Commerce, presented Williams with a big Paul Revere silver bowl. Harry Carlson, a member of the sports committee of the Boston Chamber, gave him a plaque, whose inscription he did not read in its entirety, out of deference to Williams' distaste for this sort of fuss. Mayor Collins, seated in a wheelchair, presented the Jimmy Fund with a thousand-dollar check.

Then the occasion himself stooped to the microphone, and his voice sounded, after the others, very Californian; it seemed to be coming, excellently amplified, from a great distance, adolescently young and as smooth as a butternut. His thanks for the gifts had not died from our ears before he glided, as if helplessly, into "In spite of all the terrible things that have been said about me by the knights of the keyboard up there. . . ." He glanced up at the press rows suspended behind home plate. The crowd tittered, appalled. A frightful vision flashed upon me, of the press gallery pelting Williams with erasers, of Williams clambering up the foul screen to slug journalists, of a riot, of Mayor Collins being crushed. ". . . And they *were* terrible things," Williams insisted, with level melancholy, into the mike. "I'd like to forget them, but I can't." He paused, swallowed his memories, and went on, "I want to say that my years in Boston have been the greatest thing in my life." The crowd, like an immense sail going limp in a change of wind, sighed with relief. Taking all the parts himself, Williams then acted out a vivacious little morality drama in which an imaginary tempter came to him at the beginning of his career and said, "Ted, you can play anywhere you like." Leaping nimbly into the role of his younger self (who in biographical actuality had yearned to be a Yankee), Williams gallantly chose Boston over all the other cities, and told us that Tom Yawkey was the greatest owner in baseball and we were the greatest fans. We applauded ourselves lustily. The umpire came out and dusted the plate. The voice of doom announced over the loudspeakers that after Williams' retirement his uniform number, 9, would be permanently retired—the first time the Red Sox had so honored a player. We cheered. The national anthem was played. We cheered. The game began.

Williams was third in the batting order, so he came up in the bottom of the first inning, and Steve Barber, a young pitcher born two months before Williams began playing in the major leagues, offered him four pitches, at all of which he disdained to swing, since none of them were within the strike zone. This demonstrated simultaneously that Williams' eyes were razor-sharp and that Barber's control wasn't. Shortly, the bases were full, with Williams on second. "Oh, I hope he gets held up at third! That would be wonderful," the girl beside me moaned, and, sure enough, the man at bat walked and Williams was delivered into our foreground. He struck the pose of Donatello's David, the third-base bag being Goliath's head. Fiddling with his cap, swapping small talk with the Oriole third basemen (who seemed delighted to have him drop in), swinging his arms with a sort of prancing nervousness, he looked fine—flexible, hard, and not unbecomingly substantial through the middle. The long neck, the small head, the knickers whose cuffs were worn down near his ankles—all these clichés of sports cartoon iconography were rendered in the flesh.

With each pitch, Williams danced down the baseline, waving his arms and stirring dust, ponderous but menacing, like an attacking goose. It occurred to about a dozen humorists at once to shout "Steal home! Go, go!" Williams' speed afoot was never legendary. Lou Clinton, a young Sox outfielder, hit a fairly deep fly to center field. Williams tagged up and ran home. As he slid across the plate, the ball, thrown with unusual heft by Jackie Brandt, the Oriole center fielder, hit him on the back.

"Boy, he was really loafing, wasn't he?" one of the collegiate voices behind me said.

"It's cold," the other voice explained. "He doesn't play well when it's cold. He likes heat. He's a hedonist."

The run that Williams scored was the second and last of the inning. Gus Triandos, of the Orioles, quickly evened the score by plunking a home run over the handy left-field wall. Williams, who had had this wall at his back for twenty years,[13] played the ball flawlessly. He didn't budge. He just stood still, in the center of the little patch of grass that his patient footsteps had worn brown, and, limp with lack of interest, watched the ball pass overhead. It was not a very interesting game. Mike Higgins, the Red Sox manager, with nothing to lose, had restricted his major-league players to the left-field line—along with Williams, Frank Malzone, a first-rate third baseman, played the game—and had peopled the rest of the terrain with unpredictable youngsters fresh, or not so fresh, off the farms. Other than Williams' recurrent appearances at the plate, the *maladresse* of the Sox infield was the sole focus of suspense; the second baseman turned every grounder into a juggling act, while the shortstop did a breathtaking impersonation of an open window. With this sort of assistance, the Orioles wheeled their way into a 4–2 lead. They had early replaced Barber with another young pitcher, Jack Fisher. Fortunately (as it turned out), Fisher is no cutie; he is willing

---

[13] In his second season (1940) he was switched to left field, to protect his eyes from the right-field sun.

to burn the ball through the strike zone, and inning after inning this tactic punctured Higgins' string of test balloons.

Whenever Williams appeared at the plate—pounding the dirt from his cleats, gouging a pit in the batter's box with his left foot, wringing resin out of the bat handle with his vehement grip, switching the stick at the pitcher with an electric ferocity—it was like having a familiar Leonardo appear in a shuffle of *Saturday Evening Post* covers. This man, you realized—and here, perhaps, was the difference, greater than the difference in gifts—really desired to hit the ball. In the third inning, he hoisted a high fly to deep center. In the fifth, we thought he had it; he smacked the ball hard and high into the heart of his power zone, but the deep right field in Fenway and the heavy air and a casual east wind defeated him. The ball died. Al Pilarcik leaned his back against the big "380" painted on the right-field wall and caught it. On another day, in another park, it would have been gone. (After the game, Williams said, "I didn't think I could hit one any harder than that. The conditions weren't good.")

The afternoon grew so glowering that in the sixth inning the arc lights were turned on—always a wan sight in the day-time, like the burning headlights of a funeral procession. Aided by the gloom, Fisher was slicing through the Sox rookies, and Williams did not come to bat in the seventh. He was second up in the eighth. This was almost certainly his last time to come to the plate in Fenway Park, and instead of merely cheering, as we had at his three previous appearances, we stood, all of us, and applauded. I had never before heard pure applause in a ballpark. No calling, no whistling, just an ocean of handclaps, minute after minute, burst after burst, crowding and running together in continuous succession like the pushes of surf at the edge of the sand. It was a sombre and considered tumult. There was not a boo in it. It seemed to renew itself out of a shifting set of memories as the Kid, the Marine, the veteran of feuds and failures and injuries, the friend of children, and the enduring old pro evolved down the bright tunnel of twenty-two summers toward this moment. At last, the umpire signalled for Fisher to pitch; with the other players, he had been frozen in position. Only Williams had moved during the ovation, switching his bat impatiently, ignoring everything except his cherished task. Fisher wound up, and the applause sank into a hush.

Understand that we were a crowd of rational people. We knew that a home run cannot be produced at will; the right pitch must be perfectly met and luck must ride with the ball. Three innings before, we had seen a brave effort fail. The air was soggy, the season was exhausted. Nevertheless, there will always lurk, around the corner in a pocket of our knowledge of the odds, an indefensible hope, and this was one of the times, which you now and then find in sports, when a density of expectation hangs in the air and plucks an event out of the future.

Fisher, after his unsettling wait, was low with the first pitch. He put the second one over, and Williams swung mightily and missed. The crowd grunted, seeing that classic swing, so long and smooth and quick, exposed. Fisher threw the third time, Williams swung again, and there it was. The ball climbed on a diagonal line into the vast volume of air over center field. From my angle, behind third base, the ball seemed less an object in flight than the tip of a towering, motionless construct, like the Eiffel Tower or the Tappan Zee Bridge. It was in the books while it was still in the sky. Brandt ran back to the deepest corner of the outfield grass, the ball descended beyond his reach and struck in the crotch where the bullpen met the wall, bounced chunkily, and vanished.

Like a feather caught in a vortex, Williams ran around the square of bases at the center of our beseeching screaming. He ran as he always ran out home runs—hurriedly, unsmiling, head down, as if our praise were a storm of rain to get out of. He didn't tip his cap. Though we thumped, wept, and chanted "We want Ted" for minutes after he hid in the dugout, he did not come back. Our noise for some seconds passed beyond excitement into a kind of immense open anguish, a wailing, a cry to be saved. But immortality is nontransferable. The papers said that the other players, and even the umpires on the field, begged him to come out and acknowledge us in some way, but he refused. Gods do not answer letters.

Every true story has an anticlimax. The men on the field refused to disappear, as would have seemed decent, in the smoke of Williams' miracle. Fisher continued to pitch, and escaped further harm. At the end of the inning, Higgins sent Williams out to his left-field position, then instantly replaced him with Carrol Hardy, so we had a long last look at Williams as he ran out there and then back, his uniform jogging, his eyes steadfast on the ground. It was nice, and we were grateful, but it left a funny taste.

One of the scholasticists behind me said, "Let's go. We've seen everything. I don't want to spoil it." This seemed a sound aesthetic decision. Williams' last word had been so exquisitely chosen, such a perfect fusion of expectation, intention, and execution, that already it felt a little unreal in my head, and I wanted to get out before the castle collapsed. But the game, though played by clumsy midgets under the feeble glow of the arc lights, began to tug at my attention, and I loitered in the runway until it was over. Williams' homer had, quite incidentally, made the score 4–3. In the bottom of the ninth inning, with one out, Marlin Coughtry, the secondbase juggler, singled. Vic Wertz, pinch-hitting, doubled off the left-field wall, Coughtry advancing to third. Pumpsie Green walked, to load the bases. Willie Tasby hit a double-play ball to the third baseman, but in making the pivot throw Billy Klaus, an ex-Red Sox infielder, reverted to form and threw the ball past the first baseman and into the Red Sox dugout. The Sox won, 5–4. On the car radio as I drove home I heard that Williams, his own man to the end, had decided not to accompany the team to New York. He had met the little death that awaits athletes. He had quit.

QUESTIONS AND EXERCISES

1. Updike's essay opens with a paragraph containing a good deal of information as well as an unmistakably subjective and impressionistic method of presentation. The writer tells us, for instance, that the day was "overcast, chill, and uninspirational," the first two terms giving only sensory data, the third an emotional tone of sorts. What other conspicuous combinations of fact and feeling do you find in this paragraph?

2. The essay's central method is narrative, the description of a sequence of events on a given September afternoon. But in order to lend depth to his own sense of the occasion, Updike must also provide some treatment of Williams' earlier career. Discuss in detail the means by which he fits this material in, giving special attention to the quality of the transitions and the rearrangements of strict chronology.

3. At what point does the essay become most frankly subjective? Would it be accurate to say that here Updike himself commands more interest than Williams? Why, or why not? And why do you suppose Updike did not *open* his essay with this nostalgic reminiscence of boyhood impressions?

4. Cite pertinent examples that demonstrate the pains Updike takes to provide detail and commentary of the sort that a real baseball fan would not require, in order to appeal to a wider audience.

5. Does the essay simply re-create a set of events and the feelings that go with them, or do you find some strongly implicit thesis or governing idea? If so, can you describe the sort of reader whose assumptions and views would *not* qualify him as a sympathetic reader of this essay?

6. The whole essay is, in one sense, a statement about being part of an audience. In several places the writer directly describes the various

sorts of baseball fans who were near him in the stands on the day of the game. Does this appeal to the sympathies of a wider audience, by giving each reader someone to identify with? Explain. By what other means does Updike convey the feeling that his experience has not only been highly individual, but more nearly communal?

7. Do you discover any places where Updike is obviously twisting evidence in Williams' favor? Does he do this in such a way as to alienate the reader, or does it seem rather to be part of his deliberate technique for commanding the sympathetic attention of his audience? How does his essay compare with Rosten's "The Intellectual and the Mass Media" in this respect?

8. Suppose that you were about to write a lengthy essay on some subject similar to Updike's, using a primarily narrative technique and attempting, in part, to re-create the feelings and sensations of a particular event at a given place and time. What characteristics of your own mind and personality (as you conceive them) would you want to make conspicuous in your treatment of the subject? And how would you go about making such revelations? Write a few paragraphs about this, specifying exactly the nature of your would-be subject, and then, if the prospects seem good, try writing the essay itself. If the prospects seem bad, write a few hundred words explaining why.

9. Take a good look at Updike's opening description of Fenway Park. Try to produce a descriptive paragraph of your own—describing whatever you like—that achieves the same sense of personal involvement in the scene. Write another, on the same scene, in which you try to create a feeling of detachment, purely passive witness.

10. Explain, in about 250–300 words, how Updike (or someone else) might have written on approximately the same subject without using much narrative.

11. Write a 700-word essay that can be regarded as the last word in the Ted Williams controversy. Try to avoid mealy-mouthed compromise and cautious emptiness. This exercise is recommended only for the brash.

CHAPTER FOUR

The Arrangement of Parts

1

When we read essays, we participate in a straight-line process of verbal communication; that is, we move in sequence of time from one part of the discourse to the next, and then on to the next, until we reach what is called the end. The process within the individual sentence is similar, as we move from each word to the one following until we reach terminal punctuation. Linear progression is so intrinsic to both our reading and thinking that we take it for granted. It seldom occurs to us that meanings can be transmitted in any other way, hence we do not think of sequence itself as a particularly distinctive principle of organization. Yet in the arrangement of parts no other principle is so important as sequence, since it is a constant to which all strategies of presentation are related.

If our biological equipment for perceiving things were radically changed, the structure of our discourse would change too. In some forms of experience, we do have the power to take in a number of elements or parts simultaneously, or at least in such rapid succession that the perceptions *seem* simultaneous. Imagine, for instance, looking at a painting which depicts five different animal heads, arranged in an X shape, against a white background. We see all of the heads at once, and can perceive instantly the whole pattern formed by their individual relations to one another. Suppose that we were able to treat five different paragraphs of print, or even five sentences, in the same way, not just seeing but *understanding* them all at the same time. The printed, bound book would become quaintly obsolete, as would most of our habits of expressive organization.

But we cannot perceive more than one verbal meaning at a time, and so we are stuck, like it or not, with linear organization of parts in discourse. This means that in arranging a composition of any length or complexity, the writer must constantly take into account the most capricious and imperfect of the reader's faculties—his memory. The substance of paragraph 2 must still be available in the reader's mind by the time he reaches paragraph 10, and the same is true for all of the other parts of the composition. If the essay's arranged sequence does not aid the memory in every possible way, then the real structure of its meanings will be lost. Of course, not all parts of the essay need be remembered at the same moment, or with the same intensity; but this fact complicates rather than simplifies the arranging of parts.

Anyone who has read more than a few essays will know that, although linear organization is common to all of them, some capitalize on it, emphasize it, more than others. The continuous narration of a journey, for example, calls attention to its own sequential structure; a different kind of narration, in which the whole journey is represented by a number of isolated vignettes or descriptions of events along the way, is less patently sequential, and may even present its parts in an order different from that of the actual happening. Or suppose that the writer is describing several different activities going on simultaneously in various parts of a large city; or listing several causes, not related to each other, that help to produce a common effect. In these instances, the order of presentation is not of crucial importance, and the positions of the several parts may be perfectly interchangeable. But where each event explains, or modifies, or extends another, where the various causes are linked together in a chain leading to the end effect, sequence is far more certainly fixed.

Imagine that, instead of being printed in books or magazines, essays were marketed in "decks," like playing cards, with each paragraph or distinct part printed on a separate card, and the whole deck thoroughly shuffled. Imagine, further, that all of the little helpful signs of linkage and transition were removed. In some cases it would be fairly easy to reconstruct the correct order. In others, there would be much uncertainty. In a few, it might even appear that there was no single correct order, that the meaning of the entire deck remained equally clear after each shuffling. For certain special purposes, this last type, the "undertermined" presentation, may be very effective.

An essay whose aim is to recreate the feel of a particular place and time—one's home town during boyhood—might simply put together in random order a number of impressionistic descriptive passages in such a way that the reader would feel no need of directedness, no sense that he is supposed to imagine himself travelling from one part of the town to another as the essay progresses. In different circumstances, an apparently random sequence of parts might effectively invite the reader to *impose* an order of his own, thus involving him not only as a spectator but as a participant. In fact, however, essays of this type are extremely rare. Our Western culture has traditionally encouraged values that lead us to expect purposeful directedness in discourse. In an earlier chapter we observed that practically all essays are propelled by some kind of thesis or argument, and the structure of thesis and argument cannot be left entirely to chance.

2

As he asserts, persuades, and proves, driving his intention through the various linked parts of the essay toward its culminative effect, the essayist must constantly define and classify elements in experience. *Definition* and *classification*, especially when they work together, provide the stuff of which an essay's structural components are made. To classify something is to locate it in a group with all other things of its type; to define it is to distinguish it from all other things, specifying its uniqueness. Thus in one sense classification is an *inclusive* process, definition an *exclusive* one. The one expands and the other contracts the focus of awareness. Definition makes experience convincingly the author's own; classification makes it recognizable for his audience. Thus in "Hub Fans Bid Kid Adieu" John Updike both classifies the afternoon's events (he is a spectator at a sporting event, the weather is cloudy, the home team has no hope of winning the pennant, and so forth) and defines it as his own afternoon in Fenway Park so particularly that there can be no chance of confusing it with anyone else's afternoon, any time, anyplace. On a smaller scale the essay contains lesser classifications (Ted Williams as a great hitter, for instance) and precise definitions (Ted Williams as the greatest all-round hitter of all time). Obviously the two processes are mutually dependent on each other. The particular involves the general, and vice versa. In every attempt to isolate something, to individuate and make it distinct, the process relies largely on making connections, relating X to what lies outside it. Within almost any single brief passage the interaction is quietly at work: "Languages are more to us than systems of thought-transference. They are invisible garments that drape themselves about our spirit and give a predetermined form to all its symbolic expression. When the expression is of unusual significance, we call it literature." This quotation is from the first paragraph of Edward Sapir's "Language and Literature," one of the essays included in this chapter. The opening sentence starts out as if it were going to define or classify: "Languages are . . . ," but its actual function is to label one definition as insufficient. This strategy is a familiar one in discourse. In making a proposition, we may not only affirm X but also deny not-X, thus emphasizing the special distinctness of what we are saying by deliberately contrasting it with what we *do not* mean. And yet in order to deny not-X we must formulate it, and hence produce the idea of it in the mind of the reader. Thus even in the simplest case of the "not-that-but-this" locution, the desire to limit and define closely must produce an accompanying gesture of expansion. In Sapir's sentence, the expansiveness is even more pronounced, for he is not even rejecting absolutely the definition of languages as "systems of thought-transference." In fact his phrasing—"more to us than"—plainly shows that this definition *is* applicable as far as it goes. Having retained the phrase "systems of thought-transference" as a literal definition not entirely adequate to the purpose, Sapir can go on in the next sentence to fulfill the promise of "more," which he accomplishes by metaphorical means, likening our spirit to our body and our language to the clothing in which our body is dressed. The result is a combined richness of meaning that no single assertion could have produced. The effort to define and distinguish has also been an effort to complicate and extend.

What happens within a brief passage can be found happening also among the larger structural units of the whole essay. One element of meaning—it may be a whole paragraph or that part of a paragraph that develops a single thought—is laid next to another element in a relation which may be contrastive, or additive, or both. This relationship may follow two principal forms: *progression* and *parallelism*. Both are used as ways of connecting any given passage in the text with the passages that precede and follow it, for the express purpose of reinforcing the reader's memory and thus lending coherence to the effect of the whole.

Progression is the form of advance, the introduction of a new step or phase in the presentation of the essay's substance. Progressive arrangement gives the reader the satisfying sense that he is moving along toward an eventual conclusion. Obviously, no essay needs to be thrusting forward all the time; on the other hand, no essay can afford to neglect progression altogether. The progression must be sufficiently conspicuous and frequent so that stagnation does not set in and so that the reader, at any given point, can know or remember what the author is driving at.

The most obvious type of progression is *narrative*, in which the several stages in a sequence of events appear in the order of their occurrence. If the author sees his subject as having in itself the shape of evolving action, a straight story-like sequence may provide the most natural form of organization. Even where it is necessary to frequently interrupt the narrative flow in order to introduce different kinds of progressive movement or expansion through parallel

ROCHESTER INSTITUTE OF TECHNOLOGY LIBRARY

meanings, momentum is relatively easy to maintain if a strong sense of narrative progress has been established at the beginning. The author can then count on the element of suspense, the reader's urge to find out what happens next. Trouble arises, usually, when the narrative movement is not established as dominant from the start, so that the reader cannot know for sure whether he is reading an account of an action that will be completed, or a logical argument, or an analytic commentary, or whatever.

In essays, as in stories and novels, the author may, of course, invert the order of narration in some way, beginning in the middle of the action or at the end of it and then going back to describe earlier events. If used sensibly, this is a good way of providing special emphasis when it is needed. In narrating an urban summer riot, for example, it may make good strategic sense to open by describing the height of the action—the looting, burning, and bloodshed—and then treat in sequence the build-up to and the consequences of the central event. Or, for somewhat different purposes, the author could begin with prelude and aftermath, saving the central event for the essay's close. Arrangements vary according to the author's sense of what needs to be emphasized. The only universal rule of thumb is that the natural chronology should not be rearranged unless there is an express reason for doing so. Inversion "just for the fun of it" usually produces a confusing effect and nothing more.

Progression can also be achieved through the relation of cause to effect. Like plain narrative, the cause-effect link has a chronological basis—effect follows cause in time—and therefore it is well suited to the medium of verbal discourse, where things are perceived by the reader not simultaneously but sequentially. This does not mean that cause-effect is only a subspecies of narrative. In narrative what precedes one event is another event. But a given effect, whether it be an action or a situation, may be traced to ideas, feelings, economic habits, biological facts, divine will—to any one of an infinite number of causes that are not in themselves events and that need not *immediately* precede the effect in time. There is another difference. Though limited inversions are possible and sometimes helpful in narrative, the general rule is that the narration follow the actual order of the events themselves. We almost never encounter a serious piece of writing in which the most recent action is narrated first, then the action immediately preceding it, then the one preceding that, and so on back through all the stages to a beginning. In the handling of cause and effect, however, it is perfectly acceptable practice to begin by describing an effect at hand and then move backward through the series of causes that produced it. This method would be called in-depth analysis, whereas a similar handling of plain narrative might be called sheer foolishness. To understand why this is so and why, in practice, an essayist is very likely to deal with cause after he deals with effect rather than to follow the "natural" sequence, we need to consider the normal human reaction to any interesting act or state of affairs. If our experience brings us to something that is striking, that interests us, that arrests our attention, we are far more likely to ask, "How did this come about?" than "What will be the result?", for the good reason that we are conditioned to think of the past as knowable and the future as not-so-knowable. Therefore the essayist who is concerned with causation and not just with chronological sequence often finds that, in the explanation of any process, it is most natural to work backward.

A third means of progression is the structure of *logic*. The logical connection of parts is a method almost always used in discourse whose purpose is to persuade or prove, though as a rule it is found in combination with other progressive devices. Often, and especially when the essayist is trying to create an effect of easy, relaxed informality of discourse, the hard outlines of logical organization will be intentionally softened, blurred, or veiled, so that the reader will have no feeling that he is being threatened by a formidable apparatus. But whether conspicuous or not, the forms of logic always advance an essay's substance toward its conclusion. We may note, briefly, three major types of logical progression.

1. *Induction:* This is the movement from individual observed facts or pieces of evidence to a generalized conclusion, and its function can be recognized as the basis of what we call scientific method. If I visit two hundred homes in Matawan, New Jersey and find that each of them has a living room whose walls are painted avocado green, I may conclude that all the living rooms in Matawan are painted avocado green. Obviously this technique can be persuasive in an essay only if the conclusion seems a reasonable inference from the facts, and only if the facts are accepted as reliable. Much might be said, from a logician's point of view, about the ways in which inductive method—or any logical method for that matter—can be abused. But from the writer's point of view, it is enough to remember that in order to gain the full effect of a leap forward in the essay's advance, the conclusion must seem fully supported by evidence, and the evidence should all be linked together in some fairly obvious way so that its *collective* relevance to the conclusion is clear and unambiguous. Where these conditions are met, inductive argument can be a particularly good way of both organizing the essay

and appealing to the reader, for it always begins with immediate experience and individual cases, which, after all, are the materials on which the essayist's art most naturally works. And, as with cause and effect, the normal order of actual reasoning can be reversed in the order of presentation: The conclusion can be stated first and then supported by evidence.

2. *Deduction:* This is a movement through a series of assertions that are related in such a way that a combination of some of them establishes the validity of others. The simplest and most familiar deductive form is the syllogism:

> Every edible fruit is nourishing. [MAJOR PREMISE]
>
> An apple is an edible fruit. [MINOR PREMISE]
>
> An apple is nourishing. [CONCLUSION]

or, in the so-called hypothetical form:

> P^1: If any fruit is edible, it is nourishing.
>
> P^2: There is at least one fruit, an apple, that is edible.
>
> C: Therefore an apple is nourishing.

The major premise and the minor premise, taken together, imply the conclusion. Obviously the deductive conclusion is different in kind from the inductive one, since it is the product of an almost mathematical process. The truth of each premise must be separately established; otherwise the conclusion, however logically valid, may not be true. As it is used in the essay, of course, the syllogism never appears starkly as a three-part formula. The order of elements may well be inverted, and each of them is likely to be encased in a full body of descriptive and argumentative material. In some cases, one of the premises may simply be assumed, never explicitly stated. Suppose that in an essay defending capital punishment, for instance, the author argues that proven murderers must be executed lest they corrupt their fellow prison inmates. Part of the argument might be reducible to this syllogistic form:

> P^1: It is bad for any men to associate with proven murderers.
>
> P^2: Prison convicts are men.
>
> C: It is bad for prison convicts to associate with proven murderers.

In the actual presentation this form might be concealed under any number of variant strategies. One possibility: State the conclusion first, acknowledging that to some people it may sound like an odd idea, since prison convicts are assumed to be corrupt anyway. Then develop the major premise in great detail, establishing by all available means—testimony of psychiatrists, chemical analogies, personal anecdotes, and so forth—that no man is already so bad that he cannot be made worse by the wrong sort of company. This process may take several sentences or several paragraphs. Then simply restate the conclusion, leaving the minor premise unstated on the assumption that no one would dispute it anyway.

Arrangement of parts in a deductive progression can bring to the essay an elegant shapeliness, a sense of great control and assurance. The main danger is that one of the premises may require such elaborate and diverse support that the main thrust of the total argument is lost or neglected. Perhaps the wisest course is to use deduction and induction in concert, establishing premises by inductive means and then deducing from them.

3. *Analogy:* Analogical argument is generally regarded as the least intellectually solid of the major logical forms. On the other hand, it has considerable advantages in emotional appeal and can be used to great effect, especially in supplementing other types of argument. Its procedure is to assert a particular similarity between two things (ideas, situations, persons, or whatever) by pointing out their unquestionable similarity in a number of other respects. One could argue by analogical means that dogs, like cats, must loathe water, since dogs are similar to cats in so many other demonstrable ways. Another analogical argument—familiar enough to all of us nowadays—asserts that any negotiation with the Communist bloc is bound to result in disgrace for the United States, the analogue being Chamberlain's sellout to Hitler at Munich. But it is possible to construct convincing analogies by drawing the lines of comparison very precisely and in great numbers.

Arrangement of parts in analogical method requires a close knitting-together of the several points of similarity. As a rule it is preferable to make the cross-references point by point, in the most systematic way, rather than to describe all of the characteristics of the first analogue before starting on the second. This procedure spares the reader the annoyance of checking back to verify the correspondences. It is also wise to subordinate analogy to other methods, making clear to the reader that it is only a minor contribution to the essay's total substance.

The other general type of relation between parts is *parallelism*. It provides a lateral development of substance, complementing and reinforcing the forward movement of *progression*. Imagine a purely progressive essay structure, one in which each segment represents an advance through some connective means—narrative, causal, or logical—to the next. It would be an unusual essay. The purposes of the good essay nearly always demand that, at various points in the progression, a given functional part be doubled, trebled, or multiplied still more, in order to give weight to the discourse. Where this occurs, we have parts in parallel. Practically speaking, any two elements are in parallel when they share the same relation to a third element. The essayist may describe in sequence two (or more) causes that work independently toward the same effect, two (or more) simultaneous events that immediately precede another event, two (or more) examples that establish a premise, and so forth. In a sense, although these parallel parts can only be encountered by the reader one at a time, they want to be taken together as elements of a single function. And the parallel relation can be strengthened further, made more conspicuous, by adding to similarity of function some other connectives between the parts. The most common grounds for such additional connection are *similarity* and *proximity*. If two things resemble each other strongly, or if they are close together in either space or time, we associate them with each other naturally. Consider two different cases of parallel development within the context of effect-to-cause progression, both represented here in skeletal form:

A. the air is polluted because

1. factories use low-grade fuel
2. a low cloud cover traps the poisons
3. nothing has been done to purify it

B. the air is polluted because

1. factories use low-grade fuel
2. automobiles produce lots of carbon monoxide
3. all the suburbanites are burning leaves

Clearly the parallel relation of 1, 2, and 3 is far more emphatic in B than in A, and the difference between A and B would be even more extreme if each of the causes were given a full paragraph. Still more intense connections can be made by maintaining *verbal* similarities among the three:

C. the air is polluted because
1. factories are burning low-grade fuel
2. automobiles are burning gasoline
3. suburbanites are burning leaves

In order to see more clearly how parallel connections give shape to the essay, we must consider a number of familiar applications of the principle.

Restatement is probably the most common form of parallel connection. When an assertion is important enough to require that the reader remember it well, and especially when its meaning is complicated or subtle, some kind of restatement is called for. This may be simply a literal repetition, using exactly the same words in the same sequence. More often it will be a variant phrasing whose content is a little different from the original; this has the advantage of enriching the meaning, as well as stressing it. Inexperienced writers as a rule do not consciously use restatement as often as they should, because they are afraid that it will be taken as a sign that they have run out of things to say. An accomplished essayist knows how to restate for clarity and emphasis without insulting either the reader or himself. It takes practice.

Examples frequently occur in pairs or triads. A single example may not be enough when its purpose is to illustrate or clarify the statement to which it is attached. If more than one is used, however, the author must take care to establish *separately for each of them* its special relevance to the central point.

Analysis often provides a type of parallel elaboration. When logical argument has arrived at some unified conclusion, for instance, the author may wish to break that conclusion down into its several basic elements or aspects, stating each of them in order. Analysis of a single part may occur at any point in a given structural sequence, whether narrative, causal, or logical, but it generally works best at either the beginning or end of the sequence, where it cannot interfere with or obscure the main progression.

Multiple point of view is a way of using parallel order to fill out description or definition. Although the essay usually communicates the author's personal view, he may find it desirable to add authority to his opinion by recording (or just imagining) how the situation appears to certain other persons whose vantages and values are different from his own.

The four applications of parallelism just described represent only a small fraction of the total possibilities, but they should suggest how valuable the device can be. And more must be said here about the internal arrangements that are available in any parallel structure. We start with the fact that parallel parts may be either similar to each other, or dissimilar, in terms of content, length, and verbal form. Where the arrangement of parts emphasizes similarity, the effect is one of *balance*. Where dissimilarity is emphasized, the result is *climax*. Suppose that the author is discussing a woman's beauty, and that he seeks to celebrate *competing* claims of her hair and complexion:

> Lydia's hair, lustrous by firelight, fell in bright curves about her shoulders. Its subtle fragrance mingled with the scent of the burning pine logs. No camera could have captured the beauty of it. Her skin, pale and clear as water, glimmered softly in the flickering light. No rich fabric might have matched its charm.

The parallel construction is balanced. If, on the other hand, the author wishes to establish priorities, he may produce something like this:

> Lydia's hair was beautiful. Her clear, pale skin glimmered in the flickering light. And her eyes, deep with the sublime radiance of pure love, captured and held all attention.

This is *climax*. Like balance, it can work through a sequence of paragraphs as well as through a sequence of sentences. Both effects make use of the inherent value or importance of each part, or the verbal length of each, or the structural complexity of the ideas. Both balance and climax have extraordinary power to organize material for the convenience of the reader's memory. It is worth adding that their usefulness is not restricted to parallel organization. They can operate through progressions as well.

3

Finally, a few words about *beginnings*, *endings*, and *transitions*. An opening paragraph should orient the reader at least preliminarily, but it need not (and in most cases should not) attempt to summarize in advance the entire intention and argument of the essay. Similarly, it may be helpful in the final paragraph to remind the reader of what he has just read, but except in very long and complicated essays there should be no need for a full résumé. A bad essay is likely to be dull at both ends, where the author is not actually *doing* anything, but merely prancing around in anticipation of the event or in celebration of its finish. Many writers find the quality of their work much improved if, when the essay's first draft is complete, they simply strike out the first and last paragraphs.

As for *transitions*, there is just one thing to say: Where there are any verbal signs of connection between parts—be they single words, phrases, or whole sentences—there must already be a real substantive connection. A well structured essay needs no artificial linkage between its parts.

LANGUAGE AND LITERATURE

Edward Sapir

Languages are more to us than systems of thought-transference. They are invisible garments that drape themselves about our spirit and give a predetermined form to all its symbolic expression. When the expression is of unusual significance, we call it literature.[1] Art is so personal an expression that we do not like to feel that it is bound to predetermined form of any sort. The possibilities of individual expression are infinite, language in particular is the most fluid of mediums. Yet some limitation there must be to this freedom, some resistance of the medium. In great art there is the illusion of absolute freedom. The formal restraints imposed by the material—paint, black and white, marble, piano tones, or whatever it may be—are not perceived; it is as though there were a limitless margin of elbow-room between the artist's fullest utilization of form and the most that the material is innately capable of. The artist has intuitively surrendered to the inescapable tyranny of the material, made its brute nature fuse easily with his conception.[2] The material "disappears" precisely

[1] I can hardly stop to define just what kind of expression is "significant" enough to be called art or literature. Besides, I do not exactly know. We shall have to take literature for granted.

[2] This "intuitive surrender" has nothing to do with subservience to artistic convention. More than one revolt in modern art has been dominated by the desire to get out of the material just what it is really capable of. The impressionist wants light and color because paint can give him just these; "literature" in painting, the sentimental suggestion of a "story," is offensive to him because he does not want the virtue of his particular form to be dimmed by shadows from another medium. Similarly, the poet, as never before, insists that words mean just what they really mean.

LANGUAGE AND LITERATURE: From *Language: An Introduction To The Study of Speech* by Edward Sapir, copyright, 1921, by Harcourt, Brace & World, Inc.; renewed, 1949, by Jean V. Sapir. Reprinted by permission of the publishers.

because there is nothing in the artist's conception to indicate that any other material exists. For the time being, he, and we with him, move in the artistic medium as a fish moves in the water, oblivious of the existence of an alien atmosphere. No sooner, however, does the artist transgress the law of his medium than we realize with a start that there is a medium to obey.

Language is the medium of literature as marble or bronze or clay are the materials of the sculptor. Since every language has its distinctive peculiarities, the innate formal limitations—and possibilities —of one literature are never quite the same as those of another. The literature fashioned out of the form and substance of a language has the color and the texture of its matrix. The literary artist may never be conscious of just how he is hindered or helped or otherwise guided by the matrix, but when it is a question of translating his work into another language, the nature of the original matrix manifests itself at once. All his effects have been calculated, or intuitively felt, with reference to the formal "genius" of his own language; they cannot be carried over without loss or modification. Croce [3] is therefore perfectly right in saying that a work of literary art can never be translated. Nevertheless literature does get itself translated, sometimes with astonishing adequacy. This brings up the question whether in the art of literature there are not intertwined two distinct kinds or levels of art—a generalized, non-linguistic art, which can be transferred without loss into an alien linguistic medium, and a specifically linguistic art that is not transferable.[4] I believe the distinction is entirely valid, though we never get the two levels pure in practice. Literature moves in language as a medium, but that medium comprises two layers, the latent content of language—our intuitive record of experience—and the particular conformation of a given language—the specific how of our record of experience. Literature that draws its sustenance mainly—never entirely—from the lower level, say a play of Shakespeare's, is translatable without too great a loss of character. If it moves in the upper rather than in the lower level—a fair example is a lyric of Swinburne's—it is as

[3] See Benedetto Croce, *Aesthetic*.
[4] The question of the transferability of art productions seems to me to be of genuine theoretic interest. For all that we speak of the sacrosanct uniqueness of a given art work, we know very well, though we do not always admit it, that not all productions are equally intractable to transference. A Chopin étude is inviolate; it moves altogether in the world of piano tone. A Bach fugue is transferable into another set of musical timbres without serious loss of esthetic significance. Chopin plays with the language of the piano as though no other language existed (the medium "disappears"); Bach speaks the language of the piano as a handy means of giving outward expression to a conception wrought in the generalized language of tone.

good as untranslatable. Both types of literary expression may be great or mediocre.

There is really no mystery in the distinction. It can be clarified a little by comparing literature with science. A scientific truth is impersonal, in its essence it is untinctured by the particular linguistic medium in which it finds expression. It can as readily deliver its message in Chinese [5] as in English. Nevertheless it must have some expression, and that expression must needs be a linguistic one. Indeed the apprehension of the scientific truth is itself a linguistic process, for thought is nothing but language denuded of its outward garb. The proper medium of scientific expression is therefore a generalized language that may be defined as a symbolic algebra of which all known languages are translations. One can adequately translate scientific literature because the original scientific expression is itself a translation. Literary expression is personal and concrete, but this does not mean that its significance is altogether bound up with the accidental qualities of the medium. A truly deep symbolism, for instance, does not depend on the verbal associations of a particular language but rests securely on an intuitive basis that underlies all linguistic expression. The artist's "intuition," to use Croce's term, is immediately fashioned out of a generalized human experience—thought and feeling—of which his own individual experience is a highly personalized selection. The thought relations in this deeper level have no specific linguistic vesture; the rhythms are free, not bound, in the first instance, to the traditional rhythms of the artist's language. Certain artists whose spirit moves largely in the non-linguistic (better, in the generalized linguistic) layer even find a certain difficulty in getting themselves expressed in the rigidly set terms of their accepted idiom. One feels that they are unconsciously striving for a generalized art language, a literary algebra, that is related to the sum of all known languages as a perfect mathematical symbolism is related to all the roundabout reports of mathematical relations that normal speech is capable of conveying. Their art expression is frequently strained, it sounds at times like a translation from an unknown original—which, indeed, is precisely what it is. These artists—Whitmans and Brownings—impress us rather by the greatness of their spirit than the felicity of their art. Their relative failure is of the greatest diagnostic value as an index of the pervasive presence in literature of a larger, more intuitive linguistic medium than any particular language.

Nevertheless, human expression being what it is, the greatest—or

[5] Provided, of course, Chinese is careful to provide itself with the necessary scientific vocabulary. Like any other language, it can do so without serious difficulty if the need arises.

shall we say the most satisfying—literary artists, the Shakespeares and Heines, are those who have known subconsciously to fit or trim the deeper intuition to the provincial accents of their daily speech. In them there is no effect of strain. Their personal "intuition" appears as a completed synthesis of the absolute art of intuition and the innate, specialized art of the linguistic medium. With Heine, for instance, one is under the illusion that the universe speaks German. The material "disappears."

Every language is itself a collective art of expression. There is concealed in it a particular set of esthetic factors—phonetic, rhythmic, symbolic, morphological—which it does not completely share with any other language. These factors may either merge their potencies with those of that unknown, absolute language to which I have referred—this is the method of Shakespeare and Heine—or they may weave a private, technical art fabric of their own, the innate art of the language intensified or sublimated. The latter type, the more technically "literary" art of Swinburne and of hosts of delicate "minor" poets, is too fragile for endurance. It is built out of spiritualized material, not out of spirit. The successes of the Swinburnes are as valuable for diagnostic purposes as the semi-failures of the Brownings. They show to what extent literary art may lean on the collective art of the language itself. The more extreme technical practitioners may so over-individualize this collective art as to make it almost unendurable. One is not always thankful to have one's flesh and blood frozen to ivory.

An artist must utilize the native esthetic resources of his speech. He may be thankful if the given palette of colors is rich, if the springboard is light. But he deserves no special credit for felicities that are the language's own. We must take for granted this language with all its qualities of flexibility or rigidity and see the artist's work in relation to it. A cathedral on the lowlands is higher than a stick on Mont Blanc. In other words, we must not commit the folly of admiring a French sonnet because the vowels are more sonorous than our own or of condemning Nietzsche's prose because it harbors in its texture combinations of consonants that would affright on English soil. To so judge literature would be tantamount to loving "Tristan und Isolde" because one is fond of the timbre of horns. There are certain things that one language can do supremely well which it would be almost vain for another to attempt. Generally there are compensations. The vocalism of English is an inherently drabber thing than the vowel scale of French, yet English compensates for this drawback by its greater rhythmical alertness. It is even doubtful if the innate sonority of a phonetic system counts for as much, as esthetic determinant, as the relations between the sounds, the total gamut of their similarities and contrasts. As long as the artist has the wherewithal to lay out his sequences and rhythms, it matters little what are the sensuous qualities of the elements of his material.

The phonetic groundwork of a language, however, is only one of the features that give its literature a certain direction. Far more important are its morphological peculiarities. It makes a great deal of difference for the development of style if the language can or cannot create compound words, if its structure is synthetic or analytic, if the words of its sentences have considerable freedom of position or are compelled to fall into a rigidly determined sequence. The major characteristics of style, in so far as style is a technical matter of the building and placing of words, are given by the language itself, quite as inescapably, indeed, as the general acoustic effect of verse is given by the sounds and natural accents of the language. These necessary fundamentals of style are hardly felt by the artist to constrain his individuality of expression. They rather point the way to those stylistic developments that most suit the natural bent of the language. It is not in the least likely that a truly great style can seriously oppose itself to the basic form patterns of the language. It not only incorporates them, it builds on them. The merit of such a style as W. H. Hudson's or George Moore's [6] is that it does with ease and economy what the language is always trying to do. Carlylese, though individual and vigorous, is yet not style; it is a Teutonic mannerism. Nor is the prose of Milton and his contemporaries strictly English; it is semi-Latin done into magnificent English words.

It is strange how long it has taken the European literatures to learn that style is not an absolute, a something that is to be imposed on the language from Greek or Latin models, but merely the language itself, running in its natural grooves, and with enough of an individual accent to allow the artist's personality to be felt as a presence, not as an acrobat. We understand more clearly now that what is effective and beautiful in one language is a vice in another. Latin and Eskimo, with their highly inflected forms, lend themselves to an elaborately periodic structure that would be boring in English. English allows, even demands, a looseness that would be insipid in Chinese. And Chinese, with its unmodified words and rigid sequences, has a compactness of phrase, a terse parallelism, and a silent suggestiveness that would be too tart, too mathematical, for the English genius.

[6] Aside from individual peculiarities of diction, the selection and evaluation of particular words as such.

While we cannot assimilate the luxurious period of Latin nor the pointilliste style of the Chinese classics, we can enter sympathetically into the spirit of these alien techniques.

I believe that any English poet of to-day would be thankful for the concision that a Chinese poetaster attains without effort. Here is an example: [7]

> Wu-river [8] stream mouth evening sun sink,
> North look Liao-Tung,[9] not see home.
> Steam whistle several noise, sky-earth boundless,
> Float float one reed out Middle-Kingdom.

These twenty-eight syllables may be clumsily interpreted: "At the mouth of the Yangtsze River, as the sun is about to sink, I look north toward Liao-Tung but do not see my home. The steam-whistle shrills several times on the boundless expanse where meet sky and earth. The steamer, floating gently like a hollow reed, sails out of the Middle Kingdom." [10] But we must not envy Chinese its terseness unduly. Our more sprawling mode of expression is capable of its own beauties, and the more compact luxuriance of Latin style has its loveliness too. There are almost as many natural ideals of literary style as there are languages. Most of these are merely potential, awaiting the hand of artists who will never come. And yet in the recorded texts of primitive tradition and song there are many passages of unique vigor and beauty. The structure of the language often forces an assemblage of concepts that impresses us as a stylistic discovery. Single Algonkin words are like tiny imagist poems. We must be careful not to exaggerate a freshness of content that is at least half due to our freshness of approach, but the possibility is indicated nonetheless of utterly alien literary styles, each distinctive with its disclosure of the search of the human spirit for beautiful form.

Probably nothing better illustrates the formal dependence of literature on language than the prosodic aspect of poetry. Quantitative verse was entirely natural to the Greeks, not merely because poetry grew up in connection with the chant and the dance,[11] but because

[7] Not by any means a great poem, merely a bit of occasional verse written by a young Chinese friend of mine when he left Shanghai for Canada.
[8] The old name of the country about the mouth of the Yangtsze.
[9] A province of Manchuria.
[10] I.e., China.
[11] Poetry everywhere is inseparable in its origins from the singing voice and the measure of the dance. Yet accentual and syllabic types of verse, rather than quantitative verse, seem to be the prevailing norms.

alternations of long and short syllables were keenly live facts in the daily economy of the language. The tonal accents, which were only secondarily stress phenomena, helped to give the syllable its quantitative individuality. When the Greek meters were carried over into Latin verse, there was comparatively little strain, for Latin too was characterized by an acute awareness of quantitative distinctions. However, the Latin accent was more markedly stressed than that of Greek. Probably, therefore, the purely quantitative meters modeled after the Greek were felt as a shade more artificial than in the language of their origin. The attempt to cast English verse into Latin and Greek molds has never been successful. The dynamic basis of English is not quantity,[12] but stress, the alternation of accented and unaccented syllables. This fact gives English verse an entirely different slant and has determined the development of its poetic forms, is still responsible for the evolution of new forms. Neither stress nor syllabic weight is a very keen psychologic factor in the dynamics of French. The syllable has great inherent sonority and does not fluctuate significantly as to quantity and stress. Quantitative or accentual metrics would be as artificial in French as stress metrics in classical Greek or quantitative or purely syllabic metrics in English. French prosody was compelled to develop on the basis of unit syllable-groups. Assonance, later rhyme, could not but prove a welcome, an all but necessary, means of articulating or sectioning the somewhat spineless movement of sonorous syllables. English was hospitable to the French suggestion of rhyme, but did not seriously need it in its rhythmic economy. Hence rhyme has always been strictly subordinated to stress as a somewhat decorative feature and has been frequently dispensed with. It is no psychologic accident that rhyme came later into English than in French and is leaving it sooner.[13] Chinese verse has developed along very much the same lines as French verse. The syllable is an even more integral and sonorous unit than in French, while quantity and stress are too uncertain to form the basis of a metric system. Syllable-groups—so and so many syllables per rhythmic unit—and rhyme are therefore two of the controlling factors in Chinese prosody. The third factor, the alternation of syllables with level tone and syllables with inflected (rising or falling) tone, is peculiar to Chinese.

To summarize, Latin and Greek verse depends on the principle of

---

[12] Quantitative distinctions exist as an objective fact. They have not the same inner, psychological value that they had in Greek.

[13] Verhaeren was no slave to the Alexandrine, yet he remarked to Symons, *à propos* of the translation of *Les Aubes,* that while he approved of the use of rhymeless verse in the English version, he found it "meaningless" in French.

contrasting weights; English verse, on the principle of contrasting stresses; French verse, on the principles of number and echo; Chinese verse, on the principles of number, echo, and contrasting pitches. Each of these rhythmic systems proceeds from the unconscious dynamic habit of the language, falling from the lips of the folk. Study carefully the phonetic system of a language, above all its dynamic features, and you can tell what kind of a verse it has developed—or, if history has played pranks with its psychology, what kind of verse it should have developed and some day will.

Whatever be the sounds, accents, and forms of a language, however these lay hands on the shape of its literature, there is a subtle law of compensations that gives the artist space. If he is squeezed a bit here, he can swing a free arm there. And generally he has rope enough to hang himself with, if he must. It is not strange that this should be so. Language is itself the collective art of expression, a summary of thousands upon thousands of individual intuitions. The individual goes lost in the collective creation, but his personal expression has left some trace in a certain give and flexibility that are inherent in all collective works of the human spirit. The language is ready, or can be quickly made ready, to define the artist's individuality. If no literary artist appears, it is not essentially because the language is too weak an instrument, it is because the culture of the people is not favorable to the growth of such personality as seeks a truly individual verbal expression.

.   .   .

The main point developed in Sapir's opening paragraph is that in all art the medium imposes restrictions that the great can gracefully accept. This generality is paralleled in the second paragraph's treatment of language as the particular medium of literature. The significance is the same in both cases; the whole is being held up alongside one of its parts, so that we may understand and remember that the truth being recognized here is no isolated piece of opinion, but is involved in a universal phenomenon. However, Sapir actually introduces the first paragraph by referring to the particular case of language, in order to clarify immediately the subject of his inquiry. Thus there is a movement from the particular to the general, accomplished through the transitional clause "language in particular is the most fluid of mediums," and then at the start of paragraph 2 a switch back to the particular, effected in the opening sentence. But why has Sapir followed such a relatively complicated arrangement rather than used the simpler sequence in which *all* the statements about literary art either precede or follow those about art in general? Mainly because, despite his use of a parallel relation, he does not want the parallelism itself to command central attention, but rather to introduce, in a subservient way, the more important idea that he will explore in paragraph 2—the idea that *literature* contains a non-linguistic as well as a linguistic art. And this idea, which turns out to be crucial to the larger purpose of Sapir's essay, is probably his best reason for using the introductory parallelism between art and literature, since that parallelism allows him to anticipate the idea of a deeper, broader mode of artistic being.

In any case, Sapir provides at the opening of paragraph 2 a parallelism that actually extends the parallelism of paragraph 1. Having observed that language is the medium of literature, he immediately points out that the media of various literatures differ from each other. He thus sets up a parallel relationship that can be construed approximately as follows: Art is to literature as literature is to the literature of a particular language. This relationship is worth a closer look, though, because of the way in which the author fails (no doubt deliberately) to exploit and call attention to its existence. If he had called attention to it, we would be aware of a three-member parallel construction, and the inevitable result would be a tendency to "find" also a *progressive* thrust through the set of three. As it is—because the author does not make the triad obtrusive by inserting such a phrase as "in a like manner" or "as with x, so with y," —the relation between the literature of a particular language and literature in general, that of the part to the whole, is recognized as a separate idea. This is just as well, for the similarities between art and language are not of the same type as those between language and the particular language, nor does Sapir have the same reasons for bringing them up (he does not develop the idea that a work in one aesthetic medium is non-translatable into another aesthetic medium). Each half of the parallelism has its separate use, and the combined function of the two is to establish, by recognizing the possibility of partial translation, the existence of a non-linguistic art element in literature.

Of course, causal and logical processes are at work simultaneously with the development of a parallel structure. They are not as conspicuous here as the parallelism because the succession of verbal elements does not conform to their order. Nevertheless, they are worth noticing, since their persuasive effect on an audience is no less real for having been left to work quietly. In the first paragraph, for example, the following submerged syllogism can be found:

P^1: Every art is bound by its medium.

P^2: Literature is an art.

 C: Literature is bound by its medium.

And in the second, one of a different type:

P¹: If partly successful translation is possible, then a kind of non-linguistic art must exist in literature.

P²: Partly successful translation is possible.

C: A kind of non-linguistic art exists in literature.

At this point, having established solidly his aesthetic dualism, Sapir can use paragraph 3 to clarify the distinction. Strictly speaking, his argument does not advance any further in this paragraph; he is simply going back over the same ground as before, but using different terms of expression. The parallelism between the actual symbolic algebra of science and the corresponding "deep" language of literature does help him to state his case more plainly because it accounts for the mysterious in terms of the familiar.

It is important to see exactly what Sapir does with his distinction, once it is set up. Our first reaction is likely to be that the mode of "deep" art is preferable to, better than, the linguistically restricted mode, because it is after all universal. And such an impression has already received some support at the close of paragraph 2, where the one mode seems to be represented by Shakespeare, the other by the comparatively minor poet Swinburne. But near the end of the following paragraph, whose main business is merely to clarify and not to alter the argument, Sapir introduces the names of Whitman and Browning as representing that class of writers who are "unconsciously striving for a generalized art language, a literary algebra," with the result that their performance in actual English idiom often appears to be strained and uncomfortable. Now we can see that Sapir's classification of writers uses three categories rather than only two: There are the purely linguistic writers of the Swinburne type, the would-be non-linguistic (or generalized-linguistic) writers like Browning and Whitman, and, finally, the great writers, who combine the virtues and avoid the defects of the other two groups because they know how to "trim the deeper intuition to the provincial accents of their daily speech." The three-way distinction is not particularly difficult to understand, but it is of the greatest importance that the reader take the trouble to understand it, and for this reason Sapir has contrived, through the arrangement of parts, to present it in a form that is not too facile, too pat. The reader has to work a bit to make the connections and sketch in the pattern, and this renders the whole thing more memorable for him than it would otherwise be.

The remainder of Sapir's essay shows that good writers follow, as closely as they can, the examples of Heine and Shakespeare, merging the potencies of their particular tongue with those of that great general "language" spoken by all art; in the process, Sapir discusses categorically the several prime means by which one's native language inevitably acts to form one's style. As he takes up in sequence the given phonetic, syntactic, and prosodic powers of language, Sapir is obviously using a classic parallel arrangement, for each of these cases supports his main contention in the same way, stands in the same relation to it. But there is a strongly climactic thrust as well. The phonetic qualities are described as "felicities," the morphological peculiarities as "far more important," and the prosodic element as the most illustrative of all. Now, to be sure, the progression does not run neatly in a straight line. The third element, unlike the second, is not simply *more* of the first, but is rather differ-ent in kind. Being functionally important and being highly illustra-tive are not, after all, the same thing. Nevertheless, a sense of rising importance is maintained in the series, with a very distinct suggestion of a movement through the comparative and superlative degrees.

Within each of the progressively parallel parts there are, of course, sub-structures in parallel as the several different languages are com-pared, but these hardly call for comment. What does need em-phasizing, though, is the way in which the entire concluding section of the essay relates structurally to the opening part. To grasp this, we need to understand how the triadic set composed of phonetics, structure, and prosody, is made to serve the author's argument. That argument, implicit in the final section of the essay, comes to the surface in its most compact form in paragraph 8, an appendage to the discussion of morphology. It is "that style is not an absolute, a something that is to be imposed on the language from Greek or Latin models, but merely the language itself, running in its natural grooves." Support for this position comes from every one of the categorical discussions, each showing how a language has certain great capacities to be realized, despite its restrictive limitations; and, of course, Greek and/or Latin is introduced as an example at every step in the progression, so that the reader may be reminded of what is being denied as well as what is being affirmed.

There is, in fact, a parallel relation between this entire piece of argument and the essay's introductory paragraphs. As the first part of the essay moved to a definition of the good writer by outlining for him a central position distinct from aberrant extremes on either side, so the second part moves to show, step by step, how good style in any language results from the cultivation of that language's own native genius, rather than by cross-breeding or by some other form of excess. It is true that the second part *might* have been put first, though the effect of such an arrangement would surely have been anticlimactic, but the most effective order is the one that Sapir has used. It is an arrangement that combines the advantages of controlled structure with those of "natural" flexibility. When Sapir does the unexpected—when, for instance, he interrupts the tidy progress of a set-of-three to insert a paragraph that in a more conventional essay would fall before the set or after it—we may not know for sure where he is going next, but we feel confident that he is going somewhere. An essayist who can cultivate this sense of assurance in his reader has achieved an effect far more important than that of literal intelligibility.

THE CUTENESS OF WELL-BEING: THE GIFT SHOPPE

Reed Whittemore

The Prosecution:

It was not Thorstein Veblen, but a lesser student of our social scene —in fact a friend of mine—who observed that our society has progressed from the era of the better mousetrap to the era of the funnier male barbecue apron. Veblen might have been amused by the remark, but he would not have agreed with it entirely; he would have said that although we may have become less utilitarian than we were, we were never as utilitarian as some critics of America—especially nineteenth century Englishmen—have proclaimed. We have shared, and continue to share, with the rest of humanity a fascination for hoarding and giving mostly useless but certainly showy objects.

Veblen died in 1929, and by 1929 the barbecue-apron world was upon us, though the apron itself had not, to my knowledge, made its appearance. In 1929 one could buy fancy nutcrackers, paraphernalia for the "complete" bridge table, cigarette-dispensing devices for car dashboards, and trick watches for those friends who had everything. Now one has a greater selection to choose from—a cigarette lighter that plays "Smoke Gets in Your Eyes," a bathroom clock that says, "No Loitering," whisky toothpaste—but the basic

THE CUTENESS OF WELL-BEING: THE GIFT SHOPPE: Reprinted by permission of The Macmillan Company from *The Boy From Iowa* by Reed Whittemore. © by Reed Whittemore, 1958.

gift-shoppe condition is hardly a new one. It was not new, I gather, in ancient Rome either. There seems to be a permanent need for gift shoppes; and it is in this sense that they may be thought of as utilitarian, even though the objects they display become more useless yearly.

But what is the need, the social need that is satisfied by a gift shoppe filled with Venus toothpicks, mink-trimmed clothespins, and lighted ash trays for lowbrows, together with a few more tasteful gadgets for ladies and gents of true Kulch? Veblen described the consuming of "conspicuous trinkets" as a way to demonstrate the possession of wealth; he pointed out that "no class of society, not even the most abjectly poor, foregoes all customary conspicuous consumption," and that "very much of squalor and discomfort will be endured before the last trinket or the last pretense of pecuniary decency is put away."

These quotations oversimplify Veblen's attitude toward conspicuous consumption, however. They suggest that we all aspire to be Diamond Jim Brady, which is certainly not true, particularly now when almost everyone is some sort of "have" if only by courtesy of a finance company. Veblen, being a firm economic materialist, may have emphasized money too much, but like all good money men he knew that money is a means, not an end, and that men of means have ends other than money—for example, power, status, love, comfort, heaven on earth. In the case of trinkets, indeed, money is critical only when a lot of money is clearly involved; normally the trinkets we choose do not display our bankroll so much as our character, our taste, our wit, maybe our soul. When we display them or give them we hope that the display will display *us* in a beautiful light, and will accordingly be approved by the proper parties, who will then admire us from below or bend to us from above.

Of course, it is just possible that there are a few of us, a tiny band of selfless saints, who are not looking for approval when we enter a gift shoppe. We simply want to give something nice to Uncle Sidney, and in choosing something for him, not us, we consider only *his* character, taste, wit, or soul. But such a group, if it exists, makes poor copy for both sociologists and satirists; furthermore, it probably doesn't exist. Who can say with assurance that he is not guilty of "putting on a show" when he purchases for Uncle Sidney or himself a Jayne Mansfield hot-water bottle? or even when he purchases a simple, magnificently grained Dunhill pipe? As David Riesman has observed, we are all other-directed in some measure; and other-direction is nothing more or less than the business of playing a part, not being one's self. What should be added is that self is itself something of a bastard. Our roles become us; we are not, most of us, aware of our dramatic posturings when we exhibit them, since we have been on stage like Shirley Temple from infancy.

To the extent that our displays are determined by large environmental forces that act as our stage directors, the roles we play are at least tentatively chartable. This is where the sociologists and satirists step in. Thus I take it that in war and in other times of crisis the show to be put on is a show of courage, fixed resolve, cool nerves, and stamina. There will be variations upon this, such as Falstaff's or Sad Sack's, but the heroic or stoic ideal remains for us to emulate, and if we cannot emulate it we feel obliged at least to look as if we are emulating it; otherwise we are shamed and ashamed. I also take it that in times of love the show to be put on is a show of physical and verbal prowess, as well as dedication to the loved object. There will be variations upon this too, but the conventional image of the "proper" lover will nonetheless be with us in our romantic moments, influencing if not governing our conduct. Nor are love and war the only situations where outside models plague us. *Any* social situation generates its ideal participant, to whom its poor earthly counterparts look up with envy and chagrin. This ideal may not be much—it may be something like Elvis Presley, or the man across the street whose lawn is weedless—but it is nonetheless a lofty ideal in its own prescribed context, and we are influenced by it even when we resent it, dislike it, or pity it, and therefore *re*act to it.

It is because of this inevitable and continuing interaction between the individual and the models he finds around him that studies of better mousetraps or funnier male barbecue aprons get, as this one is getting, complicated. A male barbecue apron is not just a male barbecue apron; if looked at in the properly fanciful spirit it suggests so much about our society that the mind reels. One may build a whole social history around its development, a history of a time of peace, well-being, and galloping decadence. Taking the Veblen, anthropological line toward it, for example, one may observe the sad decline in our time of the male species, a decline from his ancient barbaric condition of honorable leisure which made cooking, even the specialized cooking of a steak in the back yard, women's work. On the one hand the male's culinary role is still distinguished, by the elegant apron, from the setting of tables and the boiling of frozen peas. But on the other hand the apron *is* an apron, and since it is almost surely given the man by a woman, it is a gift that an honorable barbaric male in the old days could only have regarded as an insult. In other words the apron may be conceived as both an ambiguous and a trivial symbol of male dominance: a woman will not wear it, but the man who wears it will not look like Hotspur.

A superficially more reassuring, though equally speculative, way of looking at the apron is as a symbol of the good life, the life of the gourmet, and the life of the man of property. But it is at best a mighty cheesy symbol of all this—the property, for example, may contain only garbage cans and a $2.99 charcoal burner; so one can imagine in recent barbecue-apron history a number of annoyed barbaric males who have denied the apron these particular properties by tearing it up and sitting in blue-jeans in the parlor while the wife has burned hamburgers over a hotplate.

All in all the apron is best, with its jokes and lewd pictures upon it, as a symbol, a manifestation of the clever and cute. Not only is this meaning for it the most precise meaning it seems to have, but the meaning is shared with 90 per cent of the other items in a representative gift shoppe, items that are also incontrovertibly and forever cute. This cuteness *is* socially significant.

Ah, cuteness. Cuteness is the product of a curious kind of insecurity, of the uncommitted, the uninvolved, the intellectually idle. Cuteness is an easy way of substituting manner for matter, avoiding issues and judgments by espousing wit and style. I have too much respect for wit and style to mean by this that if one has wit and style one is therefore cute; but wit and style, good or bad, high or low, elegant or mundane, will almost surely produce some kind of cuteness as long as they are practiced in a vacuum. And there is no vacuum quite like the modern gift shoppe.

Look at that shoppe from both sides—from the side of the owner and from the side of the enterer and loiterer. The owner is committed to running a store whose function may not be described as the functions of other stores may be. There are no particular commodities or species of commodities he is committed to sell. He is committed to selling gestures rather than things—gestures of friendship or love, gestures of cleverness or wealth, gestures of sophistication or taste, but always gestures. As for the customer, the customer is of course the reason for the store, and so he is interested in gestures, not things, also. He is looking for the suitable, the timely, the tasteful, the shocking; and the thinginess of the store's contents is if anything a distraction to him as he wanders from the mobiles to the witty highball glasses. If only there were a way to communicate *directly* his understanding of the eventual recipient's understanding, then there would be no need for Operation Gift Shoppe at all. For the use value of whatever is chosen will be negligible; the thing will be looked at, not used; it will be judged not by its utility but by its adequacy as a gesture, just as the acting in a play is judged when the play is so familiar that its content no longer reaches us.

Now, when gestures solely are involved, when in other words we are obliged to display ourselves on a bare stage with no plot and no thesis to help us along, we must choose our gestures carefully. We must not be too dramatic, but not too flat either; we must be neither too serious nor too frivolous. We must indeed not be "too" anything or we will be thought of as "too too." Hence we get cute. The cute gesture is one that is not meant; it is like a mock gesture except that it does not mock anything (that would be dangerous); it is a neutral gesture that at its best displays cleverness and comprehension, at its worst displays uncertainty and an incapacity to act or assert. It is in a brief a pure gesture, untouched by conviction or feeling but loaded with "style."

The trouble with gifts is that as gestures they are bulky and sometimes expensive. A greeting card on the other hand is beautifully platonic and seldom costs more than thirty-five cents. It is no wonder, then, that in our age of cuteness clever greeting cards have come to take up more and more space in our gift shoppes and that in big cities shoppes devoted exclusively to these cards have appeared and apparently prospered. The clever card puts in (cute) words what we try laboriously to say with a (cute) gift. The clever card is not so ostentatious as a gift, though it may be "too too" in some other respect. And the *really* clever card is the most noncommittal gesture known to man.

Contemplate, first, a potentially "too too" card: a picture of a large, round, and cute elephant, above which is the simple inscription: "An Elephant." Open the card and read the pay-off lines: "—is pregnant for twenty-two months—stop complaining." I think it will be agreed that this card might be regarded as in bad taste in some quarters, namely, quarters where one simply does not talk about pregnancy. But there are increasingly few quarters like this any more, and anyway the card carries its vulgarity so openly, so archly, that the vulgarity is part of the cuteness and therefore will not seem, to most, *too* vulgar. As for its other properties, it is obviously a poor card to send to somebody who has greatly complained, but otherwise it is innocent. It may therefore be sent with impunity to all pregnant women except hypochondriacs with "old-fashioned" ideas, and when it is sent it will divulge nothing about the sender's feelings toward the sendee except that the former has been thoughtful enough to go to the store. As for its wit, well, it is not dazzling but it is passable, and whatever bite it may have is mostly removed by the fact that it is a printed card, not original with the sender. Thus even this card, which I have chosen as an example of something "too too" because it appears at first vaguely shocking, is relatively safe.

Then consider the plainer cards: "New Tepee? Enjoy Heapee."
Or: "Don't Hibernate! Celebrate!" Or even: "You make money?
You're my honey." Surely such cards can offend no one except he
who is, like myself, offended by cuteness itself. Their cartoon gaiety
and impersonal warmth are perfectly suited to the kind of display the
empty-headed person must make if he is to be invisible. The only
trouble with them is that they are not so funny as the elephant card;
they will therefore not receive so much notice. Somewhere in between the card which is bright but dangerous (not very) and the
card which is safe but not bright lies, we may imagine, the perfect
card, the ideal card, the card that the hard-working wits at Hallmark
and elsewhere toil all their lives to produce, so that any gift-shoppe
enterer and loiterer may pounce upon it and say, "This will *serve* me
perfectly without *damaging* me at all." When that card is produced
it will probably cost seventy-five cents, but it will be worth it; the
gift shoppes will be able to stock it, and it alone.

But I am being ridiculous. Of course one card will never do; nor
will one perfectly cute and idle gift. For cuteness must be, to be
serviceable, more than innocuous. It must also be novel, always
novel. The card makers and gift devisers may never rest. The elephant must be replaced tomorrow by a rhinoceros, and the barbecue
apron must be supplanted by a chef's hat. Meanwhile the poor
demented enterer and loiterer must keep abreast of each change in
cuteness's currency—though this is impossible—or he will appear in
public as precisely the bore that he is. No, there is no single solution
—no perfect card or gift, no parlor formula—for the daily recurring
challenges of cuteness. For although cuteness is a way of avoiding
commitment, it involves commitments itself, stupid commitments,
commitments to hundreds of meaningless gestures each one of which
must be (ever so slightly) different from its predecessor.

Such commitments make slaves of us, demanding everything of
us, returning nothing. Yet they are all that our gift-shoppe culture
has to offer. And now, Mr. Defense?

The Defense:
    Thank you.
    You malign us. We are not the slaves to gift shoppes that you say
we are. Let me go back. . . .
    Cuteness, despite the ease with which you have demolished it, is a
very complex social and psychic phenomenon. Unfortunately, it is
not generally approached by those interested in complexity. Instead
it is taken as meat by the polemicist (like yourself), or more frequently by the comic dramatist who, by isolating and exaggerating

its properties, produces a fine farce or diatribe against the frivolous and empty. There is nothing terribly wrong with this procedure, and some of the world's best comedies have been written about a rich and/or idle class that has lost sight of "essentials" and come to devote all its energies to some current nonsense. But the procedure is ultimately moral rather than scholarly; at the end the offending empty-heads are appropriately lectured to or punished, and life may be imagined to go on thereafter without their services. The end of Molière's *Les Précieuses ridicules* is typical:

> As for you, you jades, I don't know what keeps me from doing the same to you. We shall be the by-word and the laughing stock of everyone; and that's what you have brought upon us by your foolish nonsense. Go, hide your heads, you wretched girls; go, hide forever. (*Alone*) And as for you who caused their folly, contemptible trash, pernicious amusements of idle minds, novels, songs, verses, sonnets and rhymes—be off with you to all the devils!

Here we have a scene that might well be transferred to a modern gift shoppe—for the gift shoppe is surely a place of *concentration* of nonsense. The girls in the piece would be, instead of middle-class vamps aspiring to ladyships, daughters of Florida millionaires aspiring to be what they are. And instead of being led astray by idle poets, they would be the victims of our whole gift-shoppe-culture industry. Finally, because the middle class is no longer a bastion of common sense standing firmly against the frivolous nobility, the speaker of these lines could not be, as he is in Molière, middle class. Instead he would have to be some sort of alien—a pedagogue perhaps, or even an idle poet. With these changes, however, the play could still go on—for the essence of cuteness stays with us down the years—and if properly handled it would be both funny and instructive. The trouble is that it wouldn't be true.

It wouldn't be true in the sense that it would be an exaggeration of the truth, the kind of exaggeration that a scholar, if not a playwright, would have to temper with endless qualifications, not about the gift shoppe but about the customers. The gift shoppe is clear enough; it represents, as you have indicated, cuteness unadorned, where manner is substituted for matter, and where what passes for wit and style is practiced in a vacuum. But the customer—well, we simply *must* give that sometimes undershirted character credit for not always seeing eye to eye with the gift-shoppe owner, not always, not inevitably. He (or she) may be under constant social pressure to like the barbecue apron or the HIS and HER bath towels, and he may occasionally actually live up to the ideal of nonsense prescribed for him, in which case he is fit to be cast in a comedy and will wander about the store looking for the suitable, the timely, the tasteful, the shocking—whatever may be needed to put him in the social swim. But he (or she) is just as likely, I must insist, to go into the store with doubts and come out in a rage. Furthermore, because class distinctions in our society have become nebulous, he may come out in a rage whether he is genteel or proletarian. He is not predictable, this "average" man; he is less other-directed than he sometimes appears to be and than superficial comedies and social studies make him out to be. This is not to say that cuteness is not a staple in our culture; nor is it to say that the revision of Molière's play I proposed would be wholly false. It is only to say that there is a difference, always a difference, between a cultural fact and a personal fact. We see the culture, in this instance, in the gift shoppe and its weighty allies in advertising and industry. And having seen this we rush to place the individual *in* the culture. Well, of course he is in the culture, this average man, but he is also out of it. He may not be very far out of it, but he can be the most bebarbecue-aproned man in Minneapolis or Kansas City and still not be what the culture would, as it were, *like* him to be. As for the man who is openly a rebel, he just isn't a rare bird at all. The number of persons who in a quiet way go about fighting the very element in which they are immersed is very large, particularly when the element is cuteness.

I keep coming back to good old cuteness. Let us imagine that I, a reputable housewife in a little red rambler in a good section of town (I convert myself to Eve to make sure that nobody will come at me with the difference between male and female tastes), am in the market for something for a not very dear friend who is pregnant. I am not anxious to be in the market; as a matter of fact I wish like anything I were not in the market; but I am in the market because, to this extent, I am other-directed: I don't think I can "get away" with being merely silent. So I dash off to the gift shoppe, and after a great struggle I pick out the minimal gesture I feel I can reasonably bestow upon my acquaintance, namely, the elephant card you mentioned. I pick it out, pay for it, cart it home, sign my name to it, and send it. But do I like it? Does it represent me to the depths of my incurably frivolous soul? Not at all, not for a moment. It represents, if I am really a rebel, a compromise that I am slightly ashamed of but don't think worth not making. And it represents, if I am a sluggish society follower, a token acknowledgment of my allegiance. In neither case does my sending of the card say anything about me that a sociologist or satirist can latch on to with confidence except—and this is a big "except"—that I have not thought of a worthy alternative to the sending of the card. With the sending of the card I am really simply marking time.

We all have to mark time. We haven't the energy or the guts or the inclination or the talent or the disposition to cope with our society on all its fronts all the time, and so we retreat defensively into cuteness. This is perhaps not admirable—ideally we should always be out in the front lines standing firmly for what we stand for—but it isn't so bad either. Certainly it doesn't make us wretchedly decadent, spiritless, idle, and frivolous. We may be all these things, but our cuteness should not be taken as a sign that we are. In a society at peace, in a society of (your own word) well-being, the occasions for perpetrating some social decency or for merely keeping up with the immortal Joneses loom very large; but because they do we should not be deceived into believing that our lives have been turned over lock, stock, and barrel to them. To use the most familiar of analogies, an iceberg shows very little of itself above the surface.

The Prosecution Again:

I think it is apparent to both of us by now that we are not merely talking about cuteness. We are talking about what you were so good as to describe as "essentials." That is, we seem to agree that our society is at the moment distinguished by a great deal of *un*essential activity, one manifestation of which we have noted in the world of the gift shoppe. We differ on how seriously we should view this unessentiality, but we agree that it exists; and this suggests to me that we are both very remarkable persons, since we seem to know what an essential is.

But do we? Every profession, every walk of life, even every individual has its or his own stock of essentials, and it would take a better man than either of us to extract the essence of essentiality from all of them. The economist does battle with the social historian, the poet does battle with the philosopher, the society matron does battle with her undershirted husband about the nature of essentiality, and the battles go on endlessly without results that the combatants, at least in the visible future, will agree upon. Faced with this simple fact of the indeterminacy of essentiality, I think we must acknowledge that we are both guilty of having talked through our hats.

And yet there is one characteristic of cuteness—whether it be the cuteness of the barbecue apron or the cuteness of Noel Coward—that I wish to hang on to here, to your confusion. You have agreed with me that cuteness is a neutral gesture, that is, a gesture of inconsequence by someone who feels that some sort of display is required of him. And yet you say that this act of neutrality does not necessarily reflect upon the character of the gesturer. Now, while I agree that an occasional card is not a *significantly* idle gesture (I will even agree that sometimes cards are good cards, well intended, and therefore not idle at all), I can hardly be happy about that gesture. Indeed, the reason you give for contemplating it with complacency is wholly unacceptable to me. You say that there may be great things going on inside the person which are not revealed by the gesture—and I say, not for long.

Our social activities inevitably consist largely in gestures, and if the gestures demanded of us cannot be worthy of us, what are we to do? Must we go sit on a beach and be misanthropes? Must we forego all social amenities whenever we choose to be—though I hate to use the word in a discussion of cuteness—serious? Your iceberg position, which makes our social selves only one-seventh of our selves, is, if I may say so, probably the *basic* cuteness of our time, especially of our American Protestant time. It is this because it denies the importance of surfacing our essentialities, whatever they may be; it insists that we may all continue to be strong-minded, committed, vital persons even when we are wearing our aprons, because what is important about us is underneath. Always underneath.

I am sick and tired of this frivolous disregard for manners, style, all the outward, visible, social appurtenances of man. And I am sick and tired of it whether I find it in a gift shoppe or a parlor. In either of these locales your position is the popular position: the man in the parlor says, "That's a *delightful* Braque you have"—and thinks it stinks; your woman in the gift shoppe sends off the elephant card with displeasure and then does her best to forget the whole matter; and both of them—this is my point—think that by these acts they have in no way damaged their tough inner sensibilities. But they have, my dear friend, they have. Their disposition to cuteness or noncommitment on the surface is ultimately a disposition to the same underneath.

Bare, raw souls do nothing but vegetate. A commitment *is* a surfacing, a "sending" action, not a "sitting" action—look up its derivatives. And if we cannot commit ourselves in normal social intercourse, where in the world shall we ever display that marvelous six-sevenths of us that (*you* say) we possess underneath?

No, my friend, I cannot agree with you that Molière's *Les Précieuses ridicules* is an exaggeration of human cuteness. I can't of course vouch for its correctness as a picture of Molière's own society, and I realize that in detail the frivolities of his society must have been very different from ours. But reading the passage you quoted from, I am sent straight back to our barbecue aprons. And when the poets who caused the folly in the play are described therein as "contemptible trash," I have only to substitute for the poets *you*, my dear friend, *you*—and to say, "Be off with you to all the devils!"

QUESTIONS AND EXERCISES

1. The author has elected to cast this essay in dialogue form, taking alternately the roles of Prosecution and Defense. One of the effects of this method is to ensure (or at least to appear to ensure) that the view opposed to his own is given a fair hearing. The reader is intended to feel, at the close, that the opposition has been not just recognized but fairly and squarely crushed. Can you think of a wholly different strategy (not involving dialogue) for presenting the opinion contained in this essay? Why and in what particular ways would this other method alter the essay's substance and its effect on the reader? Would the main sequence of parts in the Prosecution's argument be radically affected?

2. Describe the method Whittemore has used in actually representing to the reader the contents of the gift shoppe. Wouldn't it have been more visually effective and intensely memorable to devote just one long paragraph to a descriptive catalogue of a shoppe's contents? Discuss.

3. Describe as systematically as possible the internal structure of the first of the Prosecution's two speeches, showing how the parts are linked in parallelism, progression, and causal or logical association. Since the model followed here is ostensibly that of a courtroom exchange, one might expect the arrangement of parts to show a persistently logical structure rather than a more loosely associative one. Is this the case?

4. The Prosecution's first paragraph makes the point—if we can assume that Veblen's view is meant to be accepted as the correct one—that modern American society is not historically or geographically unique in its attention to "mostly useless but certainly showy objects," that in fact our habits in this respect are not *recently* or *provincially* anti-utilitarian. At first glance this position does not seem consistent with the remainder of the Prosecution's argument, since he ends, does he not, by specifically indicting the gift shoppe and all that the gift shoppe stands for in modern American society. How do you account for this? Is Whittemore distinguishing between gift shoppes in general and recent gift shoppes in particular? At what point does he do this?

5. Read through paragraphs 7, 8, and 9 again. Does this passage constitute an internal structural unit of its own? Are the relations between

parts dominantly parallel, or progressive? Would it be possible to rearrange this sequence without losing most of the desired effect? Try it.

6. Starting with paragraph 10, Whittemore (as Prosecution) begins his definition of cuteness itself. What are the most important elements in this definition, and by what means are they connected with each other? Do you regard the whole definition as adequate to the occasion? Discuss.

7. Whittemore knows, as he is writing the essay, that the Prosecution will have the last word, and what that last word will be. But if the Prosecution's closing statement is to have its full crushing effect, then the preceding statement by the Defense must be made specifically vulnerable. Do you find evidence in the Prosecution's *first* speech that he is encouraging a particular response from the Defense, trapping the Defense, and deliberately withholding part of his own argument until the Defense has committed himself to a vulnerable posture? Looking at it another way, how early in the essay do you know who is going to have the better of the argument?

8. Summarize the structure, part by part, of the Defense's presentation. Regardless of length, is it more or less structurally complicated than the opening statement by the Prosecution? Why is this so?

9. In the Prosecution's concluding statement, which paragraph would you say contains the climax of the argument? By what steps does Whittemore lead up to this paragraph? Is he persuasive? Does he leave the impression that the Defense should have been given another chance for rebuttal?

10. Discuss the author's use of *transitions* (from paragraph to paragraph, section to section of the argument) in reinforcing the main structure of his presentation. Do you find any place where a transition is being used to disguise or hide a structural weakness, a substantively unconvincing connection of parts?

11. Do you notice the change in the Prosecution's *tone?* Does this change support the substance of his argument? In what way?

12. Write a 500-word essay that takes a distinct position on some controversial topic, using dialogue form. Recast this essay into regular discursive form without sacrificing any of the opinion offered on either side.

13. Write a possible rejoinder, by "the Defense," to Whittemore's conclusions. Do not merely repeat the Defense's arguments as given in the essay.

14. Try writing an essay that makes much the same point as Whittemore's, but that uses a primarily *narrative* method. It will not suffice merely to put dialogue into a narrative framework. Append an analytic paragraph discussing the changes in *connective means* that the switch from dialogue to narrative entails.

A VISIT FROM ROYALTY

Dan Jacobson

The royal visit was the most ballyhooed event that I can remember in South Africa. The royal family was dinned into us from every newspaper, every cinema, every wireless broadcast, every shop window, every decoration hung across every street. The royal family was here; the royal family was there; the royal family did this; the royal family did that. They had been in South Africa for weeks before they arrived in Johannesburg, and by that time hysteria was inescapable. A female announcer of the South African Broadcasting Corporation burst into tears over the air when the royal family came round her corner; a reporter on one of the dailies claimed that he had been stopped by "an ordinary man in the street" in one of the Reef mining towns, who had exclaimed: "What a golden eagle among men is the King!"

And at last, one rather cloudy day, the royal family came to be-flagged, ecstatic Johannesburg. I saw them in the morning, rushing up Eloff Street in an open car, with outriders on motor cycles, and a ripple of applause coming from the people, fading before it had begun; the car was gone so quickly. The royal car was followed by a succession of big American cars with nameless people in them, all moving at a breathtaking pace. The policemen relaxed, an officer took his hand away from his cap, and the people turned to one another with reluctant, drawn faces, like sleepers awakened from a dream. People began picking up their folding chairs, children ran across the street where the cars had passed, the crowds on both sides of the street broke up, wavered, walked towards the station or the tram termini, carrying the little flags they had hardly had time to wave. I do not know what the people had been expecting, for I had not been among them before the convoy of cars had come past, and had, indeed, been taken by surprise by the tired, known faces rushing past, and the quick, too-late applause. The people dispersed with no exaltation or disappointment: they were strange to see at that moment, as though one were in a thousand bedrooms as day returned and the sleepers reluctantly admitted the light between their lids.

A VISIT FROM ROYALTY: Reprinted by permission of The Macmillan Company from *Time of Arrival and Other Essays* by Dan Jacobson. © by Dan Jacobson, 1963.

In the evening the emotions were different. With night, with darkness, with the thousands of coloured lights, the crowds were awake and wild. All over Johannesburg there were huge throngs of people, walking, yelling; the bars were full and noisy; and, as one does so often in Johannesburg, one caught the feel of violence in the dark streets with their buildings towering on either side. There were no Africans about; for their own safety, perhaps, they had kept away. The liveliness of the streets that are usually empty of pedestrians after nightfall had something terrifying about it: the city was alive, bristling like an animal. And the passion that filled the people, that drove them to walk up and down the pavements, and in and out of bars, that made them wait on street corners, and change their places repeatedly on the stands, was elemental and powerful. It was curiosity.

I have never known anything like it. There was a huge animal passion of curiosity among the people, that was like a hunger, and was later to become a rage. They walked and waited and talked, with an anticipation so intense one might have thought something without which they could not live was about to be shown to them. It seemed to be some final, lasting knowledge that they were seeking; a spectacle which would satisfy them forever. And all the night was tedious and tense, until that moment would come. Then they, who lived so far from Europe, from England, from Buckingham Palace, would at last *see*.

We waited. The policemen forbade people to cross Commissioner Street, so we settled down hopefully on the stands; then became restive again. Someone threw orange peel at a policeman, who fell into a rage, and drew his baton. He said he'd kill the person who did it. But the crowd told him to shut up. They called him Major, and Colonel, and, in an even wilder flight of fancy, Field-Marshal Smuts. So the young constable put his baton away, muttering to himself. Then a new sport began. People started slipping across the road, and the policemen tried to stop them. A man would wait until all the policemen on a particular stretch of road were busy chasing someone else, and then he would dash across, a small hurrying figure running across the dark tar, with the policemen after him. If he did manage to get across, a cheer went up from the crowd; if he didn't, a groan of commiseration. People called to the police, distracting their attention to help others. It was all quite good-humoured, but eventually one of the policemen hit one of the people he had caught with his baton, and the game ended in anger.

But we soon forgot the man the police had dragged away with blood coming from his forehead. We were waiting for the two princesses to go to a ball; and now young couples who had been invited to the ball were walking down the middle of Commissioner Street, the men wearing evening suits and the girls in long dresses. So we cheered them, mockingly and enviously; for white South Africans are democrats among themselves, and do not readily admit anyone else's right to be cheered just like that, unless he is a politician or a rugby player. The people we cheered were also white South Africans, and so were embarrassed by the cheers; when we saw that we cheered even more loudly, of course; and made rude remarks about the girls. "*Sis!*" a woman next to me exclaimed, in protest against the behaviour of the crowd, "These people have got no respect." She must have been one of nature's Englishwomen, for the rest of us had no respect at all, and no shame at not having any.

But all this, we knew, was preparatory, and everyone was relieved when the last of the couples had gone, the street was cleared, and the policemen came to attention. "When they coming, General Smuts?" someone asked the policeman nearest to us. He said: "Two minutes' time," and we settled down in silence. We hunched, waiting for their coming. Then—a bright glow of car headlights, and a shout from the people farther down the road, the shout coming nearer, not yet really loud, and then it was upon us—a glimpse, a vision of pale glittering faces in a black car that was past us, again, before we could really shout, before we could really do anything. And now it was gone. There was nothing now, except for empty Commissioner Street, and the receding tail light of a motor-car and some motor cycles.

Nothing had been given us. As in the morning, there was a momentary silence, a kind of numbness. Then the animal awoke—not begrudgingly, as in the morning, but with a full throat. A roar went up from the crowd, a huge animal yell that rang in the streets. All along the road people were shouting, in a great, cheated roar. No answer had been given to them. And the yell died into silence as suddenly as it started.

A moment later the mob broke and began running down the road, past the Kensington tram terminus and towards the City Hall. People screamed and ran, from both sides of Commissioner Street. The police were unable to stop them. Jackets and dresses were flying loose, hundreds of feet were beating on the tar, hundreds of voices were screaming at the night, at nothing. A woman fell, and people jumped over her, or side-stepped to get away from what was just an obstruction in their path, and not a crying woman on the pavement. But no sooner had she been helped to her feet than she jerked away from her helpers and ran on screaming like all the others.

The princesses apparently had entered the City Hall through the door facing the Cenotaph, for our mob ran straight into another huge crowd gathered there. In the blaze of floodlights, people were pushing and screaming, and waving their hands though there was nothing to wave at, for the princesses had already gone inside. The crowd was possessed; in a rage, a frenzy, its passion unabated. Something had to be given to them—glimpses of two shining girls could not slake this thirst. So their passion focused itself on the nearest thing to hand: the car the princesses had arrived in. The car became their target—to see the car, to touch it, to hold it, to destroy it perhaps. But no, they did not want to destroy it. They just had to touch the car. They pushed and fought with one another, driving forward in surges. A woman next to me was carrying a baby in her arms, but she too was pushing, the child's face smothered in her sleeve. She screamed at me in Afrikaans, "*Eina!* You're pushing like a Kaffir!" and for a moment I remembered reading in one of the papers about the almost miraculous spirit of good will between the races that had been spread throughout the country by the royal visit. Miraculous, apparently, was the word. But that was lost, the woman, her words, the baby, as the crowd again gave a heave and we were all carried forward, this time right against the backs of the policemen who, with linked arms, were shoving us away from the car as determinedly as we were shoving towards it. The night was pandemonium; and all in a blaze of light that made every white face shine as though transfigured, that illuminated every open mouth and gleaming eye. And the police shoved the crowds back, shoved them back, until a passage was cleared and the car drove away, though a thousand voices called after it in a gasp, "Ah!" and again, as the car turned a corner, "Ah!" from the back of a thousand throats.

With some pushing I managed to make my way through the bodies and feet, hands and handbags, and finally get out of the pressure of the crowd, to the side of the City Hall. Few people seemed to be leaving: most of the crowd was still heaving about immediately around where the princesses' car had been. The last thing I remember before I left was a small, English-speaking South African, in a neat brown suit and shirtcuffs neat at his wrists, speaking to himself, or possibly to others, in the hope of whipping them into action that he himself was afraid to take. He was pointing at a group of Indian youths on the outskirts of the crowd, and his face bore that pale, fanatical look, self-absorbed, as though listening to God within himself, that white South Africans often wear when they are working up to violence on those with darker skins than their own. "Look at them," he was saying. "Look at them. Filthy f——— coolies, coming to look at the King and Queen, as if they're white men. Look at them, f——— cheeky coolies. Let's do something." His lips were trembling; the tremor spread to his hands. He stared at the Indians: he also was committing himself to a passion, perhaps one related to that of the crowds who, as the next morning's papers put it, had gathered to show their love for the princesses.

QUESTIONS AND EXERCISES

1. This essay is cast in narrative form. As in the Updike essay that you have read ("Hub Fans Bid Kid Adieu"), it seems likely at first that the author's prime intention is simply to re-create a moment in history, to let us know "what it was like." But in this case that straightforward representational aim is distinctly qualified by another intention. What is that intention? In what way is the narrative method (and the resulting organization of parts in chronological sequence) suited to it?

2. As in all narratives, the arrangement of parts is necessarily one of association in time. One segment of the action is followed by the next. The organization, then, is chiefly progressive. But the essay contains some particularly striking cases in which *parallel* construction is made the object of the reader's scrutiny. What are these, and how do they contribute to the essay's substance?

3. Does the essay strike you as a more or less complete documentary account, or is it evidently a careful and shrewd selection of material from the total experience of the author on the day in question? Is it important that the middle part of the day is omitted entirely?

4. Is Jacobson suggesting that violence and hatred stem, in some way, from the frustration of the crowd's expectations—their inability to release pent-up emotions fully when the royal car rushes too quickly past? Then why does the only represented bloodshed (the policeman hitting a man with his baton) occur *before* the princesses have driven by? Explain, considering the alternative possibilities.

5. What function is the policeman made to serve in the essay? Explain in full.

6. Could the substance of this essay be captured satisfactorily in a nonnarrative piece of writing? In an essay of 500–700 words, describe the difficulties (or impossibilities) that would be involved in such a project, and discuss the means, if any, by which they might be overcome.

7. Write a paragraph of plain narrative, describing an event as accurately as you can. Then re-write your account, making whatever additions or changes are necessary to give the paragraph some "mes-

sage," but trying to avoid heavy-handed and tacked-on moralizing. Append a commentary that explains in exactly what ways the change of intention has produced changes in the basic organization of the piece.

8. In about 800–1000 words, write a narrative account of the same events that Jacobson describes, but one that makes clear that your interpretation of them is radically opposed to his. If in fact you do agree with him, pretend that you do not.

CHAPTER FIVE

Elements of Verbal Style

The essayist has traditionally been thought of as having a special concern for style. The term "style" has been applied to many quite different characteristics of writing, and the significance of style has been debated rather hotly since men first became self-conscious about their use of language. For a sense of the thorniness and real importance of the problem, we need only to think about the oddly mixed connotations of the epithet "stylist." Is the stylist an exquisite artist-in-words or a hollow, posing, aesthetic fake? Is his mastery of the language the highest refinement of literary form, or is it only the sure sign of his own intellectual and emotional poverty? Is it not true that the writer with something really significant and urgent to say will have neither the time nor the inclination to tinker with verbal textures?

What underlies questions of this sort—what in fact causes the whole vexing uncertainty about style in prose and verse—is the peculiar nature of language as a medium. Being made up of a system of mostly arbitrary symbols (words) that must represent meanings but that also form linear "patterns" in grammar, syntax, and sound, language has a double capability in a way that the musical composer's tones or the sculptor's marble do not. The succession of written or spoken words must, of course, *mean*—otherwise it is not language—and yet in the very act of signifying, of referring to a reality outside itself, it develops qualities that seem, at least, to be separable from meaning in some way. Thus we continually draw distinctions between what is said and how it is said, between content and form, between matter and style. Something, it appears, is on the inside and something else on the outside, and literary audiences persist in distinguishing the two, despite some impressive arguments that there is no real distinction at all.

From one point of view, of course, the whole business can be made to seem rather silly. When an idea is framed in a particular sequence of words, it differs from that embodied in any other verbal sequence; with even the slightest change in the verbal formula a new meaning occurs: Thus there is no possibility of saying the same thing in two different ways. The very idea of style that had seemed to depend on verbal variability *within* a given meaning now seems to be an empty concept and the only true variable to be the changing substance. To this argument there are two possible responses, each of them important for a writer to understand. First, the fact that form must always alter as meaning alters cannot make form less real for the reader. Some kind of form exists whatever the meaning, and it is still completely legitimate to ask by what process a certain form was created. Secondly—and this is perhaps even more crucial than the first point—the writer pays attention, at least some of the time, not just to some precisely defined idea of what he *wishes* to mean, but also to his fondness for pattern, structure, and pleasure-giving sequences of sound. To put it another way, the specific form that a statement may take *cannot* as a rule, be instantly and changelessly fixed by what the writer intends to say, because his intention remains to some extent fuzzy and incompletely defined until it is committed to language. In effect, then, substance is partly created by style, and a particular written meaning may well be a compromise that involves stylistic choice.

This is a complicated matter worth thinking about, but it does not begin to take into account all of the ways in which the concept of style applies to literary work. Style has been regarded as covering *all* of a writer's working habits, including his characteristic means of argumentation, his way of defining a subject, his attitude toward his readers, and so forth—not merely his way of constructing phrases and sentences. More narrowly (less satisfactorily, too) it has been equated with plain grammatical and idiomatic correctness. According to one school of criticism, style is the author's verbal badge of distinction, showing his differentness from all other persons. According to another, it is an artful standard of beauty-in-words that any good author may achieve through diligence, taste, and care. No doubt each of these attitudes is useful in its way. For the present, though, we will consider style as something that happens in the arrangement of the language itself, something that is only accidentally related to "correctness" and that is far more important in some works than it is in others.

It is always difficult to account for the working *causes* of style; we can be a little more at ease in describing the result. In the most obvious sense, style is a consistent characteristic or group of characteristics in the verbal surface of a literary work. Theoretically, of course, the criteria that can be used in the "measurement" and description of a given piece of language are almost numberless. We can tabulate, for comparative purposes, this or that: use of the semicolon; reliance on inverted syntax; occurrence of the "r" and "o" sounds in juxtaposition; preference for participial adjectives; use of strong rhythmical stress in lengthy sentences. But the problem of defining a style, much less of recognizing it, is not nearly so bafflingly multiplex as this set of examples may suggest. The mere fact that a particular feature recurs with extraordinary frequency does not mean that that feature has any real stylistic importance, no matter how convincingly a statistical compilation may say so. In fact it will have no importance at all unless readers are aware of it without the help of analytic word-counts. Suppose painstaking inspection disclosed that in William Hazlitt's prose the preposition "to" is followed more often than not by some noun beginning with a hard consonant. Even if this feature makes Hazlitt a very unusual writer (since, let us say, only three writers in every thousand use hard-consonanted nouns after "to" as much as he does), it is unlikely that such a fact would have any significance in a reader's experience, even a reader with an acute sensitivity to the sound of language. It would remain a dry statistical finding. Still, some demonstrable and recurring characteristics do register, more or less insistently, on a reader's awareness. Which ones are these and why these rather than others? The answer cannot be absolute. The verbal features that one reader tends to "see" (or "hear") are not likely to be seen or heard by any other reader. But there is some common ground, and that ground is definable in various ways.

A culture that makes the oral recitation of literary works popular will encourage its people to discern stylistic effects in sound, whereas these effects will tend to be relatively unimportant among people who habitually read by "sight" alone. Where intellectual priorities lay emphasis on the importance of the imagination as a creative faculty, figurative language—the inventive use of the several varieties of metaphor—will loom large. A great deal depends, too, on the amount and kind of grammatical training that the educational system imposes on people while they are formally being taught the language. The patterns of perception and taste formed by these cultural forces do not change quickly. We can identify several stylistically important patterns that have been in practical use in the English tradition for hundreds of years with only slight changes of meaning; and these patterns can be enormously useful, in a practical way, to the student of the essay and of prose style. But we should warn ourselves before starting to enumerate them that any such listing must be rudimentary and hardly exhaustive.

First of all, there is a helpful distinction between the *predicating* and *qualifying* functions in a language. Practically all locutions have, as we have noted earlier, one activity in common: the definition and the classification of experience. Viewed in simple terms, this process is nothing more than the attribution of various characteristics to substantives (nouns and noun-substitutes). The clustering of characteristics around a central "thing" is done by verbs and modifiers. In the prose of a given writer, one or another means of attribution may be dominant. Thus one piece of writing will appear to be saturated with attached qualities, conditions, restrictions, and distinctions, most of which are brought in by adjectives and adverbs or by dependent clauses and phrases used as adjectives or adverbs. Another piece will do its job of collective definition through the main naming nouns and the main predicating verbs themselves. At present, taste and convention tend somewhat to favor the predicative type of expression. Nearly everyone has been told, at some stage in his study of prose composition, to avoid relying on adjectives and to steer clear of complicated sentence structure. Both pieces of advice are the same, for a lengthy participial phrase or a dependent clause of condition is related to the core of noun-and-verb precisely as a single adverb or adjective would be. And the motive for the advice seems to be not only the teacher's knowledge that you make fewer mistakes when you keep things simple, but also a deeply entrenched notion that the central predication of the sentence *ought* to be able to stand alone without all manner of supporting props.

Preference for the predicative type of expression may be a sort of rugged individualism in stylistic fashion. And it may not. But, obviously, this is only one side of the story. If the highly predicative style carries advantages of quicker *intelligibility* and a more clearly defined *sequence* of actions, the qualifying style is better able to show the *relational* aspect of thought, the way in which one thing depends on or supports another, and is likely to give the reader a greater sense of the integral coherency of experience. A couple of examples may make the distinction clearer:

> From the deeply shaded willow-grove where, for the last half-hour or so, she had been walking slowly along the bank of the little stream, Alice emerged in time to hear the unmistakable sound of conversation, rising, falling, growing eventually in the heat of what must be anger, and making it quite clear that Ralph, who had only arrived at the farm yesterday afternoon, was not getting along well with his rather evil-tempered stepmother.

> The jaguar twitched its tail, glared at him. Reginald held himself rigid. Birdsong burst all around him. Small comfort. The campfire smoke spiralled away, and hope spiralled away too. Muscles ached. Then stiffened. He thought, "It is a cat. Cats will eat anything. Get him, or he will get you." Darkness fell.

These passages are somewhat exaggerated in order to illustrate the contrast clearly, but the two different effects will be recognizable. In the first, the main predication is a single one, "Alice emerged," and everything else in the sentence modifies it either directly or indirectly. This method has the very distinct effect of making us feel how Alice's discovery is involved with and affected by her *emergence* from a peculiarly tranquil sort of activity. Everything is interlaced. There are no disjunctive leaps. In passage two, on the other hand, information is conveyed to us as if in separate bolts. There are fourteen different independent predications, each of them modified only slightly or not at all. Some of the nouns and verbs are sufficiently specialized to require no further modifying (e.g. "jaguar" not "big brown and yellow spotted cat of the jungle"; "glared" not "looked at him angrily"; "burst" not "broke out suddenly"; "spiralled" not "moved upward in a constantly widening curve"). The total effect is rather well suited, perhaps, to the fearful paralysis that has gripped Reginald. But it is more important, at this point, simply to recognize the differences in form, rather than to judge the relevance of form to content.

This consideration leads naturally to another one, the distinction between "normal" and "inverted" (or "suspended") syntax. To understand how the notion of "normal syntax" affects our sense of style, we must recall that modern English does not have a full set of case-endings to show the exact grammatical function of each noun. The first result of this is that the grammatical relation among elements of meaning, not conveniently made clear by the built-in identification of this word as "nominative" and that as "accusative," must usually be shown through an agreed-upon pattern of word-order. Thus we think of the usual core syntax of an English sentence as moving from subject to verb to object, and from this assumption there spring a number of associated assumptions that allow us to define, practically, the "regular" patterns of the syntax that we regard as allowable.

By relying on syntax to make clear the relations among words, we cut down the amount of variation that we can use in verbal arrangement, but at the same time we increase the conspicuousness of the "inverted" constructions where they do occur. This is true even in the briefest forms, though some cases are far more striking than others:

Brown the cow was.
Him she had never been able to forgive.
Quickly she ran.
Came the dawn.

In more elaborate constructions the stylistic possibilities are somewhat different in kind. Suppose that we have an extended sentence
whose core predication is modified by an interlocking system of
conditional clauses and phrases. The "natural" order of words—the
one we would be likely to use in spontaneous conversation—com-
pletes the core predication and then adds to it the necessary qualifying elements, in the order of their subordination to each other. But
in written discourse this method has the obvious disadvantage of
allowing the reader to suppose that the sentence's really important
business has been transacted in the first few words, and that what
follows is a series of merely refining and non-essential afterthoughts.
There are two basic ways of avoiding this effect: The modifying
material may be used *before* the core predication or, more spectacularly, some of it at least may be interposed between the main
subject and the main verb. In either case, the result is an effective
suspension of the sentence's *whole meaning;* that is, the reader must
hold in his mind all of the consecutive elements of modification until
their significance is made clear by the eventual appearance of the
main verb. The following two sentences are illustrative:

> When, resisting with an uncompromised vigor the temptation
> to betray his fellow conspirators, he appeared as usual in the
> Senate for the purpose of urging the government to military
> action, however late and small it might be, Claudius wept.

> After the disquieting experience that they had been through
> earlier that morning, the two very exhausted travellers, hoping
> to avoid any further contact with natives who, it seemed, were
> determined to make life unpleasant for them, struck out through
> the jungle in a new direction.

Certainly, in sentences of such complex structure, a great deal of the
"conspicuousness" would be preserved even if the order were rearranged to put the main subject and verb first. But the inversion
adds greatly to the effect. Such constructions as these must always
attract special attention to themselves, if only because they place
special demands on the reader's brain. More than this, however,
they are bound to make the reader aware of a certain contrivance
and calculation that has gone into the making of the sentence; in
other words, they make him more acutely aware of verbal structure
itself.

A thorough examination of structures in verbal style leads us
inevitably back to some of the same concepts that were crucial in
studying the arrangement of parts in the whole essay. *Parallelism,
balance, antithesis,* and *climax* are the central terms here. The four

are related to each other in ways that may make it difficult to keep them sharply distinct, but it helps if we notice at the start that *parallelism* is the concept on which all the others depend. Consider. Any statement may be seen as made up of units of verbal meaning, which may be individual words, phrases, or clauses: A full predication may be taken as a "member," or structural unit; so may a noun, or a noun-and-its-adjective, an infinitive phrase, the modified object of a preposition, a participial phrase, and so forth—in short, any word or logical sequence of words. In the use of language, any one of these units, whatever its length, must stand in either *parallel* or *oblique* relationship, grammatically, to any other unit in the same sentence. The oblique relationship is that which subordinates, modifies; the parallel relationship shows grammatical equivalence. Thus a conditional clause is obliquely related to the independent clause that it modifies, but it is related in parallel to another subordinate clause if both have the same kind of dependence on the main one:

> When all arguments have been exhausted on either side, and while it is still possible to regard ourselves as friends, let us agree to dispute no more.

Or, at the more familiar level, we distinguish between sets of adjectives in parallel and oblique relationship to each other: "the tall, stately elms" as against "the dark green palms." In the first case, each adjective directly modifies the noun; in the second, "dark" modifies "green," which in turn modifies "palms."

Parallelism, then, is a virtually unavoidable feature of ordinary English usage. It is not a remarkable stylistic feature in itself. In fact, the reader can move through most instances of parallel relationship without any particular sense of being involved in a "construction." Consider the following sentence:

> She *wept bitterly* and *ran in desperation back through the long corridors of the hotel to the room where, she was nearly certain, her sick baby had been left.*

The two italicized elements are parallel since they have the same grammatical relation to "She"; but, because of the patent difference between them in length and internal construction, few readers will be aware that anything stylistically distinctive is happening here. What counts, stylistically, is the special handling that the common parallel relationship may receive.

In any set of parallel units, whether there be two or more, it is possible to have a more or less conspicuous degree of internal structural correspondence between them. This correspondence may be a matter of grammatical and syntactical arrangement, as with paired clauses or paired complex phrases, or it may involve effects in sound and vocal accent, as in pairings of single words. Thus, converting the example just given, we might have:

> She *wept bitterly at the thought of her sick baby in the back room* and *ran desperately through the long corridors of the hotel to his side.*

It is no longer possible for even a casual reader to be unaware of the parallel relationship. Similarly, a pair like "*weeping* and *wailing*" or "*hard* vici*ssitudes* and *dark* excre*scences*" announces its parallelism unmistakably, whereas "oysters and green snails," for example, does not.

The crucial element of correspondence produces *balance*, and it is stylistically important that while parallelism itself is absolute—either it exists completely or it does not exist at all—balance is relative and measurable in degree. In extreme cases, where several kinds of correspondence work together, the balanced parallel construction makes a highly visible figure in the verbal surface:

> Sheldon had thought it all out. Until a suitable arrangement could be agreed on, he and Marilyn must remain separated, content to communicate with each other through the mail, quietly, and resolved to deal with all inconveniences by wit, cleverly.

Of course balance may and sometimes does exist between units that are in oblique, not parallel, relation:

> The ferocious and fearsomely enraged lion devoured the audacious but woefully foolish antelope.

But most of the time, balance is used (and noticed) in conjunction with parallelism, since it gains its most forceful and complementary effect in that way.

Antithesis is a special application of balanced parallelism, in which the coupled units oppose or contradict each other in some way. The term itself has been traditionally reserved for cases where the contrived balance is fairly elaborate and extended:

> They decided not to take needlessly time-consuming precautions, but to make faultlessly thorough preparations.

> On one side of the plain stood the heavily armored English foot soldiers with their raw courage, on the other the lethally armed French cavalry with their supreme assurance.

But the same principle is at work in much briefer pairings as well:

> not the heat but the humidity
> struggle between the justly virtuous and the virtuelessly unjust
> frantic dispersal, not calm gathering

If *balance* exploits similarity between parallel members, *climax* exploits dissimilarity. Especially where more than two units stand in parallel relationship within a sentence, there is a chance to arrange them in rising order of importance, verbal length, internal complexity, or all three combined. The appeal of this kind of stylistic device, which certainly needs no analysis to be made clear, is exactly like that of *progressive* arrangement, which we studied in Chapter Four. The principle of equation becomes complemented by that of progression, and the result is another form of "event" or figure in the verbal surface:

> He could not understand their hurt, their wounded pathos, their desperately heart-wrenching anguish.

> And so the three pigs built their houses of straw, of wood, and of bricks, respectively.

> It was his fondest hope someday to complete his formal education, leave his financial affairs in the hands of hired accountants, and, freed at last from all encumbering restrictions, travel around the world at his leisure, in an open boat.

> I came, I saw, I conquered.

The matters discussed thus far are chiefly matters of grammar and syntax. But style is usually understood to include a number of other variable features. There is, for one thing, *diction*, the kinds of words that an author uses. The pattern of preference may show itself along grammatical lines as an inclination toward the use of certain parts of speech. For example, a writer may consciously avoid modifiers and cultivate strong verbs. In such cases, diction is necessarily part of the larger issue of predicating-versus-qualifying structures, already discussed. But many other descriptive terms traditionally used in opposed pairings may be more useful in specific cases. We tend to distinguish sensuous diction from conceptual, Latinate from Anglo-Saxon, concrete from abstract, popular from esoteric, "artificial" from "natural," and so on. A style in diction may be characterized by a conspicuous use of (or avoidance of) slang, colloquialism, jargon, archaism, or what not. The possibilities are virtually endless. One author will use a remarkably high percentage of words that in some way involve negation. Another will show a taste for polysyllabic adverbs. A third may use "scientific" or clinical-sounding words whenever he can. And there will be many, of course, whose style, distinctive enough in other respects, displays no marked tendencies in diction.

Dictional habit is a stylistic quality that cannot be shown convincingly in an exemplary sentence or two; it is necessary to examine a sustained piece of writing. But perhaps a couple of moderately long paragraphs will suggest the possible effects:

> We could see dust coming up from the road where the troops were marching, and on the other side the awful sight of burned-over farm land, with a smoldering cellar-hole now and then, or the stiff-legged carcass of some burned horse or cow. The last rays of sunlight, all orange and hot, bounced off the big, flat river into our eyes. Jones turned to me and said he wanted to see no more. War had gotten to be more than he wanted to look at in broad day, much less at evening. He pulled out his flask and drank some of the wine, carefully, slowly. Now it would be my job to make the fire and cook some fish. I went at it with no joy, dragging branches over to the chopping block, piling the cut pieces together, cutting off the perch heads and stripping away the skin and gut.

> The infantry's progress along the throughfare produced dust, visible to us as was the not-entirely-extinguished conflagration of agricultural territory beyond, maculate with persistently smoking foundations and the rigid remains of unfortunate animals. The sun's final illumination, completely infernal and orange, reflected itself into our eyes from the interminable expanse of river. Jones turned to me and remarked that he had had sufficient experience of the war without being spectator to it in the evening as well. He produced his wine-flask and imbibed from it with immense care and in a leisurely manner. I understood that it would presently be my responsibility to build a fire and prepare the fish for supper. I commenced this business without enthusiasm, collecting the fragments of wood to be chopped, assembling the cut pieces in a stack, and subjecting the perch to decapitation, disintegumentation, and disembowelment.

The difference in diction between these two versions should be self-evident.

Another aspect of style that readers are able to notice consciously, without much prompting from the critics, is the characteristic type of *metaphorical* language and the frequency with which it is used. Strictly speaking, of course, metaphor (including simile, synechdoche, metonymy, personification, and the several other sub-species) is not a "figure of speech" or "figure of language" at all, in the way that balance, climax, and suspended syntax are. It is really a figure of *thought*, an explicit or implicit comparison of any two things for the purpose of modifying one of them through a selective transfer of qualities from the other. The significant act in metaphor is preverbal; that is, the core comparison takes place in the author's mind prior to and independent of its actual formulation in words. Thus a given metaphorical idea may be conveyed in one of several phrasal forms. But this qualification does not invalidate metaphor as a stylistic fact. Metaphor is a device of extraordinary importance, and hardly less so in prose than in poetry. Like habits in syntax, metaphorical tendencies often provide clear insights to the emotional and intellectual behavior of the author.

Several kinds of questions may be asked about the metaphors in a given passage. Do they call attention to themselves as special events because of their extreme length or internal complexity, or because they bring together things that seem on the surface to be radically *dis*similar? Or are they mostly "quiet," brief extensions of meaning through appropriate but unstartling comparison? Do they depend mainly on the force of *visual* resemblance, or on some other kind of correspondence? Do they supplant, or merely supplement, literal meanings? Do they reinforce each other in groups and clusters, or does each more or less make its own separate effect without forming part of a larger pattern? It may help here to compare three cases of metaphorical style:

> The social revolution that lies before us will be a cupcake, all sweetly sugared over with political platitudes on top, and carefully papered underneath so that the baking of it might cause no actual mess.

> Her answer was like music to his ears, a gentle strain of affirming melody that gave promise of diviner flights to come. He was lifted up and carried along by it.

> If we are to complete this line of reasoning, we must proceed step by step, and each step must be taken in procedural accordance with the one before it. There must be no variance. Each is like the other, exactly, and yet they will lead to something. It is a laying-down of concrete sidewalk.

In the first example we have a metaphor that would attract our attention in almost any context, not only because it is obviously loaded wih stinging irony, but mainly because we are not prepared, at first glance, to see the connection between cupcake and social revolution. It gains an extra conspicuousness, perhaps, through the way it provides a bonus insight (about the paper cup underneath) after making a perfectly sound point with the icing. In the second passage, which has been kept as mercifully short as possible, we have inconspicuous metaphor of the sort that has grown stale, clichéd. The comparisons have no power to startle us or refresh our perception. Quiet metaphor need not fall into this kind of atrophy, of course, but the danger is always there. In the final selection, we find illustrated the technique in which metaphor is used to clinch and clarify an already adequate literal account. Without a larger context, it is hard to judge whether the metaphor would in itself have been sufficient; but clearly the author is taking no chances, which may be just as well.

Finally, there is *sound*, harder to describe or analyze honestly than any other element in the composite that is style. In one sense, sound is necessarily less important in prose than in verse, since the nature of verse requires that it be, to some extent, a *regularly* composed pattern of sound, whereas in prose no such demand is imposed. But the same principles that underlie the recognizable "melody" of good verse may work with equal energy (though to a different effect) in prose. Fundamentally, two things are involved here: phonetic quality and stress.

Any succession of spoken sounds may strike us as pleasurable or unpleasurable. Now it is true that our response is more often determined by what the words mean than we are generally inclined to suspect. The felicity of "sound" in a phrase like "the whispering pine" is really little more than a felicity in the described object that we vaguely associate with the sound of the words that name it, as may be seen by considering another phrase substantially similar in phonetic make-up, "the whiskery swine." But certainly this is not the whole story; if we cannot identify some sounds as intrinsically pleasant, we can agree that some combinations are distinctly unpleasant, simply because they put a speaker to physical inconvenience in pronouncing them. "Teach such children" sounds rough or "bad," not because the "ch" sound is unpleasant in itself, but because the sequence of sounds forces the mouth and tongue into an awkward sequence of formations. Or we may find offensive the repetition of the same sound (partial or whole rhyme) in words obliquely related, where sound and grammatical structure seem to be working at cross-purposes. Thus, "the rippling pealing of the bells" sounds clumsy and banal (as "rippling peal" would not), while "the rippling, pealing bells," though it makes perhaps less sense, seems more audibly appropriate because the "rhymed" words are grammatically parallel. If these examples seem to suggest that the achievement of good sound in prose is mainly a negative process of avoiding tongue-twisters and awkward jingles, that is exactly the point. Of course it is also possible, in more positive terms, to discover certain phonetic patternings and combinations that impress us with symmetry, rising gradation, or elegant alternation of complementary effects. Consider, for example, the sound made by this passage, taken from the De Quincey essay in Chapter Two:

> The second Sister is called *Mater Suspiriorum*, Our Lady of Sighs. She never scales the clouds, nor walks abroad upon the winds. She wears no diadem. And her eyes, if they were ever seen, would be neither sweet nor subtle; no man could read their story; they would be found filled with perishing dreams, and with wrecks of forgotten delirium. But she raises not her eyes; her head, on which sits a dilapidated turban, droops for ever, for ever fastens on the dust. She weeps not. She groans not. But she sighs inaudibly at intervals.

No single sentence here is without some beautiful grouping of sounds. But of course we cannot account for the audible charm of this passage without going beyond phonetic content to consider rhythm, of which De Quincey is one of the acknowledged masters in prose.

Rhythm is caused, in English, by the distribution through the entire syllabic surface of certain syllables that receive stress, or vocal emphasis, when the language is spoken aloud. If, in their alternation, the ratio between stressed and non-stressed syllables becomes predictably regular, we say that the language is metered, that is, measured. Critics have traditionally agreed that prose-rhythm must never become so regular as to sound metrical. Prose, it is argued, should leave meter, like rhyme, to the regulated structuring of verse. Nevertheless, most sensitive readers insist that good prose has a cadence of some sort, though it may be difficult to classify accurately. Critics and writers of ancient times were able to identify a great many distinct *cursus*, or rhythmic "runs," proper selection of which was regarded as especially important at the end of the sentence, and interest in this sound-craft survived into the seventeenth century in England. For modern writers and readers, these recognizable patterns of cadence simply do not exist. Instead, our sense of rhythmic flow seems to come from three more general types of effect: 1. Sometimes the rhythm of prose becomes nearly metrical, and thus attracts special notice:

> Úndĕr thĕ búrdĕn ŏf dárknĕss thĕy lábŏřed, aňd thĕir wórk wŏuld nót bĕ dóne ŭntíl lŏng ăftĕr súnriše hăd cóme tŏ thĕ fíelds.

2. Sometimes a particular sequence of stressed and non-stressed syllables, not in itself metrically regular, will be repeated precisely in a following construction, creating rhythmic *balance* of a special kind:

> Whĕn Í rĕmémbĕr thĕ gréat feásts ŏf thát wintĕr, ĭt seéms tŏ me thăt ă lóng time hăs pássed qúicklỹ.

3. Now and then there occurs a sustained locution (an elaborate clause, perhaps, or a suspended compound phrase) in which the run of irregularly alternating stressed and non-stressed syllables is un-impeded by punctuation, by phonetic awkwardness, by the juxta-position of heavy stresses, or, in short, by hiatus of any kind. Under these circumstances a sense of rhythm has a chance to generate itself in the mind of the reader—it will not be the same for all readers—and the overall effect is like that of any surprisingly sustained con-tinuous performance, for example, by a gymnast or a jazz drummer. In the following passage, supply your own scansion for the italicized "run":

> Toward evening, with the air beginning to take on a chill, we came to a quiet garden, rather small, *in whose softly scented avenues and arbors it seemed probable that children of gods might celebrate forever the intoxicating joy of immortality itself.*

With this discussion of sound we complete our consideration of the elements that compose verbal style. In the three essays that fol-low, you will find fully illustrated some of the effects that have been described here.

CRIME AND PUNISHMENT

Samuel Johnson

Audi,
Nulla unquam de morte hominis cunctatio longa est.
Juvenal.

When a man's life is in debate,
The judge can ne'er too long deliberate.
Dryden.

Saturday, 20th April 1751

Power and superiority are so flattering and delightful that, fraught with temptation and exposed to danger as they are, scarcely any virtue is so cautious, or any prudence so timorous, as to decline them. Even those that have most reverence for the laws of right are pleased with showing that not fear but choice regulates their behaviour, and would be thought to comply rather than obey. We love to overlook the boundaries which we do not wish to pass, and, as the Roman satirist remarks, "He that has no design to take the life of another is yet glad to have it in his hands."

From the same principle, tending yet more to degeneracy and corruption, proceeds the desire of investing lawful authority with terror and governing by force rather than persuasion. Pride is unwilling to believe the necessity of assigning any other reason than her own will, and would rather maintain the most equitable claims by violence and penalties than descend from the dignity of command to dispute and expostulation.

It may, I think, be suspected that this political arrogance has sometimes found its way into legislative assemblies and mingled with deliberations upon property and life. A slight perusal of the laws by which the measures of vindictive and coercive justice are established will discover so many disproportions between crimes and punishments, such capricious distinctions of guilt, and such confusion of remissness and severity as can scarcely be believed to have been produced by public wisdom, sincerely and calmly studious of public happiness.

The learned, the judicious, the pious Boerhaave relates that he never saw a criminal dragged to execution without asking himself: "Who knows whether this man is not less culpable than me?" On the days when the prisons of this city are emptied into the grave let every spectator of the dreadful procession put the same question to his own heart. Few among those that crowd in thousands to the legal massacre and look with carelessness, perhaps with triumph, on the utmost exacerbations of human misery would then be able to return without horror and dejection. For who can congratulate himself upon a life passed without some act more mischievous to the peace or prosperity of others than the theft of a piece of money?

It has been always the practice when any particular species of robbery becomes prevalent and common, to endeavour its suppression by capital denunciations. Thus one generation of malefactors is commonly cut off and their successors are frighted into new expedients. The art of thievery is augmented with greater variety of fraud, and subtleized to higher degrees of dexterity and more occult methods of conveyance. The law then renews the pursuit in the heat of anger and overtakes the offender again with death. By this practice capital inflictions are multiplied, and crimes very different in their degrees of enormity are equally subjected to the severest punishment that man has the power of exercising upon man.

The lawgiver is undoubtedly allowed to estimate the malignity of an offence, not merely by the loss or pain which single acts may produce, but by the general alarm and anxiety arising from the fear of mischief and insecurity of possession. He therefore exercises the right which societies are supposed to have over the lives of those that compose them, not simply to punish a transgression but to maintain order and preserve quiet. He enforces those laws with severity that are most in danger of violation, as the commander of a garrison doubles the guard on that side which is threatened with the enemy.

This method has been long tried, but tried with so little success that rapine and violence are hourly increasing. Yet few seem willing to despair of its efficacy; and of those who employ their speculations upon the present corruption of the people some propose the introduction of more horrid, lingering, and terrific punishments, some are inclined to accelerate the executions, some to discourage pardons, and all seem to think that lenity has given confidence to wickedness and that we can only be rescued from the talons of robbery by inflexible rigour and sanguinary justice.

Yet since the right of setting an uncertain and arbitrary value upon life has been disputed, and since experience of past times gives us little reason to hope that any reformation will be effected by a periodical havoc of our fellow beings, perhaps it will not be useless to consider what consequences might arise from relaxations of the law and a more rational and equitable adoption of penalties to offences.

Death is, as one of the ancients observed, τὸ τῶν φοβερῶν φοβερῶτατον, of dreadful things the most dreadful, an evil beyond which nothing can be threatened by sublunary power or feared from human enmity or vengeance. This terror should, therefore, be reserved as the last resort of authority, as the strongest and most operative of prohibitory sanctions, and placed before the treasure of life to guard from invasion what cannot be restored. To equal robbery with murder is to reduce murder to robbery, to confound in common minds the gradations of iniquity, and incite the commission of a greater crime, to prevent the detection of a less. If only murder were punished with death very few robbers would stain their hands in blood; but when by the last act of cruelty no new danger is incurred, and greater security may be obtained, upon what principle shall we bid them forbear?

It may be urged that the sentence is often mitigated to simple robbery. But surely this is to confess that our laws are unreasonable in our own opinion. And, indeed, it may be observed that all but murderers have at their last hour the common sensations of mankind pleading in their favour.

From this conviction of the inequality of the punishment to the offence proceeds the frequent solicitation of pardons. They who would rejoice at the correction of a thief are yet shocked at the thought of destroying him. His crime shrinks to nothing compared with his misery, and severity defeats itself by exciting pity.

The gibbet, indeed, certainly disables those who die upon it from infesting the community; but their death seems not to contribute more to the reformation of their associates than any other method of separation. A thief seldom passes much of his time in recollection or anticipation, but from robbery hastens to riot, and from riot to robbery, nor, when the grave closes upon his companion, has any other care than to find another.

The frequency of capital punishments, therefore, rarely hinders the commission of a crime, but naturally and commonly prevents its detection, and is, if we proceed only upon prudential principles, chiefly for that reason to be avoided. Whatever may be urged by casuists or politicians, the greater part of mankind, as they can never think that to pick the pocket and to pierce the heart is equally criminal, will scarcely believe that two malefactors so different in guilt can be justly doomed to the same punishment. Nor is the necessity of submitting the conscience to human laws so plainly evinced, so clearly stated, or so generally allowed, but that the pious, the tender, and the just will always scruple to concur with the community in an act which their private judgment cannot approve.

He who knows not how often rigorous laws produce total impunity, and how many crimes are concealed and forgotten for fear of hurrying the offender to that state in which there is no repentance, has conversed very little with mankind. And whatever epithets of reproach or contempt this compassion may incur from those who confound cruelty with firmness, I know not whether any wise man would wish it less powerful or less extensive.

If those whom the wisdom of our laws has condemned to die had been detected in their rudiments of robbery they might, by proper discipline and useful labour, have been disentangled from their habits: they might have escaped all the temptations to subsequent crimes, and passed their days in reparation and penitence. And detected they might all have been, had the prosecutors been certain that their lives would have been spared. I believe every thief will confess that he has been more than once seized and dismissed, and that he has sometimes ventured upon capital crimes because he knew that those whom he injured would rather connive at his escape than cloud their minds with the horrors of his death.

All laws against wickedness are ineffectual unless some will inform and some will prosecute. But till we mitigate the penalties for mere violations of property information will always be hated and prosecution dreaded. The heart of a good man cannot but recoil at the thought of punishing a slight injury with death, especially when he remembers that the thief might have procured safety by another crime from which he was restrained only by his remaining virtue.

The obligations to assist the exercise of public justice are indeed strong; but they will certainly be overpowered by tenderness for life. What is punished with severity contrary to our ideas of adequate retribution will be seldom discovered; and multitudes will be suffered to advance from crime to crime till they deserve death, because, if they had been sooner prosecuted, they would have suffered death before they deserved it.

This scheme of invigorating the laws by relaxation and extirpating wickedness by lenity is so remote from common practice, that I might reasonably fear to expose it to the public, could it be supported only by my own observations. I shall, therefore, by ascribing it to its author, Sir Thomas More, endeavour to procure it that attention which I wish always paid to prudence, to justice, and to mercy.

QUESTIONS AND EXERCISES

1. Having read Johnson's essay once, can you identify any characteristics of its verbal style? Even if you are unable to specify the
   recurring effects exactly, would you say that the style distinguishes
   itself most conspicuously in diction? In sound? In syntax? In figurative language? Does your judgment about this dominant effect
   change after successive readings, or does it simply intensify? Is the
   effect that you are discussing increased (or made more noticeable)
   when the piece is read aloud?

2. Would you say that, on the whole, this language relies more heavily
   on predication than on modification? If so, where do you find
   sentences that are striking exceptions to the rule? If not, what kind
   of modifying elements does Johnson seem to prefer? Can you see
   any relation between such a preference and the nature of the subject
   that he is discussing?

3. The essay contains, obviously, a great amount of Latinate diction.
   How, specifically, does this tend to affect your understanding of
   the essay's substance? Does the level of diction generally promote
   visibility, the making of images? Are there any parts of the essay
   that you think might be improved by an increase in visible effect,
   and hence a suitable change in diction? Discuss.

4. Does *parallel* construction, as Johnson handles it, tend to draw attention to itself, or does it for the most part escape notice? What part
   does *balance* play here? How many distinct cases of parallelism
   (balanced or otherwise) are there in the essay's opening sentence?
   Are the several cases of parallelism in this sentence arranged in such
   a way as to produce larger parallel constructions? If not, what
   changes in wording would be necessary to bring about this complication of parallelism?

5. Without looking back, do you recall any especially clever or striking metaphors? Does Johnson use very little metaphor? Or is his
   figurative language usually of the unobtrusive type? What about
   the bird-of-prey metaphor at the close of paragraph 7? Does it
   come as a surprise? Explain. Does Johnson extend this piece of
   metaphorical thinking elsewhere in the essay? Discuss any risks
   that might have been involved in using it more freely, as far as the
   force of his main argument is concerned.

6. What impresses you (if anything) about the *sound* of Johnson's
   language? You might try scanning some single paragraph to see
   whether the heavily stressed syllables in fact fall into any sort of
   pattern. Are there places where it appears that the writer has deliberately sought to make his language sound harsh, in order to
   jibe with what he is saying? Specify.

7. Looking back over the papers you have written during this term, do you find places in your prose where you have used *parallelism* more by reflex or thoughtless habit than from necessity? Have you used *pairs* of nouns, of verbs, of modifiers, of phrases where one would have done the job adequately? Do these practices tend to show up in clusters? Are there particular kinds of subjèct-matter that seem to encourage you to write this way? What are they? Can you see any advantage in this type of habitual doubling, whatever its faults? Try rewriting one such passage to eliminate *all* parallel construction. Then write a short paragraph of commentary, explaining why you find the revision satisfying or unsatisfying.

8. Select a paragraph from Johnson's essay that strikes you as especially freighted with abstract words. Rewrite it, preserving as much of the original substance as you can, but emphasizing the concrete, the tangible. Are you able to do this consistently by just substituting one word for another, or do you tend to get involved in additional verbiage? You might compare your results with those of someone else in the class.

9. Write a 300-word description of your own taste in metaphors. Do you enjoy using metaphor in your writing? Do you find that you are often willing to let a metaphor stand alone, or do you normally combine it with some literal phrasing of the same idea? Do long, elaborate, figurative constructions make you uneasy or impatient or both, and can you explain why, using an example invented by yourself?

10. Write a page of argument on nuclear testing (or some other comparably serious question), imitating Johnson's manner and verbal style as closely as you can. Write a second page in counter-argument to the first, using a style as un-Johnsonian as possible.

ÆS TRIPLEX

Robert Louis Stevenson

The changes wrought by death are in themselves so sharp and final, and so terrible and melancholy in their consequences, that the thing stands alone in man's experience, and has no parallel upon earth. It outdoes all other accidents because it is the last of them. Sometimes it leaps suddenly upon its victims, like a Thug; sometimes it lays a regular siege and creeps upon their citadel during a score of years. And when the business is done, there is sore havoc made in other people's lives, and a pin knocked out by which many subsidiary friendships hung together. There are empty chairs, solitary walks, and single beds at night. Again, in taking away our friends, death does not take them away utterly, but leaves behind a mocking, tragical, and soon intolerable residue, which must be hurriedly concealed. Hence a whole chapter of sights and customs striking to the mind, from the pyramids of Egypt to the gibbets and dule trees of mediæval Europe. The poorest persons have a bit of pageant going towards the tomb; memorial stones are set up over the least memorable; and, in order to preserve some show of respect for what remains of our old loves and friendships, we must accompany it with much grimly ludicrous ceremonial, and the hired undertaker parades before the door. All this, and much more of the same sort, accompanied by the eloquence of poets, has gone a great way to put humanity in error; nay, in many philosophies the error has been embodied and laid down with every circumstance of logic; although in real life the bustle and swiftness, in leaving people little time to think, have not left them time enough to go dangerously wrong in practice.

As a matter of fact, although few things are spoken of with more fearful whisperings than this prospect of death, few have less influence on conduct under healthy circumstances. We have all heard of cities in South America built upon the side of fiery mountains, and how, even in this tremendous neighbourhood, the inhabitants are not a jot more impressed by the solemnity of mortal conditions than if they were delving gardens in the greenest corner of England. There are serenades and suppers and much gallantry among the myrtles overhead; and meanwhile the foundation shudders underfoot, the bowels of the mountain growl, and at any moment living ruin may leap sky-high into the moonlight, and tumble man and his merry-making in the dust. In the eyes of very young people, and very dull old ones, there is something indescribably reckless and desperate in such a picture. It seems not credible that respectable married people, with umbrellas, should find appetite for a bit of supper within quite a long distance of a fiery mountain; ordinary life begins to smell of high-handed debauch when it is carried on so close to a catastrophe; and even cheese and salad, it seems, could hardly be relished in such circumstances without something like a defiance of the Creator. It should be a place for nobody but hermits dwelling in prayer and maceration, or mere born-devils drowning care in a perpetual carouse.

And yet, when one comes to think upon it calmly, the situation of these South American citizens forms only a very pale figure for the state of ordinary mankind. This world itself, travelling blindly and swiftly in overcrowded space, among a million other worlds travelling blindly and swiftly in contrary directions, may very well come by a knock that would set it into explosion like a penny squib. And what, pathologically looked at, is the human body with all its organs, but a mere bagful of petards? The least of these is as dangerous to the whole economy as the ship's powder-magazine to the ship; and with every breath we breathe, and every meal we eat, we are putting one or more of them in peril. If we clung as devotedly as some philosophers pretend we do to the abstract idea of life, or were half as frightened as they make out we are, for the subversive accident that ends it all, the trumpets might sound by the hour and no one would follow them into battle—the blue-peter might fly at the truck, but who would climb into a sea-going ship? Think (if these philosophers were right) with what a preparation of spirit we should affront the daily peril of the dinner-table: a deadlier spot than any battle-field in history, where the far greater proportion of our ancestors have miserably left their bones! What woman would ever be lured into marriage, so much more dangerous than the wildest sea? And what would it be to grow old? For, after a certain distance, every step we take in life we find the ice growing thinner below our feet, and all around us and behind us we see our contemporaries going through. By the time a man gets well into the seventies, his continued existence is a mere miracle; and when he lays his old bones in bed for the night, there is an overwhelming probability that he will never see the day. Do the old men mind it, as a matter of fact? Why, no. They were never merrier; they have their grog at night, and tell the raciest stories; they hear of the death of people about their own age, or even younger, not as if it was a grisly warning, but with a simple childlike pleasure at having outlived some one else; and when a draught might puff them out like a guttering candle, or a bit of a stumble shatter them like so much glass, their old hearts keep sound and unaffrighted, and they go on, bubbling with laughter, through years of man's age compared to which the valley at Balaklava was as safe and peaceful as a village cricket-green on Sunday. It may fairly be questioned (if we look to the peril only) whether it was a much more daring feat for Curtius to plunge into the gulf, than for any old gentleman of ninety to doff his clothes and clamber into bed.

Indeed, it is a memorable subject for consideration, with what unconcern and gaiety mankind pricks on along the Valley of the Shadow of Death. The whole way is one wilderness of snares, and the end of it, for those who fear the last pinch, is irrevocable ruin. And yet we go spinning through it all, like a party for the Derby.

Perhaps the reader remembers one of the humorous devices of the deified Caligula: how he encouraged a vast concourse of holiday-makers on to his bridge over Baiæ bay; and when they were in the height of their enjoyment, turned loose the Prætorian guards among the company, and had them tossed into the sea. This is no bad miniature of the dealings of nature with the transitory race of man. Only, what a chequered picnic we have of it, even while it lasts! and into what great waters, not to be crossed by any swimmer, God's pale Prætorian throws us over in the end!

We live the time that a match flickers; we pop the cork of a ginger-beer bottle, and the earthquake swallows us on the instant. Is it not odd, is it not incongruous, is it not, in the highest sense of human speech, incredible, that we should think so highly of the ginger-beer, and regard so little the devouring earthquake? The love of Life and the fear of Death are two famous phrases that grow harder to understand the more we think about them. It is a well-known fact that an immense proportion of boat accidents would never happen if people held the sheet in their hands instead of making it fast; and yet, unless it be some martinet of a professional mariner or some landsman with shattered nerves, every one of God's creatures makes it fast. A strange instance of man's unconcern and brazen boldness in the face of death!

We confound ourselves with metaphysical phrases, which we import into daily talk with noble inappropriateness. We have no idea of what death is, apart from its circumstances and some of its consequences to others; and although we have some experience of living, there is not a man on earth who has flown so high into abstraction as to have any practical guess at the meaning of the word *life*. All literature, from Job and Omar Khayam to Thomas Carlyle or Walt Whitman, is but an attempt to look upon the human state with such largeness of view as shall enable us to rise from the consideration of living to the Definition of Life. And our sages give us about the best satisfaction in their power when they say that it is a vapour, or a show, or made out of the same stuff with dreams. Philosophy, in its more rigid sense, has been at the same work for ages; and after a myriad bald heads have wagged over the problem, and piles of words have been heaped one upon another into dry and cloudy volumes without end, philosophy has the honour of laying before us, with modest pride, her contribution towards the subject: that life is a Permanent Possibility of Sensation. Truly a fine result! A man may very well love beef, or hunting, or a woman; but surely, surely, not a Permanent Possibility of Sensation! He may be afraid of a precipice, or a dentist, or a large enemy with a club, or even an undertaker's man; but not certainly of abstract death. We may trick with the word life in its dozen senses until we are weary of tricking; we may argue in terms of all the philosophies on earth, but one fact remains true throughout—that we do not love life, in the sense that we are greatly preoccupied about its conservation; that we do not, properly speaking, love life at all, but living. Into the views of the least careful there will enter some degree of providence; no man's eyes are fixed entirely on the passing hour; but although we have some anticipation of good health, good weather, wine, active employment, love, and self-approval, the sum of these anticipations does not amount to anything like a general view of life's possibilities and issues; nor are those who cherish them most vividly, at all the most scrupulous of their personal safety. To be deeply interested in the accidents of our existence, to enjoy keenly the mixed texture of human experience, rather leads a man to disregard precautions, and risk his neck against a straw. For surely the love of living is stronger in an Alpine climber roping over a peril, or a hunter riding merrily at a stiff fence, than in a creature who lives upon a diet and walks a measured distance in the interest of his constitution.

There is a great deal of very vile nonsense talked upon both sides of the matter: tearing divines reducing life to the dimensions of a mere funeral procession, so short as to be hardly decent; and melancholy unbelievers yearning for the tomb as if it were a world too far away. Both sides must feel a little ashamed of their performances now and again when they draw in their chairs to dinner. Indeed, a good meal and a bottle of wine is an answer to most standard works upon the question. When a man's heart warms to his viands, he forgets a great deal of sophistry, and soars into a rosy zone of contemplation. Death may be knocking at the door, like the Commander's statue; we have something else in hand, thank God, and let him knock. Passing bells are ringing all the world over. All the world over, and every hour, some one is parting company with all his aches and ecstasies. For us also the trap is laid. But we are so fond of life that we have no leisure to entertain the terror of death. It is a honeymoon with us all through, and none of the longest. Small blame to us if we give our whole hearts to this glowing bride of ours, to the appetites, to honour, to the hungry curiosity of the mind, to the pleasure of the eyes in nature, and the pride of our own nimble bodies.

We all of us appreciate the sensations; but as for caring about the Permanence of the Possibility, a man's head is generally very bald, and his senses very dull, before he comes to that. Whether we regard life as a lane leading to a dead wall—a mere bag's end, as the French say—or whether we think of it as a vestibule or gymnasium, where we wait our turn and prepare our faculties for some more noble destiny; whether we thunder in a pulpit, or pule in little atheistic poetry-books, about its vanity and brevity; whether we look justly for years of health and vigour, or are about to mount into a bath-chair, as a step towards the hearse; in each and all of these views and situations there is but one conclusion possible: that a man should stop his ears against paralysing terror, and run the race that is set before him with a single mind. No one surely could have recoiled with more heartache and terror from the thought of death than our respected lexicographer; and yet we know how little it affected his conduct, how wisely and boldly he walked, and in what a fresh and lively vein he spoke of life. Already an old man, he ventured on his Highland tour; and his heart, bound with triple brass, did not recoil before twenty-seven individual cups of tea. As courage and intelligence are the two qualities best worth a good man's cultivation, so it is the first part of intelligence to recognise our precarious estate in life, and the first part of courage to be not at all abashed before the fact. A frank and somewhat headlong carriage, not looking too anxiously before, not dallying in maudlin regret over the past, stamps the man who is well armoured for this world.

And not only well armoured for himself, but a good friend and a good citizen to boot. We do not go to cowards for tender dealing; there is nothing so cruel as panic; the man who has least fear for his own carcase, has most time to consider others. That eminent chemist who took his walks abroad in tin shoes, and subsisted wholly upon tepid milk, had all his work cut out for him in considerate dealings with his own digestion. So soon as prudence has begun to grow up in the brain, like a dismal fungus, it finds its first expression in a paralysis of generous acts. The victim begins to shrink spiritually; he develops a fancy for parlours with a regulated temperature, and takes his morality on the principle of tin shoes and tepid milk. The care of one important body or soul becomes so engrossing, that all the noises of the outer world begin to come thin and faint into the parlour with the regulated temperature; and the tin shoes go equably forward over blood and rain. To be overwise is to ossify; and the scruple-monger ends by standing stockstill. Now the man who has his heart on his sleeve, and a good whirling weathercock of a brain, who reckons his life as a thing to be dashingly used and cheerfully hazarded, makes a very different acquaintance of the world, keeps all his pulses going true and fast, and gathers impetus as he runs, until, if he be running towards anything better than wildfire, he may shoot up and become a constellation in the end. Lord look after his health, Lord have a care of his soul, says he; and he has at the key of the position, and swashes through incongruity and peril towards his aim. Death is on all sides of him with pointed batteries, as he is on all sides of all of us; unfortunate surprises gird him round; mim-mouthed friends and relations hold up their hands in quite a little elegiacal synod about his path: and what cares he for all this? Being a true lover of living, a fellow with something pushing and spontaneous in his inside, he must, like any other soldier, in any other stirring, deadly warfare, push on at his best pace until he touch the goal. "A peerage or Westminster Abbey!" cried Nelson in his bright, boyish, heroic manner. These are great incentives; not for any of these, but for the plain satisfaction of living, of being about their business in some sort or other, do the brave, serviceable men of every nation tread down the nettle danger, and pass flyingly over all the stumbling-blocks of prudence. Think of the heroism of Johnson, think of that superb indifference to mortal limitation that set him upon his dictionary, and carried him through triumphantly until the end! Who, if he were wisely considerate of things at large, would ever embark upon any work much more considerable than a halfpenny post card? Who would project a serial novel, after Thackeray and Dickens had each fallen in mid-course? Who would find heart enough to begin to live, if he dallied with the consideration of death?

And, after all, what sorry and pitiful quibbling all this is! To forego all the issues of living in a parlour with a regulated temperature—as if that were not to die a hundred times over, and for ten years at a stretch! As if it were not to die in one's own lifetime, and without even the sad immunities of death! As if it were not to die, and yet be the patient spectators of our own pitiable change! The Permanent Possibility is preserved, but the sensations carefully held at arm's length, as if one kept a photographic plate in a dark chamber. It is better to lose health like a spendthrift than to waste it like a miser. It is better to live and be done with it, than to die daily in the sickroom. By all means begin your folio; even if the doctor does not give you a year, even if he hesitates about a month, make one brave push and see what can be accomplished in a week. It is not only in finished undertakings that we ought to honour useful labour. A spirit goes out of the man who means execution, which outlives the most untimely ending. All who have meant good work with their whole hearts, have done good work, although they may die before they have the time to sign it. Every heart that has beat strong and cheerfully has left a hopeful impulse behind it in the world, and bettered the tradition of mankind. And even if death catch people, like an open pitfall, and in mid-career, laying out vast projects, and planning monstrous foundations, flushed with hope, and their mouths full of boastful language, they should be at once tripped up and silenced: is there not something brave and spirited in such a termination? and does not life go down with a better grace, foaming in full body over a precipice, than miserably straggling to an end in sandy deltas? When the Greeks made their fine saying that those whom the gods love die young, I cannot help believing they had this sort of death also in their eye. For surely, at whatever age it overtake the man, this is to die young. Death has not been suffered to take so much as an illusion from his heart. In the hot-fit of life, a-tip-toe on the highest point of being, he passes at a bound on to the other side. The noise of the mallet and chisel is scarcely quenched, the trumpets are hardly done blowing, when, trailing with him clouds of glory, this happy-starred, full-blooded spirit shoots into the spiritual land.

QUESTIONS AND EXERCISES

1. Stevenson was one of the most-praised English stylists of all time, called by one reviewer "the Shakespeare of our prose." Can you tell by what kinds of criteria his *stylistic* reputation may have been established?

2. Does Stevenson's prose seem more or less "formal" than Johnson's? Is this difference primarily a matter of grammar and syntax, of diction, or of what? Discuss this question carefully, using Stevenson's paragraph 2 and Johnson's paragraphs 5 through 7 for particular reference.

3. Is there anything odd about the term "elegiacal synod" in paragraph 9? Are there other dictional surprises of this same type? Where?

4. Does Stevenson's frequent use of parallelism and climax involve him, usually, in a grammatically complex or "difficult" sentence structure? Taking paragraph 6 as your sample, explain how Stevenson is able to write such long sentences as these without using more subordinating and suspended constructions.

5. Smoothness and continuity are supposed to be qualities of Stevenson's verbal style. How does he achieve these effects in this essay, and in paragraph 4 particularly? Bear in mind what was said concerning transitions in Chapter Four.

6. Compare Stevenson's figurative language with Johnson's.

7. In general, does Stevenson's management of language imply a *formal* relationship between reader and author, or a somewhat *informal* one? In what ways is this accomplished? Is the result appropriate to the essay's substance?

8. Stevenson makes several key phrases memorable by repeating them

a number of times. Do you think this device of phrasal repetition is a good thing for the essay, and does it achieve anything more than simply assisting the memory?

9. Make a list of subjects that you think could be dealt with in the style used in this essay. Write a brief commentary explaining some of your choices.

10. Subject for a critical paper: Are there any glaring inconsistencies in Stevenson's argument here, and does his verbal style tend to disclose or conceal these inconsistencies? Cite the text as frequently and specifically as possible. This is not an easy topic. Stay clear of it unless you are prepared to produce serious critical analysis.

11. Write a paragraph on any subject (even, if necessary, a paragraph of pure nonsense) with the chief goal of having it sound "good" and "melodious" when read aloud. Add another paragraph, *in the same style*, seriously evaluating and accounting for the success of the first.

12. Write a fairly long paragraph (100–200 words) on a subject you know something about, but use nothing but syntactically straightforward and simple declarative sentences—you need not *try* to make it look like childish babble. Then rewrite, using as much balanced parallelism, climax, subordination, and inverted order as you can without becoming ungrammatical or hopelessly unclear.

THE STATE OF FUNK

D. H. Lawrence

What is the matter with the English, that they are so scared of everything? They are in a state of blue funk, and they behave like a lot of mice when somebody stamps on the floor. They are terrified about money, finance, about ships, about war, about work, about Labour, about Bolshevism, and, funniest of all, they are scared stiff of the printed word. Now this is a very strange and humiliating state of mind, in a people which has always been so dauntless. And for the nation, it is a very dangerous state of mind. When a people falls into a state of funk, then God help it. Because mass funk leads some time or other to mass panic, and then—one can only repeat, God help us.

There is, of course, a certain excuse for fear. The time of change

THE STATE OF FUNK: From *Assorted Articles* by D. H. Lawrence. Copyright 1928, 1929, 1930 by D. H. Lawrence. Reprinted by permission of Alfred A. Knopf, Inc.

is upon us. The need for change has taken hold of us. We are changing, we have got to change, and we can no more help it than leaves can help going yellow and coming loose in autumn, or than bulbs can help shoving their little green spikes out of the ground in spring. We are changing, we are in the throes of change, and the change will be a great one. Instinctively, we feel it. Intuitively, we know it. And we are frightened. Because change hurts. And also, in the periods of serious transition, everything is uncertain, and living things are most vulnerable.

But what of it? Granted all the pains and dangers and uncertainties, there is no excuse for falling into a state of funk. If we come to think of it, every child that is begotten and born is a seed of change, a danger to its mother, at childbirth a great pain, and, after birth, a new responsibility, a new change. If we feel in a state of funk about it, we should cease having children altogether. *If* we fall into a state of funk, indeed, the best thing is to have no children. But why fall into a state of funk?

Why not look things in the face like men, and like women? A woman who is going to have a child says to herself: Yes, I feel uncomfortable, sometimes I feel wretched, and I have a time of pain and danger ahead of me. But I have a good chance of coming through all right, especially if I am intelligent, and I bring a new life into the world. Somewhere I feel hopeful, even happy. So I must take the sour with the sweet. There is no birth without birth pangs.

It is the business of men, of course, to take the same attitude towards the birth of new conditions, new ideas, new emotions. And sorry to say, most modern men don't. They fall into a state of funk. We all of us know that ahead of us lies a great social change, a great social readjustment. A few men look it in the face and try to realize what will be best. We none of us *know* what will be best. There is no ready-made solution. Ready-made solutions are almost the greatest danger of all. A change is a slow flux, which must happen bit by bit. And it must *happen*. You can't drive it like a steam engine. But all the time you can be alert and intelligent about it, and watch for the next step, and watch for the direction of the main trend. Patience, alertness, intelligence, and a human good will and fearlessness, that is what you want in a time of change. Not funk.

Now England is on the brink of great changes, radical changes. Within the next fifty years the whole framework of our social life will be altered, will be greatly modified. The old world of our grandfathers is disappearing like thawing snow, and is as likely to cause a flood. What the world of our grandchildren will be, fifty years hence, we don't know. But in its social form it will be very different from our world of today. We've got to change. And in our power to change, in our capacity to make new intelligent adaptation to new conditions, in our readiness to admit and fulfill new needs, to give expression to new desires and new feelings, lies our hope and our health. Courage is the great word. Funk spells sheer disaster.

There is a great change coming, bound to come. The whole money arrangement will undergo a change: what, I don't know. The whole industrial system will undergo a change. Work will be different and pay will be different. The owning of property will be different. Class will be different, and human relations will be modified and perhaps simplified. If we are intelligent, alert, and undaunted, then life will be much better, more generous, more spontaneous, more vital, less basely materialistic. If we fall into a state of funk, impotence, and persecution, then things may be very much worse than they are now. It is up to us. It is up to men to be men. While men are courageous and willing to change, nothing terribly bad can happen. But once men fall into a state of funk, with the inevitable accompaniment of bullying and repression, then only bad things can happen. To be firm is one thing. But bullying is another. And bullying of any sort whatsoever can have nothing but disastrous results. And when the mass falls into a state of funk, and you have mass bullying, then catastrophe is near.

Change in the whole social system is inevitable not merely because conditions change—though partly for that reason—but because people themselves change. We change, you and I, we change and change vitally, as the years go on. New feelings arise in us, old values depreciate, new values arise. Things we thought we wanted most intensely we realize we don't care about. The things we built our lives on crumble and disappear, and the process is painful. But it is not tragic. A tadpole that has so gaily waved its tail in the water must feel very sick when the tail begins to drop off and little legs begin to sprout. The tail was its dearest, gayest, most active member, all its little life was in its tail. And now the tail must go. It seems rough on the tadpole; but the little green frog in the grass is a new gem, after all.

As a novelist, I feel it is the change inside the individual which is my real concern. The great social change interests me and troubles me, but it is not my field. I know a change is coming—and I know we must have a more generous, more human system based on the life values and not on the money values. That I know. But what steps to take I don't know. Other men know better.

My field is to know the feelings inside a man, and to make new feelings conscious. What really torments civilized people is that they are full of feelings they know nothing about; they can't realize them, they can't fulfil them, they can't *live* them. And so they are tortured. It is like having energy you can't use—it destroys you. And feelings are a form of vital energy.

I am convinced that the majority of people today have good, generous feelings which they can never know, never experience, because of some fear, some repression. I do not believe that people would be villains, thieves, murderers, and sexual criminals if they were freed from legal restraint. On the contrary, I think the vast majority would be much more generous, good-hearted, and decent if they felt they dared be. I am convinced that people want to be more decent, more good-hearted than our social system of money and grab allows them to be. The awful fight for money, into which we are all forced, hurts our good nature more than we can bear. I am sure this is true of a vast number of people.

And the same is true of our sexual feelings; only worse. There, we start all wrong. Consciously, there is supposed to be no such thing as sex in the human being. As far as possible, we never speak of it, never mention it, never, if we can help it, even think of it. It is disturbing. It is—somehow—wrong.

The whole trouble with sex is that we daren't speak of it and think of it naturally. We are not secretly sexual villains. We are not secretly sexually depraved. We are just human beings with living sex. We are all right, if we had not this unaccountable and disastrous *fear* of sex. I know, when I was a lad of eighteen, I used to remember with shame and rage in the morning the sexual thoughts and desires I had had the night before. Shame, and rage, and terror lest anybody else should have to know. And I *hated* the self that I had been, the night before.

Most boys are like that, and it is, of course, utterly wrong. The boy that had excited sexual thoughts and feelings was the living, warm-hearted, passionate me. The boy that in the morning remembered these feelings with such fear, shame and rage was the social mental me: perhaps a little priggish, and certainly in a state of funk. But the two were divided against one another. A boy divided against himself; a girl divided against herself; a people divided against itself; it is a disastrous condition.

And it was a long time before I was able to say to myself: I am *not* going to be ashamed of my sexual thoughts and desires, they are me myself, they are part of my life. I am going to accept myself sexually as I accept myself mentally and spiritually, and know that I am one time one thing, one time another, but I am always myself. My sex is me as my mind is me, and nobody will make me feel shame about it.

It is long since I came to that decision. But I remember how much freer I felt, how much warmer and more sympathetic towards people. I had no longer anything to hide from them, no longer anything to be in a funk about, lest they should find it out. My sex was me, like my mind and my spirit. And the other man's sex was him, as his mind was him, and his spirit was him. And the woman's sex was her, as her mind and spirit were herself too. And once this quiet admission is made, it is wonderful how much deeper and more real the human sympathy flows. And it is wonderful how difficult the admission is to make, for man or woman: the tacit, natural admission, that allows the natural warm flow of the blood sympathy, without repression and holding back.

I remember when I was a very young man I was enraged when with a woman, if I was reminded of her sexual actuality. I only wanted to be aware of her personality, her mind and spirit. The other had to be fiercely shut out. Some part of the natural sympathy for a woman had to be shut away, cut off. There was a mutilation in the relationship all the time.

Now, in spite of the hostility of society, I have learned a little better. Now I know that a woman is her sexual self too, and I can feel the normal sex sympathy with her. And this silent sympathy is utterly different from desire or anything rampant or lurid. If I can really sympathize with a woman in her sexual self, it is just a form of warm-heartedness and compassionateness, the most natural life-flow in the world. And it may be a woman of seventy-five, or a child of two, it is the same. But our civilization, with its horrible fear and funk and repression and bullying, has almost destroyed the natural flow of common sympathy between men and men, and men and women.

And it is this that I want to restore into life: just the natural warm flow of common sympathy between man and man, man and woman. Many people hate it, of course. Many men hate it that one should tacitly take them for sexual, physical men instead of mere social and mental personalities. Many women hate it the same. Some, the worst, are in a state of rabid funk. The papers call me "lurid" and a "dirty-minded fellow." One woman, evidently a woman of education and means, wrote to me out of the blue: "You, who are a mixture of the missing link and the chimpanzee, etc."—and told me my name stank in men's nostrils: though, since she was Mrs. Something or other, she might have said women's nostrils. And these people think they are being perfectly well-bred and perfectly "right." They are safe inside the convention, which also agrees that we are sexless creatures and social beings merely, cold and bossy and assertive, cowards safe inside a convention.

Now I am one of the least lurid mortals, and I don't at all mind being likened to a chimpanzee. If there is one thing I don't like it is cheap and promiscuous sex. If there is one thing I insist on it is that sex is a delicate, vulnerable, vital thing that you mustn't fool with. If there is one thing I deplore it is heartless sex. Sex must be a real flow, a real flow of sympathy, generous and warm, and not a trick thing, or a moment's excitation, or a mere bit of bullying.

And if I write a book about the sex relations of a man and a woman, it is not because I want all men and women to begin having indiscriminate lovers and love affairs, off the reel. All this horrid scramble of love affairs and prostitution is only part of the funk, bravado, and *doing it on purpose*. And bravado and *doing it on purpose* is just as unpleasant and hurtful as repression, just as much a sign of secret fear.

What you have to do is to get out of the state of funk, sex funk. And to do so, you've got to be perfectly decent, and you have to accept sex fully in the consciousness. Accept sex in the consciousness, and let the normal physical awareness come back, between you and other people. Be tacitly and simply aware of the sexual being in every man and woman, child and animal; and unless the man or woman is a bully, be sympathetically aware. It is the most important thing just now, this gentle physical awareness. It keeps us tender and alive at a moment when the great danger is to go brittle, hard, and in some way dead.

Accept the sexual, physical being of yourself, and of every other creature. Don't be afraid of it. Don't be afraid of the physical functions. Don't be afraid of the so-called obscene words. There is nothing wrong with the words. It is your fear that makes them bad, your needless fear. It is your fear which cuts you off physically even from your nearest and dearest. And when men and women are physically cut off, they become at last dangerous, bullying, cruel. Conquer the fear of sex, and restore the natural flow. Restore even the so-called obscene words, which are part of the natural flow. If you don't, if you don't put back a bit of the old warmth into life, there is savage disaster ahead.

QUESTIONS AND EXERCISES

1. Lawrence uses a great deal of parallel construction in this essay, but the effect is quite different from that of the Johnson and Stevenson essays. What makes the difference?

2. Does Lawrence's insistent use of phrasal and clausal duplication serve any useful purpose? Do you find it irritating eventually?

Does it seem likely that the irritation itself contributes to the essay's force, and was deliberately cultivated by Lawrence? In which paragraph is this tendency most noticeable?

3. In rereading the essay, do you find any important departures from direct and simple English syntax? Does Lawrence's sparing use of subordinating constructions have anything to do with the emphatic effect that he achieves through repetition of terms and phrases?

4. What variety in diction, particularly in adverbs and adjectives, does this essay show? Does the author depend much on highly specific modifiers? Highly specific diction of any sort? Do you imagine that the level of his diction here might be offensive to some part of his audience? What part?

5. In how many different ways is Lawrence able to say "no," convey denial and negation?

6. Glance through the essay again, looking specifically for Lawrence's use of figurative language. Which instances strike you as conveying his point most strongly? Do the various local metaphors seem related to some one central and unifying idea? Explain. Would it have been appropriate for Lawrence to use more elaborately lengthy metaphors here?

7. Compared with most English prose, this essay would be called informal. Is it accurate to say that this informality is of the kind that we find in *spoken*, conversational English? What are the signs of this type of informality, exactly? Do you find the essay actually easier to read aloud than, say, the Stevenson essay?

8. An experiment: Choose a subject about which you feel strongly enough to argue and persuade; then, write out your argument as *rapidly* as you can, to see how much you can get said in fifteen minutes. Compare the resulting style with Lawrence's. Then try the same subject again, on your own, taking your time, but aiming consciously at Lawrence's feeling of urgent impetuousness.

9. Write a short critical essay (200–400 words) on Lawrence's use of extremely short sentences and non-sentences, using these devices yourself.

10. Explain, in about 500 words, how Lawrence's prose style is suited to his subject.

11. Choose one of the longer paragraphs from "The State of Funk" and rewrite it in a style that you regard as *inappropriate* to its substance. Attach an analytic outline specifying the individual ways in which you have tried to get this effect.

12. In his last two paragraphs, Lawrence switches over to the imperative ("Accept the sexual, physical being of yourself," etc.). Has he used it at all earlier? What is its effect here? Write a 300-word commentary on this, including some comparison of these final paragraphs with those that open the essay.

CHAPTER SIX

Style and Self

In Chapter Three, where we discussed the author's relationship to the world, to the audience, and to his work, we promised to discuss later the special problem of the *stylistic* self. Now that we have looked at some of the basic elements of stylistic performance, it is time to turn to this question. But keep in mind that in this chapter we will not try to establish definitions or analytic guidelines; we will try simply to stimulate critical thinking on an important and complex problem.

As we saw earlier, the identity of the author and his manner of treating a subject can, in certain ways, greatly qualify and even radically alter the substance, so that we find ourselves saying of a particular work, "here his real subject is himself, whether he knows it or not." Usually he does know it. The kind and degree of an author's personal involvement is something over which he can and generally does exercise personal control. It is even possible that, among several of his essays in which the "personal" element appears strong, more than one version of the "self" will intrude. The writer who projects a deeply introspective strain of philosophical thoughtfulness in one essay may very well appear as a rather whimsical person in the next. There need be no dishonesty in this kind of change. The reader who finds an improbable variety of selves in an essayist may sense a root dishonesty. More likely, though, he will find that the different faces he has been shown are not really different faces at all, but different facial expressions, all perfectly consistent with the author's "real" self insofar as it can be known at all.

When we move from the larger matters of strategy, structure, and selection of material to actual verbal arrangement, however, there is some change in circumstances. When a man speaks or writes, he is engaging in an activity in which he has been establishing habits since he was about two years old. Certain ways of using language are familiar and comfortable for him, and others are not. This does not mean that every time he says something aloud or in print he must surely reveal a self strangely and sharply different from everyone else. The habits of expression that he has formed may, after all, be so "normal" that we say of him, as of most people, that he sounds like everybody else. The point, rather, is that if he does have a distinctive style, it will not be easy for him to get rid of it or alter it. His way of using language has been adapted to fit his vision of the world; it is not an attitude or pose adaptable to special occasions. But of course, fakery is still possible, if more difficult. A writer who has had long and expert experience of stylistic masters in his own tongue, may be particularly tempted sometimes to indulge in a kind of mimicry. We can usually tell, when reading an author whom we know reasonably well (in print, if not in person), whether or not he is affecting some style other than his own. Since the author's own voice or style is not just an added ornament but rather the most precise refinement of his essay's substance, the identification of that voice can be for the reader one of the most rewarding sensations of literary experience. And the location of personal style is fixed by a combination of the verbal elements described in the preceding chapter.

We tend naturally to think that the surest signs of projected self in an author's style will be discovered in his vocabulary, so that if we inspect his *diction* carefully we will have the best clue to his mind and personality. But self is only one of the prime determinants of style. Subject is another and the intended audience a third. If we think sensibly for a moment about the priorities here and about our actual experience in reading essays with widely divergent styles, we must see that, as far as the choice of words is concerned, subject and audience are the chief factors. It is true that the author's self will determine his favorite subjects, his audience, and thus, by extension, the total character of his diction. But we are thinking here in terms of the individual essay and the reader's response to it.

Much more can be learned, relatively speaking, from the author's habitual way of framing sentences, the organizing syntax and grammatical patterns that have become second nature to him. These are not liable to change as much as subject matter changes, though of course in the long run, one does tend to use different constructions for narrating than for logical reasoning. Even within the limited framework of possibilities that the English language offers—a language only vestigially inflected, as we have seen, and therefore not as syntactically flexible as, say, Latin—there is plenty of room for the development of distinctive patterns. The calm and august deliberateness of Johnson is caught and permanently held in the formal grandeur of his recurrent balance and antithesis, the gradual but ceaseless advance of logical good sense, clause by carefully matched clause. In Lawrence's prose we can detect a personality more volatile, mercurial, more suddenly given to impulse and the immediate expression of feelings; the shorter and less formally structured sentences reveal this, in repetition, just as effectively as any other element in the style. Or consider the difference between these two possible formulations of the same thought (using the same diction):

> Capital punishment is only superficially repugnant. Society is threatened continuously by morally depraved outcasts. They know the universal weaknesses of the human condition and they prey on them. Mild forms of punitive justice will not deter these men from the most savage crimes, but capital punishment provides a better safeguard. We cannot help recognizing this.

> When we consider the effects of capital punishment as a deterrent against the most savage crimes, we cannot help recognizing that, because of the invaluable protection thus provided a public that otherwise remains helpless in face of continuous threats from morally depraved outcasts who prey on universal weaknesses of the human condition, such a safeguard, however superficially repugnant it may be, is preferable to any milder form of punitive justice.

Though it is difficult to formulate in words the differences between the two selves suggested here, we understand at first contact that the passages represent two different intellectual temperaments. The closer integration of elements in the second passage may suggest a more purposeful and energetic character, with more of a built-in inclination to arrive at conclusions, to use each piece of opinion or data as a means of getting to another. The writer has a clear sense of the importance of structures, of cause-and-effect, of distinctions in rank and priority. The author of the first passage, on the other hand, appears above all else, to be striving for clarity within each unit of expression. He shows less concern for structure than for simplicity. His implicit logic is not, after all, remarkably weaker than that of the other writer. But the integrated web of subordinating connections among the various elements in the thought is not thoroughly projected into the syntax and the grammatical structure. Now of course it would be foolish to try for any reliable inference about the author's character on the basis of such a tiny sample, but we may learn something by playing the game. At least, if we were asked to which of these two writers the adjectives "plain," "straightforward," "dogged," "tight-lipped" could apply, we should not hesitate long before answering.

In addition to diction and syntax, metaphor ranks high as a means by which the personal quality in a style is set. Of course, many writers (like many people) have no particular attachment to figurative expression. But where metaphor is important, it is likely to be the most active stylistic element. And the chances are that it will be the most personally and intimately revealing. For whereas the diction must lie within the accepted vocabulary of the language, and the variation in syntactical forms is hedged in by limits of that language's elasticity, metaphor is (or at least may be) the work of the private imagination, without regulators. The likenesses, similarities, connections, that a man sees in life give us a fantastically direct insight into his central self. It may be the sheer, outrageous capriciousness of the metaphors that strikes us; or the elaborate method through which each one is worked out, justified in fine detail; or the nearly obsessive way in which a whole cluster of metaphors works consistently around a single theme. As usual in matters of style, the reader will find it hard to say what discovery, precisely, the author's figurative language has made possible. He may be able to do no more than say, "I have discovered that this is a man who can think of likening a philosophical dilemma to a field full of bullocks, and then actually bring it off." But this single impression may turn out to cut closer to the heart of things than all the diction-sifting and syntax-study in the world.

When we say, "Style is the man himself," we can mean a number of different things. It should by now be clear that the most permanent features of a man's verbal style provide a reliable index to his intellect and to his way of thinking and viewing life. It may not show the "whole self," but it will show that aspect of the self with which we as readers must be most concerned—the author's full sensibility engaged with whatever in life is most seriously important to it. As for his *moral* self—his peculiar type of goodness or evil—that is rather harder to get at, and it is probably wiser to look for it in the long-range content of his works than in the arrangement of phrases. It was once quite fashionable to say that a fundamentally bad man cannot write with distinction—his moral slovenliness will project itself into a slipshod way of handling sentences—and that a man of virtue must write well. While it would be smug to deny the existence of any such correspondences as these, we can at least doubt that they really involve morality. And even if they did, the division of all writers into the camps of good and evil really would not go far to *individuate* each man as a special self.

By the same token, we should not confuse a man's real self with what is popularly thought of as "personality." "Personality," in this sense, is little more than the aggregate of trivial qualities of temporary social behavior, designed to impress and ingratiate; its cultivation is particularly disastrous for a writer's style, not merely because it takes the shallow for the deep, but also because it tends to equate the "personal" with what is most novel, most different-from-everything-else, most "unique." And the search for that extreme differentness inevitably leads to excesses of cuteness and forced freshness, clownishly "bright" violence to the language, and all manner of unusual behavior for its own sake. The writer who really is a wild and fire-hot eccentric of genius will not have to *try* to make his style distinctive. For other people, the attempt normally ends up looking merely ridiculous. And it is nearly as absurd to look for and expect that kind of violent differentness in what we read.

The real value of self in style has less to do with differentness (whether extreme or modest) than with something that may be best conveyed by the rather Victorian word "sincerity." It is more important to sound like yourself than to sound different from everybody else. The two things are not the same. If I want above all to differentiate my appearance, I can go out every day dressed in a suit of bright green and chartreuse sequins in stripes, with iridescent red sunbursts sewn on. However attractive such a vision may be in itself, it does not necessarily have a thing to do with who I am. Of course, my brown worsted suit-and-vest may not be very relevant either, but at least it does not positively distract attention from me. In style, the object is to discover, by trial, what verbal manner is naturally easy and versatile, true to the qualities of your intellect. It is in this sense, and this sense only, that self-consciousness can be a good thing for a writer.

In the three essays that follow, it will probably be obvious that three rather different styles are at work. How much each style is personal, a real extension of the man, will not be easy for you to judge from a single essay. But the important element—the feeling that the author is speaking, here at least, with honest force and without tricky pretensions—should be within the range of judgment.

WEAPONS: WAR OF THE ICONS

Marshall McLuhan

When the Russian girl Valentina Tereshkova, quite without pilot training, went into orbit on June 16, 1963, her action, as reacted to

---

WEAPONS: WAR OF THE ICONS: From *Understanding Media* by Marshall McLuhan. Copyright © 1964. McGraw-Hill Book Company. Used by permission.

in the press and other media, was a kind of defacing of the images of the male astronauts, especially the Americans. Shunning the expertise of American astronauts, all of whom were qualified test pilots, the Russians don't seem to feel that space travel is related enough to the airplane to require a pilot's "wings." Since our culture forbids the sending of a woman into orbit, our only repartee would have been to launch into orbit a group of space children, to indicate that it is, after all, child's play.

The first sputnik or little "fellow-traveler" was a witty taunting of the capitalist world by means of a new kind of technological image or icon, for which a group of children in orbit might yet be a telling retort. Plainly, the first lady astronaut is offered to the West as a little Valentine—or heart throb—suited to our sentimentality. In fact, the war of the icons, or the eroding of the collective countenance of one's rivals, has long been under way. Ink and photo are supplanting soldiery and tanks. The pen daily becomes mightier than the sword.

The French phrase *"guerre des nerfs"* of twenty-five years ago has since come to be referred to as "the cold war." It is really an electric battle of information and of images that goes far deeper and is more obsessional than the old hot wars of industrial hardware.

The "hot" wars of the past used weapons that knocked off the enemy, one by one. Even ideological warfare in the eighteenth and nineteenth centuries proceeded by persuading individuals to adopt new points of view, one at a time. Electric persuasion by photo and movie and TV works, instead, by dunking entire populations in new imagery. Full awareness of this technological change had dawned on Madison Avenue ten years ago when it shifted its tactics from the promotion of the individual product to the collective involvement in the "corporate image," now altered to "corporate posture."

Parallel to the new cold war of information exchange is the situation commented on by James Reston in a *New York Times* release from Washington:

> Politics has gone international. The British Labor Leader is here campaigning for Prime Minister of Britain, and fairly soon John F. Kennedy will be over in Italy and Germany campaigning for reelection. Everybody's now whistle-stopping through somebody else's country, usually ours.
>
> Washington has still not adjusted to this third-man role. It keeps forgetting that anything said here may be used by one side or another in some election campaign, and that it may, by accident, be the decisive element in the final vote.

If the cold war in 1964 is being fought by informational technology, that is because all wars have been fought by the latest technology available in any culture. In one of his sermons John Donne commented thankfully on the blessing of heavy firearms:

> So by the benefit of this light of reason they have found out *Artillery*, by which warres come to quicker ends than heretofore . . .

The scientific knowledge needed for the use of gunpowder and the boring of cannon appeared to Donne as "the light of reason." He failed to notice another advance in the same technology that hastened and extended the scope of human slaughter. It is referred to by John U. Nef in *War and Human Progress:*

> The gradual abandonment of armor as a part of the equipment of soldiers during the seventeenth century freed some metal supplies for the manufacture of firearms and missiles.

It is easy to discover in this a seamless web of interwoven events when we turn to look at the psychic and social consequences of the technological extensions of man.

Back in the 1920s King Amanullah seems to have put his finger on this web when he said, after firing off a torpedo:

"I feel half an Englishman already."

The same sense of the relentlessly interwoven texture of human fate was touched by the schoolboy who said:

"Dad, I hate war."

"Why, son?"

"Because war makes history, and I hate history."

The techniques developed over the centuries for drilling gun-barrels provided the means that made possible the steam engine. The piston shaft and the gun presented the same problems in boring hard steel. Earlier, it had been the lineal stress of perspective that had channeled perception in paths that led to the creation of gunfire. Long before guns, gunpowder had been used explosively, dynamite style. The use of gunpowder for the propelling of missiles in trajectories waited for the coming of perspective in the arts. This liaison of events between technology and the arts may explain a matter that has long puzzled anthropologists. They have repeatedly tried to explain the fact that nonliterates are generally poor shots with rifles, on the grounds that, with the bow and arrow, proximity to game was more important than distant accuracy, which was almost impossible to achieve—hence, say some anthropologists, their imitation of hunted beasts by dressing in skins to get close to the herd. It is also pointed out that bows are silent, and when an arrow missed, animals rarely fled.

If the arrow is an extension of the hand and the arm, the rifle is an extension of the eye and teeth. It may be to the point to remark that it was the literate American colonists who were first to insist on a rifled barrel and improved gunsights. They improved the old muskets, creating the Kentucky rifle. It was the highly literate Bostonians who outshot the British regulars. Marksmanship is not the gift of the native or the woodsman, but of the literate colonist. So runs this argument that links gunfire itself with the rise of perspective, and with the extension of the visual power in literacy. In the Marine Corps it has been found that there is a definite correlation between education and marksmanship. Not for the nonliterate is our easy selection of a separate, isolated target in space, with the rifle as an extension of the eye.

If gunpowder was known long before it was used for guns, the same is also true of the use of the lodestone or magnet. Its use in the compass for lineal navigation had, also, to wait for the discovery of lineal perspective in the arts. Navigators took a long time to accept the possibility of space as uniform, connected, and continuous. Today in physics, as in painting and sculpture, progress consists in giving up the idea of space as either uniform, continuous, or connected. Visuality has lost its primacy.

In the Second World War the marksman was replaced by automatic weapons fired blindly in what were called "perimeters of fire" or "fire lanes." The old-timers fought to retain the bolt-action Springfield which encouraged single-shot accuracy and sighting. Spraying the air with lead in a kind of tactual embrace was found to be good by night, as well as by day, and sighting was unnecessary. At this stage of technology, the literate man is somewhat in the position of the old-timers who backed the Springfield rifle against perimeter fire. It is this same visual habit that deters and obstructs literate man in modern physics, as Milic Capek explains in *The Philosophical Impact of Modern Physics*. Men in the older oral societies of middle Europe are better able to conceive the nonvisual velocities and relations of the subatomic world.

Our highly literate societies are at a loss as they encounter the new structures of opinion and feeling that result from instant and global information. They are still in the grip of "points of view" and of habits of dealing with things one at a time. Such habits are quite crippling in any electric structure of information movement, yet they could be controlled if we recognized whence they had been acquired. But literate society thinks of its artificial visual bias as a thing natural and innate.

Literacy remains even now the base and model of all programs of industrial mechanization; but, at the same time, it locks the minds and senses of its users in the mechanical and fragmentary matrix that is so necessary to the maintenance of mechanized society. That is why the transition from mechanical to electric technology is so very traumatic and severe for us all. The mechanical techniques, with their limited powers, we have long used as weapons. The electric techniques cannot be used aggressively except to end all life at once, like the turning off of a light. To live with both of these technologies at the same time is the peculiar drama of the twentieth century.

In his *Education Automation*, R. Buckminster Fuller considers that weaponry has been a source of technological advance for mankind because it requires continually improved performance with ever smaller means. "As we went from the ships of the sea to the ships of the air, the performance per pound of the equipment and fuel became of even higher importance than on the sea."

It is this trend toward more and more power with less and less hardware that is characteristic of the electric age of information. Fuller has estimated that in the first half century of the airplane the nations of the world have invested two and a half trillion dollars by subsidy of the airplane as a weapon. He added that this amounts to sixty-two times the value of all the gold in the world. His approach to these problems is more technological than the approach of historians, who have often tended to find that war produces nothing new in the way of invention.

"This man will teach us how to beat him," Peter the Great is said to have remarked after his army had been beaten by Charles XII of Sweden. Today, the backward countries can learn from us how to beat us. In the new electric age of information, the backward countries enjoy some specific advantages over the highly literate and industrialized cultures. For backward countries have the habit and understanding of oral propaganda and persuasion that was eroded in industrial societies long ago. The Russians had only to adapt their traditions of Eastern icon and image-building to the new electric media in order to be aggressively effective in the modern world of information. The idea of the Image, that Madison Avenue has had to learn the hard way, was the only idea available to Russian propaganda. The Russians have not shown imagination or resourcefulness in their propaganda. They have merely done that which their religious and cultural traditions taught them; namely, to build images.

The city, itself, is traditionally a military weapon, and is a collective shield or plate armor, an extension of the castle of our very skins. Before the huddle of the city, there was the food-gathering phase of man the hunter, even as men have now in the electric age returned psychically and socially to the nomad state. Now, however, it is called information-gathering and data-processing. But it is global, and it ignores and replaces the form of the city which has, therefore, tended to become obsolete. With instant electric technology, the globe itself can never again be more than a village, and the very nature of city as a form of major dimensions must inevitably dissolve like a fading shot in a movie. The first circumnavigation of the globe in the Renaissance gave men a sense of embracing and possessing the earth that was quite new, even as the recent astronauts have again altered man's relation to the planet, reducing its scope to the extent of an evening's stroll.

The city, like a ship, is a collective extension of the castle of our skins, even as clothing is an extension of our individual skins. But weapons proper are extensions of hands, nails, and teeth, and come into existence as tools needed for accelerating the processing of matter. Today, when we live in a time of sudden transition from mechanical to electric technology, it is easier to see the character of all previous technologies, we being detached from all of them for the time being. Since our new electric technology is not an extension of our bodies but of our central nervous systems, we now see all technology, including language, as a means of processing experience, a means of storing and speeding information. And in such a situation all technology can plausibly be regarded as weapons. Previous wars can now be regarded as the processing of difficult and resistant materials by the latest technology, the speedy dumping of industrial products on an enemy market to the point of social saturation. War, in fact, can be seen as a process of achieving equilibrium among unequal technologies, a fact that explains Toynbee's puzzled observation that each invention of a new weapon is a disaster for society, and that militarism itself is the most common cause of the breaking of civilizations.

By militarism, Rome extended civilization or individualism, literacy, and lineality to many oral and backward tribes. Even today the mere existence of a literate and industrial West appears quite naturally as dire aggression to nonliterate societies; just as the mere existence of the atom bomb appears as a state of universal aggression to industrial and mechanized societies.

On the one hand, a new weapon or technology looms as a threat to all who lack it. On the other hand, when everybody has the same technological aids, there begins the competitive fury of the homogenized and the egalitarian pattern against which the strategy of social class and caste has often been used in the past. For caste and class are techniques of social slow-down that tend to create the stasis of tribal societies. Today we appear to be poised between two ages—one of detribalization and one of retribalization.

> Between the acting of a dreadful thing,
> And the first motion, all the interim is
> Like a Phantasma, or a hideous Dream:
> The genius and the mortal instruments
> Are then in council; and the state of man,
> Like to a little Kingdom, suffers then
> The nature of an insurrection.
>   (*Julius Caesar*, Brutus, II, i)

If mechanical technology as extension of parts of the human body had exerted a fragmenting force, psychically and socially, this fact appears nowhere more vividly than in mechanical weaponry. With the extension of the central nervous system by electric technology, even weaponry makes more vivid the fact of the unity of the human family. The very inclusiveness of information as a weapon becomes a daily reminder that politics and history must be recast in the form of "the concretization of human fraternity."

This dilemma of weaponry appears very clearly to Leslie Dewart in his *Christianity and Revolution*, when he points to the obsolescence of the fragmented balance-of-power techniques. As an instrument of policy, modern war has come to mean "the existence and end of one society to the exclusion of another." At this point, weaponry is a self-liquidating fact.

QUESTIONS AND EXERCISES

1. Do you find the author's argument easy to understand the first time through? If not, is the difficulty caused by his use of unusual or complicated sentence structure, obscure vocabulary, or rarified figurative language? If not, then by what? Is this difficulty really a characteristic of style, and does it suggest anything at all about the quality of the author as a man?

2. Describe the style-characteristics of paragraph 8 (beginning with "The techniques) as precisely as you can. The next-to-last sentence in this paragraph is much longer and more complicated than any of the others. Is this by design, do you think, or by chance? Explain.

3. What is there in the essay's diction that suggests familiarity, ease, and general *relaxation* in the writer? Does this characteristic (whether you think it is genuine or part of a pose) have anything to do with the subject of the essay?

4. McLuhan quotes a good deal from other authorities, especially toward the end of the essay. If his own style is highly individuated, then these quotations should strike the reader as stylistically conspicuous. That is, one should be aware of a different set of linguistic habits in moving from the McLuhan text to the inserted quotation back again. Do you find this to be the case? Discuss.

5. Write a one-page (250-word) explanation of the difference between the mechanical and electric technologies as the essay conceives of them.

6. Write an essay of about 500 words, imitating McLuhan's style as closely as you can. Add a paragraph explaining exactly your methods and procedures in this imitative attempt.

7. Invent what you regard as a worthwhile writing exercise based on the McLuhan essay, and write out the directions as exactly as possible. Then do the exercise yourself, adding a paragraph in which you comment on its effectiveness as a means of stylistic practice.

8. Write an essay of about 300–500 words on the current scene in clothing fashions; make the style as deliberately different and strange as you can without badly damaging its intelligibility. Add a paragraph commenting on what the style has done to the substance of your essay.

HOW TO BECOME
A MAN OF GENIUS

George Bernard Shaw

The secret at the bottom of the whole business is simply this: there is no such thing as a man of genius. I am a man of genius myself, and ought to know. What there is, is a conspiracy to pretend that there are such persons, and a selection of certain suitable individuals to assume the imaginary character. The whole difficulty is to get selected.

On reflection I perceive that this explanation is too straightforward for anyone to understand. Let me try to come at it by another way. You will at least admit that Man, having, as he cynically believes, excellent private reasons for not thinking much of himself, has a praiseworthy desire to improve on himself—an aspiration after better things is what you probably call it. Now when a child wants something it has not got, what does it do? It pretends to have it. It gets astride of a walking stick and insists on a general conspiracy to pass that stick off as a horse. When it grows to manhood it gives up pretending that walking sticks are horses, not in the least because it has risen superior to the weakness of conspiring to cherish illusions, but because on leaving the nursery it has passed into a sphere in which real horses are attainable, at which point the pretence becomes unnecessary. The moment it becomes unnecessary, the pressure which kept all eyes closed to its absurdity ceases. Here you have the whole explanation of the fact that the grown man is more "sensible" than the child, or the civilized man than the savage. Because he is able to attain more, he pretends less. With regard to the things that are beyond his attainment, he pretends as arrantly as his five-year-old boy.

For example, he wants, as aforesaid, to improve on himself. But is such a want possible, seeing that Man, whatever he may suppose to the contrary, most certainly cannot conceive anything that is outside his own experience, and therefore in a sense cannot conceive anything higher than himself, nor desire a thing without conceiving it? But that difficulty is very easily got over. Pray, amiable sir or madam, what is the thing you call yourself? Is it yourself as you are with people you like or as you are with people who rub you the wrong way? Is it yourself before dinner or after it? Is it yourself saying your prayers or driving a bargain, listening to a Beethoven symphony or being hustled by a policeman to make way for a public procession, buying a present for your first love or paying your taxes, fascinating everyone in your best clothes or hiding your slippers and curl papers from the public eye? If your enemy might select some one moment of your life to judge you by, would you not come out mean, ugly, cowardly, vulgar, sensual, even though you be another Goethe; or if you might choose the moment yourself, would you not come out generous and handsome, though you may be, on an average of all your moments, a most miserly and repulsive person? At worst, you are brave when there is no danger, and openhanded when you are not asked for anything, as one may see by your sympathy with the heroes of your favorite novels and plays.

Our experience does, then, provide us with material for a concept of a superhuman person. You have only to imagine someone always as good as you were in the very loftiest ten seconds of your life, always as brave as you felt when you read The Three Musketeers, always as wise at a moment's notice as the books into which philosophers have garnered the corrected errors of their lifetime, always as selfless as you have felt in your hour of utmost satiety, always as beautiful and noble as your wife or husband appeared to you at the climax of the infatuation which led you to the matrimonial experiment which you may or may not have regretted ever since, and there you have your poet, your hero, your Cleopatra or whatever else you may require in the superhuman line, by a simple rearrangement of your own experience, much of which was itself arrived at by the same process.

Wise indeed and wisest among men would be he who could now say to me: Why should I deceive myself thus foolishly? Why not fix my affections, my hopes, my enthusiasms on men and women as they are, varying from day to day, and but rarely seeing the highest heaven through the clouds, instead of on these ideal monsters who never existed and never will exist, and for whose sake men and women now despise one another and make the earth ridiculous with Pessimism, which is the inevitable end of all Idealism? But the average man is not yet wise: he will have his ideals just as the child will have his walking stick horse. And the lower he is, the more extravagant are his demands. Everyone has noticed how severely fastidious a thorough-paced blackguard is about the character and conduct of the woman to whom he proposes to confide the honor of his name, whereas your great man scandalises his acquaintances by his tolerance of publicans and sinners. Again, if you are a dramatist writing plays for a theatre in a disreputable quarter, where every boy in the gallery is a pickpocket, your hero must be positively singing like a kettle with ebullient honesty, a thing which no law abiding audience could bear for half an hour.

Observe now that the actor who plays to the thieves' gallery is not really an outrageously honest man: he only lends himself to the desire of the audience to pretend that he is. But do not therefore conclude that he enjoys his position through no merit of his own. If that were so, why should he, and not the "extra gentleman" who silently carries a banner, and who vehemently covets his salary and his place in the cast, be the hero of the play? Clearly because of the superior art with which the hero is able to lend himself to the conspiracy. The audience craves intensely for every additional quarter inch of depth of belief in their illusion, and for every quarter inch they will pay solid money; whilst they will no less feelingly avoid the actor who fails to bear it out, or who, worse still, destroys it. Therefore the actor, though he may not have the merit they ascribe to him, has the merit of counterfeiting it well; and in this, as in all other things, it takes, as Dumas *fils* well said, "a great deal of merit to make even a small success." But that is only because the competition for leading parts is so tremendous in the modern world. The public is not exacting: it will choose the better of two actors for its hero when it has any choice; but it will have its hero anyhow, even when the best actor is a very bad one, as he often is.

Now let us go from the microcosm to the macrocosm—from the

cheap theatre to Shakespeare's great stage of "all the world," which, also, be it observed, has its thieves' gallery. On that stage there are many parts to be cast, since the audience will have its ideal king, its President, its statesman, its saint, its hero, its poet, its Helen of Troy, and its man of genius. No one can *be* these figments; but somebody must act them or the gallery will pull the house down. Napoleon, called on, as a man who had won battles, to cast himself for Emperor, grasped the realities of the situation, and, instead of imitating the ideal Cæsar or Charlemagne, took lessons from Talma. Other king's parts are hereditary: your Romanoff, your Hohenzollern, your Guelph walks through his part at his ease, knowing that with a crown on his head his "How d'ye do?" will enchant everyone with its affability, his three platitudes and a peroration pass for royal eloquence, and his manners and his coat seem in the perfection of taste. The divinity that hedges a king wrecks itself as effectually on a born Republican as on an English court tailor. I have seen a book by an American lady in which the Princess of Wales is ecstatically compared to "a vestal kneeling at some shrine." In England a judge is as likely as not to be some vulgar promoted advocate who makes coarse jokes over breach-of-promise cases; passes vindictive sentences with sanctimonious unction; and amuses himself off the bench like an ostler. But he is always spoken and written of as a veritable Daniel come to judgment. Mr. Gladstone's opinions on most social subjects are too childish to be intelligible to the rising generation; and Lord Salisbury makes blunders about the functions of governing bodies which would disqualify him for employment as a vestry clerk: but both gentlemen are highly successful in the parts of eminent statesmen. The fool of the family scrapes through an examination in the Greek testament by the bishop's chaplain; buttons his collar behind instead of before; and is straightway revered as a holy man. And the policeman, with his club and buttons, represents unspeakable things to the child in the street. The public has invested them all with the attributes of its ideals; and thenceforth the man who betrays the truth about them profanes those ideals and is dealt with accordingly.

It is now plain how to proceed in order to become a man of genius. You must strike the public imagination in such a fashion that they will select you as the incarnation of their ideal of a man of genius. To do this no doubt demands some extraordinary qualities, and sufficient professional industry; but it is by no means necessary to be what the public will pretend that you are. On the contrary, if you believe in the possibility of the ideal yourself without being vain enough to fancy that you realize it—if you retire discouraged because you find that you are not a bit like it—if you do not know, as every conjuror knows, that the imagination of the public will make up for all your deficiencies and fight for your complete authenticity as a fanatic fights for his creed, then you will be a failure. "Act well your part: there all the honor lies."

It is possible, however, that circumstances may cast you for such a humble part that it may be difficult even by any extremity of good acting to raise it to any prominence. You must then either be content in obscurity or else do what Sothern did with the part of Lord Dundreary in "Our American Cousin" or what Frederic Lemaître did with the part of Robert Macaire in "L'Auberge des Adrets." You must throw over the author's intention and create for yourself a fantastic leading part out of the business designed for a mere walking gentleman or common melodramatic villain. This is the resource to which I myself have been driven. Very recently the production of a play of mine [*Arms and the Man*] in New York led to the appearance in the New York papers of a host of brilliant critical and biographical studies of a remarkable person called Bernard Shaw. I am supposed to be that person; but I am not. There is no such person; there never was any such person; there never will or can be any such person. You may take my word for this, because I invented him, floated him, advertised him, impersonated him, and am now sitting here in my dingy second floor lodging in a decaying London Square, breakfasting off twopenn'orth of porridge and giving this additional touch to his make-up with my typewriter. My exposure of him will not shake the faith of the public in the least: they will only say "What a cynic he is!", or perhaps the more sympathetic of them may say, "What a pity he is such a cynic!"

It is a mistake, however, to suppose that a man must be either a cynic or an idealist. Both of them have as a common basis of belief the conviction that mankind as it really is is hateful. From this dismal and disabling infidelity the idealist escapes by pretending that men can be trained and preached and cultivated and governed and educated and self-repressed into something quite different from what they really are. The cynic sees that this regeneration is an imposture, and that the selfish and sensual Yahoo remains a Yahoo underneath the scholar's gown, the priest's cassock, the judge's ermine, the soldier's uniform, the saint's halo, the royal diadem and the poet's wreath. But pray where do these idealists and cynics get their fundamental assumption that human nature needs any apology? What is the objection to man as he really is and can become any more than to the solar system as it really is? All that can be said is that men, even when they have done their best possible, cannot be ideally kind, ideally honest, ideally chaste, ideally brave and so on. Well, what does that matter, any more than the equally important fact that they have no eyes in the back of their heads (a most inconvenient arrangement), or that they live a few score years instead of a few thousand? Do fully occupied and healthy people ever cry for the moon, or pretend they have got it under a glass case, or believe that they would be any the better for having it, or sneer at themselves and other people for not having it? Well, the time is coming when grown up people will no more cry for their present ideals than they now do for the moon.

Even the idealist system itself is no proof of any want of veracity on the part of the human race. Moral subjects require some power of thinking: and the ordinary man very seldom thinks, and finds it so difficult when he tries that he cannot get on without apparatus. Just as he cannot calculate without symbols and measure without a foot rule, so, when he comes to reason deductively, he cannot get on without hypotheses, postulates, definitions and axioms that do not hold good of anything really existent. The actions of a capitalist as deduced by a political economist, the path of a bullet as deduced by a physicist, do not coincide with the reality, because the reality is the result of many more factors than the economist or physicist is able to take into account with his limited power of thinking. He must simplify the problem if he is to think it at all. And he does this by imagining an ideal capitalist, void of all but mercenary motives, an ideal gun, pointed in an ideal direction with ideal accuracy and charged with ideal gunpowder and an ideal bullet governed in its motion solely by the ideal explosion of the ideal powder and by gravitation. Allow him all these fictions and he can deduce an ideal result for you, which will be contradicted by the first bargain you drive or the first shot you fire, but which is nevertheless the only *thinkable* result so far. Bit by bit we shall get hold of the omitted factors in the calculation, replace the fictitious ones by real ones, and so bring our conclusions nearer to the facts. It is just the same in our attempts to think about morals. We are forced to simplify the problems by dividing men into heroes and villains, women into good women and bad women, conduct into virtue and vice, and character into courage and cowardice, truth and falsehood, purity and licentiousness, and so forth. All that is childish; and sometimes, when it comes into action in the form of one man, dressed up as Justice, ordering the slaughter of another man, caged up as Crime, it is sufficiently frightful. Under all circumstances, its pageant of kings, bishops, judges and the rest, is to the eye of the highest intellect about as valid in its pretension to reality as the Lord Mayor's Show in

London is valid in its pretension to dignity. We shall get rid of it all some day. America has already got rid of two of its figures, the king and the subject, which were once esteemed vital parts of the order of nature, and defended with unmeasured devotion and bloodshed, as indeed they still are in many places. The America of to-day is built on the repudiation of royalty. The America of to-morrow will be built on the repudiation of virtue. That is the negative side of it. The positive side will be the assertion of real humanity, which is to morality as time and space are to clocks and diagrams.

QUESTIONS AND EXERCISES

1. Looking over the affirmative and the negative content of Shaw's language in this essay, do you find any strongly marked characteristics that might be clues to the man himself? Select an especially stylized paragraph, and try rewriting it to get rid of the negations.

2. Comment on Shaw's use of series and climax, citing specific examples. How does he use these devices to let the reader know more about himself?

3. Much of the success of Shaw's style is supposed to derive from his ability to surprise and even to shock his reader. Do you find jolts of this kind in the verbal surface of this essay? Explain how they work, and how their context is prepared for them by the author.

4. Shaw seems to assume a certain kind of relationship with the reader. What is this relationship (is it, for instance, intimately warm or coolly formal) and how does it affect the style of the piece?

5. A rhetorical question is one to which no actual answer is expected. Is Shaw's frequent use of rhetorical questions particularly consistent with his style generally in this essay? In what ways?

6. It might be argued that in his last two paragraphs Shaw loses contact with the main substance of his essay and produces a digressive inquiry into another matter. Write a 750-word essay agreeing or disagreeing with this proposition, and support your opinion with specific textual evidence, including, if possible, style.

7. In an essay of whatever length you find suitable, defend *idealism* against Shaw's attack. Use a style that is as Shavian (Shaw-ish) as you can make it.

8. Since Shaw set out deliberately to make himself something of a literary personality, it may be that this personal life-style of his is related to his verbal style. Comment on this idea in an analytic essay, making clear what notions about Shaw's personality you had before reading this essay.

BODY AND SOUL

William Golding

East Coast blanked out from North Carolina right up to the Canadian border; a half-continent under a pat of fog; nothing visible but the extreme tip of the Empire State Building; planes grounded. Fog, the airman's common cold; all the resources of science are squeaking and gibbering under it; lights blink unseen, radar echoes quiver and ping; the gigantic aircraft lumber round the ramps and aprons like death's-head moths in cold weather; money leaks away. We, the privileged, sit in a sort of underground air-raid shelter, racked by public-address systems and blasts of furious air-conditioning. Evening drags into night. Everything is astonishingly dirty, and time itself is stale. We sit.

Most passengers drift away, to go by train, or try a night's sleep in the airport hotel. But I am going too far to get there any way but by jet. Tomorrow I give the first of three lectures in Los Angeles, on the other side of America. Here it is midnight, or past midnight, or feels like midnight. I am late already, and must go by what flight I can. I cannot telegraph anyone, even though I shall land at the wrong airport.

A loudspeaker honks and burbles. Incredibly, and for the next hour, we have take-off and landing limits. Our plane is getting through; and sure enough, presently it bumbles out of the fog from the runway. I go with our group to Gate Nine, shudder into a freezing night with a dull grey roof. The jet crawls towards us, howling and whistling with rage, perhaps at the fog or perhaps at the human bondage which keeps it only just under control. For a moment or two, it faces us—no, is end-on to us; for here there is no touch of human, or animal, or insect, no face—only four holes that scream like nothing else in creation. Then it huddles round and is still. Doors open and two streams of passengers ooze out. Their faces are haggard. They ignore the night that has caught up with them. They stagger, or walk with the stiff gait of stage sleep-walkers. One or two look stunned, as if they know it is midnight more or less but cannot remember if it is today or tomorrow midnight and why

BODY AND SOUL: © 1962 by William Golding. Reprinted from his volume, *The Hot Gates and Other Occasional Pieces*, by permission of Harcourt, Brace & World, Inc. and Faber & Faber Ltd.

or what. Strange vehicles flashing all over with red lights come out of the darkness, not for the passengers, but to tend the jet. They crouch under the wings and the front end, attach themselves by tubes while all their lights flash, and lights on the jet flash, and the engines sink from a wail to a moan—a note, one might think, of resignation, as if the machine now recognizes that it is caught and will have to do the whole thing over again. But for half an hour they feed it well, while it sucks or they blow, and we stand, imprisoned by the freezing cold and our own need to be somewhere else. Jet travel is a great convenience.

Then we are in, fastening safety belts, and I peer out of the window with a naïveté which seems to increase as I grow older; and a succession of blue lights flick by faster and faster; and there is an eternity of acceleration at an angle of forty-five degrees, while the whistling holes under the wings seem no longer angry but godlike— see what we can do! Look, no hands! The "No Smoking, Fasten Your Safety Belts" notice disappears. Cupping my hands round my face, squinting sideways and down, I can make out that there is a white pat of fog slipping by beneath us, and over it a few stationary stars. An air hostess demonstrates the use of the oxygen masks.

Comfort, warmth flowing back into rigid hands, comparative silence, stillness except for an occasional nudge as the plane pierces a furlong of turbulence; I try to think of what our airspeed means: it remains nothing but arithmetic. The interior of the plane is like a very superior bus. Am thawed and relaxed. They say that this is not the latest mark of jet—do jets come any faster or bigger or plusher?

Glasses tinkle. Air Hostess brings round drinks—not what happens in a bus. Select Bourbon. (Always live off the country as far as possible.) I also secrete the TWA swizzlestick as a memento. Do not cross America often this way. Another Bourbon. That makes the two obligatory drinks before an American dinner. Am cheerful now —but second drink did not contain swizzlestick and wonder if I am detected? Air Hostess approaches for the third time and I cower— but no. She is English and recognizes a fellow-countryman. Speaks Kensingtonian, which sounds odd at this place and altitude. (Note to intending immigrants. Kensingtonian despised in a man. Gets him called a pouf. Do not know exactly what this term means, but cannot think it complimentary. On the other hand, Kensingtonian in a girl widely approved of, Americans think it cute.)

Peripeteia! English Air Hostess has read my books and seen me on English telly! I instantly acquire overwhelming status. Feel utterly happy and distinguished in a nice, diffident, English sort of way. Neighbour puts away his briefcase—we all have briefcases—then talks to me. Is physicist, naturally. Tells me about jets sucking air in at one end and blowing result of combustion out at the other. Encourage him, from a pure sense of *joie de vivre*. Rash, this, very. Tells me about navigation lights, navigation, fluids, including the sea, acceleration—Bourbon now dying down. Make my way forward to lavatory in diffident but distinguished manner, watched by all the unhappy briefcases who haven't been on telly, or haven't been noticed there by an Air Hostess. Lavatory wonderful, buttons everywhere. Push the lot, just to tell grandchildren. Tiny, ultimate fraction of our airstream is scooped in somewhere and directed to blow a jet vertically up out of the pan. Could balance celluloid balls on it and shoot them down with a rifle, as at fairs.

Return to seat and physicist continues course. American Air Hostess comes and talks. More status. Physicist goes to sleep. English Air Hostess comes and talks about London, Paris, Rome, Athens. American Air Hostess counters with Hawaii and Japan. Slight loss of status. I would like to go to sleep. Body here, can see it sitting in the seat. Soul still leaving Atlantic coast. Time? AHs have got on to books. It's the beard, I think. Beard down here on the deck, just beard. Beard in jet v. distinguished. Bourbon quite dead. Return to lavatory for a bit of peace in less distinguished manner. Jet still playing and cannot be bothered to push all the buttons. Return. Physicist says "Di!" very loudly in his sleep. Die? Diana? Diathermy? AHs wander away. Nod. Have instant vision of Ann with sweeper on carpet. She switches it off, switches off all the sweepers in the world, they fade, whining—am started awake—oh my God, my God! "No Smoking, Fasten Your Safety Belts"—briefcases stirring like sea-life under returning tide.

Am awake, dammit, or rather body is awake; soul two thousand miles behind, passing through Nashville, Tennessee, shall never be whole again, body mouldering in the jet, soul marching on towards Denver. Time? Bump, rumble, rumble, lights, lights! Los Angeles. Time? Enter Belshazzar's Hall. Body finds hall moving slowly, but they can't fool body. Body knows the movement is the world turning to catch up. More halls, enough for whole dynasties of Belshazzars.

Soul will enjoy this when it catches up. More halls, *Mene, mene.* Briefcases have vanished. Tunnels, fountains, lights, music, palms, lights, more halls—they would have to put *Mene, mene* out by roneograph, or use the public-address system. *A message for Mr. Belshazzar!* Am delirious, I think. Find broom supporting man in centre of hundredth hall. Body asks broom politely, "Which way is out, Bud?" Broom answers politely, "Don't arst me, Bud, we just built it." More halls. Movement of earth deposits body in cab which hurls it ten thousand miles through lights to a recommended English-type hotel. Body recognizes bed as English. Has knobs at each corner. Body falls on bed, giggling at thought of soul now plodding through Death Valley. Body undresses so as to get an hour or two of sleep, telephone rings. Bearleader would like to show body the sights. Body dresses and descends. Nice bearleader drives body through sunny Los Angeles and up the heights where the fire was. Body sees mountain road of burnt houses for film stars. Only thing left is row of swimming pools built on stilts out over the gorge, since there is nowhere else for them.

Descent to Pacific. Waves coming the wrong way—no, that was the Atlantic. Sherry in house. Lunch in university. Forty thousand students, or is it seventy? Own campus police and bus service. After lunch, body looks at lecture notes, but cannot bring itself to care. Body gives first lecture and hears its mouth making the appropriate noises. Soul not really necessary in this game. Has drinks beneath original Beerbohm cartoons. Has dinner with the Christmas Story lining the road outside, each tableau the size of a cottage with full-size figures in plaster and floodlit. Party after dinner. Body is told about the definitive Dickens and the Boswell factory. Body is nearly frightened to hear itself advise against the export of American novels. Stick to cars, it says. Soul would be very angry if it could hear that. Body finds itself getting smaller, or is it larger? Is led away, and falls on English-type bed with knobs at each corner.

At two o'clock in the morning there seemed to be a second person present. With the sort of effort one makes to achieve binocular vision, they united themselves; and soul in body, I was looking at the ceiling of a hotel bedroom in Los Angeles. The luxury of being whole was such that I could not sleep, but smoked till I felt like stockfish. The real trouble was that I had a defect of imagination which would not let me believe I was where I was, and yet I knew I was in Los Angeles. Being whole, I was immediately frightened at the vision of tomorrow's lecture and began to compose it in my sleepless head. That way the day dawned, and just as I ran out of cigarettes, my nice bearleader telephoned to set up the morning's sightseeing. We saw the Mormon temple, with a gold angel on the tower, far larger than any God has in heaven. We saw the colossal Medical Centre where the corridors run clean out of perspective to infinity at a point; where the patient is taken in at one end and can be served up as a complete set of demonstration slides at the other. We saw the beach—and for a moment I was really where I was—watching the waves turn over, and stunned by the acute realization that this had been here all the time, had not been created in Europe and exported to form part of a set. I lectured again, pleaded for an evening in bed, but sneaked off on my own—*peccavi*—and had dinner; filet mignon and a bottle of burgundy-type wine. (Note for wines-men: it was an Almaden '57; suffered like all California wines from that fatal inferiority complex—but once convinced you were a friend, it would offer you what it had). At two in the morning carried my filet mignon and my burgundy-type wine back to my English-type bed, and lay with my head full of tomorrow's lecture. Dawn.

Nice bearleader came and took me to see the San Gabriel mountains with snow on them and the Chinese Theatre, its pavements with footprints, handprints, graffiti of film stars on them; showed me Hollywood, Gangster's Corner, Mae West's hotel, the William Andrews Clarke Memorial Library. For ten ridiculously exciting seconds I held the MS of *The Importance of Being Earnest* in my hands. (You, too, have been awarded an Oscar!) We finished that jaunt in a bowling alley, where the beer was good, the telly in colour and the machines for setting up the pins seemed, in their implacable devotion, to be much more intelligent than anything else in sight.

I lecture, meet students, and pack grip in a flash. Meet faculty. Party. *N*th, I think. Now I am taken to dinner in an English-type restaurant to make me feel at home. Recognize it as English instantly, because the bartender and all the waiters are in full hunting kit. At one moment they gather round a table and sing "Happy Birthday" in close harmony. Los Angeles is the mostest, am utterly happy. What other place et cetera. Am eating abalone, the local must, and talking in six directions at once, but am suddenly seized and rushed away to jet, leaving soul still continuing conversations. Body loses way down to plane and is nearly sucked through engine, ha ha. Acceleration and fifty miles *square* of lights tilts under us. This is the latest mark of jet, they say, can see no difference, that is the Pacific down there, time, eleven o'clock.

American Air Hostess brings round Bourbon. Secrete swizzlestick. Another Bourbon. American Southern Belle-type Air Hostess, v. pretty, guesses I am English and a writer (beard in jet), comes and sits! Immense status. SBAH did Creative Writing Course at College. Said to her Prof.: "Ah aim to be a writer." Prof. said: "What do you know about life?" SBAH said: "Ah hev written a critical essay on Thomas Wolfe and a short story which ah would like you to read." Prof. read story, said: "Go and be an Air Hostess" —"So heah ah em!" Delightful girl, there ought to be a lot more of them and there probably are. Supper. Go to lavatory and discover this really *is* the latest mark of jet. Tiny, ultimate fraction of our airstream is scooped in somewhere, led into the pan and merely chases itself round and round and round.

Am tucked up solicitously for the night, but am still able to see out of the window, my goodness me, no sleep with a view like that. America sliding by, 650 miles an hour airspeed with 150 miles an hour tail wind; 800 miles an hour over the ground—no cloud. Cities, gleaming, glowing ravishments slide under us six miles down, lines of phosphorescence scored at right-angles to each other. Moon and snow. Stars, perceptibly wheeling. More molten cities. Body understands that America is crust of earth with fire inside, must break out somewhere, hence these scores, these right-angled lava cracks, these chessboard patterns of luminosity (with here and there a wink of veritable incandescence like the white spark on a red coal), but all soft as the tiny lights of a shock cradle. Garish street lamps, Christmas Decorations, traffic signals, window displays, sky signs, now softened, softened. Body lines up jet-hole with city—sees it swallow a whole street six miles long in seconds, how to take the children to school, scoop! three blocks of run-down houses, park, Motel, Motel, Motel, parking lot, cemetery, jump the sparking traffic lights, scoop! Drugstore, Charlies Cheeseburgers, Eats, Frolic Fashion House, Beautician, Physician, Mortician, Realty, News Office WinnDixie MountjoyToyTownSurplusWarStockCrossroadsChurchofChrist (Airconditioning)Square!MayoraltyFireStationPoliceStation HowardJohnsonSquare!LightsLightsSquare!LightsLightsLights RiverSquare! All sucked in and blown out, scooped up, hurled back, august, imperial, god-like, America, oh from up here and at this power, even unto weeping, America The—

SBAH is tinkling glasses and switching on lights. My God. BREAKFAST! Four hours out from Los Angeles—where soul is still engaged in fierce discussion of freedom, birth control, how to be happy though British, Emblems—four hours out, there is ahead of us the distinction between grey and black that betokens dawn over the curved Atlantic. Sure enough, the sweeper is switched off for a thirty-minutes' descent. Poor soul, no longer the centre of my sinful earth, but setting out just now on that long climb over the Rockies. Fasten your safety belts. And the time is. . . .

QUESTIONS AND EXERCISES

1. What is the effect of beginning the essay with a series of abrupt non-sentences? Does the entire first paragraph sustain this effect,

even though it eventually uses complete sentences? If so, how is this accomplished?

2. What is the nature and significance of the style-change in paragraph 12? At what point is there another major shift in the stylistic character of the piece?

3. The author is British, but the scene is American. How does Golding exploit this circumstance stylistically?

4. No one, presumably, would deny that the verbal style in this essay is highly specialized, "different," and obtrusive. Is its conspicuous oddness more a result of the essay's substance or of the author's particular self? Explain.

5. An essay of this type bears a certain obvious resemblance to a lyric poem. Suppose that the substance of this essay were translated into good metered and rhymed stanzas? Would such a translation be likely to improve or even to preserve the central effect that Golding has achieved? Why?

6. One of the things Golding has tried to capture in his style is the sensation of great velocity. Write a page of narrative in which you try for precisely the reverse effect—that of stasis, fixity, eventlessness. Add an analytic paragraph explaining how, technically, you have tried to gain the desired result.

7. Try writing a brief description in which you drastically depart from the usual syntax, grammatical structure, and vocabulary of English, retaining just enough to be intelligible. Test the result on some willing victim, to see whether you are actually intelligible or not. If not, rewrite.

8. Write an evaluative analysis of Golding's impressions of America, relating the stylistic technique to other devices used to produce the whole result.

CHAPTER SEVEN

Value

When the categories of analysis and critical description are exhausted, when all has been said that needs to be said about structure, style, rhetorical strategy, and the like, the reader may or may not be in an improved position to speak about the whole value of the piece he has read. The capacity to judge value—to say not merely what a thing is but whether it is good or not—is one that no textbook can pretend to deliver by formula. But value judgments are real as well as necessary acts, and certainly there is some point in discussing, briefly, the means by which they may reliably be formed. Analytic skill is not always a great asset here: We may be tempted to settle for dissection of the work rather than make a whole assessment of its quality. But the right kind of heightened critical awareness can, if sensibly controlled, sharpen the faculty of judgment as well as that of enjoyment.

An act of judgment tends, by its very nature, to be a selfish act. Not always, but very often, the particular evaluation of this or that element in our experience is little more than an act of self-assertion, or even of aggression, that is committed less because we feel the real need for a judgment than because we feel the real need for showing the world that *we* are there, importantly, in the presence of things worth judging. In fact, this aggressiveness may be a sign of health and vigor. If a person is trying to exercise discrimination and taste, he will be foolish to assume a fake attitude of passive impartiality. And there are often especially good reasons for making deeply personal assessments of an essay, since the essayist is above all else appealing to persons, man to man; he is not addressing a collective audience in an amphitheater or a jury in a courtroom. The manifest energy of his own distinctive views seems to call for an answering energy of judgment from the reader. Perhaps the most important consequence of this potentially aggressive instinct to put things in their deserved places is a tendency among readers to like an essay (or any piece of literature) more as they come to know it better. Familiarity, in this sense, rarely breeds contempt. By making itself intelligible to the reader, an essay has collaborated with him in an achievement not unlike an act of possession. For the reader, it is the next best thing to having written it himself. Of course, there are numerous exceptions. And there is a point of diminishing returns. Familiarity should not be permitted to deteriorate into a dull acquaintance with the repetitiously obvious. In the main, though, the principle is a sound one, and is what prompts us, in our best moments, to avoid snap judgments.

Many things are at stake here. Is it better for us, somehow more sane and wholesome, to admire and approve than to despise and reject? If so, then critical charity would be the usual practice among rational men; "if you can't say something nice, don't say anything at all." No doubt there is some virtue in this idea, however syrupy it seems. An intellectual life devoted largely to pernicious and negative judgments is likely to poison itself eventually. On the other hand, consider the nightmarish consequences of being able to like everything. The human mind has only a certain amount of power to grasp and organize its reality; if it does not select and discriminate amongst the infinitely various shadings of quality and value in experience, it will be lost in weltering chaos. Matthew Arnold saw the task of criticism as the identifying and preserving of the very best that has been thought and said during the course of human civilization. There may not be much of the very best; and for the ordinary reader, who is, after all, reacting to literature in other ways than the purely critical, there must be a gradation of value within the less sublime regions. Yet Arnold's idea remains absolutely right. We should have a sense of the very highest that human mind and art can accomplish. Perhaps a single reader will find that special illumination or radiance only a handful of times during his entire life. (If this volume contains even one or two essays that meet such a test, it is a remarkable volume.) But the recognition of such high achievement —the feeling that one is in the presence of unalterably profound truths, artfully expressed, that strike deep to the heart of the human situation—ought not imply the consequent *disapproval* of everything else. To distinguish the splendid from the very good is not to condemn the very good; there is room enough for condemnation when we distinguish the good from the mediocre. At each level on an absolute scale, a given work will probably be comparable to some other work in our acquaintance. In wise proportions, the twin evaluations of a thing in itself and as compared with other things can produce mature criticism and intelligent habits of taste. But the right mixture is not easily come by.

It was once regarded as a great mark of critical sophistication to say that a literary work should be judged not by some absolute standard but on its own terms. This idea has become a yawning cliché, no matter how well intended; and, what is worse, if accepted in its simplest form it badly distorts literary realities by implying that only one type of judgment is legitimate. We can at least try to put first things first.

The question to be asked first and most persistently about any literary production must be "So what?" This question goes directly to the *magnitude* of the writer's achievement, and no amount of misguided democratic chatter about the equal value of all literary projects can dispel it. Although the value of an essay on the economic effects of bad architectural taste *can* be *compared* with that of an essay on trends in window-shade design during the late 1940's, no serious reader really supposes that one is as "good" as the other, as long as both are written well. The elements that constitute magnitude or greatness are few, but they are powerful.

If an essay develops a universally recognizable theme, whether directly or by implication, it has a greater magnitude than the essay whose interest is topical and provincial. This judgment is not the result of elaborate mathematical calculations. We are not merely deciding that the greater the essay the greater the number of readers who can be interested in it. Magnitude is established only when the reader becomes consciously aware that the substance of the statement is so real and so much a part of basic human experience that it must appeal widely, not just geographically but in time. Rarely does a reader experience that exalted feeling, the sensation of knowing that what is before him is in no way restricted to his own time and place, yet is sharply pertinent there. This larger value does not at all imply that there is anything mean, petty, or deficient in an essay like Reed Whittemore's "The Cuteness of Well-Being" or John Kenneth Galbraith's "The Decline of the Machine." Though the appeal of each of these essays is in part circumscribed by temporal or geographical considerations, each points to certain essentially human truths that transcend the particularity of the moment, whereas Faulkner's "An Innocent at Rinkside" and Updike's "Hub Fans Bid Kid Adieu" are of a different order, not as "big," as we can recognize by imagining what sort of an audience either of them would find in Burma or the twenty-third century. Topical and local interest may renew itself, of course, quite abruptly, and the intensely topical essay will always have great interest for the historian or antiquarian. Again, it must be stressed that commentary on the present scene is the life blood of most essay-writing, and there is no intention here to call for a change in that state of affairs. If we had nothing but solemnly "universalized" disquisitions on Love, Death, Truth, Sport, and so on, the literary prospect would be dreary indeed. Still, special honor is due the graceful joining of the topical and universal.

Second, there is the question of *originality*, or, to use an older-fashioned word, "inventiveness." The really fine essay will succeed, one way or another, in showing us some aspect of the world as we have never seen it before. But the notion of originality needs some careful qualifying. It is not enough that an essay says something that has never been said before in a way that has never been used before. That differentness or newness must recognizably come from its author's total grasp of experience rather than from technical experimentation. The best sort of originality announces itself quietly; not until the reader has finished the essay, perhaps, does he realize how truly original it is. Sensitivity to this element of literary merit is not something that can be taught or inculcated by helpful hints, but at least one practical question can and should be asked repeatedly by a serious reader: Is the author faking? This involves two related matters. First, we should be able to determine before we have read very far in the essay whether or not it was written because the author really had something to say. If not, if he was only casting about for an occasion or subject because he thought it high time to write an essay, the signs of artificiality and contrivance usually give him away. At the worst, we may not be inclined to believe what he says; at the best, it will not matter to us very much that he has said it. Closely related is the question of the writer's honesty in developing his thesis. A good essay always gives the impression that the force of its representation and argument is solidly backed by the author's clear understanding of whatever may be pertinent to the subject. But where the advancing statement depends on special manipulation, selection, suppression, or arbitrary interpretation of evidence, where we see that clever management is being used to make up for a deficient intellectual integrity, our judgment of the result must be highly unfavorable. Too many readers are excessively reluctant to pass judgment on failings of this sort, assuming that after all "the author knows best what he is doing." But sharp practice in literary expression deserves exactly the same treatment that it gets in other places.

Finally, of course, there is the essay's sheer artistic competence—the element that we have in mind (or should have in mind) when we say that a work must be judged on its own terms. How well, we ask, does the piece succeed in fulfilling the intention that it has set for itself? Within the limits of these intentions, what sort of achievement has been realized? Thus perfection of form and technique should be thought of not as categorically separate from magnitude, but as that quality that permits magnitude to emerge fully where the other conditions of excellence have been met.

The essayist's mastery of his material, the professional skill that he brings to the difficult task of verbal composition itself, can be measured in a great many ways, most of which are probably familiar to you. Some of the more useful criteria are always worth special mention: internal consistency, proportioned harmony of parts, control, wholeness, grace. Examples of success and failure in these various regards might well be endless. Here, a single hypothetical case will be used to represent the whole range. Suppose that an essay on that popular subject, capital punishment, announces itself distinctly as an argumentative piece; that is, the first paragraph informs the reader that such and such a case is going to be made for the abolition of the death penalty. Words like "prove," "show," and "demonstrate" promise the well-disciplined logical assault to come. But then the author uses up most of his space on an informative account of the history of capital punishment, with only occasional reminders of the thesis thrown in as if to show that he has not reneged on his original promise. Now, it is just possible that, in a situation like this, the author is trying to make use of an immense irony: his real point being that the history of the phenomenon itself *is* argument enough, the sort of self-evident testimony that makes all further reasoning superfluous. More likely, though, he is not conscious of his inconsistency, and his essay is a poor one. Or—to take up another sort of difficulty—imagine that the essay is to be composed of a series of paragraphs in each of which the author first puts a particular positive argument and then demolishes the relevant counter-argument (for example, paragraph 1 argues first that taking human life is morally evil, and second that capital punishment for murderers does not especially deter other murderers from taking human life). But near the end of the essay the author apparently tires of this pattern and decides to omit the second, demolishing part of one paragraph in order to move more quickly to his impassioned summary and conclusion. The result may be disastrous for the credible force of his essay, for he has inadvertently made possible the impression that he has no retort to make against one of his opponent's best counter-arguments and thus has slyly omitted it. Or perhaps he *has* slyly omitted it. Either way the impression is damaging. A third form of malfunction might be the use of a jaunty or colloquial style to express a highly structured and formally arranged argument. Another might be a digression disproportionately long, or a failure to use visual effects where the reader has been led to expect them, or the simple failure to complete an anticipated parallelism or climax.

An essay can be bad for other reasons than its positively definable errors or deformities. There may be errors of omission as well, missed opportunities that, if a reader becomes aware of them, can completely undercut whatever strength the essay may possess in other respects. A common failing is the writer's inability to provide at crucial points the concrete imagery or examples that would have fixed his argument in the reader's memory. Another is the inadequate definition of those terms on which the ensuing argument is to depend. A third is the failure to cite outside authorities in cases where it is impossible to go forward on the strength of mere personal opinion. And in some essays, of course, the reader may sense important omissions, although he may never be able to say exactly what it is that he misses.

But—and this should be the point to remember—*if* an essayist has avoided all the technical pitfalls and has polished his essay until it is a technically perfect piece of verbal machinery, he has been able to do so not just because he has literary skill but because his intention, the substance of his essay as he conceived it, had from the outset something of magnitude and honest originality in it.

In reading the essays that follow, you should not assume that there is some neat and predictable alternation of the very bad and the very good. There are no clay pigeons here. Still, the hope is that you will find some of these four more satisfying than others, and be able to say why.

I. R.: THE OPIATE OF THE ELITE

Benjamin DeMott

June 1960

Fifty years ago it would have been difficult to name in a phrase the unique quality or principle of American intellectual life—there was still too much Europe (subjects, disciplines, scholarship, learning) left in the thinking mind. Nowadays, though, the peculiar national

I.R.: THE OPIATE OF THE ELITE: From *Hells & Benefits* by Benjamin DeMott. Copyright © 1962 by Benjamin DeMott, Basic Books, Inc., New York.

note sounds louder, and the problem is easier to solve. Where but in America, after all, is last week's Marxist this week's analysand and next week's hipster or priest? Where but in America is the life of a word one season? [1] Where but in America do the national heroes of yesteryear—Huck and Jim, Ishmael and Queequeeg—become (at an interesting critic's awakening) mere male lovers caught in the act? Where but in America is the thinking man's favorite reading a volume of paperback philosophy that "shows him" how Aquinas and Hegel (or Plato and Pepys or Darwin and Hakluyt or Melville and Mighty Mouse) are one? The ground of this taste and behavior, the center from which the new illumination flows, is the principle of *Instant Redefinition*, an item which when properly identified and celebrated may well rank at the level of the twin-burger and sidecar among major American contributions to culture.

Highbrows are not of course the only people aware of or responsible for this contribution. A nod must go to the common semanticist, that bird of no especially elegant feather who long ago began amusing himself with paradoxes of functional name-changing (If I enter the room by the window, the window "is" a door; if I look through the door to see what is in the room, the door "is" a window), and thereby helped to lay the shifty foundation for IR. And an award of some sort is also due those political and commercial giants who, by playing the game of Redefinition tirelessly over the years, have done much to create an audience capable of recognizing achievement in the field. It was an amateur name-changer from Wisconsin, a character who had never heard of Korzybski, who (ages ago) first managed to enchant the nation with the trick of spinning terms: I have 350 *Communists*, 175 *sympathizers*, 35 *partyliners* . . . And by the same token it is the unsung adman who, whether working with ordinary domestic redefinitions (Surf equals soap, Crest equals health), or on projects of international reverberation (Puerto Rico equals money), has functioned as the indispensable link between the superb verbal agility of the Elite and homely inarticulateness of the mob. Nor should it be forgotten, in any serious effort to apportion credit, that some of the most daring ventures in IR have come (astonishingly) from stodgy enterprises like banks and investment

[1] Who can remember when a *square* was a figure and a *sick comedian* was an ill man? Who can recognize the *Model T* now that it is called a *Classic Car?* Was there not a time—hardly a wink ago, it seems—when *vodka* meant drunken, rough-bearded commissars, not smart Martinis? a time when *Spring* was not a cigarette, when the *summit* was not a conference, when *sitting* was not a job—a time when *Beats* could be counted and *Hips* reduced, when a *package* was something you carried instead of negotiated with Paramount and Bennett Cerf? There was, there was, but we shall not see its like again.

houses. Hayden, Stone and Company for example burst forth this year with a market letter that quoted a text of Micah ("What does the Lord require of thee but to do justice, to love mercy, and to walk humbly with thy God?") and subsequently redefined it as "this bullish psychology." Shields and Company, in the days of the artful and famous Mr. Walter Gutman, produced classic work in the genre, notably a stunning redefinition of the modern artist as a *growth stock:*

> . . . people with money are speculating in art like [*sic*] they do in stocks. . . . If you want to make money there's a great group of only partially recognized talent to choose from, here are some of the names—Forst, Leslie, Segal, Grillo, Wolf-Kahn, Frank, Katz, McElroy—the Museum of Modern Art is showing work of 16 younger artists—there's money in art, I know from experience. You can become a Friend of the Whitney Museum if you want to along with Armand Erpf of Loeb, Rhoades & Co., and Joseph Hirshhorn of uranium riches, Roy Neuberger and Howard Lipman who somehow or other get there first and most quietly each year with one of the most spectacular stocks—this year it was Universal Match—they were in long before the people I know told me about it.

This commendable IR activity on the fringes of intellectual life should not, however, be allowed to obscure the truth that the original achievements in the line were uniquely the product of the Elite —founding fathers whose gifts enabled them to see Lewis Carroll as Kafka, St. Augustine as Sorel, years before anyone dreamt of a market for such insights. And happily (as any evening's random reading testifies) the Elite continues to be responsible for the most strikingly ingenious applications in the field. While clods, authorities, and experts even at this date deal dully and seriously with the question whether the Guggenheim Museum of Frank Lloyd Wright is an honorable, useful, or adequate *museum,* IR apprentices writing in art journals and gallery catalogues shuck off all that boredom by renaming the place completely. (Soaring above the brutally exigent fact that the object discussed is a building in which nothing but pictures and fire extinguishers are hung, one critic declares that Wright's museum "is" a Dadaist Funhouse: argument over, redefinition complete.) Or again: while dryasdust scholars and statisticians pore over census figures and eye-wearying tables from the Bureau of Labor Statistics, laboring to buttress tiresome answers to tiresome questions about the nature of recent shifts in what is called the "pyramid of society," a free-spirited IR man leaps forward to quicker and more amusing questions. Why say *pyramid* at all? why not a new name?—bulb? hourglass? fishing bob? Addressing himself to the matter in an analytical *Horizon* article called "The Future American Class System" (illustrated in analytical red, white and blue), Mr. Stimson Bullitt wrote: "the shape of society . . . will resemble not an hourglass but a fishing bob, or a pair of coolie hats laid brim to brim with a spike projecting from the apex of each. More of the people will be clustered near the equator which divides the two classes. However, the spread between the two extremes of talent—the spikes at top and bottom—will be greater than in the past." Old pyramid becomes new bob and the reader escapes with not a single statistic jangling his brain.

As these examples indicate, part of the fascination which masters of IR undoubtedly will exercise over future historians stems from their lightfootedness, their nearly divine power of leaping with perfect poise from summit to summit, avoiding the pathetic grubbing after facts or documents or truth which so often gravels the readers of learned men, and yet invariably achieving a triumphant transformation of whatever their winged labels touch. The pedant is miserably passive; he cannot sweep aside the mouldering heaps of biographical information that assure him that such a figure as, say, Dostoeyevski, was a tormented soul throughout his life—a neurotic, an alienated mind. But the nimble IR racer, rapid and active, travels under lighter burdens of knowledge. He can say, as Professor Sidney Hook said in his recent *Political Power and Personal Freedom*, that "under the Czarist regime Dostoeyevski in his most fruitful years was a conformist." What is more, the IR-ist can move quite as swiftly in reverse. What is Richard Nixon? asked Mr. Norman Mailer in his *Advertisements for Myself*, and answered: a hipster like Thelonius Monk and Heidegger. Who is Freud? asked Mr. Erich Fromm in his book about that thinker, and answered: a "very insecure" type. What is a poem by T. S. Eliot? asked Professor Marshall McLuhan in his "Media Log" (1960) and answered: "a direct application of the method of the popular radio-tube grid circuit. . . ."

To be sure, the IR-ist does much more than protect the thrill-seeking reader against sluggish information and odious truth. In the recent past, indeed, there have been occasions when nothing but his gift stood between the public and misconceptions that could have done appalling damage to the nation's key institutions. Not long ago, for example, evidence was put in circulation that told heavily against the reputations of several eastern universities. Editors throughout the country were in receipt of well-authenticated reports indicating that some of America's unknown middle-western institutions of learning, colleges of no réclame whatever (Kalamazoo, for one), were having extraordinary success in producing serious intellectuals and scientists—a greater success (proportionally) than that of Harvard and Yale. What could such news mean except that these long-chuckled-at-schools, objects of mockery and condescension, stood for purposefulness of teaching, intensity of thought, unduplicated in the institutions known to be The Best? Plainly the national interest demanded that Americans believe that their greatest institutions are large, exclusive, and famous: was it not likely that uncertainty about the preeminence of Yale and Harvard would lead directly to uncertainty about Cadillacs or even about Time, Inc.? A brilliant IR agent, Mr. David Riesman, asked himself this question and thereafter threw himself manfully into the breach, managing in one superlative paragraph to crush the enemy by redefining successful education as Boobism:

> . . . many of the leading and most distinguished universities (Harvard, Yale, and Princeton for example) have turned out relatively few scientists in proportion to their graduates, whereas a number of small and often impoverished liberal arts colleges, primarily in the middle West, have turned out, in proportion to their enrollments, a great many. . . . In other words, the very lack of cosmopolitanism of some of these colleges (especially perhaps in the middle West), and the lack of cosmopolitanism of the students who . . . went there, meant that a teacher of even moderate quality and interest in his students could accumulate disciples quite readily. Conversely, the inferior record of the great cosmopolitan universities in recruiting undergraduates into academic careers has in my judgment been partly due to the fact that students who went there have had many other choices in mind. (Likewise their social science professors, busy with graduate students, with consultantships, and with all the opportunities and temptations of a metropolis, have also had other alternatives to looking for disciples among their undergraduate students.) That is, such students have found other ways to spend their time, even other intellectual ways, than in the laboratory or in the office of the favorite professor. They could envisage themselves (assuming they eschewed business) becoming diplomats, journalists, or TV script-writers, along with a thousand other opportunities offered by the big city. ("The College Professor," in *Education in the Age of Science*, ed. Brand Blandshard, 1959.)

Had it not been for Mr. Riesman, the public might have persisted in the delusion that a man devoted to teaching isn't a neurotic "looking for disciples" among undergraduates, and could even have convinced itself that only sociologists regard earnest and capable teaching as a product of naivete and narrowness.

True, opportunities for service of this sort do not occur daily:

the life of an IR agent is not lived at a continuous pitch of vibrant selflessness. Still, these men have saved more than the reputation of Harvard. More than once a writer who has felt that *his* reputation was being encroached upon by mere imitators has shrewdly reconstituted himself as an IR man simply to set the record straight. Thus, when William Faulkner was asked (by the English Club at the University of Virginia) to say a word about Salinger's *Catcher in the Rye,* he answered as follows:

> His [Salinger's] story was [of] an intelligent, very sensitive young man who was—[in] this day and time—an anachronism, was almost an obsolescence, trying to cope with a struggle with the present day world which he was not fitted for, when he didn't want money, he didn't want position, anything, he just wanted to find man and wanted something to love, and he couldn't. There was nothing there. The nearest he came to it was his sister who was a child and though she tried to love him she couldn't understand his problem. The only other human beings he ran into he had preconceptions to doubt . . . (*Faulkner in the University,* ed. F. L. Gwynn and J. L. Blotner, 1959.)

Sentences like these neatly redefine Holden Caulfield as Quentin Compson of *The Sound and the Fury,* and clarify the important question of precedence. And beyond such minor rescues, there have been moments when, owing to nothing more than a single judicious application of IR, whole art forms that have suffered neglect or even opprobrium have been restored to their proper significance. A season or so ago Random House brought out an unpretentious looking, gaily-jacketed volume of Mr. Stephen Becker about the history of funnies and cartoons—an item called *Comic Art in America* that was richly illustrated with old strips, cartoons, and big print. Suspecting no IR trap, one picked up the book prepared for a nostalgic evocation of the Sunday afternoons of youth—and was stunned to read:

> The drawing style is more complex than we might think at first glance, seeing the free use of white space, straight lines and patches of black. The backgrounds are not complicated, but they contribute to the sense of reality. . . . His line was already clean and sure; his backgrounds were open and uncluttered. . . . The facial expressions were beautifully simple . . .

What are these sentences about? Why, about *Jiggs* and *Smitty!* Ugliness redefined as art, a technical appreciation of *kitsch,* a recovery comparable to Lascaux! Although (as is the case with many works of IR) skimming sentences in Mr. Becker's book is like trying to stand up on a turntable, it should be said that the moment at which assurances vanish in *Comic Art in America*, the moment of redefinition when *Skippy* and *Tillie* become *draftsmanship*, is a trifle more moving (literally) than a page of the usual IR paperback claiming that Freud's other name is Marx. For while the latter names are often no more than mere counters, Jiggs and Lester De Pester have genuine reverberations: in altering his relationship to them the average reader alters a whole landscape of mind.

By studying this or any other IR alteration—funnies as art, painting as growth stock, Nixon as hipster—a researcher could doubtless arrive at a model of the new-style thinking mind. But since it is improbable that such a project is yet under way, the present moment has to be thought of simply as another time of transition, a period just preceding the formalization of an exciting new conceptual scheme in psychology. This is not to say that the transition will be absolutely smooth: a current of opposition to IR does flow. As might be expected (what intellectual advance was ever easily accomplished?), a few clerks and greybeards profess to regard the emergence of IR as a sign of failing cultural health. Some persist in claiming that a mark of a sophisticated or truly educated mind has always been disbelief that a mere switch of labels, the mere shout of a magic word, can suffice to alter the essential nature of the object named. And there is, of course, a battered shard or two of evidence that supports this view. That a belief in word magic is characteristic of the childish mind is suggested by certain fantasies called *children's books* (the boy Roland, in Stephane Nelly's book of that name, says "Crack" and mink skins come to life, chalk animals burst off the blackboard). That certain superstitious inquirers of the dead past have inveighed against the idle shifting of labels can be demonstrated by the example of Sir Thomas Browne, who three centuries ago warned against those who thrust "new names or notions upon Authentic Virtues and Vices." And as is well known, one or two dour minds of the present age (Orwell, for instance) have urged that the so-called perversion of IR which issues in Great Redefinitions like War is Peace and Peace is War is nothing less than the key to the monstrosity of totalitarianism.

But what is missing from all antediluvian prejudice of this kind is (clearly) any deep historical sense, any truly sensitive awareness of the differences between former ages and our own. As already indicated, the grand record of intellectual history over the past thirty years amply establishes the advent of a period (our own) when men are able to persuade themselves that by attaching a new label to their cast of thought, replacing zeal with zen, they in fact make themselves new. Moreover, the present age has convictions about the very *nature* of ideas that are unique and that explain in themselves the gap between traditionalist standards and those of IR. In our age a valuable idea—a jazz bassoon, a recessed filter—dawns in the mind of a thinker who is styled an *Idea Man;* the latter talks the idea (also called a gimmick or stick) into his Dictet and a thousand mere technicians (idealess men) carry it out, while the Idea Man retires to invite his Muse again. In the classical model of the intellectual life the situation is different. A new idea is regarded as meaningless until documented, until its originator succeeds in relating it to an existent body of thought, in underpinning it with observation, in assessing it with an eye toward revealing both its strengths and weaknesses. Or again, to mention only one more of a dozen major differences in modes of thought between this and earlier ages: in today's ad agency it is possible to have a name for a soap or a moon-shot before the soap exists—not one name (Fab, Vel) but a dozen, each of them a name without a referent. But in the older world it was assumed that thoughtful men would have no dealings with words that stood for nothing: a new label (the indeterminancy principle, dementia praecox in remission, Joe Christmas) could be justified only if it were a name for a complicated series of experiments, emotional responses, imaginative probings and weighings of experience, only if it finally signified a genuine accretion of knowledge, imaginative, moral, or scientific. Looked at as a fossilic survival, the sense of intellection just described may possess certain attractions, may inspire a quiver of nostalgia—but to allow the fancy too much play here would be foolish. If the present age is one in which intellectual endeavor becomes increasingly a matter of "having an Idea" in the "new-name" sense, if the characteristic term of praise in this age is not "thorough," or "complete," or "solid," but *suggestive,* it does not follow that IR is the cause rather than the consequence of this development. Intelligent men who comprehend the direction of the future will in short strike no ostrich-like posture at this moment, but assume cheerfully that since former ages admit to having had nothing but a beast in view, it is not less than wise to welcome the new.

Whether the welcome will be enthusiastic anywhere on earth except here is perhaps a question. Certainly England has shown signs of resistance. The principle of snappy redefinition, the idea of altering a situation by the mere tossing forth of a new epithet, continues to be regarded by English fogies young and old as a subject mainly for jokes. IR is never encountered as part of the armor of a young, passionate Englishman who regards himself (as Norman Mailer regards himself) as the heroic talent of the age; instead it appears only in the tiny handbooks of such humorists as Stephen Potter, who seem determined not to allow IR to become more than another gamesman's ploy. But the strength of this resistance can be exaggerated: America is, after all, not quite alone. When account is taken both of its enormous cultural influence and of the voice of the political master of IR, the Soviet Free Thinker—that immensely forceful redefiner of such terms as Evolution and God—it seems improbable that foreign places will not willy-nilly enter the new dispensation soon. And for this reason, if for no other, it is interesting to speculate about the future of the label IR itself. At the moment it is still feasible to stand back, as it were, and view the initials as mere symptoms of the condition that they pretend to define—but ages hence the case will be otherwise: the IR factor will be the unifying principle of all culture, the blessed and blessing softener of the universal brain. There will be churches then, surely, perhaps even some IR saints. And the latter will be chosen (inevitably) from IR's first generation—today's highbrow Americans, those unique characters who already are everything by starts and nothing long, swervers from one vocabulary to another, name-changers, Real Shifty Guys, figures who have yet to say (and never will) "Teach me to stand still." A vision to excite every ambitious soul! For the light it casts on the activity of such sou's (before the moment of their exaltation), and upon the Mental Age they represent, and hence upon the future of The Mind, the principle of IR deserves to be treated even now, if not with adoration, then with (at the least) only an extremely *wary* contempt.

QUESTIONS AND EXERCISES

1. So what? If you have trouble with this question, try question 3.
2. A frequent sign that something has gone wrong with an essay (or its reader) is the positive awareness, as one reads through it, of an alternative way of saying all this. The really well-made essay will probably strike us as having been constructed in the best possible way and will not give our minds a chance to wander off in search of alternatives. Is DeMott's essay open to comment in this respect? If so, how and where?
3. Do you believe that the author has said something necessary here? Or has he deliberately manufactured an opportunity to display his ironical sense of things? Try to identify the elements in the essay that produce your response.

4. Does the author's representation of IR remain consistent? That is, do all of his examples represent a single identifiable tendency in our use of language? Discuss fully, specifying variations if and when they occur.

5. Comment on the writer's sense of structural proportion as it is revealed in this essay. Where does he define the underlying cause of IR? Would it have been better to leave causes out of consideration altogether?

6. Assess the universal appeal of this essay, as compared with its topical interest. Do you find places (sentences, paragraphs) in which the topical is converted to genuinely universal terms? Explain how this is done.

7. Write a two-page commentary on the sources of the effect of sincerity (or its opposite) in this essay.

8. Write a highly condensed account of the criteria according to which this essay would be judged successful. Are these the criteria that your first reading of the essay naturally suggested? Discuss.

9. Take any long paragraph from "I. R.: The Opiate of the Elite" and rewrite it in such a way as to produce, if possible, a more persuasive effect on an audience. (Preserve its original length.)

10. Discuss analytically DeMott's use of humor in this essay.

SOOTFALL AND FALLOUT

E. B. White

Turtle Bay, October 18, 1956

This is a dark morning in the apartment, but the block is gay with yellow moving vans disgorging Mary Martin's belongings in front of a house a couple of doors east of here, into which (I should say from the looks of things) she is moving. People's lives are so exposed at moments like this, their possessions lying naked in the street, the light of day searching out every bruise and mark of indoor living. It is an unfair exposé—end tables with nothing to be at the end of, standing lamps with their cords tied up in curlers, bottles of

---

SOOTFALL AND FALLOUT: (Turtle Bay, October 18, 1956) From *The Points of My Compass* by E. B. White. Copyright © 1956 by E. B. White. Originally appeared in *The New Yorker* and reprinted by permission of Harper & Row, Publishers and Hamish Hamilton Ltd.

vermouth craning their long necks from cartons of personal papers, and every wastebasket carrying its small cargo of miscellany. The vans cause a stir in the block. Heads appear in the windows of No. 230, across the way. Passers-by stop on the sidewalk and stare brazenly into the new home through the open door. I have a mezzanine seat for the performance; like a Peeping Tom, I lounge here in my bathrobe and look down, held in the embrace of a common cold, before which scientists stand in awe although they have managed to split the atom, infect the topsoil with strontium 90, break the barrier of sound, and build the Lincoln Tunnel.

What a tremendous lot of stuff makes up the cumulus called "the home"! The trivet, the tiny washboard, the fire tools, the big copper caldron large enough to scald a hog in, the metal filing cabinets, the cardboard filing cabinets, the record player, the glass and the china invisible in their barrels, the carpet sweeper. (I wonder whether Miss Martin knows that she owns an old-fashioned carpet sweeper in a modern shade of green.) And here comes a bright little hacksaw, probably the apple of Mr. Halliday's eye. When a writing desk appears, the movers take the drawers out, to lighten the load, and I am free to observe what a tangle Mary Martin's stationery and supplies are in—like my wife's, everything at sixes and sevens. And now the bed, under the open sky above Forty-eighth Street. And now the mattress. A wave of decency overtakes me. I avert my gaze.

The movers experience the worst trouble with two large house plants, six-footers, in their great jars. The jars, on being sounded, prove to be a third full of water and have to be emptied into the gutter. Living things are always harder to lift, somehow, than inanimate objects, and I think any mover would rather walk up three flights with a heavy bureau than go into a waltz with a rubber plant. There is really no way for a man to put his arms around a big house plant and still remain a gentleman.

Out in back, away from the street, the prospect is more pleasing. The yellow cat mounts the wisteria vine and tries to enter my bedroom, stirred by dreams of a bullfinch in a cage. The air is hazy, smoke and fumes being pressed downward in what the smog reporter of the *Times* calls "a wigwam effect." I don't know what new gadget the factories of Long Island are making today to produce such a foul vapor—probably a new jet applicator for the relief of nasal congestion. But whatever it is, I would swap it for a breath of fresh air. On every slight stirring of the breeze, the willow behind Mary Martin's wigwam lets drop two or three stylish yellow leaves, and they swim lazily down like golden fish to where Paul, the handyman, waits with his broom. In the ivy border along the wall, watchful of the cat, three thrushes hunt about among the dry leaves. I can't pronounce "three thrushes," but I can see three thrushes from this window, and this is the first autumn I have ever seen three at once. An October miracle. I think they are hermits, but the visibility is so poor I can't be sure.

This section of Manhattan boasts the heaviest sootfall in town, and the United States of America boasts the heaviest fallout in the world, and when you take the sootfall and the fallout and bring smog in on top of them, I feel I am in a perfect position to discuss the problem of universal pollution. The papers, of course, are full of the subject these days, as they follow the Presidential campaigners around the nation from one contaminated area to another.

I have no recent figures on sootfall in the vicinity of Third Avenue, but the *Times* last Saturday published some figures on fallout from Dr. Willard F. Libby, who said the reservoir of radioactive materials now floating in the stratosphere from the tests of all nations was roughly twenty-four billion tons. That was Saturday. Sunday's *Times* quoted Dr. Laurence H. Snyder as saying, "In assessing the potential harm [of weapons-testing], statements are always qualified by a phrase such as 'if the testing of weapons continues at the present rate . . .' This qualification is usually obsolete by the time the statement is printed." I have an idea the figure twenty-four billion tons may have been obsolete when it appeared in the paper. It may not have included, for instance, the radioactive stuff from the bomb the British set off in Australia a week or two ago. Maybe it did, maybe it didn't. The point of Dr. Snyder's remark is clear; a thermonuclear arms race is, as he puts it, self-accelerating. Bomb begets bomb. A begets H. Anything you can build, I can build bigger.

"Unhappily," said Governor Harriman the other night, "we are still thinking in small, conventional terms, and with unwarranted complacency."

The habit of thinking in small, conventional terms is, of course, not limited to us Americans. You could drop a leaflet or a Hubbard squash on the head of any person in any land and you would almost certainly hit a brain that was whirling in small, conventional circles. There is something about the human mind that keeps it well within the confines of the parish, and only one outlook in a million is non-parochial. The impression one gets from campaign oratory is that the sun revolves around the earth, the earth revolves around the United States, and the United States revolves around whichever city the speaker happens to be in at the moment. This is what a friend of mine used to call the Un-Copernican system. During a Presidential race, candidates sometimes manage to create the impression that their thoughts are ranging widely and that they have abandoned conventional thinking. I love to listen to them when they are in the throes of these quadrennial seizures. But I haven't heard much from either candidate that sounded unconventional—although I have heard some things that sounded sensible and sincere. A candidate could easily commit political suicide if he were to come up with an unconventional thought during a Presidential tour.

I think Man's gradual, creeping contamination of the planet, his sending up of dust into the air, his strontium additive in our bones, his discharge of industrial poisons into rivers that once flowed clear, his mixing of chemicals with fog on the east wind add up to a fantasy of such grotesque proportions as to make everything said on the subject seem pale and anemic by contrast. I hold one share in the corporate earth and am uneasy about the management. Dr. Libby said there is new evidence that the amount of strontium reaching the body from topsoil impregnated by fallout is "considerably less than the seventy percent of the topsoil concentration originally estimated." Perhaps we should all feel elated at this, but I don't. The correct amount of strontium with which to impregnate the topsoil is *no* strontium. To rely on "tolerances" when you get into the matter of strontium 90, with three sovereign bomb testers already testing, independently of one another, and about fifty potential bomb testers ready to enter the stratosphere with their contraptions, is to talk with unwarranted complacency. I belong to a small, unconventional school that believes that *no* rat poison is the correct amount to spread in the kitchen where children and puppies can get at it. I believe that *no* chemical waste is the correct amount to discharge into the fresh rivers of the world, and I believe that if there is a way to trap the fumes from factory chimneys, it should be against the law to set these deadly fumes adrift where they can mingle with fog and, given the right conditions, suddenly turn an area into another Donora, Pa.

"I have seen the smoky fury of our factories—rising to the skies," said President Eisenhower pridefully as he addressed the people of Seattle last night. Well, I can see the smoky fury of our factories drifting right into this room this very minute; the fury sits in my throat like a bundle of needles, it explores my nose, chokes off my breath, and makes my eyes burn. The room smells like a slaughterhouse. And the phenomenon gets a brief mention in the morning press.

One simple, unrefuted fact about radioactive substances is that scientists do not agree about the "safe" amount. All radiation is harmful, all of it shortens life, all is cumulative, nobody keeps track of how much he gets in the form of X-rays and radio-therapy, and all of it affects not only the recipient but his heirs. Both President Eisenhower and Governor Stevenson have discussed H-bomb testing and the thermonuclear scene, and their views differ. Neither of them, it seems to me, has quite told the changing facts of life on earth. Both tend to speak of national security as though it were still capable of being dissociated from universal well-being; in fact, sometimes in these political addresses it sounds as though this nation, or any nation, through force of character or force of arms, could damn well rise *above* planetary considerations, as though we were greater than our environment, as though the national verve somehow transcended the natural world.

"Strong we shall stay free," said President Eisenhower in Pittsburgh. And Governor Stevenson echoed the statement in Chicago: ". . . only the strong can be free."

This doctrine of freedom through strength deserves a second look. It would have served nicely in 1936, but nobody thought of it then. Today, with the H-bomb deterring war, we are free and we are militarily strong, but the doctrine is subject to a queer, embarrassing amendment. Today it reads, "Strong we shall stay free, *provided we do not have to use our strength*." That's not quite the same thing. What was true in 1936, if not actually false today, is at best a mere partial, or half, truth. A nation wearing atomic armor is like a knight whose armor has grown so heavy he is immobilized; he can hardly walk, hardly sit his horse, hardly think, hardly breathe. The H-bomb is an extremely effective deterrent to war, but it has little virtue as a *weapon* of war, because it would leave the world uninhabitable.

For a short while following the release of atomic energy, a strong nation was a secure nation. Today, no nation, whatever its thermonuclear power, is a strong nation in the sense that it is a fully independent nation. All are weak, and all are weak from the same cause: each depends on the others for salvation, yet none likes to admit this dependence, and there is no machinery for interdependence. The big nations are weak because the strength has gone out of their arms —which are too terrifying to use, too poisonous to explode. The little nations are weak because they have always been relatively weak and now they have to breathe the same bad air as the big ones. Ours is a balance, as Mr. Stevenson put it, not of power but of terror. If anything, the H-bomb rather favors small nations that don't as yet possess it; they feel slightly more free to jostle other nations, having discovered that a country can stick its tongue out quite far these days without provoking war, so horrible are war's consequences.

The atom, then, is a proper oddity. It has qualified the meaning of national security, it has very likely saved us from a third world war, it has given a new twist to the meaning of power, and it has already entered our bones with a cancer-producing isotope. Furthermore, it has altered the concept of personal sacrifice for moral principle. Human beings have always been willing to shed their blood for what they believed in. Yesterday this was clear and simple; we would pay in blood because, after the price was exacted, there was still a chance to make good the gain. But the modern price tag is not blood. Today our leaders and the leaders of other nations are, in effect, saying, "We will defend our beliefs not alone with our blood—by God, we'll defend them, if we have to, with our genes." This is bold, resolute talk, and one can't help admiring the spirit of it. I admire the spirit of it, but the logic of it eludes me. I doubt whether any noble principle—or any ignoble principle, either, for that matter —can be preserved at the price of genetic disintegration.

The thing I watch for in the speeches of the candidates is some hint that the thermonuclear arms race may be bringing people nearer together, rather than forcing them farther apart. I suspect that because of fallout we may achieve a sort of universality sooner than we bargained for. Fallout may compel us to fall in. The magic-carpet ride on the mushroom cloud has left us dazed—we have come so far so fast. There is a passage in Anne Lindbergh's book *North to the Orient* that captures the curious lag between the mind and the body during a plane journey, between the slow unfolding of remembered images and the swift blur of modern flight. Mrs. Lindbergh started her flight to the Orient by way of North Haven, her childhood summer home. "The trip to Maine," she wrote, "used to be a long and slow one. There was plenty of time in the night, spattered away in the sleeper, in the morning spent ferrying across the river at Bath, in the afternoon syncopated into a series of calls on one coast town after another—there was plenty of time to make the mental change coinciding with our physical change. . . . But on this swift flight to North Haven in the *Sirius* my mind was so far behind my body that when we flew over Rockland Harbor the familiar landmarks below me had no reality."

Like the girl in the plane, we have arrived, but the familiar scene lacks reality. We cling to old remembered forms, old definitions, old comfortable conceptions of national coziness, national self-sufficiency. The Security Council meets solemnly and takes up Suez, eleven sovereign fellows kicking a sovereign ditch around while England threatens war to defend her "lifelines," when modern war itself means universal contamination, universal deathliness, and the end of ditches. I would feel more hopeful, more *secure*, if the Councilmen suddenly changed their tune and began arguing the case for mud turtles and other ancient denizens of ponds and ditches. That is the thing at stake now, and it is what will finally open the Canal to the world's ships in perfect concord.

Candidates for political office steer clear of what Mrs. Luce used to call "globaloney," for fear they may lose the entire American Legion vote and pick up only Norman Cousins. Yet there are indications that supranational ideas are alive in the back of a few men's minds. Through the tangle of verbiage, the idea of "common cause" skitters like a shy bird. Mr. Dulles uses the word "interdependent" in one sentence, then returns promptly to the more customary, safer word "independent." We give aid to Yugoslavia to assure her "independence," and the very fact of the gift is proof that neither donor nor recipient enjoys absolute independence any more; the two are locked in mortal *inter*dependence. Mr. Tito says he is for "new forms and new laws." I haven't the vaguest notion of what he means by that, and I doubt whether he has, either. Certainly there are no *old* laws, if by "laws" he means enforceable rules of conduct by which the world community is governed. But I'm for new forms, all right. Governor Stevenson, in one of his talks, said, "Nations have become so accustomed to living in the dark that they find it hard to learn to live in the light." What light? The light of government? If so, why not say so? President Eisenhower ended a speech the other day with the phrase "a peace of justice in a world of law." Everything else in his speech dealt with a peace of justice in a world of anarchy.

The riddle of disarmament, the riddle of peace, seems to me to hang on the interpretation of these conflicting and contradictory phrases—and on whether or not the men who use them really mean business. Are we independent or interdependent? We can't possibly be both. Do we indeed seek a peace of justice in a world of law, as the President intimates? If so, when do we start, and how? Are we for "new forms," or will the old ones do? In 1945, after the worst blood bath in history, the nations settled immediately back into old forms. In its structure, the United Nations reaffirms everything that caused World War II. At the end of a war fought to defeat dictators, the U.N. welcomed Stalin and Péron to full membership, and the Iron Curtain quickly descended to put the seal of authority on this inconsistent act. The drafters of the Charter assembled in San Francisco and defended their mild, inadequate format with the catchy phrase "Diplomacy is the art of the possible." Meanwhile, a little band of physicists met in a squash court and said, "The hell with the art of the possible. Watch this!"

The world organization debates disarmament in one room and, in the next room, moves the knights and pawns that make national arms imperative. This is not justice and law, and this is not light. It is not new forms. The U.N. is modern in intent, old-fashioned in shape. In San Francisco in 1945, the victor nations failed to create a constitution that placed a higher value on principle than on sovereignty, on common cause than on special cause. The world of 1945 was still a hundred percent parochial. The world of 1956 is still almost a hundred percent parochial. But at last we have a problem that is clearly a community problem, devoid of nationality—the problem of the total pollution of the planet.

We have, in fact, a situation in which the deadliest of all weapons, the H-bomb, together with its little brother, the A-bomb, is the latent source of great agreement among peoples. The bomb is universally hated, and it is universally feared. We cannot escape it with collective security; we shall have to face it with united action. It has given us a few years of grace without war, and now it offers us a few millenniums of oblivion. In a paradox of unbelievable jocundity, the shield of national sovereignty suddenly becomes the challenge of national sovereignty. And, largely because of events beyond our control, we are able to sniff the faint stirring of a community ferment—something every man can enjoy.

The President speaks often of "the peaceful uses of atomic energy," and they are greatly on his mind. I believe the peaceful use of atomic energy that should take precedence over all other uses is this: stop it from contaminating the soil and the sea, the rain and the sky, and the bones of man. That is elementary. It comes ahead of "goodwill" ships and it comes ahead of cheap power. What good is cheap power if your child already has an incurable cancer?

The hydrogen-garbage-disposal program unites the people of the earth in a common anti-litterbug drive for salvation. Radioactive dust has no nationality, is not deflected by boundaries; it falls on Turk and Texan impartially. The radio-strontium isotope finds its way into the milk of Soviet cow and English cow with equal ease. This simple fact profoundly alters the political scene and calls for political leaders to echo the physicists and say, "Never mind the art of the possible. Watch this!"

To me, living in the light means an honest attempt to discover the germ of common cause in a world of special cause, even against the almost insuperable odds of parochialism and national fervor, even in the face of the dangers that always attend political growth. Actually, nations are already enjoying little pockets of unity. The European coal-steel authority is apparently a success. The U.N., which is usually impotent in political disputes, has nevertheless managed to elevate the world's children and the world's health to a community level. The trick is to encourage and hasten this magical growth, this benign condition—encourage it and get it on paper, while children still have healthy bones and before we have all reached the point of no return. It will not mean the end of nations; it will mean the true beginning of nations.

Paul-Henri Spaak, addressing himself to the Egyptian government the other day, said, "We are no longer at the time of the absolute sovereignty of states." We are not, and we ought by this time to know we are not. I just hope we learn it in time. In the beautiful phrase of Mrs. Lindbergh's, there used to be "plenty of time in the night." Now there is hardly any time at all.

Well, this started out as a letter and has turned into a discourse. But I don't mind. If a candidate were to appear on the scene and come out for the dignity of mud turtles, I suppose people would hesitate to support him, for fear he had lost his reason. But he would have my vote, on the theory that in losing his reason he had kept his head. It is time men allowed their imagination to infect their intellect, time we all rushed headlong into the wilder regions of thought where the earth again revolves around the sun instead of around the Suez, regions where no individual and no group can blithely assume the right to sow the sky with seeds of mischief, and where the sovereign nation at last begins to function as the true friend and guardian of sovereign man.

P.S. (May 1962). The dirty state of affairs on earth is getting worse, not better. Our soil, our rivers, our seas, our air carry an ever-increasing load of industrial wastes, agricultural poisons, and military debris. The seeds of mischief are in the wind—in the warm sweet airs of spring. Contamination continues in greater force and new ways, and with new excuses: the Soviet tests last autumn had a double-barrelled purpose—to experiment and to intimidate. This was the first appearance of the diplomacy of dust; the breaking of the moratorium by Russia was a high crime, murder in the first degree. President Kennedy countered with the announcement that he would reply in kind unless a test-ban agreement could be reached by the end of April. None was reached, and our tests are being conducted. One more nation, France, has joined the company of testers. If Red China learns the trick, we will probably see the greatest pyrotechnic display yet, for the Chinese love fireworks of all kinds.

I asked myself what I would have done, had I been in the President's shoes, and was forced to admit I would have taken the same course—test. The shattering of the moratorium was for the time being the shattering of our hopes of good nuclear conduct. In a darkening and dirt-ridden world the course of freedom must be maintained even by desperate means, while there is a time of grace, and the only thing worse than being in an arms race is to be in one and not compete. The President's decision to resume testing in the atmosphere was, I believe, a correct decision, and I think the people who protest by lying down in the street have not come up with an alternative course that is sensible and workable. But the time of grace will run out, sooner or later, for all nations. We are in a vast riddle, all of us—dependence on a strength that is inimical to life— and what we are really doing is fighting a war that uses the lives of future individuals, rather than the lives of existing young men. The President did his best to lighten the blow by pointing out that fallout isn't as bad as it used to be, that our tests would raise the background radiation by only one percent. But this is like saying that it isn't dangerous to go in the cage with the tiger because the tiger is taking a nap. I am not calmed by the news of fallout's mildness, or deceived by drowsy tigers. The percentages will increase, the damage will mount steadily unless a turn is made somehow. Because our adversary tests, we test; because we test, they test. Where is the end of this dirty habit? I think there is no military solution, no economic solution, only a political solution, and this is the area to which we should give the closest attention and in which we should show the greatest imaginative powers.

These nuclear springtimes have a pervasive sadness about them, the virgin earth having been the victim of rape attacks. This is a smiling morning; I am writing where I can look out at our garden piece, which has been newly harrowed, ready for planting. The rich brown patch of ground used to bring delight to eye and mind at this fresh season of promise. For me the scene has been spoiled by the maggots that work in the mind. Tomorrow we will have rain, and the rain falling on the garden will carry its cargo of debris from old explosions in distant places. Whether the amount of this freight is great or small, whether it is measurable by the farmer or can only be guessed at, one thing is certain: the character of rain has changed, the joy of watching it soak the waiting earth has been diminished, and the whole meaning and worth of gardens has been brought into question.

QUESTIONS AND EXERCISES

1. The main part of this essay, as the dateline indicates, was written well over ten years ago. To what extent is it "dated"? What are

the details that seem most to limit and restrict its relevance today? Would you say that the essay will become less and less relevant as time passes, or is it now about as out-of-date as it will ever be? Explain.

2. How effective is the relationship between nuclear fallout and the lesser forms of pollution, as White tries to develop it here? Specifically, consider the way in which his concern about fallout eventually takes over the essay altogether. Is this good strategy? Is the timing right?

3. What is your most serious adverse criticism of this essay? If the fault is one that could be removed without altering totally the nature of the piece, explain how this might be done.

4. What have Mary Martin's household goods to do with the main substance of this essay?

5. Was it a good idea for White to add a "postscript" in 1962, or should he have rewritten the entire essay? Explain your conclusions.

6. Would you say that the author has tried to use here the style of spoken conversation? Are there formal signs of this? Explain. Is the style suited to such a serious subject?

7. Write about 700 words describing the structural organization of this essay and commenting on its effectiveness in carrying the substance.

8. Write two or three pages about the *importance* of White's essay (or about its unimportance, if that is the way you feel). Speak from your own present point of view, not that of 1956.

9. In a commentary of about 500 words, assess the element of *originality* in "Sootfall and Fallout."

THE GREATNESS OF HUCKLEBERRY FINN

Lionel Trilling

In 1876 Mark Twain published *The Adventures of Tom Sawyer* and in the same year he began what he called "another boys' book." He set little store by the new venture and said that he had undertaken it "more to be at work than anything else." His heart was not in it—"I like it only tolerably well as far as I have got," he said,

THE GREATNESS OF HUCKLEBERRY FINN: Introduction by Lionel Trilling to Mark Twain's *The Adventures of Huckleberry Finn*, Rinehart Edition. Introduction copyright 1948 by Lionel Trilling. Reprinted by permission of Holt, Rinehart and Winston, Inc.

"and may possibly pigeonhole or burn the MS when it is done." He pigeonholed it long before it was done and for as much as four years. In 1880 he took it out and carried it forward a little, only to abandon it again. He had a theory of unconscious composition and believed that a book must write itself; the book which he referred to as "Huck Finn's Autobiography" refused to do the job of its own creation and he would not coerce it.

But then in the summer of 1882 Mark Twain was possessed by a charge of literary energy which, as he wrote to a friend, was more intense than any he had experienced for many years. He worked all day and every day, and periodically he so fatigued himself that he had to recruit his strength by a day or two of smoking and reading in bed. It is impossible not to suppose that this great creative drive was connected with—was perhaps the direct result of—the visit to the Mississippi he had made earlier in the year, the trip which forms the matter of the second part of *Life on the Mississippi*. His boyhood and youth on the river he so profoundly loved had been at once the happiest and most significant part of Mark Twain's life; his return to it in middle age stirred vital memories which revived and refreshed the idea of *Huckleberry Finn*. Now at last the book was not only ready but eager to write itself. But it was not to receive much conscious help from its author. He was always full of second-rate literary schemes and now, in the early weeks of the summer, with *Huckleberry Finn* waiting to complete itself, he turned his hot energy upon several of these sorry projects, the completion of which gave him as much sense of satisfying productivity as did his eventual absorption in *Huckleberry Finn*.

When at last *Huckleberry Finn* was completed and published and widely loved, Mark Twain became somewhat aware of what he had accomplished with this book that had been begun as journey-work and depreciated, postponed, threatened with destruction. It is his masterpiece, and perhaps he learned to know that. But he could scarcely have estimated it for what it is, one of the world's great books and one of the central documents of American culture.

2

Wherein does its greatness lie? Primarily in its power of telling the truth. An awareness of this quality as it exists in *Tom Sawyer* once led Mark Twain to say of the earlier work that "it is *not* a boys' book at all. It will be read only by adults. It is written only for adults." But this was only a manner of speaking, Mark Twain's way of asserting, with a discernible touch of irritation, the degree of truth he had achieved. It does not represent his usual view either of boys' books or of boys. No one, as he well knew, sets a higher value on truth than a boy. Truth is the whole of a boy's conscious demand upon the world of adults. He is likely to believe that the adult world is in a conspiracy to lie to him, and it is this belief, by no means unfounded, that arouses Tom and Huck and all boys to their moral sensitivity, their everlasting concern with justice, which they call fairness. At the same time it often makes them skillful and profound liars in their own defense, yet they do not tell the ultimate lie of adults: they do not lie to themselves. That is why Mark Twain felt that it was impossible to carry Tom Sawyer beyond boy-hood—in maturity "he would lie just like all the other one-horse men of literature and the reader would conceive a hearty contempt for him."

Certainly one element in the greatness of *Huckleberry Finn*—as also in the lesser greatness of *Tom Sawyer*—is that it succeeds first as a boys' book. One can read it at ten and then annually ever after, and each year find that it is as fresh as the year before, that it has changed only in becoming somewhat larger. To read it young is like planting a tree young—each year adds a new growth-ring of mean-ing, and the book is as little likely as the tree to become dull. So, we may imagine, an Athenian boy grew up together with the *Odyssey*. There are few other books which we can know so young and love so long.

The truth of *Huckleberry Finn* is of a different kind from that of *Tom Sawyer*. It is a more intense truth, fiercer and more com-plex. *Tom Sawyer* has the truth of honesty—what it says about things and feelings is never false and always both adequate and beautiful. *Huckleberry Finn* has this kind of truth, too, but it has also the truth of moral passion; it deals directly with the virtue and depravity of man's heart.

Perhaps the best clue to the greatness of *Huckleberry Finn* has been given to us by a writer who is as different from Mark Twain as it is possible for one Missourian to be from another. T. S. Eliot's poem, "The Dry Salvages," the third of his *Four Quartets*, begins with a meditation on the Mississippi, which Mr. Eliot knew in his St. Louis boyhood. These are the opening lines:

> I do not know much about gods; but I think that the river
> Is a strong brown god . . .

And the meditation goes on to speak of the god as

> almost forgotten
> By the dwellers in cities—ever, however, implacable,

Keeping his seasons and rages, destroyer, reminder of
What men choose to forget. Unhonoured, unpropitiated
By worshippers of the machine, but waiting, watching and waiting.[1]

Huckleberry Finn is a great book because it is about a god—about, that is, a power which seems to have a mind and will of its own, and which, to men of moral imagination, appears to embody a great moral idea.

Huck himself is the servant of the river-god, and he comes very close to being aware of the divine nature of the being he serves. The world he inhabits is perfectly equipped to accommodate a deity, for it is full of presences and meanings which it conveys by natural signs and also by preternatural omens and taboos: to look at the moon over the left shoulder, to shake the tablecloth after sundown, to handle a snakeskin, are ways of offending the obscure and prevalent spirits. Huck is at odds, on moral and aesthetic grounds, with the only form of Christianity he knows, and his very intense moral life may be said to derive from his love of the river. He lives in a perpetual adoration of the Mississippi's power and charm. Huck, of course, always expresses himself better than he can know, but nothing draws upon his gift of speech like his response to his deity. After every sally into the social life of the shore, he returns to the river with relief and thanksgiving; and at each return, regular and explicit as a chorus in a Greek tragedy, there is a hymn of praise to the god's beauty, mystery, and strength, and to his noble grandeur in contrast with the pettiness of men.

Generally the god is benign, a being of long sunny days and spacious nights. But, like any god, he is also dangerous and deceptive. He generates fogs which bewilder, and he contrives echoes and false distances which confuse. His sandbars can ground and his hidden snags can mortally wound a great steamboat. He can cut away the solid earth from under a man's feet and take his house with it. The sense of the danger of the river is what saves the book from any touch of the sentimentality and moral ineptitude of most works of the imagination which contrast the life of nature with the life of society.

The river itself is only divine; it is not ethical and good. But its nature seems to foster the goodness of those who love it and try to fit themselves to its ways. And we must observe that we cannot make —that Mark Twain does not make—an absolute opposition between the river and human society. To Huck much of the charm of the

[1] Copyright, 1943, by T. S. Eliot, reprinted by permission of Harcourt, Brace & World.

river life is human: it is the raft and the wigwam and Jim. He has not run away from Miss Watson and the Widow Douglas and his brutal father to a completely individualistic liberty, for in Jim he finds his true father, very much as Stephen Dedalus in James Joyce's *Ulysses* finds his true father in Leopold Bloom.[2] The boy and the Negro slave form a family, a primitive community—and it is a community of saints.

Huck's intense and even complex moral quality may possibly not appear on a first reading, for one may be caught and convinced by his own estimate of himself, by his brags about his lazy hedonism, his avowed preference for being alone, his dislike of civilization. The fact is, of course, that he is involved in civilization up to his ears. His escape from society is but his way of reaching what society ideally dreams of for itself. Responsibility is the very essence of his character, and it is perhaps to the point that the original of Huck, a boyhood companion of Mark Twain's named Tom Blankenship, did, like Huck, "light out for the Territory," only to become a justice of the peace in Montana, "a good citizen and greatly respected."

Huck does indeed have all the capacities for simple happiness he says he has, but circumstances and his own moral nature make him the least carefree of boys—he is always "in a sweat" over the predicament of someone else. He has a great sense of the sadness of human life, and although he likes to be alone, the words "lonely" and "loneliness" are frequent with him. The note of his special sensibility is struck early in the story: "Well, when Tom and me got to the edge of the hilltop we looked away down into the village and could see three or four lights twinkling where there were sick folks, maybe; and the stars over us was sparkling ever so fine; and down by the village was the river, a whole mile broad, and awful still and grand." The identification of those three or four lonely lights as the lamps of sick-watches defines Huck's character.

His sympathy is quick and immediate. When the circus audience laughs at the supposedly drunken man who tries to ride the horse, Huck is only miserable: "It wasn't funny to me . . . ; I was all of a tremble to see his danger." When he imprisons the intending murderers on the wrecked steamboat, his first thought is of how to get someone to rescue them, for he considers "how dreadful it was,

[2] In Joyce's *Finnegans Wake* both Mark Twain and Huckleberry Finn appear frequently. The theme of rivers is, of course, dominant in the book; and Huck's name suits Joyce's purpose, as so many names do, for Finn is one of the many names of his hero. Mark Twain's love of and gift for the spoken language makes another reason for Joyce's interest in him.

even for murderers, to be in such a fix. I says to myself, there ain't no telling but I might come to be a murderer myself yet, and then how would I like it?" But his sympathy is never sentimental. When at last he knows that the murderers are beyond help, he has no inclination to false pathos. "I felt a little bit heavy-hearted about the gang, but not much, for I reckoned that if they could stand it I could." His will is genuinely good and therefore he has no need to torture himself with guilty second thoughts.

Not the least remarkable thing about Huck's feeling for people is that his tenderness goes along with the assumption that his fellow men are likely to be dangerous and wicked. He travels incognito, never telling the truth about himself and never twice telling the same lie, for he trusts no one and the lie comforts him even when it is not necessary. He instinctively knows that the best way to keep a party of men away from Jim on the raft is to beg them to come aboard to help his family stricken with smallpox. And if he had not already had the knowledge of human weakness and stupidity and cowardice, he would soon have acquired it, for all his encounters forcibly teach it to him—the insensate feud of the Grangerfords and Shepherdsons, the invasion of the raft by the Duke and the King, the murder of Boggs, the lynching party, and the speech of Colonel Sherburn. Yet his profound and bitter knowledge of human depravity never prevents him from being a friend to man.

No personal pride interferes with his well-doing. He knows what status is and on the whole he respects it—he is really a very *respectable* person and inclines to like "quality folks"—but he himself is unaffected by it. He himself has never had status, he has always been the lowest of the low, and the considerable fortune he had acquired in *The Adventures of Tom Sawyer* is never real to him. When the Duke suggests that Huck and Jim render him the personal service that accords with his rank, Huck's only comment is, "Well, that was easy so we done it." He is injured in every possible way by the Duke and the King, used and exploited and manipulated, yet when he hears that they are in danger from a mob, his natural impulse is to warn them. And when he fails of his purpose and the two men are tarred and feathered and ridden on a rail, his only thought is, "Well, it made me sick to see it; and I was sorry for them poor pitiful rascals, it seemed like I couldn't ever feel any hardness against them any more in the world."

And if Huck and Jim on the raft do indeed make a community of saints, it is because they do not have an ounce of pride between them. Yet this is not perfectly true, for the one disagreement they ever have is over a matter of pride. It is on the occasion when Jim and Huck have been separated by the fog. Jim has mourned Huck as dead, and then, exhausted, has fallen asleep. When he awakes and finds that Huck has returned, he is overjoyed; but Huck convinces him that he has only dreamed the incident, that there has been no fog, no separation, no chase, no reunion, and then allows him to make an elaborate "interpretation" of the dream he now believes he has had. Then the joke is sprung, and in the growing light of the dawn Huck points to the debris of leaves on the raft and the broken oar.

> "Jim looked at the trash, and then looked at me, and back at the trash again. He had got the dream fixed so strong in his head that he couldn't seem to shake it loose and get the facts back into its place again right away. But when he did get the thing straightened around he looked at me steady without ever smiling, and says:
>
> " 'What do dey stan' for? I'se gwyne to tell you. When I got all wore out wid work, en wid de callin' for you, en went to sleep, my heart wuz mos' broke bekase you wuz los', en I didn' k'yer no mo' what became er me en de raf'. En when I wake up en fine you back agin, all safe en soun', de tears come, en I could a got down on my knees en kiss yo' foot, I's so thankful. En all you wuz thinkin' 'bout wuz how you could make a fool uv ole Jim wid a lie. Dat truck dah is *trash*; en trash is what people is dat puts dirt on de head er dey fren's en makes 'em ashamed.'
>
> "Then he got up slow and walked to the wigwam, and went in there without saying anything but that."

The pride of human affection has been touched, one of the few prides that has any true dignity. And at its utterance, Huck's one last dim vestige of pride of status, his sense of his position as a white man, wholly vanishes: "It was fifteen minutes before I could work myself up to go and humble myself to a nigger; but I done it, and I warn't ever sorry for it afterward, neither."

This incident is the beginning of the moral testing and development which a character so morally sensitive as Huck's must inevitably undergo. And it becomes an heroic character when, on the urging of affection, Huck discards the moral code he has always taken for granted and resolves to help Jim in his escape from slavery. The intensity of his struggle over the act suggests how deeply he is involved in the society which he rejects. The satiric brilliance of the episode lies, of course, in Huck's solving his problem not by doing "right" but by doing "wrong." He has only to consult his conscience, the conscience of a Southern boy in the middle of the last century, to know that he ought to return Jim to slavery. And as soon as he makes the decision according to conscience and decides to inform on Jim, he has all the warmly gratifying emotions of conscious virtue. "Why, it was astonishing, the way I felt as light as a feather right straight off, and my troubles all gone . . . I felt good and all washed clean of sin for the first time I had ever felt so in my life, and I knowed I could pray now." And when at last he finds that he cannot endure his decision but must change it and help Jim in his escape, it is not because he has acquired any new ideas about slavery—he believes that he detests Abolitionists; he himself answers when he is asked if the explosion of a steamboat boiler had hurt anyone, "No'm, killed a nigger," and of course he finds nothing wrong in the responsive comment, "Well, it's lucky because sometimes people do get hurt." Ideas and ideals can be of no help to him in his moral crisis. He no more condemns slavery than Tristram and Lancelot condemn marriage; he is as consciously *wicked* as any illicit lover of romance and he consents to be damned for a personal devotion, never questioning the justice of the punishment he has incurred.

Huckleberry Finn was once barred from certain libraries and schools for its alleged subversion of morality. The authorities had in mind the book's endemic lying, the petty thefts, the denigrations of respectability and religion, the bad language and the bad grammar. We smile at that excessive care, yet in point of fact *Huckleberry Finn* is indeed a subversive book—no one who reads thoughtfully the dialectic of Huck's great moral crisis will ever again be wholly able to accept without some question and some irony the assumptions of the respectable morality by which he lives, nor will ever again be certain that what he considers the clear dictates of moral reason are not merely the engrained customary beliefs of his time and place.

3

We are not likely to miss in *Huckleberry Finn* the subtle, implicit moral meaning of the great river. But we are likely to understand these moral implications as having to do only with personal and individual conduct. And since the sum of individual pettiness is on the whole pretty constant, we are likely to think of the book as applicable to mankind in general and at all times and in all places, and we praise it by calling it "universal." And so it is; but like many books to which that large adjective applies, it is also local and particular. It has a particular moral reference to the United States in the period after the Civil War. It was then when, in Mr. Eliot's phrase, the river was forgotten, and precisely by the "dwellers in cities," by the "worshippers of the machine."

The Civil War and the development of the railroads ended the great days when the river was the central artery of the nation. No contrast could be more moving than that between the hot, turbulent energy of the river life of the first part of *Life on the Mississippi* and the melancholy reminiscence of the second part. And the war that brought the end of the rich Mississippi days also marked a change in the quality of life in America which, to many men, consisted of a deterioration of American moral values. It is of course a human habit to look back on the past and to find it a better and more innocent time than the present. Yet in this instance there seems to be an objective basis for the judgment. We cannot disregard the testimony of men so diverse as Henry Adams, Walt Whitman, William Dean Howells, and Mark Twain himself, to mention but a few of the many who were in agreement on this point. All spoke of something that had gone out of American life after the war, some simplicity, some innocence, some peace. None of them was under any illusion about the amount of ordinary human wickedness that existed in the old days, and Mark Twain certainly was not. The difference was in the public attitude, in the things that were now accepted and made respectable in the national ideal. It was, they all felt, connected with new emotions about money. As Mark Twain said, where formerly "the people had desired money," now they "fall down and worship it." The new gospel was, "Get money. Get it quickly. Get it in abundance. Get it in prodigious abundance. Get it dishonestly if you can, honestly if you must." [3]

With the end of the Civil War capitalism had established itself. The relaxing influence of the frontier was coming to an end. Americans increasingly became "dwellers in cities" and "worshippers of the machine." Mark Twain himself became a notable part of this new dispensation. No one worshipped the machine more than he did, or thought he did—he ruined himself by his devotion to the Paige typesetting machine by which he hoped to make a fortune even greater than he had made by his writing, and he sang the praises of the machine age in *A Connecticut Yankee in King Arthur's Court*. He associated intimately with the dominant figures of American business enterprise. Yet at the same time he hated the new way of life and kept bitter memoranda of his scorn, commenting on the low morality or the bad taste or the smugness and dullness of the men who were shaping the national ideal and directing the destiny of the nation.

[3] *Mark Twain in Eruption*, edited by Bernard De Voto, p. 77.

Mark Twain said of *Tom Sawyer* that it "is simply a hymn, put into prose form to give it a worldly air." He might have said the same, and with even more reason, of *Huckleberry Finn*, which is a hymn to an older America forever gone, an America which had its great national faults, which was full of violence and even of cruelty, but which still maintained its sense of reality, for it was not yet enthralled by money, the father of ultimate illusion and lies. Against the money-god stands the river-god, whose comments are silent—sunlight, space, uncrowded time, stillness and danger. It was quickly forgotten once its practical usefulness had passed, but, as Mr. Eliot's poem says, "The river is within us. . . ."

4

In form and style *Huckleberry Finn* is an almost perfect work. Only one mistake has ever been charged against it, that it concludes with Tom Sawyer's elaborate, too elaborate, game of Jim's escape. Certainly this episode is too long—in the original draft it was much longer—and certainly it is a falling-off, as almost anything would have to be, from the incidents of the river. Yet it has a certain formal aptness—like, say, that of the Turkish initiation which brings Molière's *Le Bourgeois Gentilhomme* to its close. It is a rather mechanical development of an idea, and yet some device is needed to permit Huck to return to his anonymity, to give up the role of hero, to fall into the background which he prefers, for he is modest in all things and could not well endure the attention and glamour which attend a hero at a book's end. For this purpose nothing could serve better than the mind of Tom Sawyer with its literary furnishings, its conscious romantic desire for experience and the hero's part, and its ingenious schematization of life to achieve that aim.

The form of the book is based on the simplest of all novel-forms, the so-called picaresque novel, or novel of the road, which strings its incidents on the line of the hero's travels. But, as Pascal says, "rivers are roads that move," and the movement of the road in its own mysterious life transmutes the primitive simplicity of the form: the road itself is the greatest character in this novel of the road, and the hero's departures from the river and his returns to it compose a subtle and significant pattern. The linear simplicity of the picaresque novel is further modified by the story's having a clear dramatic organization: it has a beginning, a middle and an end, and a mounting suspense of interest.

As for the style of the book, it is not less than definitive in American literature. The prose of *Huckleberry Finn* established for written prose the virtues of American colloquial speech. This has nothing to do with pronunciation or grammar. It has something to do with ease and freedom in the use of language. Most of all it has to do with the structure of the sentence, which is simple, direct, and fluent, maintaining the rhythm of the word-groups of speech and the intonations of the speaking voice.

In the matter of language, American literature had a special problem. The young nation was inclined to think that the mark of the truly literary product was a grandiosity and elegance not to be found in the common speech. It therefore encouraged a greater breach between its vernacular and its literary language than, say, English literature of the same period ever allowed. This accounts for the hollow ring one now and then hears even in the work of our best writers in the first half of the last century. English writers of equal stature would never have made the lapses into rhetorical excess that are common in Cooper and Poe and that are to be found even in Melville and Hawthorne.

Yet at the same time that the language of ambitious literature was high and thus always in danger of falseness, the American reader was keenly interested in the actualities of daily speech. No literature, indeed, was ever so taken up with matters of speech as ours was. "Dialect," which attracted even our serious writers, was the accepted common ground of our popular humorous writing. Nothing in social life seemed so remarkable as the different forms which speech could take—the brogue of the immigrant Irish or the mispronunciation of the German, the "affection" of the English, the reputed precision of the Bostonian, the legendary twang of the Yankee farmer, and the drawl of the Pike County man. Mark Twain, of course, was in the tradition of humor that exploited this interest, and no one could play with it nearly so well. Although today the carefully spelled-out dialects of nineteenth-century American humor are likely to seem dull enough, the subtle variations of speech of *Huckleberry Finn*, of which Mark Twain was justly proud, are still part of the liveliness and flavor of the book.

Out of his knowledge of the actual speech of America Mark Twain forged a classic prose. The adjective may seem a strange one, yet it is apt. Forget the misspellings and the faults of grammar, and the prose will be seen to move with the greatest simplicity, directness, lucidity, and grace. These qualities are by no means accidental. Mark Twain, who read widely, was passionately interested in the problems of style; the mark of the strictest literary sensibility is everywhere to be found in the prose of *Huckleberry Finn*.

It is this prose that Ernest Hemingway had chiefly in mind when he said that "all modern American literature comes from one book by Mark Twain called *Huckleberry Finn.*" Hemingway's own prose stems from it directly and consciously; so does the prose of the two modern writers who most influenced Hemingway's early style, Gertrude Stein and Sherwood Anderson (although neither of them could maintain the robust purity of their model); so, too, does the best of William Faulkner's prose, which, like Mark Twain's own, reinforces the colloquial tradition with the literary tradition. Indeed, it may be said that almost every contemporary writer who deals conscientiously with the problems and possibility of prose must feel, directly or indirectly, the influence of Mark Twain. He is the master of the style that escapes the fixity of the printed page, that sounds in our ears with the immediacy of the heard voice, the very voice of unpretentious truth.

AN INTRODUCTION TO HUCKLEBERRY FINN

T. S. Eliot

The Adventures of Huckleberry Finn is the only one of Mark Twain's various books which can be called a masterpiece. I do not suggest that it is his only book of permanent interest; but it is the only one in which his genius is completely realized, and the only one which creates its own category. There are pages in *Tom Sawyer* and in *Life on the Mississippi* which are, within their limits, as good as anything with which one can compare them in *Huckleberry Finn;* and in other books there are drolleries just as good of their kind. But when we find one book by a prolific author which is very much superior to all the rest, we look for the peculiar accident or concourse of accidents which made that book possible. In the writing of *Huckleberry Finn* Mark Twain had two elements which, when treated with his sensibility and his experience, formed a great book: these two are the Boy and the River.

Huckleberry Finn is, no doubt, a book which boys enjoy. I cannot speak from memory: I suspect that a fear on the part of my parents lest I should acquire a premature taste for tobacco, and perhaps

AN INTRODUCTION TO HUCKLIBERRY FINN: The Cressent Press, London, 1950. Reprinted by permission of Esme Valerie Eliot.

other habits of the hero of the story, kept the book out of my way. But *Huckleberry Finn* does not fall into the category of juvenile fiction. The opinion of my parents that it was a book unsuitable for boys left me, for most of my life, under the impression that it was a book suitable only for boys. Therefore it was only a few years ago that I read for the first time, and in that order, *Tom Sawyer* and *Huckleberry Finn*.

Tom Sawyer did not prepare me for what I was to find its sequel to be. *Tom Sawyer* seems to me to be a boys' book, and a very good one. The River and *the* Boy make their appearance in it; the narrative is good; and there is also a very good picture of society in a small mid-Western river town (for St. Petersburg is more Western than Southern) a hundred years ago. But the point of view of the narrator is that of an adult observing a boy. And Tom is the ordinary boy, though of quicker wits, and livelier imagination, than most. Tom is, I suppose, very much the boy that Mark Twain had been: he is remembered and described as he seemed to his elders, rather than created. Huck Finn, on the other hand, is the boy that Mark Twain still was, at the time of writing his adventures. We look at Tom as the smiling adult does: Huck we do not look at—we see the world through his eyes. The two boys are not merely different types; they were brought into existence by different processes. Hence in the second book their roles are altered. In the first book Huck is merely the humble friend—almost a variant of the traditional valet of comedy; and we see him as he is seen by the conventional respectable society to which Tom belongs, and of which, we feel sure, Tom will one day become an eminently respectable and conventional member. In the second book their nominal relationship remains the same; but here it is Tom who has the secondary role. The author was probably not conscious of this, when he wrote the first two chapters: *Huckleberry Finn* is not the kind of story in which the author knows, from the beginning, what is going to happen. Tom then disappears from our view; and when he returns, he has only two functions. The first is to provide a foil for Huck. Huck's persisting admiration for Tom only exhibits more clearly to our eyes the unique qualities of the former and the commonplaceness of the latter. Tom has the imagination of a lively boy who has read a good deal of romantic fiction: he might, of course, become a writer—he might become Mark Twain. Or rather, he might become the more commonplace aspect of Mark Twain. Huck has not imagination, in the sense in which Tom has it: he has, instead, vision. He sees the real world; and he does not judge it—he allows it to judge itself.

Tom Sawyer is an orphan. But he has his aunt; he has, as we learn later, other relatives; and he has the environment into which he fits. He is wholly a social being. When there is a secret band to be formed, it is Tom who organizes it and prescribes the rules. Huck Finn is alone: there is no more solitary character in fiction. The fact that he has a father only emphasizes his loneliness; and he views his father with a terrifying detachment. So we come to see Huck himself in the end as one of the permanent symbolic figures of fiction; not unworthy to take a place with Ulysses, Faust, Don Quixote, Don Juan, Hamlet and other great discoveries that man has made about himself.

It would seem that Mark Twain was a man who—perhaps like most of us—never became in all respects mature. We might even say that the adult side of him was boyish, and that only the boy in him, that was Huck Finn, was adult. As Tom Sawyer grown up, he wanted success and applause (Tom himself always needs an audience). He wanted prosperity, a happy domestic life of a conventional kind, universal approval, and fame. All of these things he obtained. As Huck Finn he was indifferent to all these things; and being composite of the two, Mark Twain both strove for them, and resented their violation of his integrity. Hence he became the humorist and even clown: with his gifts, a certain way to success, for everyone could enjoy his writings without the slightest feeling of discomfort, self-consciousness or self-criticism. And hence, on the other hand, his pessimism and misanthropy. To be a misanthrope is to be in some way divided; or it is a sign of an uneasy conscience. The pessimism which Mark Twain discharged into *The Man That Corrupted Hadleyburg* and *What is Man?* springs less from observation of society, than from his hatred of himself for allowing society to tempt and corrupt him and give him what he wanted. There is no wisdom in it. But all this personal problem has been diligently examined by Mr. Van Wyck Brooks; and it is not Mark Twain, but *Huckleberry Finn,* that is the subject of this introduction.

You cannot say that Huck himself is either a humorist or a misanthrope. He is the impassive observer: he does not interfere, and, as I have said, he does not judge. Many of the episodes that occur on the voyage down the river, after he is joined by the Duke and the King (whose fancies about themselves are akin to the kind of fancy that Tom Sawyer enjoys) are in themselves farcical; and if it were not for the presence of Huck as the reporter of them, they would be no more than farce. But, seen through the eyes of Huck, there is a deep human pathos in these scoundrels. On the other hand, the story of the feud between the Grangerfords and the Shepherdsons is a masterpiece in itself: yet Mark Twain could not have written it so, with that economy and restraint, with just the right details and no more, and leaving to the reader to make his own moral reflections, unless he had been writing in the person of Huck. And the *style* of the book, which is the style of Huck, is what makes it a far more convincing indictment of slavery than the sensationalist propaganda of *Uncle Tom's Cabin*. Huck is passive and impassive, apparently always the victim of events; and yet, in his acceptance of his world and of what it does to him and others, he is more powerful than his world, because he is more *aware* than any other person in it.

Repeated readings of the book only confirm and deepen one's admiration of the consistency and perfect adaptation of the writing. This is a style which at the period, whether in America or in England, was an innovation, a new discovery in the English language. Other authors had achieved natural speech in relation to particular characters—Scott with characters talking Lowland Scots, Dickens with cockneys: but no one else had kept it up through the whole of a book. Thackeray's Yellowplush, impressive as he is, is an obvious artifice in comparison. In *Huckleberry Finn* there is no exaggeration of grammar or spelling or speech, there is no sentence or phrase to destroy the illusion that these are Huck's own words. It is not only in the way in which he tells his story, but in the details he remembers, that Huck is true to himself. There is, for instance, the description of the Grangerford interior as Huck sees it on his arrival; there is the list of the objects which Huck and Jim salvaged from the derelict house:

> "We got an old tin lantern, and a butcher-knife without any handle, and a bran-new Barlow knife worth two bits in any store, and a lot of tallow candles, and a tin candlestick, and a gourd, and a tin cup, and a ratty old bedquilt off the bed, and a reticule with needles and pins and beeswax and buttons and thread and all such truck in it, and a hatchet and some nails, and a fish-line as thick as my little finger, with some monstrous hooks on it, and a roll of buckskin, and a leather dog-collar, and a horseshoe, and some vials of medicine that didn't have no label on them; and just as we was leaving I found a tolerable good curry-comb, and Jim he found a ratty old fiddle-bow, and a wooden leg. The straps was broke off of it, but barring that, it was a good enough leg, though it was too long for me and not long enough for Jim, and we couldn't find the other one, though we hunted all round.
>
> "And so, take it all round, we made a good haul."

This is the sort of list that a boy reader should pore over with delight; but the paragraph performs other functions of which the boy reader would be unaware. It provides the right counterpoise to the horror of the wrecked house and the corpse; it has a grim precision which tells the reader all he needs to know about the way of life of the human derelicts who had used the house; and (especially the wooden leg, and the fruitless search for its mate) reminds us at the right moment of the kinship of mind and the sympathy between the boy outcast from society and the negro fugitive from the injustice of society.

Huck in fact would be incomplete without Jim, who is almost as notable a creation as Huck himself. Huck is the passive observer of men and events, Jim the submissive sufferer from them; and they are equal in dignity. There is no passage in which their relationship is brought out more clearly than the conclusion of the chapter in which, after the two have become separated in the fog, Huck in the canoe and Jim on the raft, Huck, in his impulse of boyish mischief, persuades Jim for a time that the latter had dreamt the whole episode.

> ". . . my heart wuz mos' broke bekase you wuz los', en I didn' k'yer no mo' what become er me en de raf'. En when I wake up en fine you back agin', all safe en soun', de tears come en I could a got down on my knees en kiss' yo' foot, I's so thankful. En all you wuz thinkin' 'bout wuz how you could make a fool uv ole Jim wid a lie. Dat truck dah is *trash;* en trash is what people is dat puts dirt on de head er dey fren's en makes 'em ashamed.' . . .
>
> "It was fifteen minutes before I could work myself up to go and humble myself to a nigger—but I done it, and I warn't ever sorry for it afterwards, neither."

This passage has been quoted before; and if I quote it again, it is because I wish to elicit from it one meaning that is, I think, usually overlooked. What is obvious in it is the pathos and dignity of Jim, and this is moving enough; but what I find still more disturbing, and still more unusual in literature, is the pathos and dignity of the boy, when reminded so humbly and humiliatingly, that his position in the world is not that of other boys, entitled from time to time to a practical joke; but that he must bear, and bear alone, the responsibility of a man.

It is Huck who gives the book style. The River gives the book its form. But for the River, the book might be only a sequence of adventures with a happy ending. A river, a very big and powerful river, is the only natural force that can wholly determine the course of human peregrination. At sea, the wanderer may sail or be carried by winds and currents in one direction or another; a change of wind or tide may determine fortune. In the prairie, the direction of movement is more or less at the choice of the caravan; among mountains there will often be an alternative, a guess at the most likely pass. But the river with its strong, swift current is the dictator to the raft or to the steamboat. It is a treacherous and capricious dictator. At one season, it may move sluggishly in a channel so narrow that, encountering it for the first time at that point, one can hardly believe that it has travelled already for hundreds of miles, and has yet many hundreds of miles to go; at another season, it may obliterate the low Illinois shore to a horizon of water, while in its bed it runs with a speed such that no man or beast can survive in it. At such times, it carries down human bodies, cattle and houses. At least twice, at St. Louis, the western and the eastern shores have been separated by the fall of bridges, until the designer of the great Eads Bridge devised a structure which could resist the floods. In my own childhood, it was not unusual for the spring freshet to interrupt railway travel; and then the traveller to the East had to take steamboat from the levee up to Alton, at a higher level on the Illinois shore, before he could begin his rail journey. The river is never wholly chartable; it changes its pace, it shifts its channel, unaccountably; it may suddenly efface a sandbar, and throw up another bar where before was navigable water.

It is the River that controls the voyage of Huck and Jim; that will not let them land at Cairo, where Jim could have reached freedom; it is the River that separates them and deposits Huck for a time in the Grangerford household; the River that re-unites them, and then compels upon them the unwelcome company of the King and the Duke. Recurrently we are reminded of its presence and its power.

> "When I woke up, I didn't know where I was for a minute. I set up and looked around, a little scared. Then I remembered. The river looked miles and miles across. The moon was so bright I could a counted the drift-logs that went a-slipping along, black and still, hundreds of yards out from shore. Everything was dead quiet, and it looked late, and *smelt* late. You know what I mean—I don't know the words to put it in.
>
> "It was kind of solemn, drifting down the big still river, laying on our backs looking up at the stars, and we didn't ever feel like talking loud, and it warn't often that we laughed, only a little kind of a low chuckle. We had mighty good weather as a general thing, and nothing ever happened to us at all, that night, nor the next, nor the next.
>
> "Every night we passed towns, some of them away up on black hillsides, nothing but just a shiny bed of lights, not a house could you see. The fifth night we passed St. Louis, and it was like the whole world lit up. In St. Petersburg they used to say there was

twenty or thirty thousand people in St. Louis, but I never believed it till I see that wonderful spread of lights at two o'clock that still night. There warn't a sound there; everybody was asleep."

We come to understand the River by seeing it through the eyes of the Boy; but the Boy is also the spirit of the River. *Huckleberry Finn*, like other great works of imagination, can give to every reader whatever he is capable of taking from it. On the most superficial level of observation, Huck is convincing as a boy. On the same level, the picture of social life on the shores of the Mississippi a hundred years ago is, I feel sure, accurate. On any level, Mark Twain makes you see the River, as it is and was and always will be, more clearly than the author of any other description of a river known to me. But you do not merely see the River, you do not merely become acquainted with it through the senses: you experience the River. Mark Twain, in his later years of success and fame, referred to his early life as a steamboat pilot as the happiest he had known. With all allowance for the illusions of age, we can agree that those years were the years in which he was most fully alive. Certainly, but for his having practised that calling, earned his living by that profession, he would never have gained the understanding which his genius for expression communicates in this book. In the pilot's daily struggle with the River, in the satisfaction of activity, in the constant attention to the River's unpredictable vagaries, his consciousness was fully occupied, and he absorbed knowledge of which, as an artist, he later made use. There are, perhaps, only two ways in which a writer can acquire the understanding of environment which he can later turn to account: by having spent his childhood in that environment—that is, living in it at a period of life in which one experiences much more than one is aware of; and by having had to struggle for a livelihood in that environment—a livelihood bearing no direct relation to any intention of writing about it, of *using* it as literary material. Most of Joseph Conrad's understanding came to him in the latter way. Mark Twain knew the Mississippi in both ways: he had spent his childhood on its banks, and he had earned his living matching his wits against its currents.

Thus the River makes the book a great book. As with Conrad, we are continually reminded of the power and terror of Nature, and the isolation and feebleness of Man. Conrad remains always the European observer of the tropics, the white man's eye contemplating the Congo and its black gods. But Mark Twain is a native, and the River God is his God. It is as a native that he accepts the River God, and it is the subjection of Man that gives to Man his dignity. For without some kind of God, Man is not even very interesting.

Readers sometimes deplore the fact that the story descends to the level of *Tom Sawyer* from the moment that Tom himself re-appears. Such readers protest that the escapades invented by Tom, in the attempted "rescue" of Jim, are only a tedious development of themes with which we were already too familiar—even while admitting that the escapades themselves are very amusing, and some of the incidental observations memorable.[1] But it is right that the mood of the end of the book should bring us back to that of the beginning. Or, if this was not the right ending for the book, what ending would have been right?

In *Huckleberry Finn* Mark Twain wrote a much greater book than he could have known he was writing. Perhaps all great works of art mean much more than the author could have been aware of meaning: certainly, *Huckleberry Finn* is the one book of Mark Twain's which, as a whole, has this unconsciousness. So what seems to be the rightness, of reverting at the end of the book to the mood of *Tom Sawyer*, was perhaps unconscious art. For Huckleberry Finn, neither a tragic nor a happy ending would be suitable. No worldly success or social satisfaction, no domestic consummation would be worthy of him; a tragic end also would reduce him to the level of those whom we pity. Huck Finn must come from nowhere and be bound for nowhere. His is not the independence of the typical or symbolic American Pioneer, but the independence of the vagabond. His existence questions the values of America as much as the values of Europe; he is as much an affront to the "pioneer spirit" as he is to "business enterprise"; he is in a state of nature as detached as the state of the saint. In a busy world, he represents the loafer; in an acquisitive and competitive world, he insists on living from hand to mouth. He could not be exhibited in any amorous encounters or engagements, in any of the juvenile affections which are appropriate to Tom Sawyer. He belongs neither to the Sunday School nor to the Reformatory. He has no beginning and no end. Hence, he can only disappear; and his disappearance can only be accomplished by bringing forward another performer to obscure the disappearance in a cloud of whimsicalities.

Like Huckleberry Finn, the River itself has no beginning or end. In its beginning, it is not yet the River; in its end, it is no longer the River. What we call its headwaters is only a selection from among the innumerable sources which flow together to compose it. At what point in its course does the Mississippi become what the Mississippi *means*? It is both one and many; it is the Mississippi of this book only after its union with the Big Muddy—the Missouri; it derives some of

[1] *e.g.*, "*Jim* don't know anybody in China."

its character from the Ohio, the Tennessee and other confluents. And at the end it merely disappears among its deltas: it is no longer there, but it is still where it was, hundreds of miles to the North. The River cannot tolerate any design, to a story which is its story, that might interfere with its dominance. Things must merely happen, here and there, to the people who live along its shores or who commit themselves to its current. And it is as impossible for Huck as for the River to have a beginning or end—a *career*. So the book has the right, the only possible concluding sentence. I do not think that any book ever written ends more certainly with the right words:

> "But I reckon I got to light out for the Territory ahead of the rest, because Aunt Sally she's going to adopt me and civilize me, and I can't stand it. I been there before."

QUESTIONS AND EXERCISES

1. Each of these essays was written as an introduction to an edition of *Huckleberry Finn:* Trilling's in 1948, Eliot's in 1950. Both introductions enthusiastically praise the novel, but the similarity between them does not end there. Specify as precisely as possible how they resemble each other in content. In structure.

2. Do the two essays seem to have been written with the same audience in mind, or do differences in tone, strategy, style, and content suggest that Eliot is consciously addressing himself to a group of readers who are in some respects unlike those Trilling anticipates? Note, in particular, any details that reveal that the essay is directed not only at those for whom introductions are usually intended— people who probably have never read the particular book before— but also at experienced literary "experts" who have a long-standing interest in the novel.

3. Which of the two writers puts more of himself into his introduction? How do you account for this difference? Does this element of personal or autobiographical interest suit well the essay in which it appears? How, if at all, does the author justify its inclusion?

4. Both Trilling and Eliot give special attention to the questionable success of the novel's ending. Is this part of the discussion well integrated with the rest of the essay? Explain.

5. Like most introductions, these essays not only interpret the quality of the work in question but also provide a certain amount of information—facts about the literary tradition, about Mark Twain's other writings, about the process of the book's composition, about its reputation—that helps the reader to *locate* the novel, to see where it fits into larger schemes of experience. Which essay has more of

this information? Can you relate this difference between them to other, more fundamental differences?

6. If you had never read *Huckleberry Finn* and had to take an examination on its form, style, and content half an hour from now, which of these two introductions would you want to reread in your desperate preparation? Why?

7. Which of these essays strikes you as having the greater *magnitude?* That is, which one undertakes more ambitiously and successfully to say things about the novel that are truly important and difficult to express well? If you find that each has its own kind of magnitude, and that the kinds are not really comparable, say so. And explain.

8. If you were serving as editorial consultant to the publisher of either of these editions of *Huckleberry Finn,* what suggestions might you make to Trilling or Eliot about ways in which his essay should be augmented or otherwise improved?

9. Is one of these writers much better known to you than the other as an eminent literary figure? How, if at all, does your knowledge of his position in the world of letters affect your judgment of his essay? Be honest.

10. Write a 500-word commentary on Trilling's consistent (or inconsistent) development of the nature-versus-society relationship that he sees in *Huckleberry Finn.*

11. In a short analytic essay, discuss the appropriateness of Eliot's use of quotation.

12. Write your own introduction—a reasonably brief one—to *Huckleberry Finn* or to some other novel that you know well. This exercise may require some preliminary research.

13. Both Trilling and Eliot praise the verbal style of Mark Twain's narrator-hero. Try writing an introduction to the Trilling and Eliot pieces, using Huck's kind of language. As usual with an exercise of this type, it will help to append a concise discussion of the reasons for your success or failure in using this particular style for this purpose.

CHAPTER EIGHT

An Essayist

The foregoing chapters have suggested various ways essays may be grouped. We may organize them according to the type of subject matter, the presence or absence of substantive argument, the relative importance of personality as against objectivity, the nature of the audience for whom they are designed, and even by the hard-to-measure qualities of verbal style. They may be classified, too, by length, by place of composition, and by historical period. For purposes of academic exercise, any one of these groupings can be quite useful, particularly as it shows the technical variations and developments that are possible. Whether any of these categories corresponds, however, to the natural reading habits of people who read essays, is another question. For readers of rather specialized interest, it may be habitual to read, say, only essays on politics, or essays that moralize, or essays written in the early part of the nineteenth century, or essays composed in a colloquial style. Most readers, though, will find it natural to read essays grouped by author. Good reasons for this practice have been suggested earlier. The essay is, above all, a personal mode of expression, a manifestation—even in the most detached and objective cases—of intellectual and emotional substance that springs directly from the writer's specifically interested self. We read a great many pieces by a single man because we find ourselves interested in what he talks about, engaged by what he says, and admiring of the way he says it. When we take up a volume of his essays, the rewards may be comparable in weight and value with those afforded by great novels and plays. The author's idiom, in both thought and language, becomes familiar, his strategies and maneuvers can be anticipated without becoming tediously predictable, his recurrent and preoccupying concerns begin to take on shape and pattern. Essays reinforce and complement each other with marvelously appropriate cross-reference, until in a very real sense the whole collection assumes its own integrity as an accomplishment. And through all of this, the elements of variety, surprise, and a constantly renewed freshness of attack provide the kind of agility that the novel or play seldom provides. Of course, one need not go through an entire volume at one sitting. A few essays may yield the fullest effect without producing fatigue. In this chapter we shall study the work of a single important essayist as represented by five of his pieces. While it would be pleasant to have this sample inspire the reader to read more, our immediate purpose is to see how these five essays form a group in which the total meaning of each is greatly broadened and enriched.

It may at first seem strange that the author chosen here is Aldous Huxley, who is better known as a novelist than as an essayist. But in fact he was not limited even to these two roles; in addition to writing prose fiction and essays, he enjoyed some success in poetry and drama. And it is this very diversity in his talent, the widespread liveliness of his interest, that makes him a particularly apt example. He is not easily cowed into silence by any aspect of experience, no matter how formidable; if there is something interesting at hand, and something to be done with it or said about it or asked of it, he has a try. The essays do, of course, speak for themselves in one sense, and so the introduction here will be brief; but a certain amount of general and biographical information may help us to know the man whose character shapes the substance of these works.

Huxley was born in 1894, into a family in which personal distinction and achievement were usual. He was related, through his mother, to Matthew Arnold. His grandfather, Thomas Henry Huxley, had been recognized as one of the two or three most eminent Victorian men of science, a brilliant biologist, defender of Darwin's doctrine of evolution, who exerted lasting influence in public affairs, particularly in education. Aldous' father, Leonard Huxley, was a noted classical scholar. And an elder brother, Julian, has established himself as a leading thinker with a rare capacity for relating the data of biological science to human religious and social practices.

The young man showed quite early that he was made of the same stuff. His years at Eton and at Balliol in Oxford were distinguished ones. A first volume of poems appeared in 1916, when he was twenty-two, and from then until well into the 1950's, every year brought the publication of some new work, often two or three. During the earlier part of his life he travelled extensively through Europe, Asia, and the Americas, settling eventually in California. He remained remarkably active and intellectually ambitious throughout his life, although he suffered the great hardship of deteriorating eyesight, which left him almost totally blind long before his death. People who knew him or heard him lecture remember a very tall man, terribly gaunt, with a deeply lined face and a voice capable of astonishing, expressive feats. His personal presence was an event.

During the early 1950's, Huxley's experiments with the cactus-derived drug mescaline led him to speculate about the nature of human consciousness, and *The Doors of Perception* (1954) brought him for a while rather sensational publicity. But he had long since made a name for himself as one of the most inventive and intellectually challenging novelists of his time. His first major piece of fiction, *Crome Yellow* (1921), is an account of events at a society house-party, a situation well suited to his strategy, which reappears in several later novels, of putting his characters in circumstances where they can talk long and well, often expressing the author's own ideas. This use of conversation in the novel has an obvious connection with the art of the essayist. The mere description or narration of events gives way continually to the demands of self-expressive substance.

Another house-party novel, *Antic Hay* (1925), carries on the same conversational device. But by now it becomes clear that Huxley is less interested in the wit of opinion for its own sake than in forming some serious judgments of the relation between society and the individual. Increasingly he is led to the pessimistic conclusion that social entanglements of all sorts must be avoided by anyone who wishes to explore philosophically the "interior universe" of his own mind. *Point Counter Point* (1928) portrays sharply the nearly impossible attempt by moral people to survive in a world where human relationships culminate often in insignificance and stagnation, sometimes in open violence and ferocity. *Brave New World* (1932) ironically envisions a possible way out, a "utopian" world of the future so decontaminated, organized, and essentially dehumanized that it can only horrify. Having to deal with other people as persons and with our own not particularly pleasing bodies as bodies may be unpleasant, but the totalitarian cure seems far worse. Subsequent novels show no real change in this dark view of the world, which emerges more and more in the non-fiction as well. *Ends and Means*, a long prose commentary published in 1937, develops in detail the argument that although everyone seems to agree on the content of the ideal human society—"liberty, peace, justice, and brotherly love"—there is no agreement about the means of achieving that content, and since any particular means must necessarily condition and shape the end, alter it, the agreement on ideals does us no practical good whatever. Faced with this dilemma, Huxley strongly implies that the only viable life is that of "non-attachment"; it was this conviction that led him, during the 1940's, to a deep study of mystic and Eastern philosophies.

All this while, Huxley was also producing shorter essays of the type that you are about to read. From the time of his first collection,

On the Margin (1923), up to the *Themes and Variations* of 1950 and the *Tomorrow and Tomorrow and Tomorrow* of 1956, he voiced his views on an astounding variety of subjects. Customs, history, politics, psychology, religion, language, nature, music, painting, literature, exotic places, all come under his scrutiny, and the results are always impressive if not consistently good. What usually distinguishes his view is a finely-honed ironical awareness of the contradictions that perplex human life, tempered by an equally strong awareness of the moral need to find order and intelligibility in experience. The progress of his thought in language is not unlike that of the most important speaking characters in his novels, though generally a bit more formal in tone and structure. A further point needs special emphasis if only because it is so frequently overlooked in cataloging a writer's powers: Huxley writes interestingly because, for one thing, he *knows* a great deal. He has simply absorbed more impressions, facts, opinions, visions, textures, and feelings than most people, and he has thought about them enough to have something worth saying about them.

In a Preface to the *Collected Essays* of 1958, Huxley defines the essay as "a literary device for saying almost everything about almost anything." He goes on to discuss the variability of the form in terms of three basic types. The first is personal, and its substance is the author himself, allowing his reader to know him "through the keyhole of anecdote and description." He next defines the objective essay as that in which the author, seeking the concretely particular, addresses himself to "setting forth, passing judgment upon, and drawing general conclusions from, the relevant data." Finally, there is what Huxley calls the essay of the abstract-universal, in which the quest for grand generalization and distilled truth leaves little room for either the concrete or the personal. Each type has its inherent danger: The personal essay may degenerate into the merely cute, the objective into the dully informative, the abstract into algebra. As Huxley sees it, the majority of essays and essayists owe their success almost solely to one or another of these three kinds of activity. But the rare great essay is that in which all three flow effortlessly together, naturally intertwining the personal with the universal, the concrete with the abstract, the fact with the inner awareness. And it is clear, too, though Huxley does not say so explicitly, that he regards the talent for successful abstraction as the highest and most elusive of the three. This does not mean that every essayist should try to reach after universality; some clearly cannot and ought not do so. But where the three are legitimately joined, the reader will share in the fullest possible response to life.

The first two essays reprinted here originally appeared in Huxley's 1929 volume, *Do What You Will,* the next two in *The Olive Tree* of 1936, and the last in the collection of 1956, *Tomorrow and Tomorrow and Tomorrow.* It is suggested that all of these essays be read at a single sitting. The questions and exercises should wait, this time, until the reader has formed an aggregate impression.

WORDSWORTH IN THE TROPICS

Aldous Huxley

In the neighborhood of latitude fifty north, and for the last hundred years or thereabouts, it has been an axiom that Nature is divine and morally uplifting. For good Wordsworthians—and most serious-minded people are now Wordsworthians, either by direct inspiration or at second hand—a walk in the country is the equivalent of going to church, a tour through Westmorland is as good as a pilgrimage to Jerusalem. To commune with the fields and waters, the woodlands and the hills, is to commune, according to our modern and northern ideas, with the visible manifestations of the "Wisdom and Spirit of the Universe."

The Wordsworthian who exports this pantheistic worship of Nature to the tropics is liable to have his religious convictions some-what rudely disturbed. Nature, under a vertical sun, and nourished by the equatorial rains, is not at all like that chaste, mild deity who presides over the *Gemüthlichkeit*, the prettiness, the cozy sublimities of the Lake District. The worst that Wordsworth's goddess ever did to him was to make him hear

> Low breathings coming after me, and sounds
> Of undistinguishable motion, steps
> Almost as silent as the turf they trod;

was to make him realize, in the shape of "a huge peak, black and huge," the existence of "unknown modes of being." He seems to have imagined that this was the worst Nature *could* do. A few weeks in Malaya or Borneo would have undeceived him. Wandering in the hothouse darkness of the jungle, he would not have felt so serenely

WORDSWORTH IN THE TROPICS: Copyright 1929, 1956 by Aldous Huxley. From *Collected Essays* by Aldous Huxley. Reprinted by permission of Harper & Row, Publishers and Chatto and Windus Ltd.

certain of those "Presences of Nature," those "Souls of Lonely Places," which he was in the habit of worshipping on the shores of Windermere and Rydal. The sparse inhabitants of the equatorial forest are all believers in devils. When one has visited, in even the most superficial manner, the places where they live, it is difficult not to share their faith. The jungle is marvelous, fantastic, beautiful; but it is also terrifying, it is also profoundly sinister. There is something in what, for lack of a better word, we must call the character of great forests—even in those of temperate lands—which is foreign, appalling, fundamentally and utterly inimical to intruding man. The life of those vast masses of swarming vegetation is alien to the human spirit and hostile to it. Meredith, in his "Woods of Westermaine," has tried reassuringly to persuade us that our terrors are unnecessary, that the hostility of these vegetable forces is more apparent than real, and that if we will but trust Nature we shall find our fears transformed into serenity, joy, and rapture. This may be sound philosophy in the neighborhood of Dorking; but it begins to be dubious even in the forests of Germany—there is too much of them for a human being to feel himself at ease within their enormous glooms; and when the woods of Borneo are substituted for those of Westermaine, Meredith's comforting doctrine becomes frankly ridiculous.

It is not the sense of solitude that distresses the wanderer in equatorial jungles. Loneliness is bearable enough—for a time, at any rate. There is something actually rather stimulating and exciting about being in an empty place where there is no life but one's own. Taken in reasonably small doses, the Sahara exhilarates, like alcohol. Too much of it, however (I speak, at any rate, for myself), has the depressing effect of the second bottle of Burgundy. But in any case it is not loneliness that oppresses the equatorial traveller: it is too much company; it is the uneasy feeling that he is an alien in the midst of an innumerable throng of hostile beings. To us who live beneath a temperate sky and in the age of Henry Ford, the worship of Nature comes almost naturally. It is easy to love a feeble and already conquered enemy. But an enemy with whom one is still at war, an unconquered, unconquerable, ceaselessly active enemy—no; one does not, one should not, love him. One respects him, perhaps; one has a salutary fear of him; and one goes on fighting. In our latitudes the hosts of Nature have mostly been vanquished and enslaved. Some few detachments, it is true, still hold the field against us. There are wild woods and mountains, marshes and heaths, even in England. But they are there only on sufferance, because we have chosen, out of our good pleasure, to leave them their freedom. It has not been worth our while to reduce them to slavery. We love them because we are the masters, because we know that at any moment we can overcome them as we overcame their fellows. The inhabitants of the tropics have no such comforting reasons for adoring the sinister forces which hem them in on every side. For us, the notion "river" implies (how obviously!) the notion "bridge." When we think of a plain, we think of agriculture, towns, and good roads. The corollary of mountain is tunnel; of swamp, an embankment; of distance, a railway. At latitude zero, however, the obvious is not the same as with us. Rivers imply wading, swimming, alligators. Plains mean swamps, forests, fevers. Mountains are either dangerous or impassable. To travel is to hack one's way laboriously through a tangled, prickly, and venomous darkness. "God made the country," said Cowper, in his rather too blank verse. In New Guinea he would have had his doubts; he would have longed for the man-made town.

The Wordsworthian adoration of Nature has two principal defects. The first, as we have seen, is that it is only possible in a country where Nature has been nearly or quite enslaved to man. The second is that it is only possible for those who are prepared to falsify their immediate intuitions of Nature. For Nature, even in the temperate zone, is always alien and inhuman, and occasionally diabolic. Meredith explicitly invites us to explain any unpleasant experiences away. We are to interpret them, Pangloss fashion, in terms of a preconceived philosophy; after which, all will surely be for the best in the best of all possible Westermaines. Less openly, Wordsworth asks us to make the same falsification of immediate experience. It is only very occasionally that he admits the existence in the world around him of those "unknown modes of being" of which our immediate intuitions of things make us so disquietingly aware. Normally what he does is to pump the dangerous Unknown out of Nature and refill the emptied forms of hills and woods, flowers and waters, with something more reassuringly familiar—with humanity, with Anglicanism. He will not admit that a yellow primrose is simply a yellow primrose—beautiful, but essentially strange, having its own alien life apart. He wants it to possess some sort of soul, to exist humanly, not simply flowerily. He wants the earth to be more than earthy, to be a divine person. But the life of vegetation is radically unlike the life of man: the earth has a mode of being that is certainly not the mode of being of a person. "Let Nature be your teacher," says Wordsworth. The advice is excellent. But how strangely he himself puts it into practice! Instead of listening humbly to what the teacher says, he shuts his ears and himself dictates the lesson he desires to hear. The pupil knows better than his master; the worshipper substitutes his own oracles for those of the god. Instead of accepting the lesson as it is given to his immediate intuitions, he distorts it rationalistically into the likeness of a parson's sermon or a professorial lecture. Our direct intuitions of Nature tell us that the world is bottomlessly strange: alien, even when it is kind and beautiful; having innumerable modes of being that are not our modes; always mysteriously not personal, not conscious, not moral; often hostile and sinister; sometimes even unimaginably, because inhumanly, evil. In his youth, it would seem, Wordsworth left his direct intuitions of the world unwarped.

> The sounding cataract
> Haunted me like a passion: the tall rock,
> The mountain, and the deep and gloomy wood,
> Their colors and their forms, were then to me
> An appetite; a feeling and a love,
> That had no need of a remoter charm,
> By thought supplied, nor any interest
> Unborrowed from the eye.

As the years passed, however, he began to interpret them in terms of a preconceived philosophy. Procrustes-like, he tortured his feelings and perceptions until they fitted his system. By the time he was thirty,

> The immeasurable height
> Of woods decaying, never to be decayed,
> The stationary blasts of waterfalls—
> The torrents shooting from the clear blue sky,
> The rocks that muttered close upon our ears,
> Black drizzling crags that spake by the wayside
> As if a voice were in them, the sick sight
> And giddy prospect of the raving stream,
> The unfettered clouds and regions of the heavens,
> Tumult and peace, the darkness and the light—
> Were all like workings of one mind, the features
> Of the same face, blossoms upon one tree,
> Characters of the great Apocalypse,
> The types and symbols of eternity,
> Of first, and last, and midst, and without end.

"Something far more deeply interfused" had made its appearance on the Wordsworthian scene. The god of Anglicanism had crept under the skin of things, and all the stimulatingly inhuman strangeness of Nature had become as flatly familiar as a page from a textbook of metaphysics or theology. As familiar and as safely simple. Pantheistically interpreted, our intuitions of Nature's endless varieties of impersonal mysteriousness lose all their exciting and disturbing quality. It makes the world seem delightfully cozy, if you can pretend that all the many alien things about you are really only manifestations of one person. It is fear of the labyrinthine flux and complexity of phenomena that has driven men to philosophy, to science, to theology—fear of the complex reality driving them to invent a simpler, more manageable, and, therefore, consoling fiction. For simple, in comparison with the external reality of which we have direct intuitions, childishly simple is even the most elaborate and subtle system devised by the human mind. Most of the philosophical systems hitherto popular have not been subtle and elaborate even by human standards. Even by human standards they have been crude, bald, preposterously straightforward. Hence their popularity. Their simplicity has rendered them instantly comprehensible. Weary with much wandering in the maze of phenomena, frightened by the inhospitable strangeness of the world, men have rushed into the systems prepared for them by philosophers and founders of religions, as they would rush from a dark jungle into the haven of a well-lit, commodious house. With a sigh of relief and a thankful feeling that here at last is their true home, they settle down in their snug metaphysical villa and go to sleep. And how furious they are when any one comes rudely knocking at the door to tell them that their villa is jerry-built, dilapidated, unfit for human habitation, even nonexistent! Men have been burnt at the stake for even venturing to criticize the color of the front door or the shape of the third-floor windows.

That man must build himself some sort of metaphysical shelter in the midst of the jungle of immediately apprehended reality is obvious. No practical activity, no scientific research, no speculation is possible without some preliminary hypothesis about the nature and the purpose of things. The human mind cannot deal with the universe directly, nor even with its own immediate intuitions of the universe. Whenever it is a question of thinking about the world or of practically modifying it, men can only work on a symbolic plan of the universe, only a simplified, two-dimensional map of things abstracted by the mind out of the complex and multifarious reality of immediate intuition. History shows that these hypotheses about the nature of things are valuable even when, as later experience reveals, they are false. Man approaches the unattainable truth through a succession of errors. Confronted by the strange complexity of things, he invents, quite arbitrarily, a simple hypothesis to explain and justify the world. Having invented, he proceeds to act and think in terms of this hypothesis, as though it were correct. Experience gradually shows him where his hypothesis is unsatisfactory and how it should be modified. Thus, great scientific discoveries have been made by men seeking to verify quite erroneous theories about the nature of things. The discoveries have necessitated a modification of the original hypotheses, and further discoveries have been made in the effort to verify the modifications—discoveries which, in their turn, have led to yet further modifications. And so on, indefinitely. Philosophical and religious hypotheses, being less susceptible of experimental verification than the hypotheses of science, have undergone far less modification. For example, the pantheistic hypothesis of Wordsworth is an ancient doctrine, which human experience has hardly modified throughout history. And rightly, no doubt. For it is obvious that there must be some sort of unity underlying the diversity of phenomena; for if there were not, the world would be quite unknowable. Indeed, it is precisely in the knowableness of things, in the very fact that they are known, that their fundamental unity consists. The world which we know, and which our minds have fabricated out of goodness knows what mysterious things in themselves, possesses the unity which our minds have imposed upon it. It is part of our thought, hence fundamentally homogeneous. Yes, the world is obviously one. But at the same time it is no less obviously diverse. For if the world were absolutely one, it would no longer be knowable, it would cease to exist. Thought must be divided against itself before it can come to any knowledge of itself. Absolute oneness is absolute nothingness: homogeneous perfection, as the Hindus perceived and courageously recognized, is equivalent to non-existence, is nirvana. The Christian idea of a perfect heaven that is something other than a non-existence is a contradiction in terms. The world in which we live may be fundamentally one, but it is a unity divided up into a great many diverse fragments. A tree, a table, a newspaper, a piece of artificial silk are all made of wood. But they are, none the less, distinct and separate objects. It is the same with the world at large. Our immediate intuitions are of diversity. We have only to open our eyes to recognize a multitude of different phenomena. These intuitions of diversity are as correct, as well justified, as is our intellectual conviction of the fundamental homogeneity of the various parts of the world with one another and with ourselves. Circumstances have led humanity to set an ever-increasing premium on the conscious and intellectual comprehension of things. Modern man's besetting temptation is to sacrifice his direct perceptions and spontaneous feelings to his reasoned reflections; to prefer in all circumstances the verdict of his intellect to that of his immediate intuitions. "L'homme est visiblement fait pour penser," says Pascal; "c'est toute sa dignité et tout son mérite; et tout son devoir est de penser comme il faut." Noble words; but do they happen to be true? Pascal seems to forget that man has something else to do besides think: he must live. Living may not be so dignified or meritorious as thinking (particularly when you happen to be, like Pascal, a chronic invalid); but it is, perhaps unfortunately, a necessary process. If one would live well, one must live completely, with the whole being— with the body and the instincts, as well as with the conscious mind. A life lived, as far as may be, exclusively from the consciousness and in accordance with the considered judgments of the intellect, is a stunted life, a half-dead life. This is a fact that can be confirmed by daily observation. But consciousness, the intellect, the spirit, have acquired an inordinate prestige; and such is men's snobbish respect for authority, such is their pedantic desire to be consistent, that they go on doing their best to lead the exclusively conscious, spiritual, and intellectual life, in spite of its manifest disadvantages. To know is pleasant; it is exciting to be conscious; the intellect is a valuable instrument, and for certain purposes the hypotheses which it fabricates are of great practical value. Quite true. But, therefore, say the moralists and men of science, drawing conclusions only justified by their desire for consistency, therefore *all* life should be lived from the head, consciously, *all* phenomena should at *all* times be interpreted in terms of the intellect's hypotheses. The religious teachers are of a slightly different opinion. All life, according to them, should be lived spiritually, not intellectually. Why? On the grounds, as we discover when we push our analysis far enough, that certain occasional psychological states, currently called spiritual, are extremely agreeable and have valuable consequences in the realm of social behavior. The unprejudiced observer finds it hard to understand why these people should set such store by consistency of thought and action. Because oysters are occasionally pleasant, it does not follow that one should make of oysters one's exclusive diet. Nor should one take castor-oil every day because castor-oil is occasionally good for one. Too much consistency is as bad for the mind as it is for the body. Consistency is contrary to nature, contrary to life. The only completely consistent people are the dead. Consistent intellectualism and spirituality may be socially valuable, up to a point; but they make, gradually, for individual death. And individual death, when the slow murder has been consummated, is finally social death. So that the social utility of pure intellectualism and pure spirituality is only apparent and temporary. What is needed is, as ever, a compromise. Life must be lived in different ways at different moments. The only satisfactory way of existing in the modern, highly specialized world is to live with two personalities. A Dr. Jekyll that does the metaphysical and scientific thinking, that transacts business in the city, adds up figures, designs machines, and so forth. And a natural, spontaneous Mr. Hyde to do the physical, instinctive living in the intervals of work. The two personalities should lead their unconnected lives apart, without poaching on one another's preserves or inquiring too closely into one another's activities. Only by living discreetly and inconsistently can we preserve both the man and the citizen, both the intellectual and the spontaneous animal being, alive within us. The solution may not be very satisfactory; but it is, I believe now (though once I thought differently), the best that, in the modern circumstances, can be devised.

The poet's place, it seems to me, is with the Mr. Hydes of human nature. He should be, as Blake remarked of Milton, "of the devil's party without knowing it"—or preferably with the full consciousness of being of the devil's party. There are so many intellectual and moral angels battling for rationalism, good citizenship, and pure spirituality; so many and such eminent ones, so very vocal and authoritative! The poor devil in man needs all the support and advocacy he can get. The artist is his natural champion. When an artist deserts to the side of the angels, it is the most odious of treasons. How unforgivable, for example, is Tolstoy! Tolstoy, the perfect Mr. Hyde, the complete embodiment, if ever there was one, of non-intellectual, non-moral, instinctive life—Tolstoy, who betrayed his own nature, betrayed his art, betrayed life itself, in order to fight against the devil's party of his earlier allegiances, under the standard of Dr. Jesus-Jekyll. Wordsworth's betrayal was not so spectacular: he was never so wholly of the devil's party as Tolstoy. Still, it was bad enough. It is difficult to forgive him for so utterly repenting his youthful passions and enthusiasms, and becoming, personally as well as politically, the anglican tory. One remembers B. R. Haydon's account of the poet's reactions to that charming classical sculpture of Cupid and Psyche. "The devils!" he said malignantly, after a long-drawn contemplation of their marble embrace. "The devils!" And he was not using the word in the complimentary sense in which I have employed it here: he was expressing his hatred of passion and life, he was damning the young man he had himself been—the young man who had hailed the French Revolution with delight and begotten an illegitimate child. From being an ardent lover of the nymphs, he had become one of those all too numerous

woodmen who expel
Love's gentle dryads from the haunts of life,
And vex the nightingales in every dell.

Yes, even the nightingales he vexed. Even the nightingales, though the poor birds can never, like those all too human dryads, have led him into sexual temptation. Even the innocuous nightingales were moralized, spiritualized, turned into citizens and anglicans—and along with the nightingales, the whole of animate and inanimate Nature.

The change in Wordsworth's attitude toward Nature is symptomatic of his general apostasy. Beginning as what I may call a natural aesthete, he transformed himself, in the course of years, into a moralist, a thinker. He used his intellect to distort his exquisitely acute and subtle intuitions of the world, to explain away their often disquieting strangeness, to simplify them into a comfortable metaphysical unreality. Nature had endowed him with the poet's gift of seeing more than ordinarily far into the brick walls of external reality, of intuitively comprehending the character of the bricks, of feeling the quality of their being, and establishing the appropriate relationship with them. But he preferred to think his gifts away. He preferred, in the interests of a preconceived religious theory, to ignore the disquieting strangeness of things, to interpret the impersonal diversity of Nature in terms of a divine, anglican unity. He chose, in a word, to be a philosopher, comfortably at home with a man-made and, therefore, thoroughly comprehensible system, rather than a poet adventuring for adventure's sake through the mysterious world revealed by his direct and undistorted intuitions.

It is a pity that he never traveled beyond the boundaries of Europe. A voyage through the tropics would have cured him of his too easy and comfortable pantheism. A few months in the jungle would have convinced him that the diversity and utter strangeness of Nature are at least as real and significant as its intellectually discovered unity. Nor would he have felt so certain, in the damp and stifling darkness, among the leeches and the malevolently tangled rattans, of the divinely anglican character of that fundamental unity. He would have learned once more to treat Nature naturally, as he treated it in his youth; to react to it spontaneously, loving where love was the appropriate emotion, fearing, hating, fighting whenever Nature presented itself to his intuition as being, not merely strange, but hostile, inhumanly evil. A voyage would have taught him this. But Wordsworth never left his native continent. Europe is so well gardened that it resembles a work of art, a scientific theory, a neat metaphysical system. Man has re-created Europe in his own image. Its tamed and temperate Nature confirmed Wordsworth in his philosophizings. The poet, the devil's partisan were doomed; the angels triumphed. Alas!

FASHIONS IN LOVE

Aldous Huxley

Human nature does not change, or, at any rate, history is too short for any changes to be perceptible. The earliest known specimens of art and literature are still comprehensible. The fact that we can understand them all and can recognize in some of them an unsurpassed artistic excellence is proof enough that not only men's feelings and instincts, but also their intellectual and imaginative powers, were in the remotest times precisely what they are now. In the fine arts it is only the convention, the form, the incidentals that change: the fundamentals of passion, of intellect and imagination remain unaltered.

It is the same with the arts of life as with the fine arts. Conventions and traditions, prejudices and ideals and religious beliefs, moral systems and codes of good manners, varying according to the geographical and historical circumstances, mold into different forms the unchanging material of human instinct, passion, and desire. It is a stiff, intractable material—Egyptian granite, rather than Hindu bronze. The artists who carved the colossal statues of Rameses II may have wished to represent the Pharaoh standing on one leg and waving two or three pairs of arms over his head, as the Indians still represent the dancing Krishna. But with the best will in the world they could not have imposed such a form upon the granite. Similarly, those artists in social life whom we call statesmen, moralists, founders of religions, have often wished to mold human nature into forms of superhuman elegance; but the material has proved too stubborn for them, and they have had to be content with only a relatively small alteration in the form which their predecessors had given it. At any given historical moment human behavior is a compromise (enforced from without by law and custom, from within by belief in religious or philosophical myths) between the raw instinct on the one hand and the unattainable ideal on the other—a compromise, in our sculptural metaphor, between the unshaped block of stone and the many-armed dancing Krishna.

FASHIONS IN LOVE: Copyright 1928, 1955 by Aldous Huxley. From *Collected Essays* by Aldous Huxley. Reprinted by permission of Harper & Row, Publishers and Chatto and Windus Ltd.

Like all the other great human activities, love is the product of unchanging passions, instincts, and desires (unchanging, that is to say, in the mass of humanity; for, of course, they vary greatly in quantity and quality from individual to individual), and of laws and conventions, beliefs and ideals, which the circumstances of time and place, or the arbitrary fiats of great personalities, have imposed on a more or less willing society. The history of love, if it were ever written (and doubtless some learned German, unread, alas, by me, *has* written it, and in several volumes), would be like the current histories of art—a record of succeeding "styles" and "schools," of "influences," "revolutions," "technical discoveries." Love's psychological and physiological material remains the same; but every epoch treats it in a different manner, just as every epoch cuts its unvarying cloth and silk and linen into garments of the most diverse fashion. By way of illustration, I may mention that vogue of homosexuality which seems, from all accounts, to have been universal in the Hellenic world. Plutarch attributes the inception of this mode to the custom (novel in the fifth century, according to Thucydides) of exercising naked in the palestra.[1] But whatever may have been its origin, there can be no doubt that this particular fashion in love spread widely among people who were not in the least congenitally disposed to homosexuality. Convention and public opinion molded the material of love into forms which a later age has chosen to call "unnatural." A recrudescence of this amorous mode was very noticeable in Europe during the years immediately following the War. Among the determining causes of this recrudescence a future Plutarch will undoubtedly number the writings of Proust and André Gide.

The present fashions in love are not so definite and universal as those in clothes. It is as though our age were dubiously hesitating between crinolines and hobble skirts, trunk hose and Oxford trousers. Two distinct and hostile conceptions of love coexist in the minds of men and women, two sets of ideals, of conventions, of public opinions, struggle for the right to mold the psychological and physiological material of love. One is the conception evolved by the nineteenth century out of the ideals of Christianity on the one hand and romanticism on the other. The other is that still rather inchoate and negative conception which contemporary youth is in process of

---

[1] Plutarch, who wrote some five hundred years after the event, is by no means an unquestionable authority. The habit of which he and Thucydides speak may have facilitated the spread of the homosexual fashion. But that the fashion existed before the fifth century is made sufficiently clear by Homer, not to mention Sappho. Like many modern oriental peoples, the ancient Greeks were evidently, in Sir Richard Burton's expressive phrase, "omnifutuent."

forming out of the materials provided by modern psychology. The public opinion, the conventions, ideals, and prejudices which gave active force to the first convention and enabled it, to some extent at least, to modify the actual practice of love, had already lost much of their strength when they were rudely shattered, at any rate in the minds of the young, by the shock of the War. As usually happens, practice preceded theory, and the new conception of love was called in to justify existing post-War manners. Having gained a footing, the new conception is now a cause of new behavior among the youngest adolescent generation, instead of being, as it was for the generation of the War, an explanation of war-time behavior made after the fact.

Let us try to analyze these two coexisting and conflicting conceptions of love. The older conception was, as I have said, the product of Christianity and romanticism—a curious mixture of contradictions, of the ascetic dread of passion and the romantic worship of passion. Its ideal was a strict monogamy, such as St. Paul grudgingly conceded to amorous humanity, sanctified and made eternal by one of those terrific exclusive passions which are the favorite theme of poetry and drama. It is an ideal which finds its most characteristic expression in the poetry of that infinitely respectable rebel, that profoundly anglican worshiper of passion, Robert Browning. It was Rousseau who first started the cult of passion for passion's sake. Before his time the great passions, such as that of Paris for Helen, of Dido for Æneas, of Paolo and Francesca for one another, had been regarded rather as disastrous maladies than as enviable states of soul. Rousseau, followed by all the romantic poets of France and England, transformed the grand passion from what it had been in the Middle Ages—a demoniac possession—into a divine ecstasy, and promoted it from the rank of a disease to that of the only true and natural form of love. The nineteenth-century conception of love was thus doubly mystical, with the mysticism of Christian asceticism and sacramentalism, and with the romantic mysticism of Nature. It claimed an absolute rightness on the grounds of its divinity and of its naturalness.

Now, if there is one thing that the study of history and psychology makes abundantly clear, it is that there are no such things as either "divine" or "natural" forms of love. Innumerable gods have sanctioned and forbidden innumerable kinds of sexual behavior, and innumerable philosophers and poets have advocated the return to the most diverse kinds of "nature." Every form of amorous behavior, from chastity and monogamy to promiscuity and the most fantastic "perversions," is found both among animals and men. In any given human society, at any given moment, love, as we have seen, is the result of the interaction of the unchanging instinctive and physiological material of sex with the local conventions of morality and religion, the local laws, prejudices, and ideals. The degree of permanence of these conventions, religious myths, and ideals is proportional to their social utility in the given circumstances of time and place.

The new twentieth-century conception of love is realistic. It recognizes the diversity of love, not merely in the social mass from age to age, but from individual to contemporary individual, according to the dosage of the different instincts with which each is born, and the upbringing he has received. The new generation knows that there is no such thing as Love with a large L, and that what the Christian romantics of the last century regarded as the uniquely natural form of love is, in fact, only one of the indefinite number of possible amorous fashions, produced by specific circumstances at that particular time. Psychoanalysis has taught it that all the forms of sexual behavior previously regarded as wicked, perverse, unnatural, are statistically normal (and normality is solely a question of statistics), and that what is commonly called amorous normality is far from being a spontaneous, instinctive form of behavior, but must be acquired by a process of education. Having contracted the habit of talking freely and more or less scientifically about sexual matters, the young no longer regard love with that feeling of rather guilty excitement and thrilling shame which was for an earlier generation the normal reaction to the subject. Moreover, the practice of birth-control has robbed amorous indulgence of most of the sinfulness traditionally supposed to be inherent in it by robbing it of its socially disastrous effects. The tree shall be known by its fruits: where there are no fruits, there is obviously no tree. Love has ceased to be the rather fearful, mysterious thing it was, and become a perfectly normal, almost commonplace, activity—an activity, for many young people, especially in America, of the same nature as dancing or tennis, a sport, a recreation, a pastime. For those who hold this conception of love, liberty and toleration are prime necessities. A strenuous offensive against the old taboos and repressions is everywhere in progress.

Such, then, are the two conceptions of love which oppose one another today. Which is the better? Without presuming to pass judgment, I will content myself with pointing out the defects of each. The older conception was bad, in so far as it inflicted unnecessary and undeserved sufferings on the many human beings whose congenital and acquired modes of lovemaking did not conform to the fashionable Christian-romantic pattern which was regarded as being uniquely entitled to call itself Love. The new conception is bad, it seems to me, in so far as it takes love too easily and lightly. On love regarded as an amusement the last word is surely this of Robert Burns:

> I waive the quantum of the sin,
>   The hazard of concealing;
> But oh! it hardens all within
>   And petrifies the feeling.

Nothing is more dreadful than a cold, unimpassioned indulgence. And love infallibly becomes cold and unimpassioned when it is too lightly made. It is not good, as Pascal remarked, to have too much liberty. Love is the product of two opposed forces—of an instinctive impulsion and a social resistance acting on the individual by means of ethical imperatives justified by philosophical or religious myths. When, with the destruction of the myths, resistance is removed, the impulse wastes itself on emptiness; and love, which is only the product of conflicting forces, is not born. The twentieth century is reproducing in a new form the error of the early nineteenth-century romantics. Following Rousseau, the romantics imagined that exclusive passion was the "natural" mode of love, just as virtue and reasonableness were the "natural" forms of men's social behavior. Get rid of priests and kings, and men will be for ever good and happy; poor Shelley's faith in this palpable nonsense remained unshaken to the end. He believed also in the complementary paralogism that you had only to get rid of social restraints and erroneous mythology to make the Grand Passion universally chronic. Like the Mussets and Sands, he failed to see that the Grand Passion was produced by the restraints that opposed themselves to the sexual impulse, just as the deep lake is produced by the dam that bars the passage of the stream, and the flight of the aeroplane by the air which resists the impulse given to it by the motor. There would be no air-resistance in a vacuum; but precisely for that reason the machine would not leave the ground, or even move at all. Where there are no psychological or external restraints, the Grand Passion does not come into existence and must be artificially cultivated, as George Sand and Musset cultivated it—with what painful and grotesque results the episode of Venice made only too ludicrously manifest.

"J'aime et je veux pâlir; j'aime et je veux souffrir," says Musset, with his usual hysterically masochistic emphasis. Our young contemporaries do not wish to suffer or grow pale; on the contrary, they have a most determined desire to grow pink and enjoy themselves. But too much enjoyment "blunts the fine point of seldom pleasure." Unrestrained indulgence kills not merely passion, but, in the end, even amusement. Too much liberty is as life-destroying as too much restraint. The present fashion in lovemaking is likely to be short, because love that is psychologically too easy is not interesting. Such, at any rate, was evidently the opinion of the French, who, bored by the sexual license produced by the Napoleonic upheavals, reverted (so far, at any rate, as the upper and middle classes were concerned) to an almost anglican strictness under Louis-Philippe. We may anticipate an analogous reaction in the not distant future. What new or what revived mythology will serve to create those internal restraints without which sexual impulse cannot be transformed into love? Christian morality and ascetic ideals will doubtless continue to play their part, but there will no less certainly be other moralities and ideals. For example, Mr. D. H. Lawrence's new mythology of nature (new in its expression, but reassuringly old in substance) is a doctrine that seems to me fruitful in possibilities. The "natural love" which he sets up as a norm is a passion less self-conscious and highfalutin, less obviously and precariously artificial, than that "natural love" of the romantics, in which Platonic and Christian notions were essential ingredients. The restraints which Mr. Lawrence would impose on sexual impulse, so as to transform it into love, are not the restraints of religious spirituality. They are restraints of a more fundamental, less artificial nature—emotional, not intellectual. The impulse is to be restrained from promiscuous manifestations because, if it were not, promiscuity would "harden all within and petrify the feeling." The restraint is of the same personal nature as the impulse. The conflict is between a part of the personality and the personality as an organized whole. It does not pretend, as the romantic and Christian conflict pretends, to be a battle between a diabolical Lower Self and certain transcendental Absolutes, of which the only thing that philosophy can tell us is that they are absolutely unknowable, and therefore, for our purposes, nonexistent. It only claims to be, what in fact it is, a psychological conflict taking place in the more or less known and finite world of human interests. This doctrine has several great advantages over previous systems of inward restraint. It does not postulate the existence of any transcendental, non-human entity. This is a merit which will be increasingly appreciated as the significance of Kant's and Nietzsche's destructive criticism is more widely realized. People will cease to be interested in unknowable absolutes; but they will never lose interest in their own personalities. True, that "personality as a whole," in whose interests the sexual impulse is to be restrained and turned into love, is, strictly speaking, a mythological figure. Consisting, as we do, of a vast colony of souls —souls of individual cells, of organs, of groups of organs, hungersouls, sex-souls, power-souls, herd-souls, of whose multifarious activities our consciousness (the Soul with a large S) is only very imperfectly and indirectly aware—we are not in a position to know the real nature of our personality as a whole. The only thing we can do is to hazard a hypothesis, to create a mythological figure, call it Human Personality, and hope that circumstances will not, by destroying us, prove our imaginative guesswork too hopelessly wrong. But myth for myth, Human Personality is preferable to God. We do at least know something of Human Personality, whereas of God we know nothing and, knowing nothing, are at liberty to invent as freely as we like. If men had always tried to deal with the problem of love in terms of known human rather than of grotesquely imagined divine interests, there would have been less "making of eunuchs for the kingdom of heaven's sake," less persecution of "sinners," less burning and imprisoning of the heretics of "unnatural" love, less Grundyism, less Comstockery, and, at the same time, less dirty Don-Juanism, less of that curiously malignant and vengeful lovemaking so characteristic of the debauchee under a Christian dispensation. Reacting against the absurdities of the old mythology, the young have run into absurdities no less inordinate at the other end of the scale. A sordid and ignoble realism offers no resistance to the sexual impulse, which now spends itself purposelessly, without producing love, or even, in the long-run, amusement, without enhancing vitality or quickening and deepening the rhythms of living. Only a new mythology of nature, such as, in modern times, Blake, Robert Burns, and Lawrence have defined it, an untranscendental and (relatively speaking) realistic mythology of Energy, Life, and Human Personality, will provide, it seems to me, the inward resistances necessary to turn sexual impulse into love, and provide them in a form which the critical intelligence of Post-Nietzschean youth can respect. By means of such a conception a new fashion in love may be created, a mode more beautiful and convenient, more healthful and elegant, than any seen among men since the days of remote and pagan antiquity.

TIME AND THE MACHINE

Aldous Huxley

Time, as we know it, is a very recent invention. The modern time-sense is hardly older than the United States. It is a by-product of

TIME AND THE MACHINE: From *The Olive Tree* by Aldous Huxley. Copyright 1937 by Aldous Huxley; renewed 1965 by Laura A. Huxley. Reprinted by permission of Harper & Row, Publishers and Chatto and Windus Ltd.

industrialism—a sort of psychological analogue of synthetic perfumes and aniline dyes.

Time is our tyrant. We are chronically aware of the moving minute hand, even of the moving second hand. We have to be. There are trains to be caught, clocks to be punched, tasks to be done in specified periods, records to be broken by fractions of a second, machines that set the pace and have to be kept up with. Our consciousness of the smallest units of time is now acute. To us, for example, the moment 8.17 A.M. means something—something very important, if it happens to be the starting time of our daily train. To our ancestors, such an odd eccentric instant was without significance —did not even exist. In inventing the locomotive, Watt and Stevenson were part inventors of time.

Another time-emphasizing entity is the factory and its dependent, the office. Factories exist for the purpose of getting certain quantities of goods made in a certain time. The old artisan worked as it suited him with the result that consumers generally had to wait for the goods they had ordered from him. The factory is a device for making workmen hurry. The machine revolves so often each minute; so many movements have to be made, so many pieces produced each hour. Result: the factory worker (and the same is true, *mutatis mutandis*, of the office worker) is compelled to know time in its smallest fractions. In the hand-work age there was no such compulsion to be aware of minutes and seconds.

Our awareness of time has reached such a pitch of intensity that we suffer acutely whenever our travels take us into some corner of the world where people are not interested in minutes and seconds. The unpunctuality of the Orient, for example, is appalling to those who come freshly from a land of fixed meal-times and regular train services. For a modern American or Englishman, waiting is a psychological torture. An Indian accepts the blank hours with resignation, even with satisfaction. He has not lost the fine art of doing nothing. Our notion of time as a collection of minutes, each of which must be filled with some business or amusement, is wholly alien to the Oriental, just as it was wholly alien to the Greek. For the man who lives in a pre-industrial world, time moves at a slow and easy pace; he does not care about each minute, for the good reason that he has not been made conscious of the existence of minutes.

This brings us to a seeming paradox. Acutely aware of the smallest constituent particles of time—of time, as measured by clock-work and train arrivals and the revolutions of machines—industrialized man has to a great extent lost the old awareness of time in its larger divisions. The time of which we have knowledge is artificial, machine-made time. Of natural, cosmic time, as it is measured out by sun and moon, we are for the most part almost wholly unconscious. Pre-industrial people know time in its daily, monthly and seasonal rhythms. They are aware of sunrise, noon and sunset; of the full moon and the new; of equinox and solstice; of spring and summer, autumn and winter. All the old religions, including Catholic Christianity, have insisted on this daily and seasonal rhythm. Pre-industrial man was never allowed to forget the majestic movement of cosmic time.

Industrialism and urbanism have changed all this. One can live and work in a town without being aware of the daily march of the sun across the sky; without ever seeing the moon and stars. Broadway and Piccadilly are our Milky Way; our constellations are outlined in neon tubes. Even changes of season affect the townsman very little. He is the inhabitant of an artificial universe that is, to a great extent, walled off from the world of nature. Outside the walls, time is cosmic and moves with the motion of sun and stars. Within, it is an affair of revolving wheels and is measured in seconds and minutes—at its longest, in eight-hour days and six-day weeks. We have a new consciousness; but it has been purchased at the expense of the old consciousness.

WORDS AND BEHAVIOR

Aldous Huxley

Words form the thread on which we string our experiences. Without them we should live spasmodically and intermittently. Hatred itself is not so strong that animals will not forget it, if distracted, even in the presence of the enemy. Watch a pair of cats, crouching on the brink of a fight. Balefully the eyes glare; from far down in the throat of each come bursts of a strange, strangled noise of defiance; as though animated by a life of their own, the tails twitch and tremble. With aimed intensity of loathing! Another moment and surely there must be an explosion. But no; all of a sudden one of the two creatures turns away, hoists a hind leg in a more than fascist

WORDS AND BEHAVIOR: Copyright 1937 by Aldous Huxley; renewed 1965 by Laura A. Huxley. From *Collected Essays* by Aldous Huxley. Reprinted by permission of Harper & Row, Publishers and Chatto and Windus Ltd.

salute and, with the same fixed and focused attention as it had given a moment before to its enemy, begins to make a lingual toilet. Animal love is as much at the mercy of distractions as animal hatred. The dumb creation lives a life made up of discreet and mutually irrelevant episodes. Such as it is, the consistency of human characters is due to the words upon which all human experiences are strung. We are purposeful because we can describe our feelings in rememberable words, can justify and rationalize our desires in terms of some kind of argument. Faced by an enemy we do not allow an itch to distract us from our emotions; the mere word "enemy" is enough to keep us reminded of our hatred, to convince us that we do well to be angry. Similarly the word "love" bridges for us those chasms of momentary indifference and boredom which gape from time to time between even the most ardent lovers. Feeling and desire provide us with our motive power; words give continuity to what we do and to a considerable extent determine our direction. Inappropriate and badly chosen words vitiate thought and lead to wrong or foolish conduct. Most ignorances are vincible, and in the greater number of cases stupidity is what the Buddha pronounced it to be, a sin. For, consciously, or subconsciously, it is with deliberation that we do not know or fail to understand—because incomprehension allows us, with a good conscience, to evade unpleasant obligations and responsibilities, because ignorance is the best excuse for going on doing what one likes, but ought not, to do. Our egotisms are incessantly fighting to preserve themselves, not only from external enemies, but also from the assaults of the other and better self with which they are so uncomfortably associated. Ignorance is egotism's most effective defense against that Dr. Jekyll in us who desires perfection; stupidity, its subtlest stratagem. If, as so often happens, we choose to give continuity to our experience by means of words which falsify the facts, this is because the falsification is somehow to our advantage as egotists.

Consider, for example, the case of war. War is enormously discreditable to those who order it to be waged and even to those who merely tolerate its existence. Furthermore, to developed sensibilities the facts of war are revolting and horrifying. To falsify these facts, and by so doing to make war seem less evil than it really is, and our own responsibility in tolerating war less heavy, is doubly to our advantage. By suppressing and distorting the truth, we protect our sensibilities and preserve our self-esteem. Now, language is, among other things, a device which men use for suppressing and distorting the truth. Finding the reality of war too unpleasant to contemplate, we create a verbal alternative to that reality, parallel with it, but in quality quite different from it. That which we contemplate thenceforward is not that to which we react emotionally and upon which we pass our moral judgments, is not war as it is in fact, but the fiction of war as it exists in our pleasantly falsifying verbiage. Our stupidity in using inappropriate language turns out, on analysis, to be the most refined cunning.

The most shocking fact about war is that its victims and its instruments are individual human beings, and that these individual human beings are condemned by the monstrous conventions of politics to murder or be murdered in quarrels not their own, to inflict upon the innocent and, innocent themselves of any crime against their enemies, to suffer cruelties of every kind.

The language of strategy and politics is designed, so far as it is possible, to conceal this fact, to make it appear as though wars were not fought by individuals drilled to murder one another in cold blood and without provocation, but either by impersonal and therefore wholly non-moral and impassible forces, or else by personified abstractions.

Here are a few examples of the first kind of falsification. In place of "cavalrymen" or "foot-soldiers" military writers like to speak of "sabres" and "rifles." Here is a sentence from a description of the Battle of Marengo: "According to Victor's report, the French retreat was orderly; it is certain, at any rate, that the regiments held together, for the six thousand Austrian sabres found no opportunity to charge home." The battle is between sabres in line and muskets in échelon—a mere clash of ironmongery.

On other occasions there is no question of anything so vulgarly material as ironmongery. The battles are between Platonic ideas, between the abstractions of physics and mathematics. Forces interact; weights are flung into scales; masses are set in motion. Or else it is all a matter of geometry. Lines swing and sweep; are protracted or curved; pivot on a fixed point.

Alternatively the combatants are personal, in the sense that they are personifications. There is "the enemy," in the singular, making "his" plans, striking "his" blows. The attribution of personal characteristics to collectivities, to geographical expressions, to institutions, is a source, as we shall see, of endless confusions in political thought, of innumerable political mistakes and crimes. Personification in politics is an error which we make because it is to our advantage as egotists to be able to feel violently proud of our country and of ourselves as belonging to it, and to believe that all the misfortunes due to our own mistakes are really the work of the Foreigner. It is easier to feel violently toward a person than toward an abstraction;

hence our habit of making political personifications. In some cases military personifications are merely special instances of political personifications. A particular collectivity, the army or the warring nation, is given the name and, along with the name, the attributes of a single person, in order that we may be able to love or hate it more intensely than we could do if we thought of it as what it really is: a number of diverse individuals. In other cases personification is used for the purpose of concealing the fundamental absurdity and monstrosity of war. What is absurd and monstrous about war is that men who have no personal quarrel should be trained to murder one another in cold blood. By personifying opposing armies or countries, we are able to think of war as a conflict between individuals. The same result is obtained by writing of war as though it were carried on exclusively by the generals in command and not by the private soldiers in their armies. ("Rennenkampf had pressed back von Schubert.") The implication in both cases is that war is indistinguishable from a bout of fisticuffs in a bar room. Whereas in reality it is profoundly different. A scrap between two individuals is forgivable; mass murder, deliberately organized, is a monstrous iniquity. We still choose to use war as an instrument of policy; and to comprehend the full wickedness and absurdity of war would therefore be inconvenient. For, once we understood, we should have to make some effort to get rid of the abominable thing. Accordingly, when we talk about war, we use a language which conceals or embellishes its reality. Ignoring the facts, so far as we possibly can, we imply that battles are not fought by soldiers, but by things, principles, allegories, personified collectivities, or (at the most human) by opposing commanders, pitched against one another in single combat. For the same reason, when we have to describe the processes and the results of war, we employ a rich variety of euphemisms. Even the most violently patriotic and militaristic are reluctant to call a spade by its own name. To conceal their intentions even from themselves, they make use of picturesque metaphors. We find them, for example, clamoring for war planes numerous and powerful enough to go and "destroy the hornets in their nests"—in other words, to go and throw thermite, high explosives and vesicants upon the inhabitants of neighboring countries before they have time to come and do the same to us. And how reassuring is the language of historians and strategists! They write admiringly of those military geniuses who know "when to strike at the enemy's line" (a single combatant deranges the geometrical constructions of a personification); when to "turn his flank"; when to "execute an enveloping movement." As though they were engineers discussing the strength of materials and the distribution of stresses, they talk of abstract entities called "man power" and "fire power." They sum up the long-drawn sufferings and atrocities of trench warfare in the phrase, "a war of attrition"; the massacre and mangling of human beings is assimilated to the grinding of a lens.

A dangerously abstract word, which figures in all discussions about war, is "force." Those who believe in organizing collective security by means of military pacts against a possible aggressor are particularly fond of this word. "You cannot," they say, "have international justice unless you are prepared to impose it by force." "Peace-loving countries must unite to use force against aggressive dictatorships." "Democratic institutions must be protected, if need be, by force." And so on.

Now, the word "force," when used in reference to human relations, has no single, definite meaning. There is the "force" used by parents when, without resort to any kind of physical violence, they compel their children to act or refrain from acting in some particular way. There is the "force" used by attendants in an asylum when they try to prevent a maniac from hurting himself or others. There is the "force" used by the police when they control a crowd, and that other "force" which they use in a baton charge. And finally there is the "force" used in war. This, of course, varies with the technological devices at the disposal of the belligerents, with the policies they are pursuing, and with the particular circumstances of the war in question. But in general it may be said that, in war, "force" connotes violence and fraud used to the limit of the combatants' capacity.

Variations in quantity, if sufficiently great, produce variations in quality. The "force" that is war, particularly modern war, is very different from the "force" that is police action, and the use of the same abstract word to describe the two dissimilar processes is profoundly misleading. (Still more misleading, of course, is the explicit assimilation of a war, waged by allied League-of-Nations powers against an aggressor, to police action against a criminal. The first is the use of violence and fraud without limit against innocent and guilty alike; the second is the use of strictly limited violence and a minimum of fraud exclusively against the guilty.)

Reality is a succession of concrete and particular situations. When we think about such situations we should use the particular and concrete words which apply to them. If we use abstract words which apply equally well (and equally badly) to other, quite dissimilar situations, it is certain that we shall think incorrectly.

Let us take the sentences quoted above and translate the abstract word "force" into language that will render (however inadequately) the concrete and particular realities of contemporary warfare.

"You cannot have international justice unless you are prepared to impose it by force." Translated, this becomes: "You cannot have international justice unless you are prepared, with a view to imposing a just settlement, to drop thermite, high explosives and vesicants upon the inhabitants of foreign cities and to have thermite, high explosives and vesicants dropped in return upon the inhabitants of your cities." At the end of this proceeding, justice is to be imposed by the victorious party—that is, if there is a victorious party. It should be remarked that justice was to have been imposed by the victorious party at the end of the last war. But, unfortunately, after four years of fighting, the temper of the victors was such that they were quite incapable of making a just settlement. The Allies are reaping in Nazi Germany what they sowed at Versailles. The victors of the next war will have undergone intensive bombardments with thermite, high explosives and vesicants. Will their temper be better than that of the Allies in 1918? Will they be in a fitter state to make a just settlement? The answer, quite obviously, is: No. It is psychologically all but impossible that justice should be secured by the methods of contemporary warfare.

The next two sentences may be taken together. "Peaceloving countries must unite to use force against aggressive dictatorships. Democratic institutions must be protected, if need be, by force." Let us translate. "Peace-loving countries must unite to throw thermite, high explosives and vesicants on the inhabitants of countries ruled by aggressive dictators. They must do this, and of course abide the consequences, in order to preserve peace and democratic institutions." Two questions immediately propound themselves. First, is it likely that peace can be secured by a process calculated to reduce the orderly life of our complicated societies to chaos? And, second, is it likely that democratic institutions will flourish in a state of chaos? Again, the answers are pretty clearly in the negative.

By using the abstract word "force," instead of terms which at least attempt to describe the realities of war as it is today, the preachers of collective security through military collaboration disguise from themselves and from others, not only the contemporary facts, but also the probable consequences of their favorite policy. The attempt to secure justice, peace and democracy by "force" seems reasonable enough until we realize, first, that this noncommittal word stands, in the circumstances of our age, for activities which can hardly fail to result in social chaos; and second, that the consequences of social chaos are injustice, chronic warfare and tyranny.

The moment we think in concrete and particular terms of the concrete and particular process called "modern war," we see that a policy which worked (or at least didn't result in complete disaster) in the past has no prospect whatever of working in the immediate future. The attempt to secure justice, peace and democracy by means of a "force," which means, at this particular moment of history, thermite, high explosives and vesicants, is about as reasonable as the attempt to put out a fire with a colorless liquid that happens to be, not water, but petrol.

What applies to the "force" that is war applies in large measure to the "force" that is revolution. It seems inherently very unlikely that social justice and social peace can be secured by thermite, high explosives and vesicants. At first, it may be, the parties in a civil war would hesitate to use such instruments on their fellow-countrymen. But there can be little doubt that, if the conflict were prolonged (as it probably would be between the evenly balanced Right and Left of a highly industrialized society), the combatants would end by losing their scruples.

The alternatives confronting us seem to be plain enough. Either we invent and conscientiously employ a new technique for making revolutions and settling international disputes; or else we cling to the old technique and, using "force" (that is to say, thermite, high explosives and vesicants), destroy ourselves. Those who, for whatever motive, disguise the nature of the second alternative under inappropriate language, render the world a grave disservice. They lead us into one of the temptations we find it hardest to resist—the temptation to run away from reality, to pretend that facts are not what they are. Like Shelley (but without Shelley's acute awareness of what he was doing) we are perpetually weaving

> A shroud of talk to hide us from the sun
> Of this familiar life.

We protect our minds by an elaborate system of abstractions, ambiguities, metaphors and similes from the reality we do not wish to know too clearly; we lie to ourselves, in order that we may still have the excuse of ignorance, the alibi of stupidity and incomprehension, possessing which we can continue with a good conscience to commit and tolerate the most monstrous crimes:

> The poor wretch who has learned his only prayers
> From curses, who knows scarcely words enough
> To ask a blessing from his Heavenly Father,
> Becomes a fluent phraseman, absolute

And technical in victories and defeats,
And all our dainty terms for fratricide;
Terms which we trundle smoothly o'er our tongues
Like mere abstractions, empty sounds to which
We join no meaning and attach no form!
As if the soldier died without a wound:
As if the fibers of this godlike frame
Were gored without a pang: as if the wretch
Who fell in battle, doing bloody deeds,
Passed off to Heaven translated and not killed;
As though he had no wife to pine for him,
No God to judge him.

The language we use about war is inappropriate, and its inappropriateness is designed to conceal a reality so odious that we do not wish to know it. The language we use about politics is also inappropriate; but here our mistake has a different purpose. Our principal aim in this case is to arouse and, having aroused, to rationalize and justify such intrinsically agreeable sentiments as pride and hatred, self-esteem and contempt for others. To achieve this end we speak about the facts of politics in words which more or less completely misrepresent them.

The concrete realities of politics are individual human beings, living together in national groups. Politicians—and to some extent we are all politicians—substitute abstractions for these concrete realities, and having done this, proceed to invest each abstraction with an appearance of concreteness by personifying it. For example, the concrete reality of which "Britain" is the abstraction consists of some forty-odd millions of diverse individuals living on an island off the west coast of Europe. The personification of this abstraction appears, in classical fancy-dress and holding a very large toasting fork, on the backside of our copper coinage; appears in verbal form, every time we talk about international politics. "Britain," the abstraction from forty millions of Britons, is endowed with thoughts, sensibilities and emotions, even with a sex—for, in spite of John Bull, the country is always a female.

Now, it is of course possible that "Britain" is more than a mere name—is an entity that possesses some kind of reality distinct from that of the individuals constituting the group to which the name is applied. But this entity, if it exists, is certainly not a young lady with a toasting fork; nor is it possible to believe (though some eminent philosophers have preached the doctrine) that it should possess anything in the nature of a personal will. One must agree with T. H.

Green that "there can be nothing in a nation, however exalted its mission, or in a society however perfectly organized, which is not in the persons composing the nation or the society. . . . We cannot suppose a national spirit and will to exist except as the spirit and will of individuals." But the moment we start resolutely thinking about our world in terms of individual persons we find ourselves at the same time thinking in terms of universality. "The great rational religions," writes Professor Whitehead, "are the outcome of the emergence of a religious consciousness that is universal, as distinguished from tribal, or even social. Because it is universal, it introduces the note of solitariness." (And he might have added that, because it is solitary, it introduces the note of universality.) "The reason of this connection between universality and solitude is that universality is a disconnection from immediate surroundings." And conversely the disconnection from immediate surroundings, particularly such social surrounding as the tribe or nation, the insistence on the person as the fundamental reality, leads to the conception of an all-embracing unity.

A nation, then, may be more than a mere abstraction, may possess some kind of real existence apart from its constituent members. But there is no reason to suppose that it is a person; indeed, there is every reason to suppose that it isn't. Those who speak as though it were a person (and some go further than this and speak as though it were a personal god) do so, because it is to their interest as egotists to make precisely this mistake.

In the case of the ruling class these interests are in part material. The personification of the nation as a sacred being, different from and superior to its constituent members, is merely (I quote the words of a great French jurist, Léon Duguit) "a way of imposing authority by making people believe it is an authority *de jure* and not merely *de facto*." By habitually talking of the nation as though it were a person with thoughts, feelings and a will of its own, the rulers of a country legitimate their own powers. Personification leads easily to deification; and where the nation is deified, its government ceases to be a mere convenience, like drains or a telephone system, and, partaking in the sacredness of the entity it represents, claims to give orders by divine right and demands the unquestioning obedience due to a god. Rulers seldom find it hard to recognize their friends. Hegel, the man who elaborated an inappropriate figure of speech into a complete philosophy of politics, was a favorite of the Prussian government. *"Es ist,"* he had written, *"es ist der Gang Gottes in der Welt, das der Staat ist."* The decoration bestowed on him by Frederick William III was richly deserved.

Unlike their rulers, the ruled have no material interest in using inappropriate language about states and nations. For them, the reward of being mistaken is psychological. The personified and deified nation becomes, in the minds of the individuals composing it, a kind of enlargement of themselves. The superhuman qualities which belong to the young lady with the toasting fork, the young lady with plaits and a brass *soutien-gorge*, the young lady in a Phrygian bonnet, are claimed by individual Englishmen, Germans and Frenchmen as being, at least in part, their own. *Dulce et decorum est pro patria mori.* But there would be no need to die, no need of war, if it had not been even sweeter to boast and swagger for one's country, to hate, despise, swindle and bully for it. Loyalty to the personified nation, or to the personified class or party, justifies the loyal in indulging all those passions which good manners and the moral code do not allow them to display in their relations with their neighbors. The personified entity is a being, not only great and noble, but also insanely proud, vain and touchy; fiercely rapacious; a braggart; bound by no considerations of right and wrong. (Hegel condemned as hopelessly shallow all those who dared to apply ethical standards to the activities of nations. To condone and applaud every iniquity committed in the name of the State was to him a sign of philosophical profundity.) Identifying themselves with this god, individuals find relief from the constraints of ordinary social decency, feel themselves justified in giving rein, within duly prescribed limits, to their criminal proclivities. As a loyal nationalist or party-man, one can enjoy the luxury of behaving badly with a good conscience.

The evil passions are further justified by another linguistic error —the error of speaking about certain categories of persons as though they were mere embodied abstractions. Foreigners and those who disagree with us are not thought of as men and women like ourselves and our fellow-countrymen; they are thought of as representatives and, so to say, symbols of a class. In so far as they have any personality at all, it is the personality we mistakenly attribute to their class—a personality that is, by definition, intrinsically evil. We know that the harming or killing of men and women is wrong, and we are reluctant consciously to do what we know to be wrong. But when particular men and women are thought of merely as representatives of a class, which has previously been defined as evil and personified in the shape of a devil, then the reluctance to hurt or murder disappears. Brown, Jones and Robinson are no longer thought of as Brown, Jones and Robinson, but as heretics, gentiles, Yids, niggers, barbarians, Huns, communists, capitalists, fascists, liberals—whichever the case may be. When they have been called such names and assimilated to the accursed class to which the names apply, Brown, Jones and Robinson cease to be conceived as what they really are— human persons—and become for the users of this fatally inappropriate language mere vermin or, worse, demons whom it is right and proper to destroy as thoroughly and as painfully as possible. Wherever persons are present, questions of morality arise. Rulers of nations and leaders of parties find morality embarrassing. That is why they take such pains to depersonalize their opponents. All propaganda directed against an opposing group has but one aim: to substitute diabolical abstractions for concrete persons. The propagandist's purpose is to make one set of people forget that certain other sets of people are human. By robbing them of their personality, he puts them outside the pale of moral obligation. Mere symbols can have no rights—particularly when that of which they are symbolical is, by definition, evil.

Politics can become moral only on one condition: that its problems shall be spoken of and thought about exclusively in terms of concrete reality; that is to say, of persons. To depersonify human beings and to personify abstractions are complementary errors which lead, by an inexorable logic, to war between nations and to idolatrous worship of the State, with consequent governmental oppression. All current political thought is a mixture, in varying proportions, between thought in terms of concrete realities and thought in terms of depersonified symbols and personified abstractions. In the democratic countries the problems of internal politics are thought about mainly in terms of concrete reality; those of external politics, mainly in terms of abstractions and symbols. In dictatorial countries the proportion of concrete to abstract and symbolic thought is lower than in democratic countries. Dictators talk little of persons, much of personified abstractions, such as the Nation, the State, the Party, and much of depersonified symbols, such as Yids, Bolshies, Capitalists. The stupidity of politicians who talk about a world of persons as though it were not a world of persons is due in the main to self-interest. In a fictitious world of symbols and personified abstractions, rulers find that they can rule more effectively, and the ruled, that they can gratify instincts which the conventions of good manners and the imperatives of morality demand that they should repress. To think correctly is the condition of behaving well. It is also in itself a moral act; those who would think correctly must resist considerable temptations.

CANNED FISH

Aldous Huxley

An enormous new building had been added to the cannery. From now on, in straight-line and continuous production, six hundred women would daily convert three hundred and fifty tons of frozen carcasses into seven hundred thousand tins of tuna. Today the new facilities were being dedicated.

It was a solemn occasion. A rostrum had been erected on the wharf outside the factory. Bunting flapped in the fishy breeze. Mayors, senators, vice-governors were on hand to say a few well-chosen words. The new cannery, it appeared, was a triumph not only of technology, but also and above all of Private Enterprise, of the American Way of Life. It represented, we were told, two million dollars' worth of faith in the Future, of fidelity to the Past, of belief in Progress, of trust in . . . But listening to eloquence is something I have never been very good at. I looked at my companion, and my companion looked at me. Without a word we rose and tiptoed away.

A friendly engineer offered to show us round the factory. We began with the thawing tanks, into which the ocean-going trawlers discharge their refrigerated cargo. Next came the butchering tables, where the great fish are cleaned, and from which their heads, guts and tails are spirited away across the street, to a processing plant that transforms them (not without an overpowering stench) into fish meal for poultry. From the butchering tables we moved to the huge pressure cookers, the cooling shelves, the long conveyor belts of stainless steel, the machines for filling the cans, the machines for sealing and sterilizing the cans, the machines for labeling the cans, the machines for packing the cans in cartons.

So far as tunas were concerned, this was a holiday. The factory was empty; our voices reverberated in a cathedral silence. But next door, in the mackerel department, the work of canning was in full swing. Standing at an immensely long workbench, a line of over-alled women receded into the dim distance. Beyond the bench was a trough full of rapidly flowing water, and beyond the trough were

CANNED FISH: From *Tomorrow and Tomorrow and Tomorrow and Other Essays* by Aldous Huxley. Copyright 1955 by Aldous Huxley. Reprinted by permission of Harper & Row, Publishers and Chatto and Windus Ltd.

the conveyor belt and, above it, on a shelf, an inexhaustible reservoir of empty cans. From an upper story, where, invisible to us, the butchering was evidently going on, a wide-mouthed pipe descended perpendicularly. About once every minute a plug was pulled and a cataract came rushing down the pipe. Floating in the water were thousands of cross sections of mackerel. At breakneck speed they were whirled along the trough. As they passed, each woman reached out a gloved hand and dragged ashore as much as she needed for the five or six cans that she would fill before the next discharge. The cross sections were rammed into place—a big chunk, a smaller chunk, a tiny chunk, whatever piece would fit into the three-dimensional jigsaw—and the tightly packed can was placed on the conveyor belt, along which it moved, unhurrying, toward the weighers, the sealers, the sterilizers, labelers and craters. I clocked the performance and found that it took from ten to fifteen seconds to fill a can. Three hundred, on an average, every hour; two thousand four hundred in the course of a working day; twelve thousand a week.

Outside, in the hazy sunshine, a dignitary of some sort was still talking. "Liberty," he declaimed, and a second, distant loud-speaker repeated the overlapping syllables: "Liberty—berty."

Once more the plug was pulled. Another Niagara of water and sliced fish came rushing down the flume.

"Oppor—opportunity," bawled the loud-speakers. "Way of life—of life."

Buried in every language are nodules of petrified poetry, rich and unsuspected veins of fossil wisdom. Consider, for example, the French word *travail*. It is derived from Late Latin *trepalium*, the name of a kind of rack used for punishing criminals or persuading reluctant witnesses. Etymologically, work is the equivalent of torture. In English we preserve the word's original sense in relation to obstetrics (a woman "in travail") and have endowed it with the secondary meaning, not of work, but of wayfaring. Journeys in the Middle Ages were exhausting and dangerous. "Travel" is *trepalium* —torment for tourists.

The word "work" is emotionally neutral; but "toil" and the now obsolete "swink" carry unpleasant overtones. It was the same in the languages of classical antiquity. *Ponos* in Greek and *labor* in Latin signify both "work" and "suffering." "And Rachel travailed," we read in the Book of Genesis, "and she had hard labor." Two words for work, two words for pain. Moreover, when Modern English "labor" carries its primary meaning, it generally stands for work of the most disagreeable kind—compulsory work, as in the case of penal "hard labor," or the heavy, unskilled work which is performed by "laborers."

Backward-looking sentimentalists are never tired of telling us that in the Middle Ages, work was all joy and spontaneous creativity. Then what, one may ask, could have induced our ancestors to equate labor with anguish? And why, when they wanted a name for work, did they borrow it from the torture chamber?

> Who first invented work, and bound the free
> And holiday-rejoicing spirit down
> To the ever-haunting importunity
> Of business in the green fields, and the town—
> To plow, loom, anvil, spade—and, oh! most sad,
> To that dry drudgery of the desk's dry wood?
> Who but the Being unblest, alien from good,
> Sabbathless Satan, he who his unglad
> Task ever plies 'mid rotatory burnings,
> That round and round incalculably reel—
> For wrath divine hath made him like a wheel—
> In that red realm from which are no returnings,
> Where toiling and turmoiling ever and aye,
> He and his thoughts keep pensive working-day.

Lamb was quite right. In every civilization work, for all but a favored few, has always been a thing of hideous dreariness, an infernal monotony of boredom at the best and, at the worst, of discomfort or even sheer anguish. One remembers the description, in *The Golden Ass*, of the animals and humans who worked, while the owner's wife amused herself with magic and adultery, at the flour mill. Men and asses, mules and boys—they were all in travail, all on the *trepalium*, bruised, galled, strained beyond the limits of organic endurance. And the life of laborers in a medieval village, the life of journeymen and apprentices in the workshop of a master craftsman in the town, was hardly less dismal than that of their pre-Christian ancestors. In its beginnings industrialization merely aggravated an already intolerable state of affairs. The physical tortures imposed in the dark satanic mills of Georgian and Early Victorian England were worse, because more systematic, better organized, than the travail of earlier centuries. Thanks to automatic machines and labor laws, thanks to trade unions and the internal-combustion engine, thanks to hoists and belts and humanitarianism, there are now few tasks which actually hurt. The rack has been abolished. But the boredom, the frightful punctuality of wheels returning again and again to the same old position—these remain. Remain under free enterprise, remain under Socialism, remain under Communism.

Under the present technological dispensations the opportunity to escape from the tyranny of repetition comes only to a very small minority. But with the multiplication of fully automatic machines, fully automatic factories, even fully automatic industries, the case will be altered. Some of those now condemned to the task of keeping time with wheels will become the highly skilled doctors and nurses of the new, all-but-human gadgets. The rest will do—what? It remains to be seen. Only one thing seems tolerably certain. Owing to the deplorable lack of quantitative and qualitative uniformity displayed by living organisms, the fish-canning industry will be one of the last to become fully automatic. The technical procedures current today will probably be current, with only trifling modifications, a generation from now. Should we rejoice over this island of stability in a flux of change? Or should we lament? In another twenty-five or thirty years we may be in a position to answer.

And meanwhile what will have happened to the raw material of our industry? What, in a word, will the fish be up to? A generation ago the biologist and the commercial fisherman would have answered, without hesitation: "If they aren't overfished, they will be doing exactly what they are doing now." Times have changed, and today the answer to our question would probably be: "Goodness only knows." For in recent years fishes have been behaving in the most eccentric and indecorous manner. Consider, for example, the European tuna. Forty years ago individual specimens of *Thunnus thynnus* were caught, at certain seasons, in the English Channel and the North Sea; but there was no tuna-packing industry north of Portugal, and the main supply of tinned or salted tunny came from the Mediterranean islands of Sardinia and Sicily. Today there is a flourishing tunny industry in Norway.

And the tuna's is by no means an isolated or exceptional case. Fishes which, not long ago, were thought of as being exclusively tropical, are now caught off the New England coast, and fishes once regarded as natives of the temperate zone have moved into the Arctic. The North Sea has ceased to be the great fishing ground of Western Europe. Today ocean-going trawlers, equipped with freezing units, make long voyages to the coasts of Iceland and northernmost Scandinavia. The Eskimos of Greenland have given up their traditional occupation, the hunting of seals, and have taken instead to fishing for cod. What were once regarded as immutable behavior patterns have changed, almost overnight. The world of fishes is in a state of revolution. Within the next twenty or thirty years the strangest things may happen in that world—with incalculable results for all concerned in the catching and processing of sea food.

This revolution in the watery world of the fish is a consequence of a larger revolution in the earth's atmosphere—a revolution which is changing the climate of the northern hemisphere and is likely to affect profoundly the course of human history during the next few generations or even centuries. The causes of this climatic revolution are obscure, but its effects are manifest. The glaciers are everywhere melting. The snow pack on the mountains has diminished to such an extent that the Jungfrau is now thirty feet lower than it used to be when I was a boy. The Spitzbergen Archipelago, which used to be open for shipping for about four months out of the twelve, is now open for eight or nine. Russian icebreakers and cargo ships sail the once impassable seas that wash the northern coasts of the Soviet empire. In Canada and Siberia agriculture is moving steadily into higher and higher latitudes. Plants, birds and mammals, hitherto unknown in those regions, have now made their entrance and may soon take the place of the cold-loving species which are beginning to find their environment uncomfortably balmy.

This sort of thing, we should remember, has happened before, not merely in the remote geological past, but in quite recent historical times. In the early Middle Ages, Europe (and presumably the rest of the northern hemisphere) enjoyed two or three centuries of most unusual weather. There was enough sunshine in southern England to ripen grapes, and for four or five generations it was possible to drink British wine. Then, about the time of Chaucer, the climate changed again, and for a couple of centuries Europe experienced the rigors of what has been called the Little Ice Age. In Denmark and northern Germany many villages had to be abandoned. In Iceland the cultivation of cereals became impossible, and the fields, in many cases, were covered by the encroaching glaciers. Today the glaciers are in full retreat, and there is every reason to believe that in a few years rye and barley will once more be grown, to the further enrichment of a country which has already profited by the migration to its shores of innumerable fishes fleeing from the increasing warmth of the North Sea.

But if the high latitudes of the northern hemisphere become pleasantly warmer, does it not follow that the low latitudes will grow most *un*pleasantly hotter? There are some indications that this may be actually happening. In Africa, north of the equator, forests are giving place to savannas, and savannas are drying up into deserts. And what of the long, hardly intermitted drought, from which large areas of the American Southwest have recently been suffering? Is this the usual kind of cyclical dry spell, or does it presage a relatively permanent worsening of an arid or semiarid climate? Time alone will show. Meanwhile, if I had a few millions to invest for the benefit of my grandchildren, I would put them all into Canada rather than Texas. "Westward the course of empire takes its way." So wrote the good Bishop Berkeley two centuries ago. Reincarnated today, the philosopher-poet would probably turn his prophetic eyes ninety degrees to the right. Westward no longer, but northward, northward moves the course of empire. The tunas, the pilchards, the sharks and codfish—these forward-looking pioneers have already made the move, or at least are swimming in the right direction. In ever-increasing numbers, men will soon be following their example.

QUESTIONS AND EXERCISES

1. Choose at random any two of these five essays (or choose the two that you found most rewarding), and discuss the similarities between them. If you had not known beforehand, do you think you might have guessed that the same man wrote both? If so, on what sort of evidence would your guess have been based—stylistic, structural, susbtantive? If not, what evidence do you find that would positively suggest two different authors?

2. What themes or motifs recur most often in this group of Huxley essays? Having read these, would you expect the same basic attitudes and assumptions to appear in all his writings? Or does it seem possible that the concentration in this sample is accidental, or contrived by the editor? (This is a tricky question.)

3. Discounting the content and subject matter of the essays, what similarities do you see in form and strategy of presentation? Does it strike you that Huxley is highly conscious of structure in his writing? Explain.

4. What devices does the author use in attempting to make the substance of his writing *memorable*? Does he use these devices more heavily, more conspicuously, in some essays than in others? And is such a difference traceable to the differing nature of the subject matter?

5. "Words and Behavior" begins as if it were going to be a rather abstract discussion, and then it somewhat unexpectedly develops a strong topical relevance to contemporary politics and social mores. What seems to be the intended effect of this arrangement? Is it successful? Do you find the same strategy used in any other of these essays?

6. In "Canned Fish," what is the point of Huxley's concluding remarks about the great northward tendency of things? Has this anything

logically to do with the earlier parts of the essay, or does it appear that the author has simply rambled off into this subject by means of loose association? Are there odd transitions such as this in the other four essays? Does this sort of movement from one section of discourse to another seem consistent with the author's structural habits as they are otherwise revealed?

7. Discuss the *informative* function of Huxley's writing. Taking any one of the essays under consideration, point out how its structure would probably be altered if the author wished to give it a more purely informative content.

8. In "Wordsworth in the Tropics," Huxley seems to assume that his audience will know something about the ideas in Wordsworth's poetry from first-hand experience, though he does enough quoting and paraphrasing to give even an utter novice some clue to the Wordsworthian position. With this in mind, discuss the author's conception of his audience. On balance, is it more flattering than humiliating to read "Wordsworth in the Tropics"? Do you feel the same way about the other essays?

9. Is Huxley's verbal style distinctive, "personalized" in some special way? That is, do you *notice* his style as compared with that of, say, Lawrence or De Quincey? Do you find noticeable variation in style from one essay to another? Be as specific as possible in your discussion.

10. Explain carefully how Huxley arrives at his definition of love in "Fashions in Love." Why doesn't he simply open his essay with this definition? Do you find the same technique of delayed definition in any of the other essays?

11. In "Words and Behavior," what is Huxley's point in describing the personified Britain as a young lady with "a very large toasting fork"? Why, specifically, a toasting fork? Does wit and comic effect strike you as being a regular part of Huxley's equipment as a writer? Does this element in his work diminish the seriousness of his commentary on human nature and society?

12. "Time and the Machine" is a much shorter essay than the others considered here. Does its length reflect the relative unimportance of its subject? Can you easily imagine the essay, as it stands, being used as the structural framework for a much more extensive piece of writing (ten or fifteen pages perhaps)? Explain by what additions such a transformation might be accomplished. Of the other four essays, which one could most readily be reduced to a length of three or four pages? Why?

13. Which of these essays has for you the greatest absolute value, and on what grounds?

14. Describe fully what you consider to be Huxley's greatest *weakness* as an essayist, citing specific parts of the text where you can.

15. How far does Huxley succeed (and in which essays) in fusing the three kinds of excellence he sets up: the personal, the objective, and the abstract-universal?

16. Where, in these essays, does some image of the author's character, temperament, or self emerge most clearly? How important is this self-expression as part of the essays' whole achievement?

17. On what *other* subjects do you suppose Huxley would write well, and what would you expect might be his *substance* in each case?

18. Look back carefully over the pieces you have written in connection with exercises in the earlier chapters of this volume, and write a paper comparing the *consistency* you find among them to that of the Huxley group you have just read.

19. In an essay of about 800 words, explore as freely and honestly as you can your *immediate* reaction to Huxley, your first impression of the man in his work. You may wish to add a paragraph explaining what changes this first impression has undergone with subsequent readings of the essays.

20. Write a 1000-word essay *opposing* Huxley's views in "Fashions in Love" (if in fact you agree with him, try for the moment not to). Try wherever you can to take advantage of places where he seems vulnerable to counter-argument. Append a self-analytic paragraph explaining exactly what you have tried to do and exactly how your argument relates to Huxley's.

21. Write a narrative description comparable in length and type to the opening of "Canned Fish." Add a short critical commentary on the substantive or argumentative uses to which your account might be put if you decided not to let it merely stand as it is.

22. How "up to date" is Huxley's work? Discuss this in about 1000 words, including your opinion about the probable popularity of his work in the year 2000.

23. Get a copy of the *Collected Essays*, read a good number of them, and write a paper that discusses the representativeness of the five that have been included in *Style and Substance*. (This is an exercise for the unusually eager.)

Part Two

Further Readings

More Essays

OF SIMULATION AND DISSIMULATION

Francis Bacon

Dissimulation is but a faint kind of policy or wisdom; for it asketh a strong wit and a strong heart to know when to tell truth and to do it; therefore it is the weaker sort of politicians that are the greatest dissemblers. Tacitus saith, "Livia sorted well with the arts of her husband and dissimulation of her son," attributing arts or policy to Augustus and dissimulation to Tiberius. And again, when Mucianus encourageth Vespasian to take arms against Vitellius, he saith, "We rise not against the piercing judgment of Augustus, nor the extreme caution or closeness of Tiberius." These properties of arts or policy and dissimulation or closeness are indeed habits and faculties several and to be distinguished, for if a man have that penetration of judgment as he can discern what things are to be laid open and what to be secreted and what to be shewed at half lights and to whom and when (which indeed are arts of state and arts of life, as Tacitus well calleth them), to him a habit of dissimulation is a hinderance and a poorness. But if a man cannot attain to that judgment, then it is left to him generally to be close and a dissembler; for where a man cannot choose or vary in particulars, there it is good to take the safest and wariest way in general, like the going softly by one that cannot well see. Certainly, the ablest men that ever were have had all an openness and frankness of dealing and a name of certainty and veracity. But then they were like horses well managed, for they could tell passing well when to stop or turn; and at such times when they thought the case indeed required dissimulation, if then they used it, it came to pass that the former opinion spread abroad of their good faith and clearness of dealing made them almost invisible.

There be three degrees of this hiding and veiling of a man's self: the first, closeness, reservation, and secrecy, when a man leaveth himself without observation or without hold to be taken what he is; the second, dissimulation in the negative, when a man lets fall signs and arguments that he is not that he is; and the third simulation in the affirmative, when a man industriously and expressly feigns and pretends to be that he is not.

For the first of these, secrecy, it is indeed the virtue of a confessor; and assuredly the secret man heareth many confessions, for who will open himself to a blab or babbler? But if a man be thought secret, it inviteth discovery, as the more close air sucketh in the more open; and, as in confession the revealing is not for worldly use but for the ease of a man's heart, so secret men come to the knowledge of many things in that kind; while men rather discharge their minds than impart their minds. In few words, mysteries are due to secrecy. Besides (to say truth) nakedness is uncomely, as well in mind as body, and it addeth no small reverence to men's manners and actions, if they be not altogether open. As for talkers and futile persons, they are commonly vain and credulous withal; for he that talketh what he knoweth, will also talk what he knoweth not. Therefore set it down that a habit of secrecy is both politic and moral; and in this part it is good that a man's face give his tongue leave to speak; for the discovery of a man's self by the tracts of his countenance is a great weakness and betraying, by how much it is many times more marked and believed than a man's words.

For the second, which is dissimulation, it followeth many times upon secrecy by a necessity, so that he that will be secret must be a dissembler in some degree; for men are too cunning to suffer a man to keep an indifferent carriage between both and to be secret, without swaying the balance on either side. They will so beset a man with questions and draw him on and pick it out of him, that, without an absurd silence, he must shew an inclination one way; or if he do not, they will gather as much by his silence as by his speech. As for equivocations or oraculous speeches, they cannot hold out long. So that no man can be secret, except he give himself a little scope of dissimulation, which is, as it were, but the skirts or train of secrecy.

But for the third degree, which is simulation and false profession, that I hold more culpable and less politic except it be in great and rare matters: and therefore a general custom of simulation (which is this last degree) is a vice rising either of a natural falseness or fearfulness or of a mind that hath some main faults, which because a man must needs disguise, it maketh him practise simulation in other things, lest his hand should be out of use.

The advantages of simulation and dissimulation are three: first, to lay asleep opposition and to surprise, for where a man's intentions are published, it is an alarum to call up all that are against them: the second is, to reserve to a man's self a fair retreat, for if a man engage himself by a manifest declaration, he must go through or take a fall: the third is, the better to discover the mind of another, for to him that opens himself men will hardly shew themselves averse, but will (fair) let him go on and turn their freedom of speech to freedom of thought. And therefore it is a good shrewd proverb of the Spaniard, "Tell a lie and find a troth," as if there were no way of discovery but by simulation. There be also three disadvantages to set it even: the first, that simulation and dissimulation commonly carry with them a shew of fearfulness, which in any business doth spoil the feathers of round flying up to the mark: the second, that it puzzleth and perplexeth the conceits of many, that perhaps would otherwise co-operate with him and makes a man walk almost alone to his own ends: the third and greatest is that it depriveth a man of one of the most principal instruments for action, which is trust and belief. The best composition and temperature is to have openness in fame and opinion, secrecy in habit, dissimulation in seasonable use, and a power to feign if there be no remedy.

EVERYBODY'S PROTEST NOVEL

James Baldwin

In *Uncle Tom's Cabin*, that cornerstone of American social protest fiction, St. Clare, the kindly master, remarks to his coldly disapproving Yankee cousin, Miss Ophelia, that, so far as he is able to tell, the blacks have been turned over to the devil for the benefit of the whites in this world—however, he adds thoughtfully, it may turn out in the next. Miss Ophelia's reaction is, at least, vehemently right-minded: "This is perfectly horrible!" she exclaims. "You ought to be ashamed of yourselves!"

Miss Ophelia, as we may suppose, was speaking for the author; her exclamation is the moral, neatly framed, and incontestable like those improving mottoes sometimes found hanging on the walls of furnished rooms. And, like these mottoes, before which one invariably flinches, recognizing an insupportable, almost an indecent glibness, she and St. Clare are terribly in earnest. Neither of them questions the medieval morality from which their dialogue springs:

EVERYBODY'S PROTEST NOVEL: From *Notes of a Native Son* (1963). Reprinted by permission of the Beacon Press, copyright © 1949, 1955 by James Baldwin.

black, white, the devil, the next world—posing its alternatives between heaven and the flames—were realities for them as, of course,
they were for their creator. They spurned and were terrified of the
darkness, striving mightily for the light; and considered from this
aspect, Miss Ophelia's exclamation, like Mrs. Stowe's novel, achieves
a bright, almost a lurid significance, like the light from a fire which
consumes a witch. This is the more striking as one considers the
novels of Negro oppression written in our own, more enlightened
day, all of which say only: "This is perfectly horrible! You ought
to be ashamed of yourselves!" (Let us ignore, for the moment,
those novels of oppression written by Negroes, which add only a
raging, near-paranoiac postscript to this statement and actually
reinforce, as I hope to make clear later, the principles which activate
the oppression they decry.)

Uncle Tom's Cabin is a very bad novel, having, in its self-righteous,
virtuous sentimentality, much in common with *Little Women*.
Sentimentality, the ostentatious parading of excessive and spurious
emotion, is the mark of dishonesty, the inability to feel; the wet eyes
of the sentimentalist betray his aversion to experience, his fear of
life, his arid heart; and it is always, therefore, the signal of secret and
violent inhumanity, the mask of cruelty. *Uncle Tom's Cabin*—like
its multitudinous, hard-boiled descendants—is a catalogue of violence.
This is explained by the nature of Mrs. Stowe's subject matter, her
laudable determination to flinch from nothing in presenting the
complete picture; an explanation which falters only if we pause to
ask whether or not her picture is indeed complete; and what constriction or failure of perception forced her to so depend on the
description of brutality—unmotivated, senseless—and to leave un-
answered and unnoticed the only important question: what it was,
after all, that moved her people to such deeds.

But this, let us say, was beyond Mrs. Stowe's powers; she was not
so much a novelist as an impassioned pamphleteer; her book was not
intended to do anything more than prove that slavery was wrong;
was, in fact, perfectly horrible. This makes material for a pamphlet
but it is hardly enough for a novel; and the only question left to
ask is why we are bound still within the same constriction. How is it
that we are so loath to make a further journey than that made by
Mrs. Stowe, to discover and reveal something a little closer to the
truth?

But that battered word, truth, having made its appearance here,
confronts one immediately with a series of riddles and has, moreover,
since so many gospels are preached, the unfortunate tendency to
make one belligerent. Let us say, then, that truth, as used here, is

meant to imply a devotion to the human being, his freedom and fulfillment; freedom which cannot be legislated, fulfillment which cannot be charted. This is the prime concern, the frame of reference; it is not to be confused with a devotion to Humanity which is too easily equated with a devotion to a Cause; and Causes, as we know, are notoriously bloodthirsty. We have, as it seems to me, in this most mechanical and interlocking of civilizations, attempted to lop this creature down to the status of a time-saving invention. He is not, after all, merely a member of a Society or a Group or a deplorable conundrum to be explained by Science. He is—and how old-fashioned the words sound!—something more than that, something resolutely indefinable, unpredictable. In overlooking, denying, evading his complexity—which is nothing more than the disquieting complexity of ourselves—we are diminished and we perish; only within this web of ambiguity, paradox, this hunger, danger, darkness, can we find at once ourselves and the power that will free us from ourselves. It is this power of revelation which is the business of the novelist, this journey toward a more vast reality which must take precedence over all other claims. What is today parroted as his Responsibility—which seems to mean that he must make formal declaration that he is involved in, and affected by, the lives of other people and to say something improving about this somewhat self-evident fact—is, when he believes it, his corruption and our loss; moreover, it is rooted in, interlocked with and intensifies this same mechanization. Both *Gentleman's Agreement* and *The Postman Always Rings Twice* exemplify this terror of the human being, the determination to cut him down to size. And in *Uncle Tom's Cabin* we may find foreshadowing of both: the formula created by the necessity to find a lie more palatable than the truth has been handed down and memorized and persists yet with a terrible power.

It is interesting to consider one more aspect of Mrs. Stowe's novel, the method she used to solve the problem of writing about a black man at all. Apart from her lively procession of field hands, house niggers, Chloe, Topsy, etc.—who are the stock, lovable figures presenting no problem—she has only three other Negroes in the book. These are the important ones and two of them may be dismissed immediately, since we have only the author's word that they are Negro and they are, in all other respects, as white as she can make them. The two are George and Eliza, a married couple with a wholly adorable child—whose quaintness, incidentally, and whose charm, rather put one in mind of a darky bootblack doing a buck and wing to the clatter of condescending coins. Eliza is a beautiful, pious hybrid, light enough to pass—the heroine of *Quality* might, indeed, be her reincarnation—differing from the genteel mistress who has overseered her education only in the respect that she is a servant. George is darker, but makes up for it by being a mechanical genius, and is, moreover, sufficiently un-Negroid to pass through town, a fugitive from his master, disguised as a Spanish gentleman, attracting no attention whatever beyond admiration. They are a race apart from Topsy. It transpires by the end of the novel, through one of those energetic, last-minute convolutions of the plot, that Eliza has some connection with French gentility. The figure from whom the novel takes its name, Uncle Tom, who is a figure of controversy yet, is jet-black, wooly-haired, illiterate; and he is phenomenally forbearing. He has to be; he is black; only through this forbearance can he survive or triumph. (*Cf.* Faulkner's preface to *The Sound and the Fury:* These others were not Compsons. They were black:— They endured.) His triumph is metaphysical, unearthly; since he is black, born without the light, it is only through humility, the incessant mortification of the flesh, that he can enter into communion with God or man. The virtuous rage of Mrs. Stowe is motivated by nothing so temporal as a concern for the relationship of men to one another—or, even, as she would have claimed, by a concern for their relationship to God—but merely by a panic of being hurled into the flames, of being caught in traffic with the devil. She embraced this merciless doctrine with all her heart, bargaining shamelessly before the throne of grace: God and salvation becoming her personal property, purchased with the coin of her virtue. Here, black equates with evil and white with grace; if, being mindful of the necessity of good works, she could not cast out the blacks—a wretched, huddled mass, apparently, claiming, like an obsession, her inner eye—she could not embrace them either without purifying them of sin. She must cover their intimidating nakedness, robe them in white, the garments of salvation; only thus could she herself be delivered from ever-present sin, only thus could she bury, as St. Paul demanded, "the carnal man, the man of the flesh." Tom, therefore, her only black man, has been robbed of his humanity and divested of his sex. It is the price for that darkness with which he has been branded.

Uncle Tom's Cabin, then, is activated by what might be called a theological terror, the terror of damnation; and the spirit that breathes in this book, hot, self-righteous, fearful, is not different from that spirit of medieval times which sought to exorcize evil by burning witches; and is not different from that terror which activates a lynch mob. One need not, indeed, search for examples so historic or so gaudy; this is a warfare waged daily in the heart, a warfare so vast, so relentless and so powerful that the interracial handshake or the interracial marriage can be as crucifying as the public hanging or the secret rape. This panic motivates our cruelty, this fear of the dark makes it impossible that our lives shall be other than superficial; this, interlocked with and feeding our glittering, mechanical, inescapable civilization which has put to death our freedom.

This, notwithstanding that the avowed aim of the American protest novel is to bring greater freedom to the oppressed. They are forgiven, on the strength of these good intentions, whatever violence they do to language, whatever excessive demands they make of credibility. It is, indeed, considered the sign of a frivolity so intense as to approach decadence to suggest that these books are both badly written and wildly improbable. One is told to put first things first, the good of society coming before niceties of style or characterization. Even if this were incontestable—for what exactly is the "good" of society?—it argues an insuperable confusion, since literature and sociology are not one and the same; it is impossible to discuss them as if they were. Our passion for categorization, life neatly fitted into pegs, has led to an unforeseen, paradoxical distress; confusion, a breakdown of meaning. Those categories which were meant to define and control the world for us have boomeranged us into chaos; in which limbo we whirl, clutching the straws of our definitions. The "protest" novel, so far from being disturbing, is an accepted and comforting aspect of the American scene, ramifying that framework we believe to be so necessary. Whatever unsettling questions are raised are evanescent, titillating; remote, for this has nothing to do with us, it is safely ensconced in the social arena, where, indeed, it has nothing to do with anyone, so that finally we receive a very definite thrill of virtue from the fact that we are reading such a book at all. This report from the pit reassures us of its reality and its darkness and of our own salvation; and "As long as such books are being published," an American liberal once said to me, "everything will be all right."

But unless one's ideal of society is a race of neatly analyzed, hardworking ciphers, one can hardly claim for the protest novels the lofty purpose they claim for themselves or share the present optimism concerning them. They emerge for what they are: a mirror of our confusion, dishonesty, panic, trapped and immobilized in the sunlit prison of the American dream. They are fantasies, connecting nowhere with reality, sentimental; in exactly the same sense that such movies as *The Best Years of Our Lives* or the works of Mr. James M. Cain are fantasies. Beneath the dazzling pyrotechnics of these current operas one may still discern, as the controlling force, the intense theological preoccupations of Mrs. Stowe, the sick vacuities of *The Rover Boys*. Finally, the aim of the protest novel becomes something very closely resembling the zeal of those alabaster missionaries to Africa to cover the nakedness of the natives, to hurry them into the pallid arms of Jesus and thence into slavery. The aim has now become to reduce all Americans to the compulsive, bloodless dimensions of a guy named Joe.

It is the peculiar triumph of society—and its loss—that it is able to convince those people to whom it has given inferior status of the reality of this decree; it has the force and the weapons to translate its dictum into fact, so that the allegedly inferior are actually made so, insofar as the societal realities are concerned. This is a more hidden phenomenon now than it was in the days of serfdom, but it is no less implacable. Now, as then, we find ourselves bound, first without, then within, by the nature of our categorization. And escape is not effected through a bitter railing against this trap; it is as though this very striving were the only motion needed to spring the trap upon us. We take our shape, it is true, within and against that cage of reality bequeathed us at our birth; and yet it is precisely through our dependence on this reality that we are most endlessly betrayed. Society is held together by our need; we bind it together with legend, myth, coercion, fearing that without it we will be hurled into that void, within which, like the earth before the Word was spoken, the foundations of society are hidden. From this void— ourselves—it is the function of society to protect us; but it is only this void, our unknown selves, demanding, forever, a new act of creation, which can save us—"from the evil that is in the world." With the same motion, at the same time, it is this toward which we endlessly struggle and from which, endlessly, we struggle to escape.

It must be remembered that the oppressed and the oppressor are bound together within the same society; they accept the same criteria, they share the same beliefs, they both alike depend on the same reality. Within this cage it is romantic, more, meaningless, to speak of a "new" society as the desire of the oppressed, for that shivering dependence on the props of reality which he shares with the *Herrenvolk* makes a truly "new" society impossible to conceive. What is meant by a new society is one in which inequalities will disappear, in which vengeance will be exacted; either there will be no oppressed at all, or the oppressed and the oppressor will change places. But, finally, as it seems to me, what the rejected desire is, is an elevation of status, acceptance within the present community. Thus, the African, exile, pagan, hurried off the auction block and into the fields, fell on his knees before that God in Whom he must now believe; who had made him, but not in His image. This tableau, this impossibility, is the heritage of the Negro in America: *Wash me,* cried the slave to his Maker, *and I shall be whiter, whiter than snow!* For black is the color of evil; only the robes of the saved are white. It is this cry, implacable on the air and in the skull, that he must live with. Beneath the widely published catalogue of brutality— bringing to mind, somehow, an image, a memory of church-bells burdening the air—is this reality which, in the same nightmare notion, he both flees and rushes to embrace. In America, now, this country devoted to the death of the paradox—which may, therefore, be put to death by one—his lot is as ambiguous as a tableau by Kafka. To flee or not, to move or not, it is all the same; his doom is written on his forehead, it is carried in his heart. In *Native Son,* Bigger Thomas stands on a Chicago street corner watching airplanes flown by white men racing against the sun and "God-damn" he says, the bitterness bubbling up like blood, remembering a million in- dignities, the terrible, rat-infested house, the humiliation of home- relief, the intense, aimless, ugly bickering, hating it; hatred smoulders through these pages like sulphur fire. All of Bigger's life is con- trolled, defined by his hatred and his fear. And later, his fear drives him to murder and his hatred to rape; he dies, having come, through this violence, we are told, for the first time, to a kind of life, having for the first time redeemed his manhood. Below the surface of this novel there lies, as it seems to me, a continuation, a complement of that monstrous legend it was written to destroy. Bigger is Uncle Tom's descendant, flesh of his flesh, so exactly opposite a portrait that, when the books are placed together, it seems that the con- temporary Negro novelist and the dead New England woman are locked together in a deadly, timeless battle; the one uttering merciless exhortations, the other shouting curses. And, indeed, within this web of lust and fury, black and white can only thrust and counter-thrust, long for each other's slow, exquisite death; death by torture, acid, knives and burning; the thrust, the counter-thrust, the longing mak- ing the heavier that cloud which blinds and suffocates them both, so that they go down into the pit together. Thus has the cage betrayed us all, this moment, our life, turned to nothing through our terrible attempts to insure it. For Bigger's tragedy is not that he is cold or black or hungry, not even that he is American, black; but that he has accepted a theology that denies him life, that he admits the possibility of his being sub-human and feels constrained, therefore, to battle for his humanity according to those brutal criteria bequeathed him at his birth. But our humanity is our burden, our life; we need not battle for it; we need only to do what is infinitely more difficult— that is, accept it. The failure of the protest novel lies in its rejection of life, the human being, the denial of his beauty, dread, power, in its insistence that it is his categorization alone which is real and which cannot be transcended.

THE AMERICAN IDEAL

G. K. Chesterton

There is nothing the matter with Americans except their ideals. The real American is all right; it is the ideal American who is all wrong. It is the code and conception of life imposed from above, much more than the merely human faults and weaknesses working up from below.

In so far as the citizens of the Western democracy have really gone wrong, they have not inherently or quite naturally gone wrong. They have been taught wrong; instructed wrong; educated wrong; exalted and uplifted wrong. A huge heresy, rather peculiar to modern times, yet singularly uncriticized by modern critics, has actually perverted them in a way which is not really very consonant to their personalities. The real, natural Americans are candid, generous, capable of a beautiful wonder and gratitude; enthusiastic about things external to themselves; easily contented and not particularly conceited. They have been deliberately and dogmatically taught to be conceited. They have been systematically educated in a theory of enthusiasm, which degrades it into mere egotism. The American has received as a sort of religion the notion that blowing his own trumpet is as important as the trump of doom.

It is, I am almost certain, in the main an example of the hardening effect of a heresy, and even of a hostile heresy. There are more examples of it than those admit who ignore the peril of heresy. The Scots are an example; they were never naturally Calvinists; and when they break free, it is to become very romantic figures like Stevenson or Cunninghame Graham. The Americans were never naturally boomsters or business bullies. They would have been much happier and more themselves as a race of simple and warm-hearted country people eager for country sports or gazing at the wonders in country fairs. An egotistic heresy, produced by the modern

THE AMERICAN IDEAL: From *Sidelights* (1932). Reprinted by permission of A. P. Watt & Son and Messrs. Sheed & Ward Limited.

heathenry, has taught them against all their Christian instincts that boasting is better than courtesy and pride better than humility.

It is queer to note how raw and recent is the heresy; and how little it has been spotted by any heresy-hunt. We have heard much of modern polygamy or promiscuity reversing the Christian idea of purity. We have heard something, and we ought to hear more, of modern capitalism and commercialism reversing the Christian idea of charity to the poor. But we have not heard much about Advertisement, with its push, publicity and self-assertion, reversing the idea of Christian humility. Yet we can at once test the ethics of publicity by removing it from public life; by merely applying it to private life. What should we think, in a private party, if an old gentleman had written on his shirtfront in large fine flowing hand: "I am the only well-bred person in this company." What should we think of any person of taste and humour who went about wearing a placard inscribed "Please note quiet charm of my personality." What should we say if people gravely engraved on their visiting card the claim to be the handsomest or the wittiest or the most subtly, strangely attractive people about town. We should not only think, with great accuracy, that they were behaving like asses, and certainly destroying beforehand any social advantages they might really have. We should also think they were wantonly reversing and destroying a principle of social amenity and moral delicacy, recognized in all civilized states and ages, but especially emphasized in the ethics of Christianity. Yet modern business, especially in America, does really enforce this sort of publicity in public life; and has begun to press it even in private life. But the point to be emphasized here is that it is really pressed upon most of the Americans; they are goaded and driven into this sort of public life; large numbers of them would have been perfectly contented with private life. They would have endured it, even if it had retained all the old decency and dignity of private life. For this is where the critic must deal most delicately with the subtlety of their simplicity.

The Americans are always excused as a new nation; though it is no longer exactly a new excuse. But in truth these terms are very misleading; and in some ways they have rather the atmosphere of an old nation. Over whole tracts of that vast country, they are certainly what we should call an old-fashioned nation. In no nation in the world are so many people attached to a certain sort of old texts, familiar quotations, or the pieces of sentiment that were written on the pink pages of Victorian albums. A popular book was published, while I was in America, bearing the somewhat alarming name of *Heart Throbs*, from which compilation one might learn that some great and grim judge of the High Court had for his favourite poem "Grandmother's Blessing," or that some colossus of commerce, a Steel-King or an Oil-King, preferred the simple lines entitled, "Daddy's Hat." It is only fair to say that some of these hard-headed and ruthless rulers had never forgotten the real classical claims of "Love's Young Dream," or "The Seven Ages of Man." Some may sneer at these extracts, but surely not at their novelty or crudity. I do not mention them for the purpose of sneering at them, but, on the contrary, for the purpose of showing that there must be a great block of solid and normal sentiment, even of traditional sentiment. And people having that sentiment, people inheriting that tradition, would not necessarily, on their own account, have become believers in selfish, sensational self-advertisement. I suspect, as a matter of fact, that there is rather less of such callous and contemptuous egoism in America than anywhere else. The older civilizations, some of which I will venture to call the more civilized civilizations, have a great many advantages in variety of culture and a conspectus of criticism; but I should guess that their wickedness is more wicked. A Frenchman can be much more cynical and sceptical than an American; a German much more morbid and perverted than an American; an Englishman much more frozen and sophisticated with pride. What has happened to America is that a number of people who were meant to be heroic and fighting farmers, at once peasants and pioneers, have been swept by the pestilence of a particular fad or false doctrine; the ideal which has and deserves the detestable title of Making Good. The very words are a hypocrisy, that would have been utterly unintelligible to any man of any other age or creed; as meaningless to a Greek sophist as to a Buddhist monk. For they manage, by one mean twist of words, to combine the notion of making money with the entirely opposite notion of being good. But the abnormality of this notion can best be seen, as I have said, in its heathen and barbaric appeal to a brazen self-praise. Selling the goods meant incidentally, of course, lying about the goods; but it was almost worse that it meant bragging about the goods.

There is a very real sense in which certain crudities in the Americans are not so much a part of American crudity as actually a part of American culture. They are not mere outbreaks of human nature; they are something systematically impressed upon human nature. It is not for nothing that some of the most prominent features of their actual academic training are things like schools of commerce or schools of journalism. There is a vital distinction between these things and all that the world has generally meant by a school; especially the most scholastic sort of school. Even those who think little of learning Greek and Latin will agree that it carried with it a vague suggestion of admiring Greeks and Latins. The schoolboy was supposed in some sense to feel inferior. But even in a commercial academy the boy is not occupied in gazing at some great millionaire doing a straddle in wheat, with the feelings of the simplest pagan of antiquity gazing at the Colossus of Rhodes. It would not do him much good if he did; but in general practice he does not. If he learns anything, he learns to do a straddle in wheat himself, or to hope that he will do it as acrobatically as any other acrobat. He does not even learn to venerate Mr. Rockefeller, but only to imitate Mr. Rockefeller.

Nor does the practical study of journalism lead to any particular veneration for literature. The qualities inculcated and encouraged are the same as those which commerce inculcates and encourages. I say it with no particular hostility or bitterness, but it is a fact that the school of commerce or the school of journalism might almost as well be called a school of impudence or a school of swagger or a school of grab and greed.

But the point is that people are taught to be impudent or greedy, not that they are naturally impudent and greedy. As a matter of fact, they are not. And that is the whole paradox of the position, which I have already suggested and should like here to expand. I have seen in the United States young people, coming out of this course of culture, who actually pulled themselves together to be rude, as normal young people have always pulled themselves together to be polite. They were shy in fact and shameless on principle. They would ask rude questions, but they were as timid about asking a rude question as an ordinary youth about paying a compliment. They would use the most brazen methods to induce somebody to see them, and anybody who did see them would pity them for their bashfulness. They were always storming the stage in a state of stage fright.

The very simple explanation of this puzzling contradiction is that they were perfectly nice and normal people in themselves, but they had never been left to themselves by those who were always telling them to assert themselves. They had been bounced into bouncing and bullied into being bullies. And the explanation is the existence of this modern heresy, or false ideal, that has been preached to everybody by every organ of publicity and plutocracy: the theory that self-praise is the only real recommendation.

I have suggested that the American character might have developed in an infinitely more healthy and human fashion if it had not been for this heresy. Of course the American character would in any case have been very much more alert and lively and impetuous than the English character. But that has nothing to do with the particular features and fashions of commercial advertisement and ambition.

There are many other races that are more vivacious or vehement than the English and who yet live the normal life of contented country folk, and practice the traditional ideas of modesty and courtesy.

The trouble with the false commercial ideal is that it has made these men struggle against modesty as if it were morbidity; and actually try to coarsen their natural courtesy, as other men stifle a natural crudity. I do not think that bragging and go-getting are American faults. I hate them as American virtues; I think the quarrel is not so much with the men as with the gods: the false gods they have been taught to worship and still only worship with half their hearts. And these gods of the heathen are stone and brass, but especially brass; and there is an eternal struggle in that half-hearted idolatry; for often, while the gods are of brass, the hearts are of gold.

E = M C²

Albert Einstein

In order to understand the law of the equivalence of mass and energy, we must go back to two conservation or "balance" principles which, independent of each other, held a high place in pre-relativity physics. These were the principle of the conservation of energy and the principle of the conservation of mass. The first of these, advanced by Leibnitz as long ago as the seventeenth century, was developed in the nineteenth century essentially as a corollary of a principle of mechanics.

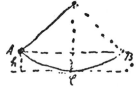

Drawing from Dr. Einstein's manuscript.

Consider, for example, a pendulum whose mass swings back and forth between the points A and B. At these points the mass m is

E=MC²: From *Out of My Later Years* (1950). Reprinted by permission of the Estate of Albert Einstein.

higher by the amount h than it is at C, the lowest point of the path (see drawing). At C, on the other hand, the lifting height has disappeared and instead of it the mass has a velocity v. It is as though the lifting height could be converted entirely into velocity, and vice versa. The exact relation would be expressed as $mgh = \frac{m}{2}v^2$, with g representing the acceleration of gravity. What is interesting here is that this relation is independent of both the length of the pendulum and the form of the path through which the mass moves.

The significance is that something remains constant throughout the process, and that something is energy. At A and at B it is an energy of position, or "potential" energy; at C it is an energy of motion, or "kinetic" energy. If this concept is correct, then the sum $mgh + m\frac{v^2}{2}$ must have the same value for any position of the pendulum, if h is understood to represent the height above C, and v the velocity at that point in the pendulum's path. And such is found to be actually the case. The generalization of this principle gives us the law of the conservation of mechanical energy. But what happens when friction stops the pendulum?

The answer to that was found in the study of heat phenomena. This study, based on the assumption that heat is an indestructible substance which flows from a warmer to a colder object, seemed to give us a principle of the "conservation of heat." On the other hand, from time immemorial it has been known that heat could be produced by friction, as in the fire-making drills of the Indians. The physicists were for long unable to account for this kind of heat "production." Their difficulties were overcome only when it was successfully established that, for any given amount of heat produced by friction, an exactly proportional amount of energy had to be expended. Thus did we arrive at a principle of the "equivalence of work and heat." With our pendulum, for example, mechanical energy is gradually converted by friction into heat.

In such fashion the principles of the conservation of mechanical and thermal energies were merged into one. The physicists were thereupon persuaded that the conservation principle could be further extended to take in chemical and electromagnetic processes—in short, could be applied to all fields. It appeared that in our physical system there was a sum total of energies that remained constant through all changes that might occur.

Now for the principle of the conservation of mass. Mass is defined by the resistance that a body opposes to its acceleration (inert mass). It is also measured by the weight of the body (heavy mass). That these two radically different definitions lead to the same value for the mass of a body is, in itself, an astonishing fact. According to the principle—namely, that masses remain unchanged under any physical or chemical changes—the mass appeared to be the essential (because unvarying) quality of matter. Heating, melting, vaporization, or combining into chemical compounds would not change the total mass.

Physicists accepted this principle up to a few decades ago. But it proved inadequate in the face of the special theory of relativity. It was therefore merged with the energy principle—just as, about 60 years before, the principle of the conservation of mechanical energy had been combined with the principle of the conservation of heat. We might say that the principle of the conservation of energy, having previously swallowed up that of the conservation of heat, now proceeded to swallow that of the conservation of mass—and holds the field alone.

It is customary to express the equivalence of mass and energy (though somewhat inexactly) by the formula $E = mc^2$, in which c represents the velocity of light, about 186,000 miles per second. E is the energy that is contained in a stationary body; m is its mass. The energy that belongs to the mass m is equal to this mass, multiplied by the square of the enormous speed of light—which is to say, a vast amount of energy for every unit of mass.

But if every gram of material contains this tremendous energy, why did it go so long unnoticed? The answer is simple enough: so long as none of the energy is given off externally, it cannot be observed. It is as though a man who is fabulously rich should never spend or give away a cent; no one could tell how rich he was.

Now we can reverse the relation and say that an increase of E in the amount of energy must be accompanied by an increase of $\dfrac{E}{c^2}$ in the mass. I can easily supply energy to the mass—for instance, if I heat it by 10 degrees. So why not measure the mass increase, or weight increase, connected with this change? The trouble here is that in the mass increase the enormous factor c^2 occurs in the denominator of the fraction. In such a case the increase is too small to be measured directly; even with the most sensitive balance.

For a mass increase to be measurable, the change of energy per mass unit must be enormously large. We know of only one sphere in which such amounts of energy per mass unit are released: namely, radioactive disintegration. Schematically, the process goes like this: An atom of the mass M splits into two atoms of the mass M' and M", which separate with tremendous kinetic energy. If we imagine these two masses as brought to rest—that is, if we take this energy of motion from them—then, considered together, they are essentially poorer in energy than was the original atom. According to the equivalence principle, the mass sum M' + M" of the disintegration products must also be somewhat smaller than the original mass M of the disintegrating atom—in contradiction to the old principle of the conservation of mass. The relative difference of the two is on the order of $\frac{1}{10}$ of one percent.

Now, we cannot actually weigh the atoms individually. However, there are indirect methods for measuring their weights exactly. We can likewise determine the kinetic energies that are transferred to the disintegration products M' and M". Thus it has become possible to test and confirm the equivalence formula. Also, the law permits us to calculate in advance, from precisely determined atom weights, just how much energy will be released with any atom disintegration we have in mind. The law says nothing, of course, as to whether—or how—the disintegration reaction can be brought about.

What takes place can be illustrated with the help of our rich man. The atom M is a rich miser who, during his life, gives away no money (*energy*). But in his will he bequeaths his fortune to his sons M' and M", on condition that they give to the community a small amount, less than one thousandth of the whole estate (*energy or mass*). The sons together have somewhat less than the father had (*the mass sum M' + M" is somewhat smaller than the mass M of the radioactive atom*). But the part given to the community, though relatively small, is still so enormously large (*considered as kinetic energy*) that it brings with it a great threat of evil. Averting that threat has become the most urgent problem of our time.

SCIENCE AND THE UNEXPECTED UNIVERSE

Loren Eiseley

A British essayist of distinction, H. J. Massingham, once remarked perceptively that woods nowadays are haunted not by ghosts, but by a silence and man-made desolation which might well take terrifying material forms. There is nothing like a stalled train in a marsh to promote such reflections—particularly if one has been transported just beyond the environs of a great city and set down in some nether world that seems to partake both of nature before man came and the residue of what will exist after him. It was night when my train halted, but a kind of flame-wreathed landscape attended by shadowy figures could be glimpsed from the window.

After a time, with a companion, I descended and strolled forward to explore this curious region. It turned out to be a perpetually burning city dump, contributing its miasmas and choking vapors to the murky sky above the city. Amidst the tended flames of this inferno I approached one of the grimy attendants who was forking over the rubbish. In the background other shadows, official and unofficial, were similarly engaged. For a moment I had the insubstantial feeling that must exist on the borders of hell, where everything, wavering among heat waves, is transported to another dimension. One could imagine ragged and distorted souls grubbed over by scavengers for what might usefully survive.

I stood in silence watching this great burning. Sodden papers were being forked into the flames and after a while it crossed my mind that this was perhaps the place where last year's lace valentines had gone, along with old Christmas trees, and the beds I had slept on in childhood.

"I suppose you get everything here," I ventured to the grimy attendant.

He nodded indifferently and drew a heavy glove across his face.

SCIENCE AND THE UNEXPECTED UNIVERSE: © 1966 by Loren C. Eiseley. This essay will be included in Dr. Eiseley's forthcoming book *The Unexpected Universe* to be published by Harcourt, Brace & World, Inc. Reprinted by permission of the author.

His eyes were red-rimmed from the fire. Perhaps they were red anyhow.

"Know what?" He swept a hand outward toward the flames. "No," I confessed.

"Babies," he growled in my ear. "Even dead babies sometimes turn up. From there." He gestured contemptuously toward the city and hoisted an indistinguishable mass upon his fork. I stepped back from the flare of light but it was only part of an old radio cabinet. Out of it had once come voices and music and laughter, perhaps from the twenties. And where were the voices traveling now? I looked at the dangling fragments of wire. They reminded me of something, but the engine bell sounded.

I made a parting gesture. Around me in the gloom dark shapes worked ceaselessly at the dampened fires. My eyes were growing accustomed to their light.

"We get it all," the dump philosopher repeated. "Just give it time to travel, we get it all."

"Be seeing you," I said irrelevantly. "Good luck."

Back in my train seat the flames and the dangling wire rose up unwillingly in memory. It had something to do with an air crash years ago and the identification of the dead. Anthropologists get strange assignments. I put the matter out of my mind as I always do, but I dozed and it came back: the box with the dangling wires. I had once fitted a seared and broken skull-cap over a dead man's brains and I had thought, peering into the scorched and mangled skull vault, it is like a beautiful, irreparably broken machine, like something consciously made to be used, and now where are the voices and the music?

"We get it all," a dark figure said in my dream. I sighed and the figure in the murk faded into the clicking of the wheels.

One can think just so much, but the archaeologist is awake to memories of the dead cultures sleeping around us, to our destiny and to the nature of the universe we profess to inhabit. I would speak of these things not as a wise man, with scientific certitude, but from a place outside, in the role, shall we say, of a city dump philosopher. Nor is this a strained figure of speech. The archaeologist is the last grubber among things mortal. He puts not men, but civilizations, to bed, and passes upon them final judgments. He finds, if imprinted upon clay, both our grocery bills and the hymns to our gods. Or he uncovers, as I once did in a mountain cavern, the skeleton of a cradled child, supplied, in the pathos of our mortality, with the carefully "killed" tools whose shadowy counterparts were intended to serve a tiny infant through the vicissitudes it would encounter beyond the dark curtain of death. Infinite care had been lavished upon objects that did not equate with the child's ability to use them in this life. Was his spirit expected to grow to manhood, or had this final projection of bereaved parental care thrust into the night, in desperate anxiety, all that an impoverished and simple culture could provide where human affection could not follow?

In a comparable but more abstract way the modern mind, the scientific mind, concerned as it is with the imponderable mysteries of existence, has sought to equip oncoming generations with certain mental weapons against the terrors of ignorance. Protectively, as in the case of the dead child bundled in a cave, science has proclaimed a universe whose laws are open to discovery and, above all, in the words of one of its greatest exponents, Francis Bacon, it has sought "not to imagine or suppose, but to *discover* what nature does or may be made to do."

To discover what nature does, however, two primary restrictions are laid upon a finite creature: he must extrapolate his laws from what exists in his or his society's moment of time and, in addition, he is limited by what his senses can tell him of the surrounding world. Later, technology may provide the extension of those senses, as in the case of the microscope and telescope. Nevertheless the same eye or ear with which we are naturally endowed must, in the end, interpret the data derived from such extensions of sight or hearing. Moreover, science since the thirteenth century has clung to the dictum of William of Ockham that hypotheses must not be multiplied excessively; that the world, in essence, is always simple, not complicated, and its secrets accessible to men of astute and sufficiently penetrating intellect. Ironically, it is in the time of our greatest intellectual and technological triumphs that one is forced to say that Ockham's long-honored precepts, however well they have served man in the reduction of superstition, and in the mastery of his environment, are, from another view, merely a more sophisticated projection of his desire for order—and for the ability to control, understand and manipulate his world.

All of these intentions are commendable enough, but perhaps we would approach them more humbly and within a greater frame of reference if we were to recognize what Massingham sensed as lying latent in his wood, or what John Donne implied over three centuries ago when he wrote:

> I am rebegot
> of absence, darknesse, death:
> Things which are not.

Donne had recognized that behind visible nature lurks an invisible and procreant void from whose incomprehensible magnitude we can only recoil. That void has haunted me ever since I handled the shattered calvarium that a few hours before had contained, in microcosmic dimensions, a similar lurking potency.

Some years previously I had written a little book of essays in which I had narrated how time had become natural in our thinking and I had gone on to speak likewise of life and man. In the end, however, I had been forced to ask How Natural is Natural—a subject that raised the hackles of some of my scientifically inclined colleagues who confused the achievements of their disciplines with certitude on a cosmic scale. My very question thus implied an ill-concealed heresy. That heresy it is my intent to pursue further. It will involve us, not in the denigration of science, but rather in a farther stretch of the imagination as we approach those distant and wooded boundaries of thought where, in the words of the old fairy tale, the fox and the hare say goodnight to each other. It is here that predictability ceases and the unimaginable begins—or, as a final heretical suspicion, we might ask ourselves whether our own little planetary fragment of the cosmos has all along concealed a mocking refusal to comply totally with human conceptions of order and secure prediction.

The world contains, for all its seeming regularity, a series of surprises resembling those that in childhood terrorized us by erupting on springs from closed boxes. The world of primitive man is not dissimilar. Lightning leaps from clouds, something invisible rumbles in the air, the living body, spilling its mysterious red fluid, lies down in a sleep from which it cannot waken. There are night cries in the forest, talking waters, guiding omens, or portents in the fall of a leaf. No longer, as with the animal, can the world be accepted as given. It has to be perceived and consciously thought about, abstracted and considered. The moment one does so one is outside of the natural; objects are each one surrounded with an aura radiating meaning to man alone. It is to a universe already suspected of being woven together by unseen forces that man brings the organizing power of primitive magic. The manikin that is believed to control the macrocosm by some sympathetic connection is already obscurely present in the poppet thrust full of needles by the witch. Crude and imperfect, magic is still man's first conscious abstraction from nature, his first attempt to link disparate objects by some unseen attraction between them.

If we now descend into the early years of modern science we find the world of the late eighteenth and early nineteenth centuries basking comfortably in the conception of the balanced world machine. Newton had established what appeared to be the reign of universal order in the heavens. The planets, indeed the whole cosmic engine, were self-regulatory. This passion for order controlled by a Divinity too vast to be concerned with petty miracle was slowly extended to earth. James Hutton glimpsed, in the long erosion and renewal of the continents by subterranean uplift, a similar "beautiful machine" so arranged that recourse to the "preternatural," or "destructive accident," such as the Mosaic Deluge, was unnecessary to account for the physical features of the planet.

Time had lengthened and through those eons, law, not chaos, reigned. The imprint of fossil raindrops similar to those of today had been discovered upon ancient shores. The marks of fossil ripples were also observable in uncovered strata, and buried trees had absorbed the sunlight of far millennia. The remote past was one with the present and, over all, a lawful similarity decreed by a Christian Deity prevailed.

In the animal world, save for the beliefs of a few hesitant thinkers, a similar web of organization was believed to exist. The balanced Newtonian clockwork of the heavens had been transferred to earth and, for a few decades, was destined to prevail in the world of life. Plants and animals would be frozen into their existing shapes, they would compete but not change, for change in this system was basically a denial of law. Hutton's world renewed itself in cycles just as the oscillations observable in the heavens were similarly self-regulatory.

Time was thus law-abiding. It contained no novelty and was self-correcting. It was, as we have indicated, a manifestation of divine law. That law was a comfort to man. The restive world of life fell under the same dominion as the equally restive particles of earth. Organisms oscillated within severely fixed limits. The smallest animalcule in a hay infusion carried a message for man, the joints of an insect assured him of divine attention. "In every nature and every portion of nature which we can descry," wrote William Paley in a book characteristic of the period, "we find attention bestowed upon even the minutest parts. The hinges in the wing of an earwig . . . are as highly wrought as if the creator had nothing else to finish. We see no signs of diminution of care by multiplicity of objects, or distraction of thought by variety. We have no reason to fear, therefore, our being forgotten, or overlooked, or neglected." Written into these lines in scientific guise is the same humanly protective gesture that long ago had heaped skin blankets, bone needles and a carved stick for killing rabbits, into the burial chamber of a child.

This undeviating balance in which life was locked was called "natural government" by the great anatomist John Hunter. It was, in a sense, like the cyclic but undeviating life of the planet earth itself. That vast elemental creature felt the fall of raindrops on its furry hide, was troubled by the drift of autumn leaves or the erosive work of wind throughout eternity. Nevertheless, the accounts of nature were strictly kept. If a continent was depressed at one point, its equivalent arose elsewhere. Whether the item in the scale was the weight of a raindrop or a dislodged boulder on a mountainside, a dynamic balance kept the great beast young and flourishing upon its course.

And as it was with earth, so with its inhabitants. "There is an equilibrium kept up among the animals by themselves," Hunter went on to contend. They kept their own numbers pruned and in proportion. Expansion was always kept within bounds. The struggle for existence was recognized before Darwin but it was only as the indefinite sway of a returning pendulum. Life was selected but it was selected for but one purpose: vigor and consistency in appearance. The mutative variant was struck down. What had been was, what would be already existed. As in the case of that great animal the earth, of the living flora and fauna it could be said that there was to be found "no vestige of a beginning,—no prospect of an end." An elemental order lay across granite, sea and shore. Each individual animal peered from age to age out of the same unyielding sockets of bone. Out of no other casements could he stare; the dweller within would see leaf and bird eternally the same. This was the scientific doctrine known as uniformitarianism. It had abolished magic as it had abolished the many changes and shape-shiftings of witch doctors and medieval necromancers. At last the world was genuinely sane under a beneficent Deity. Then came Darwin.

At first he was hailed as another Newton who had discovered the laws of life. It was true that what had once been deemed independent creations, the shells in the collector's cabinet, the flowers pressed into memory books, were now, as in the abandoned magic of the ancient past, once more joined by invisible threads of sympathy and netted together by a common ancestry. The world seemed even more understandable, more natural than natural. The fortuitous had become fashionable and the other face of "natural government" turned out to be creation. Life's pendulum of balance was an illusion.

Behind the staid face of that nature we had worshiped for so long we were unseen shape-shifters. Viewed in the long light of limitless time we were optical illusions whose very identity was difficult to fix. Still, there was much talk of progress and perfection. It was only later that we began to realize that what Charles Darwin had introduced into nature was not Newtonian predictability but absolute random novelty. Life was bent, in the phrase of Alfred Russel Wallace, upon "indefinite departure." No living thing, not even man, understood upon what journey he had embarked. Time was no longer cyclic or monotonously repetitious.[1] It was historic, novel and unreturning. Since that momentous discovery man has, whether he realizes or accepts his fate, been moving in a world of contingent forms.

Even in the supposedly stable universe of matter, as it was viewed by nineteenth-century scientists, new problems constantly appear. The discovery by physicists of antimatter particles having electric charges opposite to those that compose our world and unable to exist in concert with known matter, raises the question of whether, after all, our corner of the universe is representative of the entire potentialities that may exist elsewhere. The existence of antimatter is unaccounted for in present theories of the universe and such peculiarities as the primordial atom and the recently reported flash of the explosion at the birth of the universe, as recorded in the radio spectrum, lead on into unknown paths.

If it were not for the fact that familiarity leads to assumed knowledge we would have to admit that the earth's atmosphere of oxygen appears to be the product of a biological invention, photosynthesis, another random event that took place in archeozoic times. That single "invention," for such it was, determined the entire nature of life on this planet and there is no possibility at present of calling it preordained. Similarly the stepped-up manipulation of chance, in the shape of both mutation and recombination of genetic factors, which is one result of the sexual mechanism, would have been unprophesiable.

The brain of man, that strange green iceberg of conscious and unconscious life, was likewise unpredictable until its appearance. A comparatively short lapse of geological time has evolved a humanity that, beginning in considerable physical diversity, has increasingly converged toward a universal biological similarity marked only by a lingering and insignificant racial differentiation. With the rise of Homo sapiens and the final perfection of the human brain as a manipulator of symbolic thought, the spectrum of man's possible social behavior has widened enormously. What is essentially the same brain biologically can continue to exist in the simple ecological

[1] For purposes of space I have chosen to ignore the short-lived geological doctrine of the early nineteenth century known as catastrophism, since I have treated it at length elsewhere.

balance of the stone age, or, on the other hand, may produce those enormous inflorescences known as civilizations. These growths seemingly operate under their own laws and take distinct and irreversible pathways. In an analogous way organisms mutate and diverge through adaptive radiation from one or a few original forms.

In the domain of culture man's augmented ability to manipulate abstract ideas and to draw in this fashion enormous latent stores of energy from his brain has led to an intriguing situation: the range of his *possible* behavior is greater and more contradictory than that which can be contained within the compass of a single society, whether tribal or advanced. Thus as man's penetration into the metaphysical and abstract has succeeded, so has his capacity to follow, in the same physical body, a series of tangential roads into the future. Likeness in body has, paradoxically, led to diversity in thought. Thought, in turn, involves such vast institutional involutions as the rise of modern science with its intensified hold upon modern society.

All past civilizations of men have been localized and have had, therefore, the divergent mutative quality to which we have referred. They have offered choices to men. Ideas have been exchanged, along with technological innovations, but never on so vast, overwhelming and single-directed a scale as in the present. Increasingly there is but one way into the future, the technological way. The frightening aspect of this situation lies in the constriction of human choice. Western technology has released irrevocable forces and the "one world" which has been talked about so glibly is frequently a distraught conformity produced by the centripetal forces of Western society. So great is its power over men that any other solution, any other philosophy, is silenced. Men, unknowingly, and whether for good or ill, are making their last decisions about human destiny. To pursue the biological analogy, it is as though, instead of many adaptive organisms, a single gigantic animal embodied the only organic future of the world.

Archaeology is the science of man's evening, not his midday triumphs. I have spoken of my visit to a flame-wreathed marsh at nightfall. All in it had been substance, matter, trailing wires and old sandwich wrappings, broken toys and iron bedsteads. Yet there was nothing present that science could not reduce into its elements, nothing that was not the product of the urban world whose far-off towers had risen gleaming in the dusk beyond the marsh. There on the city dump had lain the shabby debris of life: the waxen fragment of an old record that had stolen a human heart, wilted flowers amongst smashed beer cans, the castaway knife of a murderer, along with a broken tablespoon. It was all a maze of invisible, floating connections, and would be until the last man perished. These forlorn materials had all been subjected to the dissolving power of the human mind. They had been wrenched from deep veins of rock, boiled in great crucibles and carried miles from their origins. They had assumed shapes which, although material enough, had existed first as blueprints in the profound darkness of a living brain. They had been defined before their existence, named and given shape in the puff of air that we call a word. That word had been evoked in a skull box which, with all its contained powers and lurking paradoxes, has arisen in ways we can only dimly retrace.

A great and oft-quoted scientist is reputed to have once remarked that he refused to believe that God plays at dice with the universe. But as we survey the long backward course of time, it would appear that indeed He does, that the open-endedness of time is unexpectedly an essential element of His creation. Every time an infant is born, the dice, in the shape of genes and enzymes and the intangibles of chance environment, are being rolled again, as when that smoky figure from the fire hissed in my ear the tragedy of the cast-off infants of the city. Each one of us is a statistical impossibility around which hovers a million other lives that were never destined to be born—but who, nevertheless, are being unmanifest, a lurking potential in the dark storehouse of the void.

Today in spite of that web of law, that network of forces which the past century sought to string to the ends of the universe, a strange unexpectedness lingers about our world. This change in viewpoint, which has frequently escaped our attention, can be illustrated in the remark of Heinrich Hertz, the great nineteenth-century experimenter in the electromagnetic field. "The most important problem which our conscious knowledge of nature should enable us to solve," Hertz stated, "is the anticipation of future events, so that we may arrange our present affairs in accordance with such anticipation."

There is an attraction about this philosophy which causes it to linger in the lay mind and, as a short-term prospect, in the minds of many scientists and technologists. It implies a tidiness which is infinitely attractive to man, increasingly a homeless orphan lost in the vast abysses of space and time. Hertz's remark seems to offer surcease from uncertainty, power contained, the universe understood, the future apprehended before its emergence. The previous Elizabethan age, by contrast, had often attached to its legal documents a humble obeisance to life's uncertainties expressed in the phrase, "by the mutability of fortune and favor." The men of Shakespeare's century may have known less of science but they knew only too well what unexpected overthrow was implied in the frown of a monarch or a breath of the plague.

The twentieth century, on the other hand, surveys a totally new universe. That our cosmological conceptions bear a relationship to the past is obvious, that some of the power of which Hertz dreamed lies in our hands is all too evident, but never before in human history has the mind soared higher and seen less to cheer its complacency. We have heard much of science as the endless frontier, but we whose immediate ancestors were seekers of gold among great mountains and gloomy forests are easily susceptible to a simplistic conception of the word *frontier* as something conquerable in its totality. We assume, given enough time and expenditure of energy, that the ore will be extracted and the forests computed in board feet of lumber. A tamed wilderness will subject itself to man.

Not so the wilderness beyond the stars or concealed in the infinitesimal world beneath the atom. Wise reflection will lead us to recognize that we have come upon a different and less conquerable region. Forays across its border already suggest that man's dream of mastering all aspects of Nature takes no account of his limitations in time, space, or even his own senses, augmented though they may be by his technological devices. Even the thought that he can bring to bear upon that frontier is limited in quantity by the number of trained minds that can sustain such an adventure. Ever more expensive grow the tools with which research can be sustained, ever more diverse the social problems which that research, in its technological phase, promotes. To take one single example: who would have dreamed that a tube connecting two lenses of glass would pierce into the swarming depths of our own being, force upon us incredible feats of sanitary engineering, master the plague and create that giant upsurge out of unloosened nature which we call the population explosion?

The Roman Empire is a past event in history, yet by analogy it presents us with a small scale model comparable to the endless frontier of science. A great political and military machine had expanded outward to the limits of the known world. Its lines of communication grew ever more tenuous, taxes rose fantastically, the disaffected and alienated within its borders steadily increased. By the time of the barbarian invasions the vast structure was already dying of inanition. Yet that empire lasted far longer than the world of science has yet endured.

But what of the empire of science? Does not its word leap fast as light, is it not a creator of incalculable wealth, is not space its plaything? Its weapons are monstrous, its eye is capable of peering be-yond millions of light years. There is one dubious answer to this buoyant optimism: science is human, it is of human devising and manufacture. It has not prevented war, it has perfected it. It has not abolished cruelty or corruption. It has enabled these abominations to be practiced on a scale unknown before in human history.

Science is a solver of problems, but it is dealing with the limitless, just as, in a cruder way, were the Romans. Solutions to problems create problems; their solutions, in turn, multiply into additional problems which escape out of scientific hands like noxious insects into the interstices of the social fabric. The rate of growth is geo-metric and the vibrations set up can even now be detected in our institutions. This is what the English biologist D'Arcy Thompson called the evolution of contingency. It is no longer represented by the long, slow turn of world time as the geologist has known it. Contingency has escaped into human hands and flickers unseen be-hind every whirl of our machines, every pronouncement of political policy.

Each one of us before his death looks back upon a childhood whose ways now seem as remote as those of Rome. "Daddy," the small daughter of a friend of mine recently asked, "tell me how it was in olden days." As my kindly friend groped amidst his classical history, he suddenly realized with a slight shock that his daughter wanted nothing more than an account of his own childhood. It was forty years away and it was already "olden days." "There was a time," he said slowly to the enchanted child, "called the years of the Great Depression. In those years there was a very great deal to eat, but men could not buy it. Little girls were scarcer than now. You see," he said painfully, "their fathers could not afford them and they were not born." He made a half-apologetic gesture to the empty room as if to a gathering of small reproachful ghosts. "There was a monster we never understood called Overproduction. There were," and his voice trailed hopelessly into silence, "so many dragons in that time you could not believe it. And there was a very civilized nation where little girls were taken from their parents . . ." He could not go on. The eyes from Auschwitz, he told me later, would not permit him.

Recently I passed a cemetery in a particularly bleak countryside. Adjoining the multitude of stark upthrust grey stones was an incon-gruous row of six transparent telephone booths erected in that spot for reasons best known to the communications industry. Were they placed there for the midnight convenience of the dead, or for the midday visitors who might attempt speech with the silent people beyond the fence? It was difficult to determine, but I thought the episode suggestive of our dilemma.

An instrument for communication, erected by a powerful unseen intelligence, was at my command, but I suspect, although I was oddly averse to trying, that the wires did not run in the proper direction, and that there was something disconnected or disjointed about the whole endeavor. It was, I fear, symbolic of an unexpected aspect of our universe, a universe that however strung with connecting threads is endowed with an open-ended and perverse quality we shall never completely master. Nature contains that which does not concern us, and has no intention of taking us into its confidence. It may provide us with receiving boxes of white bone as cunning in their way as the wired booths in the cemetery, but, like these, they appear to lack some essential ingredient of genuine connection. As we consider what appears to be the chance emergence of photosynthesis which turns the light of a far star into green leaves, or the creation of the phenomenon of sex which causes the cards at the gaming table of life to be shuffled with increasing frequency and into ever more diverse combinations, it should be plain that nature contains the roiling unrest of a tornado. It is not the self-contained stately palace of the eighteenth-century philosophers, a palace whose doorstep was always in precisely the same position.

From the oscillating universe beating like a gigantic heart, to the puzzling existence of antimatter, order, in a human sense, is at least partially an illusion. Ours, in reality, is the order of a time, and of an insignificant fraction of the cosmos, seen by the limited senses of a finite creature. Behind the appearance, as even one group of primitive philosophers, the Hopi, have grasped, lurks being unmanifest, whose range and number exceeds the real; this is why the unexpected will always confront us; this is why the endless frontier is really endless. This is why the half-formed chaos of the marsh moved me as profoundly as though a new prophetic shape induced by us had risen monstrously from dangling wire and crumpled cardboard.

We are more dangerous than we seem and more potent in our ability to materialize an unexpected which is drawn from our own minds. "Force maketh Nature more violent in the Returne," Francis Bacon had once written. In the end this is her primary quality. Her creature man partakes of that essence, and it is well that he consider it in contemplation and not always in action. To the unexpected nature of the universe man owes his being. More than any other living creature he contains unknowingly the shapes and forms of an uncreated future to be drawn from his own substance. The history of this unhappy century should prove a drastic warning of his powers of dissolution even when directed upon himself. Waste, uncertain marshes lie close to reality in our heads. Shapes as yet unevoked had best be left lying amidst those spectral bog lights lest the drifting smoke of dreams, as once it did, merge imperceptibly with the choking real fumes from the ovens of Belsen and Buchenwald.

"It is very unhappy, but too late to be helped," Emerson had noted in his journal, "the discovery we have made that we exist. That discovery is called the Fall of Man. Ever afterwards we suspect our instruments. We have learned that we do not see directly." Wisdom interfused with compassion should be the consequence of that discovery, for at the same moment one aspect of the unexpected universe will have been genuinely revealed. It lies deep hidden in the human heart and not at the peripheries of space. Both the light we seek and the shadows that we fear are projected from within. It is through ourselves that the organic procession pauses, hesitates or renews its journey. "We have learned to ask terrible questions," exclaimed one thinker in the dawn of Victorian science. Perhaps it is just for this that the Unseen Player in the void has rolled his equally terrible dice. It is out of the self-knowledge gained by putting dreadful questions that man achieves his final dignity.

HARLEM IS NOWHERE

Ralph Ellison

One must descend to the basement and move along a confusing mazelike hall to reach it. Twice the passage seems to lead against a blank wall; then at last one enters the brightly lighted auditorium. And here, finally, are the social workers at the reception desks; and there, waiting upon the benches rowed beneath the pipes carrying warmth and water to the floors above, are the patients. One sees white-jacketed psychiatrists carrying charts appear and vanish behind screens that form the improvised interviewing cubicles. All is an atmosphere of hurried efficiency; and the concerned faces of the patients are brightened by the friendly smiles and low-pitched voices of the expert workers. One has entered the Lafargue Psychiatric Clinic.

HARLEM IS NOWHERE: © Copyright 1964 by Ralph Ellison. Reprinted from *Shadow and Act* by Ralph Ellison, by permission of Random House, Inc.

This clinic (whose staff receives no salary and whose fee is only twenty-five cents—to those who can afford it) is perhaps the most successful attempt in the nation to provide psychotherapy for the underprivileged. Certainly it has become in two years one of Harlem's most important institutions. Not only is it the sole mental clinic in the section, it is the only center in the city wherein both Negroes and whites may receive extended psychiatric care. Thus its importance transcends even its great value as a center for psychotherapy: it represents an underground extension of democracy.

As one of the few institutions dedicated to recognizing the total implication of Negro life in the United States, the Lafargue Clinic rejects all stereotypes, and may be said to concern itself with any possible variations between the three basic social factors shaping an American Negro's personality: he is viewed as a member of a racial and cultural minority; as an American citizen caught in certain political and economic relationships; and as a modern man living in a revolutionary world. Accordingly, each patient, whether white or black, is approached dynamically as a being possessing a cultural and biological past who seeks to make his way toward the future in a world wherein each discovery about himself must be made in the here and now at the expense of hope, pain and fear—a being who in responding to the complex forces of America has become confused.

Leaving the Lafargue Clinic for a while, what are some of the forces which generate this confusion? Who is this total Negro whom the clinic seeks to know; what is the psychological character of the scene in which he dwells; how describe the past which he drags into this scene, and what is the future toward which he stumbles and becomes confused? Let us begin with the scene: Harlem.

To live in Harlem is to dwell in the very bowels of the city; it is to pass a labyrinthine existence among streets that explode monotonously skyward with the spires and crosses of churches and clutter under foot with garbage and decay. Harlem is a ruin—many of its ordinary aspects (its crimes, its casual violence, its crumbling buildings with littered areaways, ill-smelling halls and vermin-invaded rooms) are indistinguishable from the distorted images that appear in dreams, and which, like muggers haunting a lonely hall, quiver in the waking mind with hidden and threatening significance. Yet this is no dream but the reality of well over four hundred thousand Americans; a reality which for many defines and colors the world. Overcrowded and exploited politically and economically, Harlem is the scene and symbol of the Negro's perpetual alienation in the land of his birth.

But much has been written about the social and economic aspects of Harlem; we are here interested in its psychological character—a character that arises from the impact between urban slum conditions and folk sensibilities. Historically, American Negroes are caught in a vast process of change that has swept them from slavery to the condition of industrial man in a space of time so telescoped (a bare eighty-five years) that is possible literally for them to step from feudalism into the vortex of industrialism simply by moving across the Mason-Dixon line.

This abruptness of change and the resulting clash of cultural factors within Negro personality account for some of the extreme contrasts found in Harlem, for both its negative and its positive characteristics. For if Harlem is the scene of the folk-Negro's death agony, it is also the setting of his transcendence. Here it is possible for talented youths to leap through the development of decades in a brief twenty years, while beside them white-haired adults crawl in the feudal darkness of their childhood. Here a former cotton picker develops the sensitive hands of a surgeon, and men whose grandparents still believe in magic prepare optimistically to become atomic scientists. Here the grandchildren of those who possessed no written literature examine their lives through the eyes of Freud and Marx, Kierkegaard and Kafka, Malraux and Sartre. It explains the nature of a world so fluid and shifting that often within the mind the real and the unreal merge, and the marvelous beckons from behind the same sordid reality that denies its existence.

Hence the most surreal fantasies are acted out upon the streets of Harlem; a man ducks in and out of traffic shouting and throwing imaginary grenades that actually exploded during World War I; a boy participates in the rape-robbery of his mother; a man beating his wife in a park uses boxing "science" and observes Marquess of Queensberry rules (no rabbit punching, no blows beneath the belt); two men hold a third while a lesbian slashes him to death with a razor blade; boy gangsters wielding homemade pistols (which in the South of their origin are but toy symbols of adolescent yearning for manhood) shoot down their young rivals. Life becomes a masquerade, exotic costumes are worn every day. Those who cannot afford to hire a horse wear riding habits; others who could not afford a hunting trip or who seldom attend sporting events carry shooting sticks.

For this is a world in which the major energy of the imagination goes not into creating works of art, but to overcome the frustrations of social discrimination. Not quite citizens and yet Americans, full of the tensions of modern man but regarded as primitives, Negro Americans are in desperate search for an identity. Rejecting the second-class status assigned them, they feel alienated and their whole lives have become a search for answers to the questions: Who am I, What am I, Why am I, and Where? Significantly, in Harlem the reply to the greeting, "How are you?" is very often, "Oh, man, I'm *nowhere*"—a phrase revealing an attitude so common that it has been reduced to a gesture, a seemingly trivial word. Indeed, Negroes are not unaware that the conditions of their lives demand new definitions of terms like *primitive* and *modern, ethical* and *unethical, moral* and *immoral, patriotism* and *treason, tragedy* and *comedy, sanity* and *insanity.*

But for a long time now—despite songs like the "Blow Top Blues" and the eruption of expressions like *frantic, buggy* and *mad* into Harlem's popular speech, doubtless a word-magic against the states they name—calm in face of the unreality of Negro life becomes increasingly difficult. And while some seek relief in strange hysterical forms of religion, in alcohol and drugs, and others learn to analyze the causes for their predicament and join with others to correct them, an increasing number have found their way to the Lafargue Psychiatric Clinic.

In relation to their Southern background, the cultural history of Negroes in the North reads like the legend of some tragic people out of mythology, a people which aspired to escape from its own unhappy homeland to the apparent peace of a distant mountain; but which, in migrating, made some fatal error of judgment and fell into a great chasm of mazelike passages that promise ever to lead to the mountain but end ever against a wall. Not that a Negro is worse off in the North than in the South, but that in the North he surrenders and does not replace certain important supports to his personality. He leaves a relatively static social order in which, having experienced its brutality for hundreds of years—indeed, having been formed within it and by it—he has developed those techniques of survival to which Faulkner refers as "endurance," and an ease of movement within explosive situations which makes Hemingway's definition of courage, "grace under pressure," appear mere swagger. He surrenders the protection of his peasant cynicism—his refusal to hope for the fulfillment of hopeless hopes—and his sense of being "at home in the world" gained from confronting and accepting (for day-to-day living, at least) the obscene absurdity of his predicament. Further, he leaves a still authoritative religion which gives his life a semblance of metaphysical wholeness; a family structure which is relatively stable; and a body of folklore—tested in life-and-death terms against his daily experience with nature and the Southern white man—that serves him as a guide to action.

These are the supports of Southern Negro rationality (and, to an extent, of the internal peace of the United States); humble, but of inestimable psychological value,[1] they allow Southern Negroes to maintain their almost mystical hope for a future of full democracy— a hope accompanied by an irrepressible belief in some Mecca of equality, located in the North and identified by the magic place names New York, Chicago, Detroit. A belief sustained (as all myth is sustained by ritual) by identifying themselves ritually with the successes of Negro celebrities, by reciting their exploits and enumerating their dollars, and by recounting the swiftness with which they spiral from humble birth to headline fame. And doubtless the blasting of this dream is as damaging to Negro personality as the slum scenes of filth, disorder and crumbling masonry in which it flies apart.

When Negroes are barred from participating in the main institutional life of society they lose far more than economic privileges or the satisfaction of saluting the flag with unmixed emotions. They lose one of the bulwarks which men place between themselves and the constant threat of chaos. For whatever the assigned function of social institutions, their psychological function is to protect the citizen against the irrational, incalculable forces that hover about the edges of human life like cosmic destruction lurking within an atomic stockpile.

And it is precisely the denial of this support through segregation and discrimination that leaves the most balanced Negro open to anxiety.

Though caught not only in the tensions arising from his own swift history, but in those conflicts created in modern man by a revolutionary world, he cannot participate fully in the therapy which the white American achieves through patriotic ceremonies and by identifying himself with American wealth and power. Instead, he is thrown back upon his own "slum-shocked" institutions.

But these, like his folk personality, are caught in a process of chaotic change. His family disintegrates, his church splinters; his folk wisdom is discarded in the mistaken notion that it in no way applies to urban living; and his formal education (never really his own) provides him with neither scientific description nor rounded philosophical interpretation of the profound forces that are transforming his total being. Yet even his art is transformed; the lyrical ritual elements of folk jazz—that artistic projection of the only real individuality possible for him in the South, that embodiment of a

[1] Its political and economic value is the measure of both the positive and negative characteristics of American Democracy.

superior democracy in which each individual cultivated his uniqueness and yet did not clash with his neighbors—have given way to the
near-themeless technical virtuosity of bebop, a further triumph of
technology over humanism. His speech hardens; his movements are
geared to the time clock; his diet changes; his sensibilities quicken
and his intelligence expands. But without institutions to give him
direction, and lacking a clear explanation of his predicament—the
religious ones being inadequate, and those offered by political and
labor leaders obviously incomplete and opportunistic—the individual feels that his world and his personality are out of key. The
phrase "I'm nowhere" expresses the feeling borne in upon many
Negroes that they have no stable, recognized place in society. One's
identity drifts in a capricious reality in which even the most commonly held assumptions are questionable. One "is" literally, but one
is nowhere; one wanders dazed in a ghetto maze, a "displaced person" of American democracy.

And as though all this were not enough of a strain on a people's
sense of the rational, the conditions under which it lives are seized
upon as proof of its inferiority. Thus the frustrations of Negro life
(many of them the frustrations of *all* life during this historical
moment) permeate the atmosphere of Harlem with what Dr. Frederick Wertham, Director of the Lafargue Clinic, terms "free-floating
hostility," a hostility that bombards the individual from so many
directions that he is often unable to identify it with any specific
object. Some feel it the punishment of some racial or personal guilt
and pray to God; others (called "evil Negroes" in Harlem) become
enraged with the world. Sometimes it provokes dramatic mass responses, and the results are the spontaneous outbreaks called the
"Harlem riots" of 1935 and 1943.

And why have these explosive matters—which are now a problem
of our foreign policy—been ignored? Because there is an argument
in progress between black men and white men as to the true nature
of American reality. Following their own interests, whites impose
interpretations upon Negro experience that are not only false but, in
effect, a denial of Negro humanity (witness the shock when A.
Philip Randolph questions, on the basis of Negro experience, the
meaning of *treason*). Too weak to shout down these interpretations,
Negroes live nevertheless as they have to live, and the concrete conditions of their lives are more real than white men's arguments.

And it is here exactly that lies the importance of the Lafargue
Psychiatric Clinic—both as a scientific laboratory and as an expression of forthright democratic action in its scientific willingness to
dispense with preconceived notions and accept the realities of Negro,

i.e., *American* life. It recognizes that the personality damage that brought it into being represents not the disintegration of a people's fiber, but the failure of a way of life. For not only is it an antidote to this failure, it represents a victory over another of its aspects.

For ten years, while heading various psychiatric institutions, Dr. Wertham had fought for a psychiatric center in which Negroes could receive treatment. But whether he approached politicians, city agencies or philanthropists, all gave excuses for not acting. The agencies were complacent, the politicians accused him of harboring political rather than humanitarian motives; certain liberal middlemen, who stand between Negroes and philanthropic dollars, accused him of trying to establish a segregated institution. Finally it was decided to establish the clinic without money or official recognition. The results were electric. When his fellow psychiatrists were asked to contribute their services, Dr. Wertham was overwhelmed with offers. These physicians, all of whom hold jobs in institutions which discriminate against Negroes, were eager to overcome this frustration to their science; and like some Southern Negroes who consider that part of themselves best which they hide beneath their servility, they consider their most important work that which is carried out in a Harlem basement.

Here, in the basement, a frustrated science goes to find its true object: the confused of mind who seek reality. Both find the source of their frustrations in the sickness of the social order. As such, and in spite of the very fine work it is doing, a thousand Lafargue clinics could not dispel the sense of unreality that haunts Harlem. Knowing this, Dr. Wertham and his interracial staff seek a modest achievement: to give each bewildered patient an insight into the relation between his problems and his environment, and out of this understanding to reforge the will to endure in a hostile world.

WHAT I BELIEVE

E. M. Forster

I do not believe in Belief. But this is an age of faith, and there are so many militant creeds that, in self-defence, one has to formulate a

WHAT I BELIEVE: Copyright, 1939 by E. M. Forster. Reprinted from his volume, *Two Cheers for Democracy*, by permission of Harcourt, Brace & World, Inc. and Edward Arnold Ltd.

creed of one's own. Tolerance, good temper and sympathy are no longer enough in a world which is rent by religious and racial persecution, in a world where ignorance rules, and science, who ought to have ruled, plays the subservient pimp. Tolerance, good temper and sympathy—they are what matter really, and if the human race is not to collapse they must come to the front before long. But for the moment they are not enough, their action is no stronger than a flower, battered beneath a military jack-boot. They want stiffening, even if the process coarsens them. Faith, to my mind, is a stiffening process, a sort of mental starch, which ought to be applied as sparingly as possible. I dislike the stuff. I do not believe in it, for its own sake, at all. Herein I probably differ from most people, who believe in Belief, and are only sorry they cannot swallow even more than they do. My law-givers are Erasmus and Montaigne, not Moses and St. Paul. My temple stands not upon Mount Moriah but in that Elysian Field where even the immoral are admitted. My motto is: "Lord, I disbelieve—help thou my unbelief."

I have, however, to live in an Age of Faith—the sort of epoch I used to hear praised when I was a boy. It is extremely unpleasant really. It is bloody in every sense of the word. And I have to keep my end up in it. Where do I start?

With personal relationships. Here is something comparatively solid in a world full of violence and cruelty. Not absolutely solid, for Psychology has split and shattered the idea of a "Person," and has shown that there is something incalculable in each of us, which may at any moment rise to the surface and destroy our normal balance. We don't know what we are like. We can't know what other people are like. How, then, can we put any trust in personal relationships, or cling to them in the gathering political storm? In theory we cannot. But in practice we can and do. Though A is not unchangeably A or B unchangeably B, there can still be love and loyalty between the two. For the purpose of living one has to assume that the personality is solid, and the "self" is an entity, and to ignore all contrary evidence. And since to ignore evidence is one of the characteristics of faith, I certainly can proclaim that I believe in personal relationships.

Starting from them, I get a little order into the contemporary chaos. One must be fond of people and trust them if one is not to make a mess of life, and it is therefore essential that they should not let one down. They often do. The moral of which is that I must, myself, be as reliable as possible, and this I try to be. But reliability is not a matter of contract—that is the main difference between the world of personal relationships and the world of business relationships. It is a matter for the heart, which signs no documents. In other words, reliability is impossible unless there is a natural warmth. Most men possess this warmth, though they often have bad luck and get chilled. Most of them, even when they are politicians, *want* to keep faith. And one can, at all events, show one's own little light here, one's own poor little trembling flame, with the knowledge that it is not the only light that is shining in the darkness, and not the only one which the darkness does not comprehend. Personal relations are despised today. They are regarded as bourgeois luxuries, as products of a time of fair weather which is now past, and we are urged to get rid of them, and to dedicate ourselves to some movement or cause instead. I hate the idea of causes, and if I had to choose between betraying my country and betraying my friend, I hope I should have the guts to betray my country. Such a choice may scandalise the modern reader, and he may stretch out his patriotic hand to the telephone at once and ring up the police. It would not have shocked Dante, though. Dante places Brutus and Cassius in the lowest circle of Hell because they had chosen to betray their friend Julius Caesar rather than their country Rome. Probably one will not be asked to make such an agonising choice. Still, there lies at the back of every creed something terrible and hard for which the worshipper may one day be required to suffer, and there is even a terror and a hardness in this creed of personal relationships, urbane and mild though it sounds. Love and loyalty to an individual can run counter to the claims of the State. When they do—down with the State, say I, which means that the State would down me.

This brings me along to Democracy, "even Love, the Beloved Republic, which feeds upon Freedom and lives." Democracy is not a Beloved Republic really, and never will be. But it is less hateful than other contemporary forms of government, and to that extent it deserves our support. It does start from the assumption that the individual is important, and that all types are needed to make a civilisation. It does not divide its citizens into the bossers and the bossed—as an efficiency-regime tends to do. The people I admire most are those who are sensitive and want to create something or discover something, and do not see life in terms of power, and such people get more of a chance under a democracy than elsewhere. They found religions, great or small, or they produce literature and art, or they do disinterested scientific research, or they may be what is called "ordinary people," who are creative in their private lives, bring up their children decently, for instance, or help their neighbours. All these people need to express themselves; they cannot do so unless society allows them liberty to do so, and the society which allows them most liberty is a democracy.

Democracy has another merit. It allows criticism, and if there is not public criticism there are bound to be hushed-up scandals. That is why I believe in the Press, despite all its lies and vulgarity, and why I believe in Parliament. Parliament is often sneered at because it is a Talking Shop. I believe in it *because* it is a talking shop. I believe in the Private Member who makes himself a nuisance. He gets snubbed and is told that he is cranky or ill-informed, but he does expose abuses which would otherwise never have been mentioned, and very often an abuse gets put right just by being mentioned. Occasionally, too, a well-meaning public official starts losing his head in the cause of efficiency, and thinks himself God Almighty. Such officials are particularly frequent in the Home Office. Well, there will be questions about them in Parliament sooner or later, and then they will have to mind their steps. Whether Parliament is either a representative body or an efficient one is questionable, but I value it because it criticises and talks, and because its chatter gets widely reported.

So Two Cheers for Democracy: one because it admits variety and two because it permits criticism. Two cheers are quite enough: there is no occasion to give three. Only Love the Beloved Republic deserves that.

What about Force, though? While we are trying to be sensitive and advanced and affectionate and tolerant, an unpleasant question pops up: does not all society rest upon force? If a government cannot count upon the police and the army, how can it hope to rule? And if an individual gets knocked on the head or sent to a labour camp, of what significance are his opinions?

This dilemma does not worry me as much as it does some. I realise that all society rests upon force. But all the great creative actions, all the decent human relations, occur during the intervals when force has not managed to come to the front. These intervals are what matter. I want them to be as frequent and as lengthy as possible, and I call them "civilisation." Some people idealise force and pull it into the foreground and worship it, instead of keeping it in the background as long as possible. I think they make a mistake, and I think that their opposites, the mystics, err even more when they declare that force does not exist. I believe that it exists, and that one of our jobs is to prevent it from getting out of its box. It gets out sooner or later, and then it destroys us and all the lovely things which we have made. But it is not out all the time, for the fortunate reason that the strong are so stupid. Consider their conduct for a moment in the Niebelugn's Ring. The giants there have the guns, or in other words the gold; but they do nothing with it, they do not realise that they are all-powerful, with the result that the catastrophe is delayed and the castle of Walhalla, insecure but glorious, fronts the storms. Fafnir, coiled round his hoard, grumbles and grunts; we can hear him under Europe today; the leaves of the wood already tremble, and the Bird calls its warnings uselessly. Fafnir will destroy us, but by a blessed dispensation he is stupid and slow, and creation goes on just outside the poisonous blast of his breath. The Nietzchean would hurry the monster up, the mystic would say he did not exist, but Wotan, wiser than either, hastens to create warriors before doom declares itself. The Valkyries are symbols not only of courage but of intelligence; they represent the human spirit snatching its opportunity while the going is good, and one of them even finds time to love. Brünnhilde's last song hymns the recurrence of love, and since it is the privilege of art to exaggerate, she goes even further, and proclaims the love which is eternally triumphant and feeds upon freedom, and lives.

So that is what I feel about force and violence. It is, alas! the ultimate reality on this earth, but it does not always get to the front. Some people call its absences "decadence"; I call them "civilisation" and find in such interludes the chief justification for the human experiment. I look the other way until fate strikes me. Whether this is due to courage or to cowardice in my own case I cannot be sure. But I know that if men had not looked the other way in the past, nothing of any value would survive. The people I respect most behave as if they were immortal and as if society was eternal. Both assumptions are false: both of them must be accepted as true if we are to go on eating and working and loving, and are to keep open a few breathing holes for the human spirit. No millennium seems likely to descend upon humanity; no better and stronger League of Nations will be instituted; no form of Christianity and no alternative to Christianity will bring peace to the world or integrity to the individual; no "change of heart" will occur. And yet we need not despair, indeed, we cannot despair; the evidence of history shows us that men have always insisted on behaving creatively under the shadow of the sword; that they have done their artistic and scientific and domestic stuff for the sake of doing it, and that we had better follow their example under the shadow of the aeroplanes. Others, with more vision or courage than myself, see the salvation of humanity ahead, and will dismiss my conception of civilisation as paltry, a sort of tip-and-run game. Certainly it is presumptuous to say that we *cannot* improve, and that Man, who has only been in power for a few thousand years, will never learn to make use of his power. All I mean is that, if people continue to kill one another as they do, the world cannot get better than it is, and that since there are more people than formerly, and their means for destroying one another superior, the world may well get worse. What is good in people— and consequently in the world—is their insistence on creation, their belief in friendship and loyalty for their own sakes; and though Violence remains and is, indeed, the major partner in this muddled establishment, I believe that creativeness remains too, and will always assume direction when violence sleeps. So, though I am not an optimist, I cannot agree with Sophocles that it were better never to have been born. And although, like Horace, I see no evidence that each batch of births is superior to the last, I leave the field open for the more complacent view. This is such a difficult moment to live in, one cannot help getting gloomy and also a bit rattled, and perhaps short-sighted.

In search of a refuge, we may perhaps turn to hero-worship. But here we shall get no help, in my opinion. Hero-worship is a dangerous vice, and one of the minor merits of a democracy is that it does not encourage it, or produce that unmanageable type of citizen known as the Great Man. It produces instead different kinds of small men—a much finer achievement. But people who cannot get interested in the variety of life, and cannot make up their own minds, get discontented over this, and they long for a hero to bow down before and to follow blindly. It is significant that a hero is an integral part of the authoritarian stock-in-trade today. An efficiency-regime cannot be run without a few heroes stuck about it to carry off the dullness—much as plums have to be put into a bad pudding to make it palatable. One hero at the top and a smaller one each side of him is a favourite arrangement, and the timid and the bored are comforted by the trinity, and, bowing down, feel exalted and strengthened.

No, I distrust Great Men. They produce a desert of uniformity around them and often a pool of blood too, and I always feel a little man's pleasure when they come a cropper. Every now and then one reads in the newspapers some such statement as: "The coup d'état appears to have failed, and Admiral Toma's whereabouts is at present unknown." Admiral Toma had probably every qualification for being a Great Man—an iron will, personal magnetism, dash, flair, sexlessness—but fate was against him, so he retires to unknown whereabouts instead of parading history with his peers. He fails with a completeness which no artist and no lover can experience, because with them the process of creation is itself an achievement, whereas with him the only possible achievement is success.

I believe in aristocracy, though—if that is the right word, and if a democrat may use it. Not an aristocracy of power, based upon rank and influence, but an aristocracy of the sensitive, the considerate and the plucky. Its members are to be found in all nations and classes, and all through the ages, and there is a secret understanding between them when they meet. They represent the true human tradition, the one permanent victory of our queer race over cruelty and chaos. Thousands of them perish in obscurity, a few are great names. They are sensitive for others as well as for themselves, they are considerate without being fussy, their pluck is not swankiness but the power to endure, and they can take a joke. I give no examples— it is risky to do that—but the reader may as well consider whether this is the type of person he would like to meet and to be, and whether (going farther with me) he would prefer that this type should *not* be an ascetic one. I am against asceticism myself. I am with the old Scotsman who wanted less chastity and more delicacy. I do not feel that my aristocrats are a real aristocracy if they thwart their bodies, since bodies are the instruments through which we register and enjoy the world. Still, I do not insist. This is not a major point. It is clearly possible to be sensitive, considerate and plucky and yet be an ascetic too; if anyone possesses the first three qualities, I will let him in! On they go—an invincible army, yet not a victorious one. The aristocrats, the elect, the chosen, the Best People— all the words that describe them are false, and all attempts to organise them fail. Again and again Authority, seeing their value, has tried to net them and to utilise them as the Egyptian Priesthood or the Christian Church or the Chinese Civil Service or the Group Movement, or some other worthy stunt. But they slip through the net and are gone; when the door is shut, they are no longer in the room: their temple, as one of them remarked, is the Holiness of the Heart's Affection, and their kingdom, though they never possess it, is the wide-open world.

With this type of person knocking about, and constantly crossing one's path if one has eyes to see or hands to feel, the experiment of earthly life cannot be dismissed as a failure. But it may well be hailed as a tragedy, the tragedy being that no device has been found by which these private decencies can be transmitted to public affairs. As soon as people have power they go crooked and sometimes dotty as well, because the possession of power lifts them into a region where normal honesty never pays. For instance, the man who is selling newspapers outside the Houses of Parliament can safely leave his papers to go for a drink and his cap beside them: anyone who takes a paper is sure to drop a copper into the cap. But the men who are inside the Houses of Parliament—they cannot trust one another like that, still less can the Government they compose trust other governments. No caps upon the pavement here, but suspicion, treachery and armaments. The more highly public life is organised the lower does its morality sink; the nations of today behave to each other worse than they ever did in the past, they cheat, rob, bully and bluff, make war without notice, and kill as many women and children as possible; whereas primitive tribes were at all events restrained by taboos. It is a humiliating outlook—though the greater the darkness, the brighter shine the little lights, reassuring one another, signalling: "Well, at all events, I'm still here. I don't like it very much, but how are you?" Unquenchable lights of my aristocracy! Signals of the invincible army! "Come along—anyway, let's have a good time while we can." I think they signal that too.

The Saviour of the future—if ever he comes—will not preach a new Gospel. He will merely utilise my aristocracy, he will make effective the good will and the good temper which are already existing. In other words, he will introduce a new technique. In economics, we are told that if there was a new technique of distribution, there need be no poverty, and people would not starve in one place while crops were being ploughed under in another. A similar change is needed in the sphere of morals and politics. The desire for it is by no means new; it was expressed, for example, in theological terms by Jacopone da Todi over six hundred years ago. "Ordina questo amore, O tu che m'ami," he said; "O thou who lovest me— set this love in order." His prayer was not granted, and I do not myself believe that it ever will be, but here, and not through a change of heart, is our probable route. Not by becoming better, but by ordering and distributing his native goodness, will Man shut up Force into its box, and so gain time to explore the universe and to set his mark upon it worthily. At present he only explores it at odd moments, when Force is looking the other way, and his divine creativeness appears as a trivial by-product, to be scrapped as soon as the drums beat and the bombers hum.

Such a change, claim the orthodox, can only be made by Christianity, and will be made by it in God's good time: man always has failed and always will fail to organise his own goodness, and it is presumptuous of him to try. This claim—solemn as it is—leaves me cold. I cannot believe that Christianity will ever cope with the present world-wide mess, and I think that such influence as it retains in modern society is due to the money behind it, rather than to its spiritual appeal. It was a spiritual force once, but the indwelling spirit will have to be restated if it is to calm the waters again, and probably restated in a non-Christian form. Naturally a lot of people, and people who are not only good but able and intelligent, will disagree here; they will vehemently deny that Christianity has failed, or they will argue that its failure proceeds from the wickedness of men, and really proves its ultimate success. They have Faith, with a large F. My faith has a very small one, and I only intrude it because these are strenuous and serious days, and one likes to say what one thinks while speech is comparatively free: it may not be free much longer.

The above are the reflections of an individualist and a liberal who has found liberalism crumbling beneath him and at first felt ashamed. Then, looking around, he decided there was no special reason for shame, since other people, whatever they felt, were equally insecure. And as for individualism—there seems no way of getting off this, even if one wanted to. The dictator-hero can grind down his citizens till they are all alike, but he cannot melt them into a single man. That is beyond his power. He can order them to merge, he can incite them to mass-antics, but they are obliged to be born separately, and to die separately, and, owing to these unavoidable termini, will always be running off the totalitarian rails. The memory of birth and the expectation of death always lurk within the human being, making him separate from his fellows and consequently capable of intercourse with them. Naked I came into the world, naked I shall go out of it! And a very good thing too, for it reminds me that I am naked under my shirt, whatever its colour.

ON THE PAST AND FUTURE

William Hazlitt

I have naturally but little imagination, and am not of a very sanguine turn of mind. I have some desire to enjoy the present good, and some fondness for the past; but I am not at all given to building castles in the air, nor to look forward with much confidence or hope to the brilliant illusions held out by the future. Hence I have perhaps been led to form a theory, which is very contrary to the common notions and feelings on the subject, and which I will here try to explain as well as I can.—When Sterne in the Sentimental Journey told the French Minister that if the French people had a fault, it was that they were too serious, the latter replied that if that was his opinion, he must defend it with all his might, for he would have all the world against him; so I shall have enough to do to get well through the present argument.

I cannot see, then, any rational or logical ground for that mighty difference in the value which mankind generally set upon the past and future, as if the one was every thing, and the other nothing, of no consequence whatever. On the other hand, I conceive that the past is as real and substantial a part of our being, that it is as much a *bona fide*, undeniable consideration in the estimate of human life, as the future can possibly be. To say that the past is of no importance, unworthy of a moment's regard, because it has gone by, and is no longer any thing, is an argument that cannot be held to any purpose: for if the past has ceased to be, and is therefore to be accounted nothing in the scale of good or evil, the future is yet to come, and has never been any thing. Should any one choose to assert that the present only is of any value in a strict and positive sense, because that alone has a real existence, that we should seize the instant good, and give all else to the winds, I can understand what he means (though perhaps he does not himself [1]): but I cannot comprehend how this distinction between that which has a downright and sensible, and that which has only a remote and airy existence, can be applied to establish the preference of the future over the past; for both are in this point of view equally ideal, absolutely nothing, except as they are conceived of by the mind's eye, and are thus rendered present to the thoughts and feelings. Nay, the one is even more imaginary, a more fantastic creature of the brain than the other, and the interest we take in it more shadowy and gratuitous; for the future, on which we lay so much stress, may never come to pass at all, that is, may never be embodied into actual existence in the whole course of events, whereas the past has certainly existed once, has received the stamp of truth, and left an image of itself behind. It is so far then placed beyond the possibility of doubt, or as the poet has it,

> Those joys are lodg'd beyond the reach of fate.

It is not, however, attempted to be denied that though the future is nothing at present, and has no immediate interest while we are speaking, yet it is of the utmost consequence in itself, and of the utmost interest to the individual, because it *will have* a real existence, and we have an idea of it as existing in time to come. Well, then, the past also has no real existence; the actual sensation and the interest

[1] If we take away from *the present* the moment that is just gone by and the moment that is next to come, how much of it will be left for this plain, practical theory to rest upon? Their solid basis of sense and reality will reduce itself to a pin's point, a hair-line, on which our moral balance-masters will have some difficulty to maintain their footing without falling over on either side.

belonging to it are both fled; but it *has had* a real existence, and we
can still call up a vivid recollection of it as having once been; and
therefore, by parity of reasoning, it is not a thing perfectly insignificant in itself, nor wholly indifferent to the mind, whether it
ever was or not. Oh no! Far from it! Let us not rashly quit our hold
upon the past, when perhaps there may be little else left to bind us
to existence. It is nothing to have been, and to have been happy or
miserable? Or is it a matter of no moment to think whether I have
been one or the other? Do I delude myself, do I build upon a shadow
or a dream, do I dress up in the gaudy garb of idleness and folly a
pure fiction, with nothing answering to it in the universe of things
and the records of truth, when I look back with fond delight or
with tender regret to that which was at one time to me *my all*,
when I revive the glowing image of some bright reality,

> The thoughts of which can never from my heart?

Do I then muse on nothing, do I bend my eyes on nothing, when I
turn back in fancy to "those suns and skies so pure" that lighted
up my early path? Is it to think of nothing, to set an idle value
upon nothing, to think of all that has happened to me, and of all
that can ever interest me? Or, to use the language of a fine poet (who
is himself among my earliest and not least painful recollections)—

> What though the radiance which was once so bright
> Be now for ever vanish'd from my sight.
> Though nothing can bring back the hour
> Of glory in the grass, of splendour in the flower—

yet am I mocked with a lie, when I venture to think of it? Or do
I not drink in and breathe again the air of heavenly truth, when I
but "retrace its footsteps, and its skirts far off adore?" I cannot say
with the same poet—

> And see how dark the backward stream,
> A little moment past so smiling—

for it is the past that gives me most delight and most assurance of
reality. What to me constitutes the great charm of the Confessions
of Rousseau is their turning so much upon this feeling. He seems to
gather up the past moments of his being like drops of honey-dew
to distil a precious liquor from them; his alternate pleasures and
pains are the bead-roll that he tells over, and piously worships; he
makes a rosary of the flowers of hope and fancy that strewed his
earliest years. When he begins the last of the Reveries of a Solitary

Walker, "*Il y a aujourd'hui, jour des Pâques Fleures, cinquante ans depuis que j'ai premier vu Madame Warens*," what a yearning of the soul is implied in that short sentence! Was all that had happened to him, all that he had thought and felt in that sad interval of time, to be accounted nothing? Was that long, dim, faded retrospect of years happy or miserable, a blank that was not to make his eyes fail and his heart faint within him in trying to grasp all that had once vanished, because it was not a prospect into futurity? Was he wrong in finding more to interest him in it than in the next fifty years— which he did not live to see; or if he had, what then? Would they have been worth thinking of, compared with the times of his youth, of his first meeting with Madame Warens, with those times which he has traced with such truth and pure delight "in our heart's tables?" When "all the life of life was flown," was he not to live the first and best part of it over again, and once more be all that he then was?— Ye woods that crown the clear lone brow of Norman-Court, why do I revisit ye so oft, and feel a soothing consciousness of your presence, but that your high tops waving in the wind recall to me the hours and years that are forever-fled, that ye renew in ceaseless murmurs the story of long-cherished hopes and bitter disappointment, that in your solitudes and tangled wilds I can wander and lose myself, as I wander on and am lost in the solitude of my own heart; and that as your rustling branches give the loud blast to the waste below— borne on the thoughts of other years, I can look down with patient anguish at the cheerless desolation which I feel within! Without that face pale as the primrose with hyacinthine locks, forever shunning and forever haunting me, mocking my waking thoughts as in a dream, without that smile which my heart could never turn to scorn, without those eyes dark with their own lustre, still bent on mine, and drawing the soul into their liquid mazes like a sea of love, without that name trembling in fancy's ear, without that form gliding before me like Oread or Dryad in fabled groves, what should I do, how pass the listless, leaden-footed hours? Then wave, wave on, ye woods of Tuderley, and lift your high tops in the air; my sighs and vows uttered by your mystic voice breathe into me my former being, and enable me to bear the thing I am!—The objects that we have known in better days are the main props that sustain the weight of our affections, and give us strength to await our future lot. The future is like a dead wall or a thick mist hiding all objects from our view: the past is alive and stirring with objects, bright or solemn, and of unfading interest. What is it in fact that we recur to oftenest? What subjects do we think or talk of? Not the ignorant future, but the well-stored past. Othello, the Moor of Venice, amused himself and his hearers at the house of Signor Brabantio by "running through the story of his life even from his boyish days;" and oft "beguiled them of their tears, when he did speak of some disastrous stroke which his youth suffered." This plan of ingratiating himself would not have answered, if the past had been, like the contents of an old almanac, of no use but to be thrown aside and forgotten. What a blank, for instance, does the history of the world for the next six thousand years present to the mind, compared with that of the last! All that strikes the imagination or excites any interest in the mighty scene is *what has been!* [2]

Neither in itself then, nor as a subject of general contemplation, has the future any advantage over the past. But with respect to our grosser passions and pursuits it has. As far as regards the appeal to the understanding or the imagination, the past is just as good, as real, of as much intrinsic and ostensible value as the future: but there is another principle in the human mind, the principle of action or will; and of this the past has no hold, the future engrosses it entirely to itself. It is this strong lever of the affections that gives so powerful a bias to our sentiments on this subject, and violently transposes the natural order of our associations. We regret the pleasures we have lost, and eagerly anticipate those which are to come: we dwell with satisfaction on the evils from which we have escaped (*Posthæc meminisse juvabit*)—and dread future pain. The good that is past is in this sense like money that is spent, which is of no further use, and about which we give ourselves little concern. The good we expect is like a store yet untouched, and in the enjoyment of which we promise ourselves infinite gratification. What has happened to us we think of no consequence: what is to happen to us, of the greatest. Why so? Simply because the one is still in our power, and the other not—because the efforts of the will to bring any object to pass or to prevent it strengthen our attachment or aversion to that object—because the pains and attention bestowed upon any thing add to our interest in it, and because the habitual and earnest pursuit of any end redoubles the ardour of our expectations, and converts the speculative and indolent satisfaction we might otherwise feel in it into real passion. Our regrets, anxiety, and wishes are thrown

[2] A treatise on the Millennium is dull; but who was ever weary of reading the fables of the Golden Age? On my once observing I should like to have been Claude, a person said, "he should not, for that then it would by this time have been all over with him." As if it could possibly signify when we live (saving and excepting the present minute), or as if the value of human life decreased or increased with successive centuries. At that rate, we had better have our life still to come at some future period, and so postpone our existence century after century *ad infinitum.*

away upon the past; but the insisting on the importance of the future is of the utmost use in aiding our resolutions, and stimulating our exertions. If the future were no more amenable to our wills than the past; if our precautions, our sanguine schemes, our hopes and fears, were of as little avail in the one case as in the other; if we could neither soften our minds to pleasure, nor steel our fortitude to the resistance of pain beforehand; if all objects drifted along by us like straws or pieces of wood in a river, the will being purely passive, and as little able to obviate the future as to arrest the past, we should in that case be equally indifferent to both; that is, we should consider each as it affected the thoughts and imagination with certain sentiments of approbation or regret, but without the importunity of desire, the irritation of the will, throwing the whole weight of passion and prejudice into one scale, and leaving the other quite empty. While the blow is coming, we prepare to meet it, we think to ward off or break its force, we arm ourselves with patience to endure what cannot be avoided, we agitate ourselves with fifty needless alarms about it; but when the blow is once struck, the pang is over, the struggle is no longer necessary, and we cease to harass or torment ourselves about it more than we can help. It is not that the one belongs to the future, and the other to time past; but that the one is a subject of action, of uneasy apprehension, of strong passion, and that the other has passed wholly out of the sphere of action into the region of reflection—

Calm pleasures there abide, majestic pains.[3]

It would not give a man more concern to know that he should be put to the rack a year hence, than to recollect that he had been put to it a year ago, but that he hopes to avoid the one, whereas he must sit down patiently under the consciousness of the other. In this hope he wears himself out in vain struggles with fate, and puts himself to the rack of his imagination every day he has to live in the mean while. When the event is so remote or so independent of the will as to set aside the necessity of immediate action, or to baffle all attempts to defeat it, it gives us little more disturbance or emotion than if it had already taken place, or were something to happen in another state of being, or to an indifferent person. Criminals are observed to

[3] In like manner, though we know that an event must have taken place at a distance, long before we can hear the result, yet as long as we remain in ignorance of it, we irritate ourselves about it, and suffer all the agonies of suspense, as if it were still to come; but as soon as our uncertainty is removed, our fretful impatience vanishes, we resign ourselves to fate, and make up our minds to what has happened as well as we can.

grow more anxious as their trial approaches; but after the sentence is passed, they become tolerably resigned, and generally sleep sound the night before its execution.

It in some measure confirms this theory, that men attach more or less importance to past and future events, according as they are more or less engaged in action and the busy scenes of life. Those who have a fortune to make or are in pursuit of rank and power think little of the past, for it does not contribute greatly to their views: those who have nothing to do but to think, take nearly the same interest in the past as in the future. The contemplation of the one is as delightful and real as that of the other. The season of hope has an end; but the remembrance of it is left. The past still lives in the memory of those who have leisure to look back upon the way that they have trod, and can from it "catch glimpses that may make them less forlorn." The turbulence of action, and uneasiness of desire, must point to the future: it is only in the quiet innocence of shepherds, in the simplicity of pastoral ages, that a tomb was found with this inscription—"I ALSO WAS AN ARCADIAN!"

Though I by no means think that our habitual attachment to life is in exact proportion to the value of the gift, yet I am not one of those splenetic persons who affect to think it of no value at all. *Que peu de chose est la vie humaine*—is an exclamation in the mouths of satirists and philosophers, to which I cannot agree. It is little, it is short, it is not worth having, if we take the last hour, and leave out all that has gone before, which has been one way of looking at the subject. Such calculators seem to say that life is nothing when it is over, and that may in their sense be true. If the old rule—*Respice finem*—were to be made absolute, and no one could be pronounced fortunate till the day of his death, there are few among us whose existence would, upon these conditions, be much to be envied. But this is not a fair view of the case. A man's life is his whole life, not the last glimmering snuff of the candle; and this, I say, is considerable, and not *a little matter*, whether we regard its pleasures or its pains. To draw a peevish conclusion to the contrary from our own superannuated desires or forgetful indifference is about as reasonable as to say, a man never was young because he is grown old, or never lived because he is now dead. The length or agreeableness of a journey does not depend on the few last steps of it; nor is the size of a building to be judged of from the last stone that is added to it. It is neither the first nor last hour of our existence, but the space that parts these two—not our exit nor our entrance upon the stage, but what we do, feel, and think while there,—that we are to attend to in pronouncing sentence upon it. Indeed, it would be easy to show that it is the very extent of human life, the infinite number of things contained in it, its contradictory and fluctuating interests, the transition from one situation to another, the hours, months, years, spent in one fond pursuit after another; that it is, in a word, the length of our common journey with the quantity of events crowded into it, that, baffling the grasp of our actual perception, makes it slide from our memory, and dwindle into nothing in its own perspective. It is too mighty for us, and we say it is nothing! It is a speck in our fancy, and yet what canvas would be big enough to hold its striking groups, its endless subjects! It is light as vanity, and yet if all its weary moments, if all its head and heart aches were compressed into one, what fortitude would not be overwhelmed with the blow! What a huge heap, a "huge, dumb heap," of wishes, thoughts, feelings, anxious cares, soothing hopes, loves, joys, friendships, is it composed of! How many ideas and trains of sentiment, long and deep and intense, often pass through the mind in only one day's thinking or reading, for instance! How many such days are there in a year, how many years in a long life, still occupied with something interesting, still recalling some old impression, still recurring to some difficult question and making progress in it, every step accompanied with a sense of power, and every moment conscious of "the high endeavour or the glad success;" for the mind fixes chiefly on that which keeps it employed, and is wound up to a certain pitch of pleasurable excitement or lively solicitude, by the necessity of its own nature. The division of the map of life into its component parts is beautifully made by King Henry VI.

> O God! methinks it were a happy life
> To be no better than a homely swain,
> To sit upon a hill as I do now,
> To carve out dials quaintly, point by point,
> Thereby to see the minutes how they run;
> How many make the hour full complete,
> How many hours bring about the day,
> How many days will finish up the year,
> How many years a mortal man may live:
> When this is known, then to divide the time;
> So many hours must I tend my flock,
> So many hours must I take to rest,
> So many hours must I contemplate,
> So many hours must I sport myself;
> So many days my ewes have been with young,
> So many weeks ere the poor fools will yean,

So many months ere I shall shear the fleece:
So many minutes, hours, weeks, months, and years
Past over to the end they were created,
Would bring grey hairs unto a quiet grave.

I myself am neither a king nor a shepherd: books have been my fleecy charge, and my thoughts have been my subjects. But these have found me sufficient employment at the time, and enough to muse on for the time to come.—

The passions intercept and warp the natural progress of life. They paralyse all of it that is not devoted to their tyranny and caprice. This makes the difference between the laughing innocence of childhood, the pleasantness of youth, and the crabbedness of age. A load of cares lies like a weight of guilt upon the mind: so that a man of business often has all the air, the distraction and restlessness and hurry of feeling of a criminal. A knowledge of the world takes away the freedom and simplicity of thought as effectually as the contagion of its example. The artlessness and candour of our early years are open to all impressions alike, because the mind is not clogged and pre-occupied with other objects. Our pleasures and our pains come single, make room for one another, and the spring of the mind is fresh and unbroken, its aspect clear and unsullied. Hence "the tear forgot as soon as shed, the sunshine of the breast." But as we advance farther, the will gets greater head. We form violent antipathies and indulge exclusive preferences. We make up our minds to some one thing, and if we cannot have that, will have nothing. We are wedded to opinion, to fancy, to prejudice; which destroys the soundness of our judgments, and the serenity and buoyancy of our feelings. The chain of habit coils itself round the heart, like a serpent, to gnaw and stifle it. It grows rigid and callous; and for the softness and elasticity of childhood, full of proud flesh and obstinate tumours. The violence and perversity of our passions comes in more and more to overlay our natural sensibility and well-grounded affections; and we screw ourselves up to aim only at those things which are neither desirable nor practicable. Thus life passes away in the feverish irritation of pursuit and the certainty of disappointment. By degrees, nothing but this morbid state of feeling satisfies us; and all common pleasures and cheap amusements are sacrificed to the demon of ambition, avarice, or dissipation. The machine is overwrought: the parching heat of the veins dries up and withers the flowers of Love, Hope, and Joy; and any pause, any release from the rack of ecstasy on which we are stretched, seems more insupportable than the pangs which we endure. We are suspended between tormenting desires and the horrors of *ennui*. The impulse of the will, like the wheels of a carriage going down hill, becomes too strong for the driver, Reason, and cannot be stopped nor kept within bounds. Some idea, some fancy, takes possession of the brain; and however ridiculous, however distressing, however ruinous, haunts us by a sort of fascination through life.

Not only is the principle here pointed out to be seen at work in our more turbulent passions and pursuits; but even in the formal study of arts and sciences the same thing takes place, and undermines the repose and happiness of life. The eagerness of pursuit overcomes the satisfaction to result from the accomplishment. The mind is overstrained to attain its purpose; and when it is attained, the ease and alacrity necessary to enjoy it are gone. The irritation of action does not cease and go down with the occasion for it; but we are first uneasy to get to the end of our work, and then uneasy for want of something to do. The ferment of the brain does not of itself subside into pleasure and soft repose. Hence the disposition to strong *stimuli* observable in persons of much intellectual exertion, to allay and carry off the over-excitement. The *improvisatori* poets (it is recorded by Spence in his Anecdotes of Pope) cannot sleep after an evening's continued display of their singular and difficult art. The rhymes keep running in their heads in spite of themselves, and will not let them rest. Mechanics and labouring people never know what to do with themselves on a Sunday; though they return to their work with greater spirit for the relief, and look forward to it with pleasure all the week. Sir Joshua Reynolds was never comfortable out of his painting-room, and died of chagrin and regret, because he could not paint on to the last moment of his life. He used to say that he could go on retouching a picture forever, as long as it stood on his easel; but as soon as it was once fairly out of the house, he never wished to see it again. An ingenious artist of our own time has been heard to declare, that if ever the Devil got him into his clutches, he would set him to copy his own pictures. Thus the secure, self-complacent retrospect to what is done is nothing; while the anxious, uneasy looking forward to what is to come is every thing. We are afraid to dwell upon the past, lest it should retard our future progress; the indulgence of ease is fatal to excellence; and to succeed in life, we lose the ends of being!

HYPOTHESIS AND BELIEF

Christopher Isherwood

If a member of the so-called intellectual class joins any religious group or openly subscribes to its teaching, he will have to prepare himself for a good deal of criticism from his unconverted and more sceptical friends. Some of these may be sympathetic and genuinely interested; others will be covertly satirical, suspicious, or quite frankly hostile and dismayed. It will be suggested to the convert, with a greater or lesser degree of politeness, that he has sold out, betrayed the cause of reason, retreated in cowardice from "the realities of Life," and so forth. Henceforward, his conduct will be narrowly watched for symptoms of pretentiousness, priggishness, prudery and all other forms of puritanism. Certain topics will either be altogether avoided in his presence or they will be presented in the form of a challenge, to see how he will take them.

The convert himself, self-conscious and badly rattled, is almost sure to behave unnaturally. Either he will preach at his old friends and bore them; thus confirming their worst suspicions. Or he will make desperate efforts to reassure them, by his manner and conversation, that he is still "one of the gang." He will be the first to blaspheme, the first to touch upon the delicate subject. And his friends, far from feeling relieved, will be sincerely shocked.

One question, especially, he must learn to expect. It will be asked by the most candid, by those who really want to know: "Yes, of course, I can quite understand why you did it, in a way . . . but tell me, do you actually *believe* all that?" This question is particularly distressing to the convert, because, if he is to be honest, he will have to answer: "No, I don't—yet."

The "all that" to which the questioner refers will vary in detail and mode of formulation, according to the religious group the convert happens to have chosen. In essence, however, it can always be covered by what Aldous Huxley has called "the minimum working hypothesis." This word "hypothesis" is extremely significant, but it will probably be overlooked by the outside observer, who

HYPOTHESIS AND BELIEF: From *Exhumations* copyright © 1966 by Christopher Isherwood. Reprinted by permission of Simon and Schuster, Inc.

prefers to simplify his picture of the world's religions by regarding their teachings as "creeds" and "dogmas." Nevertheless, a statement of religious doctrine can be properly called a creed only by those who know it to be true. It remains a hypothesis as long as you are not quite sure. Spiritual truth is, by definition, directly revealed and experienced; it cannot be known at second hand. What is revealed truth to a Christ is merely hypothetical truth to the vast majority of his followers; but this need not prevent the followers from trusting in Christ's personal integrity and in the authenticity of his revelation, *as far as Christ himself is concerned*. One can feel sure that Einstein is neither a fraud nor a lunatic, and that he has actually discovered the law of relativity, and still fail, in a certain sense, to "believe" in the conception of Space-Time, just because one has not yet personally understood it.

There is, even nowadays, a good deal of loose and unrealistic talk about "the conflict between religion and science." I call this kind of talk unrealistic because it suggests that "Science," and hence scientists, are one hundred per cent materialistic, and that "Religion" is based upon the blind, one hundred per cent acceptance of dogmas which are incapable of scientific proof. Modern Science is, of course, very far from being materialistic. In the nineteenth century, it is true, science did pass through a phase of mechanistic materialism. But the scientist himself never has been, and never could be, an absolute materialist. The scientist is a human being. The absolute materialist, if he existed, would have to be some sort of non-human creature, completely lacking the human faculty of intuition, a mere machine for measuring and making calculations. If a human being could become a truly convinced materialist, he would never have the heroism to get up in the morning, shave, and eat his breakfast. His world-picture would be too terrible for even the boldest heart to contemplate; and, within twenty-four hours, he would have committed suicide.

Similarly, a religion based upon blind faith could not possibly survive, as all the world-religions have survived, for hundreds and thousands of years. Religion lives, and is revived, from age to age, because of the direct revelation of the few, the saints, who win for themselves a personal knowledge of spiritual reality. Religion survives *in spite* of blind faith, priestly persecution, ecclesiastical politics; in spite of superstition and ignorance amongst the masses of its adherents. Most of us cannot understand this, because our imagination refuses to grasp the gigantic influence and importance of the saint as an historical phenomenon. Whereas the persecution and the ignorance stand out brutally from the pages of history in red and black, plain for all to see. Nine times out of ten, when we use the word "Religion," we are really referring to the crimes or follies committed in religion's name.

There is no conflict between true Religion and true Science, but there is a great deal of bickering between religious dogmatists and scientific pedants. The dogmatist states his case, or rather, presents his dogmatic ultimatum. The scientifically-trained pedant reminds him, none too patiently, that his assertions cannot be verified by the microscope, the slide-rule, or the laboratory experiment. Therefore, he continues, quite rightly, the dogma is merely another hypothesis. And he will probably add that hypotheses which are incapable of scientific proof do not interest him, anyway. At this point a deadlock is reached, and the two men part in mutual annoyance.

But now let us suppose that, instead of the tiresome, dogmatic convert (who is unconvincing because he has not personally experienced the truth of what he asserts), Christ himself should enter the scientist's laboratory, and make the very same statements which the convert makes. How would the scientist react? If the scientist were a pure, non-human materialist, he would, of course, remain completely unconvinced. But, since he is a creature of emotion and intuition as well as of reason, the chances are that he would be impressed, not rationally but emotionally, by the personality of Christ and the tremendous psychological impact of such a meeting. In spite of his scientific training, he would venture to trust his intuition. He would say to himself: "Although my scientific methods of analysis cannot deal with these statements, my intuition tells me that this man has some authority for his words."

This raises the question of what we may call "the credibility of the witness." The jury in a court of law does not, or should not, judge a case entirely by scientific (i.e. rational) method: it relies, also, on intuition. It decides to believe a witness or not to believe him—sometimes in defiance of considerable circumstantial evidence. There is, also, the factor of corroboration. If two or more witnesses support each other, and make an impression of being truthful, the case is apt to turn in their favour.

When we begin to examine the assertions of the great religious teachers we shall have to behave like jurymen. Reason can help us, no doubt, and it must be brought to bear on the case; but Reason will not take us all the way. It can only deliver a provisional verdict. It can only say: "This is possible," or "Perhaps . . ." Next, we must ask ourselves: "What sort of men are telling us this? Are they charlatans? Do they seem sane? Do their lives bear out the truth of what they preach?" And, again: "Do they, substantially, agree with each other's testimony?" On this second point, however, there can be little argument. The basis of essential agreement between the great religious teachers of the world is very firm, and can easily be demonstrated by documentary evidence. Any student of comparative religion can reconstruct "the minimum working hypothesis." Nevertheless, it is quite possible to decide that Buddha, Christ, Shankara, St. Francis and Ramakrishna were all mad, or self-deluded, and therefore not to be taken seriously. If that is the verdict, then our inquiry ends.

But if the world's teachers were not mad, then, as all must agree, their teaching has universal application, and implies an obligation to put it into practice, in our own lives. And so we are faced by the next question: "Am I dissatisfied with my life as it is at present? And, if so, am I sufficiently dissatisfied to want to do anything about it?"

Here the majority and the minority definitely part company. Buddha said that human life is miserable, but he did not say that everybody thinks it is. Not all the socially underprivileged are dissatisfied, as every reformer knows, to his despair. And this is even truer of spiritual poverty than of economic lack. Life contains a number of vivid sense-pleasures, and the gaps of despondency and boredom between them can be filled more or less adequately by hard work, sleep, the movies, drink and day-dreaming. Old age brings lethargy, and morphia will help you at the end. Life is not so bad, if you have plenty of luck, a good physique and not too much imagination. The disciplines proposed by the spiritual teachers are drastic, and the lazy will shrink back from them. They are tedious, also, and this will discourage the impatient. Their immediate results are not showy, and this will deter the ambitious. Their practice is apt to make you appear ridiculous to your neighbours. Vanity, sloth and desire will all intervene to prevent a man from setting his foot upon the path of religious effort.

Disregarding all these obstacles, and they are tremendous, the beginner will have to say to himself: "Well, I am going to try. I believe that my teacher is sane and honest. I do not believe in his teachings with the whole of my mind, and I will not pretend that I do, but I have enough belief to make a start. My reason is not offended. My approach is strictly experimental. I will put myself into his hands, and trust him at least as far as I would trust my doctor. I will try to live the kind of life which he prescribes. If, at the end of three or four years, I can conscientiously say that I have done what was asked of me and had no results whatsoever, then I will give up the whole attempt as a bad job."

WRITING FOR MAGAZINES

Alfred Kazin

Chekhov, who died at forty-four, would have been a hundred years old this year, and there have been suitable tributes to him from short-story writers, people in the theater, and scholars in the field of Russian literature. I am none of these things, and my feeling about Chekhov, though warm, is backed up by nothing more than what everyone else has read of him in English. And perhaps I would in this instance have had the grace to keep quiet had it not occurred to me that there was one significant but virtually unpraised side of Chekhov's genius that I could pay tribute to.

Chekhov began as a writer for magazines—he wrote jokes, sketches, fables, feuilletons, little articles, spoofs; he literally tossed them off, sometimes from the bath-houses where he happened to sit down and write them. And later, a bit mocking as he always was about the "Chekhovian" virtues, he nevertheless said proudly: "I wrote as a bird sings. I'd sit down and write. Without thinking of how to write or about what. My things wrote themselves. I could write at any time I liked. To write a sketch, a story, a skit cost me no labor. I, like a young calf or a colt let out into the freedom of a green and radiant pasture, leaped, cavorted, kicked up my heels. I felt gay myself—and, from the sidelines, the result must have been funny."

Do you realize how revolutionary this was and is—a magazine writer who did not think he had to be solemn in order to be serious? A writer of "pieces" who was glad that they were just that—fugitive as anything can be, meant to entertain, nothing more? The trouble with magazines is that they give you just enough space to impersonate wisdom. It is impossible to do full justice to your subject; but there is room to lecture, to sermonize, to create effects. Even in the nineteenth century, when an article was not yet called a "story" (a story was supposed to entertain, to distract, to enthrall, not to give information), Edgar Allan Poe took his own role as a contributor to magazines so seriously that he grimly conceived of every offering as a demonstration of intellectual genius. Poe, who virtually invented the detective story, created in the figure of

WRITING FOR MAGAZINES: From *Contemporaries* (1962). Reprinted by permission of the author.

Dupin, the intellectual *maudit* who figures as his detective, a figure who actually represents the modern writer far more than he does any detective. Dupin is a man who discovers what no one else can see, who has a special slant on the truth in all fields. For Poe, every tale, every essay, every review, represented not only the romantic virtue of originality, but Poe's particular need to unhinge the existing world of intellectuals and littérateurs, to sign himself Q.E.D. at the end of each demonstration by Edgar Allan Poe. Poe was a literary genius who thought that he was virtually the only first-rate mind in this country, and in having to make a living from magazines, he converted necessity into the virtue of omnipresent wisdom. Everything was turned not merely into a demonstration of his rightness but into a syllogism which readers could grasp. No wonder that in planting horror and suspense as deliberately as a movie director, Poe was able to impress his name sufficiently to keep attention to his ideas. He knew his public, and what he did not get in cash he made up in living power. For in writing for a public which then as now wanted to get information slanted to give the appearance of "the inside story," a public impatient for wisdom as well as for news, Poe turned himself into his favorite figure—the wizard, the intellectual giant, the man who from the podium of the American magazine was able to enlighten the American folk, open-mouthed and grateful for the facts.

Poe, whatever his personal anguish, did not lack a good opinion of himself, for as a writer for magazines he was always immediately in touch with his public, always in sight of their rapture or terrors or humility when he made a point. In the same way, Dickens, through the constant serialization of his novels, was so much in touch with his public that he thought it necessary, in his own magazine, to explain his separation from his wife. Dostoevsky, though he complained bitterly of having to begin serialization of a novel before he had had a chance to think it out, adored playing weekly and monthly on the feelings of the inflammable Russian public. Perhaps because he was considered the most "abnormal" and uncharacteristic of the great Russian writers, he was eager to keep a column and to be constantly in touch with the Russian intellectual public.

2

The trouble with magazine writers just now is that we are put so quickly in touch with a large public, we have so obviously the brief but undeniable power to influence, to arouse, to change the thinking of people (who now as in the nineteenth century will buy dozens of magazines but grudge themselves the purchase of one book), that, often against our better selves, we become pompous, see ourselves as having to dislodge something with each article, to make a point or to contradict one. Magazine writers should be able to embody wittily the inconsequence which naturally belongs to many magazine pieces. Instead of admitting that an article may be only a small step forward in our thinking, like an entry in a notebook, or a sketch frankly meant to relieve, to lighten, to distract (even writers, when they get through with a day's hard work, would like to feel gayer when they pick up a magazine), magazine writers think that they must be pundits on all occasions, pundits in each piece of work. Each offering in a magazine is now so carefully deliberated, weighed, written, and rewritten that we have forgotten the *joy* behind Chekhov's life as a magazine writer—the joy of not writing for the ages, of the easy tone, the marginal comment, the social joke, the joy of being as unserious as one is brief, of knowing that one can be light *because* one is forced to be brief. Perhaps because one is read on Monday and can be forgotten the same day, there is an art in being inconsequent, an art which avoids the crashing and rhetorical final note, the art of appearing as light and easy as in one's heart one knows a "piece" must often be.

Of course Chekhov did not use a typewriter, and so was not tempted to clutter up his life and everyone else's with many "drafts." He, who wrote some of the most exquisite short stories ever written, did not have to *research* facts which he had absorbed as an individual. And after he had written a piece because he had a little something to tell and a little money to earn, his editors did not feel humiliated if, as it turned out, he had been off by two decimal points in reporting the annual rainfall in Minsk. Nowadays a magazine will very rarely quarrel with your opinions; it will check only your "facts." Yet Chekhov, who like so many great writers seized the immense opportunity that magazine journalism presented him with, was trusted to go out to Sakhalin Island, to write up his own report on the convict colony there, and to influence Russian public opinion.

Many of Chekhov's most beautiful things were written for magazines, and what I like most about them is the fact that, unlike so much American editorial practice today, Chekhov was allowed to be *easy*. He did not think of a story or of an article as a demonstration by a pedagogic mind in which, at the end, all themes were wrapped together and the point handed to the reader. "The open form," as one must call it, the classic style of the European feuilleton, the style of conversation, of intimacy, of pleasure and the cafés, was Chekhov's delight and his genius. He knew that a magazine writer, working not only against time but in time, with a sharper attention to immediate issues than other writers, should not pretend to iron things out, to settle all difficulties, to ape a logical perfection that his work cannot sustain. For Chekhov everything became what every good writer wants of a story—to make it truly "a slice of life." The phrase was used by the pseudo-scientific naturalists to make a slice taken out for analysis, as under a microscope. But for Chekhov it meant the moment seized in its actual and seeming insignificance. It was this, as everyone knows, which so influenced James Joyce, Virginia Woolf, Katherine Mansfield, Sherwood Anderson—writers who showed that it is because a story in a magazine must be brief that it can suggest the unexpected depth, the delicate beauty of life caught on the wing. O. Henry, like many a writer today, thought that the ending had to be "right," to give the reader a bang. The ending of a magazine piece should be a bridge to the next thought, the next issue, not a ceremonious wind-up. For a wind-up has to be planned, and the plan usually takes over the piece as a whole.

Chekhov, by not taking magazines or himself too seriously, by not thinking that he had to liberate the Russian mind every time he sent in a sketch to a journal, liberated the short story as a form from the prosiness of prose. He showed that prose could be as profound and touching and *felt* an intimation of human existence as poetry. Every writer of fiction who is any good has wanted that for prose: to give it at least *something* of the truth that is touched by poetry. But poetry is not only the oldest literary art but always the most personal, the one that most closely requires the writer to find that portion of language, of point of view, which is most solidly *his own*. It is in the art of "verse," which by its essence is quick and bright, that so many accomplished writers have learned to write prose. Criticism is interesting to me only when the critic is; when he writes easily and well and talks in nobody's voice but his own. The critics I read are those I read for pleasure. They are very often poets—Dudley Fitts, Conrad Aiken, Randall Jarrell. A poet like Auden, an old hand at writing for magazines, learned the deftness, the ease, the insinuating honesty, from writing verse. An unusually effective collection of magazine pieces, Harold Rosenberg's *The Tradition of the New*, is distinguished by the independence and wit of a man whose original language was poetry. The poet James Agee was in many respects the most eloquent magazine writer of his time, the only writer whose individual voice could be distinguished from the anonymous smoothness of *Time*. One of the reasons why so many academic scholars find it impossible to write effectively for general magazines is that they are not used to listening to their own voices, as poets are. They find their happiness in approbation, not in the English language.

Yet *Time* has incorporated the talents of many poets to create a corporate style for which the magazine gets the credit, never the writer himself. Too many magazine editors today see themselves as "creative," think of a magazine as having the stamp of an individual book. They want writers to make a product, *the* magazine, rather than to assist writers in finding their own voices. This is where the ever-increasing apparatus of rewriting, the many drafts, the copying machine, the proofs and the checkers and the researchers and the corrections, though all made necessary by the lack in this country of the corps of dependable writer-intellectuals who make possible the *New Statesman,* nevertheless serve the ambitions of the editor rather than of the writer. But only a magazine edited by a dominating writer, like Mencken, could be as much all in one tone as so many magazines now *try* to be (and the *American Mercury* displayed Mencken's passion for style, never exclusively his own opinions). The reason why such magazines succeed in this attempt, however, is that writers are often impressed by the editor's belief in his magazine, and are glad to lend their talents to his enterprise.

A writer for magazines must above all be interesting, for there is not enough of him in any one issue to justify boring the reader. Similarly, he must extract from the conditions of his work—the hurried deadline, the last-minute change—the liveliness of time itself. It is for his gaiety and ease, above all, that I honor Chekhov the magazine writer on this anniversary. A magazine is always a date, "an issue," a moment; it is created out of an exacting sense of time and it is about time. The spirit of occasion, the tone of conversation, the modesty of the passing moment, are what most belong to it. Let the magazine writer be faithful to this spirit of gaiety —and perhaps, like Chekhov, he may triumph over his own modesty.

BEYOND VIETNAM

Martin Luther King, Jr.

I come to this magnificent house of worship tonight because my conscience leaves me no other choice. I join you in this meeting

---

BEYOND VIETNAM: Reprinted by permission of Joan Daves. Copyright © 1967 by Martin Luther King, Jr.

because I am in deepest agreement with the aims and work of the organization which has brought us together: Clergy and Laymen Concerned About Vietnam. The recent statement of your executive committee are the sentiments of my own heart and I found myself in full accord when I read its opening lines: "A time comes when silence is betrayal." That time has come for us in relation to Vietnam.

The truth of these words is beyond doubt, but the mission to which they call us is a most difficult one. Even when pressed by the demands of inner truth, men do not easily assume the task of opposing their government's policy, especially in time of war. Nor does the human spirit move without great difficulty against all the apathy of conformist thought within one's own bosom and in the surrounding world. Moreover when the issues at hand seem as perplexing as they often do in the case of this dreadful conflict we are always on the verge of being mesmerized by uncertainty: but we must move on.

Some of us who have already begun to break the silence of the night have found that the calling to speak is often a vocation of agony, but we must speak. We must speak with all the humility that is appropriate to our limited vision, but we must speak. And we must rejoice as well, for surely this is the first time in our nation's history that a significant number of its religious leaders have chosen to move beyond the prophesying of smooth patriotism to the high grounds of a firm dissent based upon the mandates of conscience and the reading of history. Perhaps a new spirit is rising among us. If it is, let us trace its movements well and pray that our own inner being may be sensitive to its guidance, for we are deeply in need of a new way beyond the darkness that seems so close around us.

Over the past two years, as I have moved to break the betrayal of my own silences and to speak from the burnings of my own heart, as I have called for radical departures from the destruction of Vietnam, many persons have questioned me about the wisdom of my path. At the heart of their concerns this query has often loomed large and loud: Why are *you* speaking about the war, Dr. King? Why are *you* joining the voices of dissent? Peace and civil rights don't mix, they say. Aren't you hurting the cause of your people, they ask? And when I hear them, though I often understand the source of their concern, I am nevertheless greatly saddened, for such questions mean that the inquirers have not really known me, my commitment or my calling. Indeed, their questions suggest that they do not know the world in which they live.

In the light of such tragic misunderstanding, I deem it of signal importance to try to state clearly, and I trust concisely, why I believe that the path from Dexter Avenue Baptist Church—the church in Montgomery, Alabama where I began my pastorate—leads clearly to this sanctuary tonight.

I come to this platform tonight to make a passionate plea to my beloved nation. This speech is not addressed to Hanoi or to the National Liberation Front. It is not addressed to China or to Russia.

Nor is it an attempt to overlook the ambiguity of the total situation and the need for a collective solution to the tragedy of Vietnam. Neither is it an attempt to make North Vietnam or the National Liberation Front paragons of virtue, nor to overlook the role they can play in a successful resolution of the problem. While they both may have justifiable reason to be suspicious of the good faith of the United States, life and history give eloquent testimony to the fact that conflicts are never resolved without trustful give and take on both sides.

Tonight, however, I wish not to speak with Hanoi and the NLF, but rather to my fellow Americans who, with me, bear the greatest responsibility in ending a conflict that has exacted a heavy price on both continents.

Since I am a preacher by trade, I suppose it is not surprising that I have seven major reasons for bringing Vietnam into the field of my moral vision. There is at the outset a very obvious and almost facile connection between the war in Vietnam and the struggle I, and others, have been waging in America. A few years ago there was a shining moment in that struggle. It seemed as if there was a real promise of hope for the poor—both black and white—through the Poverty Program. There were experiments, hopes, new beginnings. Then came the build-up in Vietnam and I watched the program broken and eviscerated as if it were some idle political plaything of a society gone mad on war, and I knew that America would never invest the necessary funds or energies in rehabilitation of its poor so long as adventures like Vietnam continued to draw men and skills and money like some demonic destructive suction tube. So I was increasingly compelled to see the war as an enemy of the poor and to attack it as such.

Perhaps the more tragic recognition of reality took place when it became clear to me that the war was doing far more than devastating the hopes of the poor at home. It was sending their sons and their brothers and their husbands to fight and to die in extraordinarily high proportions relative to the rest of the population. We were taking the black young men who had been crippled by our society and sending them 8,000 miles away to guarantee liberties in Southeast Asia which they had not found in Southwest Georgia and East

Harlem. So we have been repeatedly faced with the cruel irony of watching Negro and white boys on TV screens as they kill and die together for a nation that has been unable to seat them together in the same schools. So we watch them in brutal solidarity burning the huts of a poor village but we realize that they would never live on the same block in Detroit. I could not be silent in the face of such cruel manipulation of the poor.

My third reason moves to an even deeper level of awareness, for it grows out of my experience in the ghettos of the north over the last three years—especially the last three summers. As I have walked among the desperate, rejected and angry young men I have told them that Molotov cocktails and rifles would not solve their problems. I have tried to offer them my deepest compassion while maintaining my conviction that social change comes most meaningfully through non-violent action. But they asked—and rightly so—what about Vietnam? They asked if our own nation wasn't using massive doses of violence to solve its problems, to bring about the changes it wanted. Their questions hit home, and I knew that I could never again raise my voice against the violence of the oppressed in the ghettos without having first spoken clearly to the greatest purveyor of violence in the world today—my own government. For the sake of those boys, for the sake of this government, for the sake of the hundreds of thousands trembling under our violence, I cannot be silent.

For those who ask the question, "Aren't you a Civil Rights leader?" and thereby mean to exclude me from the movement for peace, I have this further answer. In 1957 when a group of us formed the Southern Christian Leadership Conference, we chose as our motto: "To save the soul of America." We were convinced that we could not limit our vision to certain rights for black people, but instead affirmed the conviction that America would never be free or saved from itself unless the descendants of its slaves were loosed completely from the shackles they still wear. . . .

Now, it should be incandescently clear that no one who has any concern for the integrity and life of America today can ignore the present war. If America's soul becomes totally poisoned, part of the autopsy must read Vietnam. It can never be saved so long as it destroys the deepest hopes of men the world over. So it is that those of us who are yet determined that America *will* be are led down the path of protest and dissent, working for the health of our land.

As if the weight of such a commitment to the life and health of America were not enough, another burden of responsibility was placed upon me in 1964; and I cannot forget that the Nobel Prize for

Peace was also a commission—a commission to work harder than I had ever worked before for "the brotherhood of man." This is a calling that takes me beyond national allegiances, but even if it were not present I would yet have to live with the meaning of my commitment to the ministry of Jesus Christ. To me the relationship of this ministry to the making of peace is so obvious that I sometimes marvel at those who ask me why I am speaking against the war. Could it be that they do not know that the good news was meant for all men—for communist and capitalist, for their children and ours, for black and for white, for revolutionary and conservative? Have they forgotten that my ministry is in obedience to the one who loved his enemies so fully that he died for them? What then can I say to the Viet Cong or to Castro or to Mao as a faithful minister of this one? Can I threaten them with death or must I not share with them my life?

Finally, as I try to delineate for you and for myself the road that leads from Montgomery to this place I would have offered all that was most valid if I simply said that I must be true to my conviction that I share with all men the calling to be a son of the Living God. Beyond the calling of race or nation or creed is this vocation of sonship and brotherhood, and because I believe that the Father is deeply concerned especially for his suffering and helpless and outcast children, I come tonight to speak for them.

This I believe to be the privilege and the burden of all of us who deem ourselves bound by allegiances and loyalties which are broader and deeper than nationalism and which go beyond our nation's self-defined goals and positions. We are called to speak for the weak, for the voiceless, for victims of our nation and for those it calls enemy, for no document from human hands can make these humans any less our brothers.

And as I ponder the madness of Vietnam and search within myself for ways to understand and respond in compassion my mind goes constantly to the people of that peninsula. I speak now not of the soldiers of each side, not of the junta in Saigon, but simply of the people who have been living under the curse of war for almost three continuous decades now. I think of them too because it is clear to me that there will be no meaningful solution there until some attempt is made to know them and hear their broken cries.

They must see Americans as strange liberators. The Vietnamese people proclaimed their own independence in 1945 after a combined French and Japanese occupation, and before the communist revolution in China. They were led by Ho Chi Minh. Even though they quoted the American Declaration of Independence in their own document of freedom, we refused to recognize them. Instead, we decided to support France in its re-conquest of her former colony.

Our government felt then that the Vietnamese people were not "ready" for independence, and we again fell victim to the deadly western arrogance that has poisoned the international atmosphere for so long. With that tragic decision we rejected a revolutionary government seeking self-determination, and a government that had been established not by China (for whom the Vietnamese have no great love) but by clearly indigenous forces that included some communists. For the peasants this new government meant real land reform, one of the most important needs in their lives.

For nine years following 1945 we denied the people of Vietnam the right of independence. For nine years we vigorously supported the French in their abortive effort to re-colonize Vietnam.

Before the end of the war we were meeting 80 percent of the French war costs. Even before the French were defeated at Dien Bien Phu, they began to despair of the reckless action, but we did not. We encouraged them with our huge financial and military supplies to continue the war even after they had lost the will. Soon we would be paying almost the full costs of this tragic attempt at re-colonization.

After the French were defeated it looked as if independence and land reform would come again through the Geneva agreements. But instead there came the United States, determined that Ho should not unify the temporarily divided nation, and the peasants watched again as we supported one of the most vicious modern dictators—our chosen man, Premier Diem. The peasants watched and cringed as Diem ruthlessly routed out all opposition, supported their extortionist landlords and refused even to discuss re-unification with the North. The peasants watched as all this was presided over by U.S. influence and then by increasing numbers of U.S. troops who came to help quell the insurgency that Diem's methods had aroused. When Diem was overthrown they may have been happy, but the long line of military dictatorships seemed to offer no real change—especially in terms of their need for land and peace.

The only change came from America as we increased our troop commitments in support of governments which were singularly corrupt, inept and without popular support. All the while the people read our leaflets and received regular promises of peace and democracy—and land reform. Now they languish under our bombs and consider us—not their fellow Vietnamese—the real enemy. They move sadly and apathetically as we herd them off the land of their fathers into concentration camps where minimal social needs are rarely met. They know they must move or be destroyed by our bombs. So they go—primarily women and children and the aged.

They watch as we poison their water, as we kill a million acres of their crops. They must weep as the bulldozers roar through their areas preparing to destroy the precious trees. They wander into the hospitals, with at least 20 casualties from American firepower for one Vietcong-inflicted injury. So far we may have killed a million of them—mostly children. They wander into the towns and see thousands of the children, homeless, without clothes, running in packs on the streets like animals. They see the children degraded by our soldiers as they beg for food. They see the children selling their sisters to our soldiers, soliciting for their mothers.

What do the peasants think as we ally ourselves with the landlords and as we refuse to put any action into our many words concerning land reform? What do they think as we test out our latest weapons on them, just as the Germans tested out new medicine and new tortures in the concentration camps of Europe? Where are the roots of the independent Vietnam we claim to be building? Is it among these voiceless ones?

We have destroyed their two most cherished institutions: the family and the village. We have destroyed their land and their crops. We have cooperated in the crushing of the nation's only non-communist revolutionary political force—the unified Buddhist Church. We have supported the enemies of the peasants of Saigon. We have corrupted their women and children and killed their men. What liberators!

Now there is little left to build on—save bitterness. Soon the only solid physical foundations remaining will be found at our military bases and in the concrete of the concentration camps we call fortified hamlets. The peasants may well wonder if we plan to build our new Vietnam on such grounds as these? Could we blame them for such thoughts? We must speak for them and raise the questions they cannot raise. These too are our brothers.

Perhaps the more difficult but no less necessary task is to speak for those who have been designated as our enemies. What of the National Liberation Front—that strangely anonymous group we call VC or Communists? What must they think of us in America when they realize that we permitted the repression and cruelty of Diem which helped to bring them into being as a resistance group in the south? What do they think of our condoning the violence which led to their own taking up of arms? How can they believe in our integrity when now we speak of "aggression from the North" as if there were nothing more essential to the war? How can they trust us when now we charge them with violence after the murderous reign of Diem, and charge them with the violence while we pour every new weapon of death into their land? Surely we must understand their feelings even if we do not condone their actions. Surely we must see that the men we supported pressed them to their violence. Surely we must see that our own computerized plans of destruction simply dwarf their greatest acts.

How do they judge us when our officials know that their membership is less than 25 percent communist and yet insist on giving them the blanket name? What must they be thinking when they know that we are aware of their control of major sections of Vietnam and yet we appear ready to allow national elections in which this highly organized political parallel government will have no part? They ask how we can speak of free elections when the Saigon press is censored and controlled by the military junta. And they are surely right to wonder what kind of new government we plan to help form without them—the only party in real touch with the peasants. They question our political goals and they deny the reality of a peace settlement from which they will be excluded. Their questions are frighteningly relevant. Is our nation planning to build on political myth again and then shore it up with the power of new violence?

Here is the true meaning and value of compassion and non-violence when it helps us to see the enemy's point of view, to hear his questions, to know his assessment of ourselves. For from his view we may indeed see the basic weaknesses of our own condition, and if we are mature, we may learn and grow and profit from the wisdom of the brothers who are called the opposition.

So, too, with Hanoi. In the North, where our bombs now pummel the land, and our mines endanger the waterways, we are met by a deep but understandable mistrust. To speak for them is to explain this lack of confidence in western words, and especially their distrust of American intentions now. In Hanoi are the men who led the nation to independence against the Japanese and the French, the men who sought membership in the French commonwealth and were betrayed by the weakness of Paris and the willfulness of the colonial armies. It was they who led a second struggle against French domination at tremendous costs, and then were persuaded to give up the land they controlled between the 13th and 17th parallel as a temporary measure at Geneva. After 1954 they watched us conspire with Diem to prevent elections which would have surely brought Ho Chi Minh to power over a united Vietnam, and they realized they had been betrayed again.

When we ask why they do not leap to negotiate these things must be remembered. Also it must be clear that the leaders of Hanoi considered the presence of American troops in support of the Diem regime to have been the initial military breach of the Geneva Agreements concerning foreign troops, and they remind us that they did not begin to send in any large number of supplies or men until American forces had moved into the tens of thousands.

Hanoi remembers how our leaders refused to tell us the truth about the earlier North Vietnamese overtures for peace, how the President claimed that none existed when they had clearly been made. Ho Chi Minh has watched as America has spoken of peace and built up its forces, and now he has surely heard the increasing international rumors of American plans for an invasion of the North. He knows the bombing and shelling and mining we are doing are part of traditional pre-invasion strategy. Perhaps only his sense of humor and of irony can save him when he hears the most powerful nation of the world speaking of aggression as it drops thousands of bombs on a poor weak nation more than 8,000 miles away from its shores.

At this point I should make it clear that while I have tried in these last few minutes to give a voice to the voiceless on Vietnam and to understand the arguments of those who are called enemy, I am as deeply concerned about our own troops there as anything else. For it occurs to me that what we are submitting them to in Vietnam is not simply the brutalizing process that goes on in any war where armies face each other and seek to destroy. We are adding cynicism to the process of death, for they must know after a short period there that none of the things we claim to be fighting for are really involved. Before long they must know that their government has sent them into a struggle among Vietnamese, and the more sophisticated surely realize that we are on the side of the wealthy and the secure while we create a hell for the poor.

Somehow this madness must cease. We must stop now. I speak as a child of God and brother to the suffering poor of Vietnam. I speak for those whose land is being laid waste, whose homes are being destroyed, whose culture is being subverted. I speak for the poor of America who are paying the double price of smashed hopes at home and death and corruption in Vietnam. I speak as a citizen of the world, for the world as it stands aghast at the path we have taken. I speak as an American to the leaders of my own nation. The great initiative in this war is ours. The initiative to stop it must be ours.

This is the message of the great Buddhist leaders of Vietnam. Recently one of them wrote these words: "Each day the war goes on the hatred increases in the heart of the Vietnamese and in the hearts of those of humanitarian instinct. The Americans are forcing even their friends into becoming their enemies. It is curious that the Americans, who calculate so carefully on the possibilities of military victory, do not realize that in the process they are incurring deep psychological and political defeat. The image of America will never again be the image of revolution, freedom and democracy, but the image of violence and militarism."

If we continue there will be no doubt in my mind and in the mind of the world that we have no honorable intentions in Vietnam. It will become clear that our minimal expectation is to occupy it as an American colony and men will not refrain from thinking that our maximum hope is to goad China into a war so that we may bomb her nuclear installations. If we do not stop our war against the people of Vietnam immediately the world will be left with no other alternative than to see this as some horribly clumsy and deadly game we have decided to play.

The world now demands a maturity of America that we may not be able to achieve. It demands that we admit that we have been wrong from the beginning of our adventure in Vietnam, that we have been detrimental to the life of the Vietnamese people. The situation is one in which we must be ready to turn sharply from our present ways.

In order to atone for our sins and errors in Vietnam, we should take the initiative in bringing a halt to this tragic war. I would like to suggest five concrete things that our government should do immediately to begin the long and difficult process of extricating ourselves from this nightmarish conflict:

1. End all bombing in North and South Vietnam.
2. Declare a unilateral cease-fire in the hope that such action will create the atmosphere for negotiation.
3. Take immediate steps to prevent other battlegrounds in Southeast Asia by curtailing our military build-up in Thailand and our interference in Laos.
4. Realistically accept the fact that the National Liberation Front has substantial support in South Vietnam and must thereby play a role in any meaningful negotiations and in any future Vietnam government.
5. Set a date that we will remove all foreign troops from Vietnam in accordance with the 1954 Geneva Agreement.

Part of our ongoing commitment might well express itself in an offer to grant asylum to any Vietnamese who fears for his life under a new regime which included the Liberation Front. Then we must make what reparations we can for the damage we have done. We must provide the medical aid that is badly needed, making it available in this country if necessary.

Meanwhile we in the churches and synagogues have a continuing task while we urge our government to disengage itself from a disgraceful commitment. We must continue to raise our voices and our lives if our nation persists in its perverse ways in Vietnam. We must be prepared to match actions with words by seeking out every creative means of protest possible.

As we counsel young men concerning military service we must clarify for them our nation's role in Vietnam and challenge them with the alternative of conscientious objection. I am pleased to say that this is the path now being chosen by more than seventy students at my own Alma Mater, Morehouse College, and I recommend it to all who find the American course in Vietnam a dishonourable and unjust one. Moreover I would encourage all ministers of draft age to give up their ministerial exemptions and seek status as conscientious objectors. These are the times for real choices and not false ones. We are at the moment when our lives must be placed on the line if our nation is to survive its own folly. Every man of humane convictions must decide on the protest that best suits his convictions, but we must all protest.

There is something seductively tempting about stopping there and sending us all off on what in some circles has become a popular crusade against the war in Vietnam. I say we must enter that struggle, but I wish to go on now to say something even more disturbing. The war in Vietnam is but a symptom of a far deeper malady within the American spirit, and if we ignore this sobering reality we will find ourselves organizing clergy and laymen-concerned committees for the next generation. They will be concerned about Guatemala and Peru. They will be concerned about Thailand and Cambodia. They will be concerned about Mozambique and South Africa. We will be marching for these and a dozen other names and attending rallies without end unless there is a significant and profound change in American life and policy. Such thoughts take us beyond Vietnam, but not beyond our calling as sons of the living God.

In 1957 a sensitive American official overseas said that it seemed to him that our nation was on the wrong side of a world revolution. During the past 10 years we have seen emerge a pattern of suppression which now has justified the presence of U.S. military "advisors" in Venezuela. This need to maintain social stability for our investments accounts for the counterrevolutionary action of American forces in Guatemala. It tells why American helicopters are being used against guerrillas in Colombia and why American napalm and green beret forces have already been active against rebels in Peru. It is with such activity in mind that the words of the late John F. Kennedy come back to haunt us. Five years ago he said. "Those who make peaceful revolution impossible will make violent revolution inevitable."

Increasingly, by choice or by accident, this is the role our nation has taken—the role of those who make peaceful revolution impossible by refusing to give up the privileges and the pleasures that come from the immense profits of overseas investment.

I am convinced that if we are to get on the right side of the world revolution, we as a nation must undergo a radical revolution of values. We must rapidly begin the shift from a "thing-oriented" society to a "person-oriented" society. When machines and computers, profit motives and property rights are considered more important than people, the giant triplets of racism, materialism, and militarism are incapable of being conquered.

A true revolution of value will soon cause us to question the fairness and justice of many of our past and present policies. On the one hand we are called to play the Good Samaritan on life's roadside; but that will be only an initial act. One day we must come to see that the whole Jericho Road must be transformed so that men and women will not be constantly beaten and robbed as they make their journey on life's highway. True compassion is more than flinging a coin to a beggar; it is not haphazard and superficial. It comes to see that an edifice which produces beggars needs re-structuring. A true revolution of values will soon look uneasily on the glaring contrast of poverty and wealth. With righteous indignation, it will look across the seas and see individual capitalists of the West investing huge sums of money in Asia, Africa and South America, only to take the profits out with no concern for the social betterment of the countries, and say: "This is not just." It will look at our alliance with the landed gentry of Latin America and say: "This is not just." The Western arrogance of feeling that it has everything to teach others and nothing to learn from them is not just. A true revolution of values will lay hands on the world order and say of war: "This way of settling differences is not just." This business of burning human beings with napalm, of filling our nation's homes with orphans and widows, of injecting poisonous drugs of hate into the veins of peoples normally humane, of sending men home from dark and bloody battlefields physically handicapped and psychologically deranged, cannot be reconciled with wisdom, justice, and love. A nation that continues year after year to spend more money on military defense than on programs of social uplift is approaching spiritual death.

America, the richest and most powerful nation in the world, can well lead the way in this revolution of values. There is nothing, except a tragic death wish, to prevent us from re-ordering our priorities, so that the pursuit of peace will take precedence over the pursuit of war. There is nothing to keep us from molding a recalcitrant status-quo with bruised hands until we have fashioned it into a brotherhood.

This kind of positive revolution of values is our best defense against Communism. War is not the answer. Communism will never be defeated by the use of atomic bombs or nuclear weapons. Let us not join those who shout war and through their misguided passions urge the United States to relinquish its participation in the United Nations. These are days which demand wise restraint and calm reasonableness. We must not call everyone a Communist or an appeaser who advocates the seating of Red China in the United Nations and who recognizes that hate and hysteria are not the final answers to the problem of these turbulent days. We must not engage in a negative anti-Communism, but rather in a positive thrust for democracy, realizing that our greatest defense against Communism is to take offensive action in behalf of justice. We must with positive action seek to remove those conditions of poverty, insecurity and injustice which are the fertile soil in which the seed of Communism grows and develops.

These are revolutionary times. All over the globe men are revolting against old systems of exploitation and oppression and out of the wombs of a frail world new systems of justice and equality are being born. The shirtless and barefoot people of the land are rising up as never before. "The people who sat in darkness have seen a great light." We in the West must support these revolutions. It is a sad fact that, because of comfort, complacency, a morbid fear of Communism, and our proneness to adjust to injustice, the Western nations that initiated so much of the revolutionary spirit of the modern world have now become the arch anti-revolutionary spirit. Therefore, Communism is a judgment against our failure to make democracy real and follow through on the revolutions that we initiated. Our only hope today lies in our ability to recapture the revolutionary spirit and go out into a sometimes hostile world declaring eternal hostility to poverty, racism, and militarism. With this powerful commitment we shall boldly challenge the status-quo and unjust mores and thereby speed the day when "every valley shall be exalted, and every mountain and hill shall be made low, and the crooked shall be made straight and the rough places plain."

A genuine revolution of values means in the final analysis that our loyalties must become ecumenical rather than sectional. Every nation must now develop an overriding loyalty to mankind as a whole in order to preserve the best in their individual societies.

This call for a world-wide fellowship that lifts neighborly concern beyond one's tribe, race, class and nation is in reality a call for an all-embracing and unconditional love for all men. This oft misunderstood and misinterpreted concept so readily dismissed by the Nietzches of the world as a weak and cowardly force—has now become an absolute necessity for the survival of man. When I speak of love I am not speaking of some sentimental and weak response. I am speaking of that force which all of the great religions have seen as the supreme unifying principle of life. Love is somehow the key that unlocks the door which leads to ultimate reality. This Hindu-Moslem-Christian-Jewish-Buddhist belief about ultimate reality is beautifully summed up in the first epistle of Saint John:

> Let us love one another; for love is God and everyone that loveth is born of God and knoweth God. He that loveth not knoweth not God; for God is love. If we love one another, God dwelleth in us, and his love is perfected in us.

Let us hope that this spirit will become the order of the day. We can no longer afford to worship the God of Hate or bow before the altar of retaliation. The oceans of history are made turbulent by the ever-rising tides of hate. History is cluttered with the wreckage of nations and individuals that pursued this self-defeating path of hate. As Arnold Toynbee says: "Love is the ultimate force that makes for the saving choice of life and good against the damning choice of death and evil. Therefore the first hope in our inventory must be the hope that love is going to have the last word."

We are now faced with the fact that tomorrow is today. We are confronted with the fierce urgency of now. In this unfolding conundrum of life and history there is such a thing as being too late. Procrastination is still the thief of time. Life often leaves us standing bare, naked and dejected with a lost opportunity. The "tide in the affairs of men" does not remain at the flood; it ebbs. We may cry out desperately for time to pause in her passage, but time is deaf to every plea and rushes on. Over the bleached bones and jumbled residue of numerous civilizations are written the pathetic words: "Too late?" There is an invisible book of life that faithfully records our vigilance or our neglect. "The moving finger writes, and having written moves on. . . ." We still have a choice today: non-violent co-existence or violent co-annihilation.

We must move past indecision to action. We must find new ways to speak for peace in Vietnam and justice throughout the developing world—a world that borders on our doors. If we do not act we shall surely be dragged down the long dark and shameful corridors of time reserved for those who possess power without compassion, might without morality, and strength without sight.

Now let us begin. Now let us re-dedicate ourselves to the long and bitter—but beautiful—struggle for a new world. This is the calling of the sons of God, and our brothers wait eagerly for our response. Shall we say the odds are too great? Shall we tell them the struggle is too hard? Will our message be that the forces of American life militate against their arrival as full men, and we send our deepest regrets? Or will there be another message, of longing, of hope, of solidarity with their yearnings, of commitment to their cause, whatever the cost? The choice is ours, and though we might prefer it otherwise we *must* choose in this crucial moment of human history.

A COMPLAINT OF THE DECAY OF BEGGARS, IN THE METROPOLIS

Charles Lamb

The all-sweeping besom of societarian reformation—your only modern Alcides' club to rid the time of its abuses—is uplift with many-handed sway to extirpate the last fluttering tatters of the bugbear *Mendicity* from the metropolis. Scrips, wallets, bags—staves, dogs, and crutches—the whole mendicant fraternity, with all their baggage, are fast posting out of the purlieus of this eleventh persecution. From the crowded crossing, from the corners of streets and turnings of alleys, the parting Genius of Beggary is "with sighing sent."

I do not approve of this wholesale going to work, this impertinent crusado, or *bellum ad exterminationem*, proclaimed against a species. Much good might be sucked from these Beggars.

They were the oldest and the honourablest form of pauperism. Their appeals were to our common nature; less revolting to an ingenuous mind than to be a suppliant to the particular humours or caprice of any fellow-creature, or set of fellow-creatures, parochial or societarian. Theirs were the only rates uninvidious in the levy, ungrudged in the assessment.

There was a dignity springing from the very depth of their desolation; as to be naked is to be so much nearer to the being a man, than to go in livery.

The greatest spirits have felt this in their reverses; and when Dionysius from king turned schoolmaster, do we feel anything towards him but contempt? Could Vandyke have made a picture of him, swaying a ferula for a sceptre, which would have affected our minds with the same heroic pity, the same compassionate admiration, with which we regard his Belisarius begging for an *obolus*? Would the moral have been more graceful, more pathetic?

The Blind Beggar in the legend—the father of pretty Bessy—whose story doggrel rhymes and alehouse signs cannot so degrade or attenuate but that some sparks of a lustrous spirit will shine through the disguisements—this noble Earl of Cornwall (as indeed he was) and memorable sport of fortune, fleeing from the unjust sentence of his liege lord, stript of all, and seated on the flowering green of Bethnal, with his more fresh and springing daughter by his side, illumining his rags and his beggary—would the child and parent have cut a better figure doing the honours of a counter, or expiating their fallen condition upon the three-foot eminence of some sempstering shopboard?

In tale or history your Beggar is ever the just antipode to your King. The poets and romancical writers (as dear Margaret Newcastle would call them), when they would most sharply and feelingly paint a reverse of fortune, never stop till they have brought down their hero in good earnest to rags and the wallet. The depth of the descent illustrates the height he falls from. There is no medium which can be presented to the imagination without offence. There is no breaking the fall. Lear, thrown from his palace, must divest him of his garments, till he answer "mere nature"; and Cresseid, fallen from a prince's love, must extend her pale arms, pale with other whiteness than of beauty, supplicating lazar alms with bell and clap-dish.

The Lucian wits knew this very well; and, with a converse policy, when they would express scorn of greatness without the pity, they show us an Alexander in the shades cobbling shoes, or a Semiramis getting up foul linen.

How would it sound in song, that a great monarch had declined his affections upon the daughter of a baker! yet do we feel the imagination at all violated when we read the "true ballad," where King Cophetua woos the beggar maid?

Pauperism, pauper, poor man, are expressions of pity, but pity alloyed with contempt. No one properly contemns a Beggar.

Poverty is a comparative thing, and each degree of it is mocked by its "neighbour grice." Its poor rents and comings-in are soon summed up and told. Its pretences to property are almost ludicrous. Its pitiful attempts to save excite a smile. Every scornful companion can weigh his trifle-bigger purse against it. Poor man reproaches poor man in the streets with impolitic mention of his condition, his own being a shade better, while the rich pass by and jeer at both. No rascally comparative insults a Beggar, or thinks of weighing purses with him. He is not in the scale of comparison. He is not under the measure of property. He confessedly hath none, any more than a dog or a sheep. No one twitteth him with ostentation above his means. No one accuses him of pride, or upbraideth him with mock humility. None jostle with him for the wall, or pick quarrels for precedency. No wealthy neighbour seeketh to eject him from his tenement. No man sues him. No man goes to law with him. If I were not the independent gentleman that I am, rather than I would be a retainer to the great, a led captain, or a poor relation, I would choose, out of the delicacy and true greatness of my mind, to be a Beggar.

Rags, which are the reproach of poverty, are the Beggar's robes, and graceful *insignia* of his profession, his tenure, his full dress, the suit in which he is expected to show himself in public. He is never out of the fashion, or limpeth awkwardly behind it. He is not required to put on court mourning. He weareth all colours, fearing none. His costume hath undergone less change than the Quaker's. He is the only man in the universe who is not obliged to study appearances. The ups and downs of the world concern him no longer. He alone continueth in one stay. The price of stock or land affecteth him not. The fluctuations of agricultural or commercial prosperity touch him not, or at worst but change his customers. He is not expected to become bail or surety for any one. No man troubleth him with questioning his religion or politics. He is the only free man in the universe.

The Mendicants of this great city were so many of her sights, her lions. I can no more spare them than I could the Cries of London. No corner of a street is complete without them. They are as indispensable as the Ballad Singer; and in their picturesque attire as ornamental as the signs of old London. They were the standing morals, emblems, mementoes, dial-mottoes, the spital sermons, the books for children, the salutary checks and pauses to the high and rushing tide of greasy citizenry—

——————— Look
Upon that poor and broken bankrupt there.

Above all, those old blind Tobits that used to line the wall of Lincoln's-Inn Garden, before modern fastidiousness had expelled them, casting up their ruined orbs to catch a ray of pity, and (if possible) of light, with their faithful Dog Guide at their feet—whither are they fled? or into what corners, blind as themselves, have they been driven, out of the wholesome air and sun-warmth? immersed between four walls, in what withering poor-house do they endure the penalty of double darkness, where the chink of the dropt halfpenny no more consoles their forlorn bereavement, far from the sound of the cheerful and hope-stirring tread of the passenger? Where hang their useless staves? and who will farm their dogs?—Have the overseers of St. L— caused them to be shot? or were they tied up in sacks and dropt into the Thames, at the suggestion of B— the mild rector of ——?

Well fare the soul of unfastidious Vincent Bourne,—most classical, and, at the same time, most English of the Latinists!—who has treated of this human and quadrupedal alliance, this dog and man friendship, in the sweetest of his poems, the *Epitaphium in Canem*, or, *Dog's Epitaph*. Reader, peruse it; and say, if customary sights, which could call up such gentle poetry as this, were of a nature to do more harm or good to the moral sense of the passengers through the daily thoroughfares of a vast and busy metropolis.

> Pauperis hic Iri requiesco Lyciscus, herilis,
> Dum vixi, tutela vigil columenque senectæ,
> Dux cæco fidus: nec, me ducente, solebat,
> Prætenso hinc atque hinc baculo, per iniqua locorum
> Incertam explorare viam; sed fila secutus,
> Quæ dubios regerent passûs, vestigia tuta
> Fixit inoffenso gressu; gelidumque sedile
> In nudo nactus saxo, quâ prætereuntium
> Unda frequens confluxit, ibi miserisque tenebras
> Lamentis, noctemque oculis ploravit obortam.
> Ploravit nec frustra; obolum dedit alter et alter.
> Queis corda et mentem indiderat natura benignam.
> Ad latus interea jacui sopitus herile,
> Vel mediis vigil in somnis; ad herilia jussa
> Auresque atque animum arrectus, seu frustula amicè
> Porrexit sociasque dapes, seu longa diei.
> Tædia perpessus, reditum sub nocte parabat.
>   Hi mores, hæc vita fuit, dum fata sinebant,
> Dum neque languebam morbis, nec inerte senectâ
> Quæ tandem obrepsit, veterique satellite cæcum

Orbavit dominum; prisci sed gratia facti
Ne tota intereat, longos deleta per annos,
Exiguum hunc Irus tumulum de cespite fecit,
Etsi inopis, non ingratæ, munuscula dextræ;
Carmine signavitque brevi, dominumque canemque,
Quod memoret, fidumque Canem dominumque Benignum.

Poor Irus' faithful wolf-dog here I lie,
That wont to tend my old blind master's steps,
His guide and guard; nor, while my service lasted,
Had he occasion for that staff, with which
He now goes picking out his path in fear
Over the highways and crossings; but would plant,
Safe in the conduct of my friendly string,
A firm foot forward still, till he had reach'd
His poor seat on some stone, nigh where the tide
Of passers-by in thickest confluence flow'd:
To whom with loud and passionate laments
From morn to eve his dark estate he wail'd.
Nor wail'd to all in vain: some here and there,
The well-disposed and good, their pennies gave.
I meantime at his feet obsequious slept;
Not all-asleep in sleep, but heart and ear
Prick'd up at his least motion; to receive
At his kind hand my customary crumbs,
And common portion in his feast of scraps;
Or when night warn'd us homeward, tired and spent
With our long day and tedious beggary.
  These were my manners, this my way of life
Till age and slow disease me overtook,
And sever'd from my sightless master's side.
But lest the grace of so good deeds should die,
Through tract of years in mute oblivion lost,
This slender tomb of turf hath Irus reared,
Cheap monument of no ungrudging hand,
And with short verse inscribed it, to attest,
In long and lasting union to attest,
The virtues of the Beggar and his Dog.

These dim eyes have in vain explored for some months past a well-known figure, or part of the figure, of a man, who used to glide his comely upper half over the pavements of London, wheeling along with most ingenious celerity upon a machine of wood; a spectacle to natives, to foreigners, and to children. He was of a robust make, with a florid sailor-like complexion, and his head was bare to the storm and sunshine. He was a natural curiosity, a speculation to the scientific, a prodigy to the simple. The infant would stare at the mighty man brought down to his own level. The common cripple would despise his own pusillanimity, viewing the hale stoutness, and hearty heart, of this half-limbed giant. Few but must have noticed him; for the accident which brought him low took place during the riots of 1780, and he has been a groundling so long. He seemed earth-born, an Antæus, and to suck in fresh vigour from the soil which he neighboured. He was a grand fragment; as good as an Elgin marble. The nature, which should have recruited his reft legs and thighs, was not lost, but only retired into his upper parts, and he was half a Hercules. I heard a tremendous voice thundering and growling, as before an earthquake, and casting down my eyes, it was this mandrake reviling a steed that had started at his portentous appearance. He seemed to want but his just stature to have rent the offending quadruped in shivers. He was as the man-part of a centaur, from which the horse-half had been cloven in some dire Lapithan controversy. He moved on, as if he could have made shift with yet half of the body-portion which was left him. The *os sublime* was not wanting; and he threw out yet a jolly countenance upon the heavens. Forty-and-two years had he driven this out-of-door trade, and now that his hair is grizzled in the service, but his good spirits no way impaired, because he is not content to exchange his free air and exercise for the restraints of a poor-house, he is expiating his contumacy in one of those houses (ironically christened) of Correction.

Was a daily spectacle like this to be deemed a nuisance, which called for legal interference to remove? or not rather a salutary and a touching object to the passers-by in a great city? Among her shows, her museums, and supplies for ever-gaping curiosity (and what else but an accumulation of sights—endless sights—*is* a great city; or for what else is it desirable?) was there not room for one *Lusus* (not *Naturæ*, indeed, but) *Accidentium?* What if in forty-and-two-years' going about, the man had scraped together enough to give a portion to his child (as the rumour ran) of a few hundreds —whom had he injured?—whom had he imposed upon? The contributors had enjoyed their *sight* for their pennies. What if after being exposed all day to the heats, the rains, and the frosts of heaven —shuffling his ungainly trunk along in an elaborate and painful motion—he was enabled to retire at night to enjoy himself at a club of his fellow cripples over a dish of hot meat and vegetables, as the charge was gravely brought against him by a clergyman deposing before a House of Commons' Committee—was *this*, or was his truly paternal consideration, which (if a fact) deserved a statue rather than a whipping-post, and is inconsistent, at least, with the exaggeration of nocturnal orgies which he has been slandered with—a reason that he should be deprived of his chosen, harmless, nay, edifying way of life, and be committed in hoary age for a sturdy vagabond?—

There was a Yorick once, whom it would not have shamed to have sate down at the cripples' feast, and to have thrown in his benediction, ay, and his mite too, for a companionable symbol. "Age, thou hast lost thy breed."—

Half of these stories about the prodigious fortunes made by begging are (I verily believe) misers' calumnies. One was much talked of in the public papers some time since, and the usual charitable inferences deduced. A clerk in the Bank was surprised with the announcement of a five-hundred-pound legacy left him by a person whose name he was a stranger to. It seems that in his daily morning walks from Peckham (or some village therabouts) where he lived, to his office, it had been his practice for the last twenty years to drop his halfpenny duly into the hat of some blind Bartimeus, that sate begging alms by the wayside in the Borough. The good old beggar recognised his daily benefactor by the voice only; and, when he died, left all the amassings of his alms (that had been half a century perhaps in the accumulating) to his old Bank friend. Was this a story to purse up people's hearts, and pennies, against giving an alms to the blind? or not rather a beautiful moral of well-directed charity on the one part, and noble gratitude upon the other?

I sometimes wish I had been that Bank clerk.

I seem to remember a poor old grateful kind of creature, blinking and looking up with his no eyes in the sun—

Is it possible I could have steeled my purse against him?

Perhaps I had no small change.

Reader, do not be frightened at the hard words imposition, imposture—*give, and ask no questions.* Cast thy bread upon the waters. Some have unawares (like this Bank clerk) entertained angels.

Shut not thy purse-strings always against painted distress. Act a charity sometimes. When a poor creature (outwardly and visibly such) comes before thee, do not stay to inquire whether the "seven small children," in whose name he implores thy assistance, have a veritable existence. Rake not into the bowels of unwelcome truth to save a halfpenny. It is good to believe him. If he be not all that he pretendeth, *give*, and under a personate father of a family, think (if thou pleasest) that thou hast relieved an indigent bachelor. When they come with their counterfeit looks and mumping tones, think them players. You pay your money to see a comedian feign these things, which, concerning these poor people, thou canst not certainly tell whether they are feigned or not.

ARCHITECTURAL EXCERPTS:

Norman Mailer

a) A Piece for *The New York Times*

In Lyndon Johnson's book, *My Hope for America*, the fifth chapter is titled "Toward the Great Society." It contains this paragraph:

> . . . *fifty years from now, . . . there will be four hundred million Americans, four-fifths of them in urban areas. In the remainder of this century, . . . we will have to build homes, highways, and facilities equal to all those built since this country was first settled. In the next forty years we must rebuild the entire urban United States.*

It is a staggering sentence. The city we inhabit at this moment is already close to a total reconstruction of the world our parents knew in their childhood. If there is no nuclear war, if we shift from cold war to some kind of peace, and there is a worldwide rise in the standard of living, then indeed we will build a huge new country. It is possible that not one in a thousand of the buildings put up by 1899 will still be standing in the year 2000.

But what will America look like? How will its architecture appear? Will it be the architecture of a Great Society, or continue to be the architecture of an empty promiscuous panorama where no one can distinguish between hospitals and housing projects, factories and colleges, concert halls, civic centers, and airport terminals? The mind recoils from the thought of an America rebuilt completely in the shape of those blank skyscrapers forty stories high, their walls dead as an empty television screen, their form as interesting as a box of cleansing tissue propped on end. They are buildings which reveal nothing so much as the deterioration in real value of the dollar bill.

ARCHITECTURAL EXCERPTS: Reprinted from *Cannibals and Christians* by permission of the author and his agents, Scott Meredith Literary Agency, Inc., 580 Fifth Avenue, New York, New York 10036. "A Piece for *The New York Times*" originally appeared in *The New York Times* as "Cities Higher than Mountains," copyright © 1965 by Normal Mailer. "A Statement for *Architectural Forum*," copyright © 1964 by Urban America, Inc.

They are denuded of ornament (which costs money), their windows are not subtly recessed into the wall but are laid flush with the surface like a patch of collodion on the skin, there is no instant where a roof with a tower, a gable, a spire, a mansard, a ridge or even a mooring mast for a dirigible intrudes itself into the sky, reminding us that every previous culture of man attempted to engage the heavens.

No, our modern buildings go flat, flat at the top, flat as eternal monotony, flat as the last penny in a dollar. There is so much corruption in the building codes, over inflation in the value of land, feather-bedding built into union rules, so much graft, so much waste, so much public relations, and so much emptiness inflated upon so much emptiness that no one tries to do more with the roof than leave it flat.

As one travels through the arbitrary new neighborhoods of the present, those high squat dormitories which imprison the rich as well as the poor, one is not surprised that the violence is greater than it used to be in the old slum, up are the statistics for juvenile delinquency and for dope addiction. To live in the old slum jungle left many half crippled, and others part savage, but it was at least an environment which asked for wit. In the prison vistas of urban renewal, the violence travels from without to within, there is no wit —one travels down a long empty corridor to reach one's door, long as the corridors in the public schools, long as the corridors in the hospitals at the end of the road; the landscape of modern man takes on a sense of endless empty communications.

Sterile as an operating table is the future vista of suburban spread, invigorating as a whiff of deodorant is the sight of new office buildings. Small elation sits upon us as we contemplate the future, for the picturesque will be uprooted with the ugly, our populations will double, and in a city like New York, the brownstone will be replaced by a cube sixteen stories high with a huge park for parking cars and a little grass. The city will go up a little and it will go out, it will spread. We will live with glass walls in a cold climate. The entire world will come to look like Queens Boulevard. We will have been uprooted so many times that future man will come to bear the same relation to the past that a hydroponic plant bears to soil.

Yet some part of us is aware that to uproot the past too completely is a danger without measure. It must at the least produce a profound psychic discomfort. For we do not know how much our perception of the present and our estimate of the future depend upon our sense of what has gone before. To return to an old neighborhood and discover it has disappeared is a minor woe for some; it is close to a psychological catastrophe for others, an amputation where the lost nerves still feel pain. This century must appear at times like a great beast which has lost its tail, but who could argue that the amputation was not self-inflicted?

There seems at loose an impulse to uproot every vestige of the past, an urge so powerful one wonders if it is not with purpose, if it is not in the nature of twentieth-century man to uproot himself not only from his past, but from his planet. Perhaps we live on the edge of a great divide in history and so are divided ourselves between the desire for a gracious, intimate, detailed and highly particular landscape and an urge less articulate to voyage out on explorations not yet made. Perhaps the blank faceless abstract quality of our modern architecture is a reflection of the anxiety we feel before the void, a kind of visual static which emanates from the psyche of us all, as if we do not know which way to go.

If we are to spare the countryside, if we are to protect the style of the small town and of the exclusive suburb, keep the organic center of the metropolis and the old neighborhoods, maintain those few remaining streets where the tradition of the nineteenth century and the muse of the eighteenth century still linger on the mood in the summer cool of an evening, if we are to avoid a megalopolis five hundred miles long, a city without shape or exit, a nightmare of ranch houses, highways, suburbs and industrial sludge, if we are to save the dramatic edge of a city—that precise moment when we leave the outskirts and race into the country, the open country—if we are to have a keen acute sense of concentration and a breath of release, then there is only one solution: the cities must climb, they must not spread, they must build up, not by increments, but by leaps, up and up, up to the heavens.

We must be able to live in houses one hundred stories high, two hundred stories high, far above the height of buildings as we know them now. New cities with great towers must rise in the plain, cities higher than mountains, cities with room for 400,000,000 to live, or that part of 400,000,000 who wish to live high in a landscape of peaks and spires, cliffs and precipices. For the others, for those who wish to live on the ground and with the ground, there will then be new room to live—the traditional small town will be able to survive, as will the old neighborhoods in the cities. But first a way must be found to build upward, to triple and triple again the height of all buildings as we know them now.

Picture, if you please, an open space where twenty acrobats stand, each locking hands with two different partners. Conceive then of ten acrobats standing on the shoulders of these twenty, and five upon the ten acrobats, and three more in turn above them, then two, then one. We have a pyramid of figures: six thousand to eight thousand pounds is supported upon a base of twenty pairs of shoes.

It enables one to think of structures more complex, of pyramids of steel which rise to become towers. Imagine a tower half a mile high and stressed to bear a vast load. Think of six or eight such towers and of bridges built between them, even as huge vines tie the branches of one high tree to another; think of groups of apartments built above these bridges (like the shops on the Ponte Vecchio in Florence) and apartments suspended beneath each bridge, and smaller bridges running from one complex of apartments to another, and of apartments suspended from cables, apartments kept in harmonious stress to one another by cables between them.

One can now begin to conceive of a city, or a separate part of a city, which is as high as it is wide, a city which bends ever so subtly in a high wind with the most delicate flexing of its near-to-number-less parts even as the smallest strut in a great bridge reflects the passing of an automobile with some fine-tuned quiver. In the subtlety of its swayings the vertical city might seem to be ready to live itself. It might be agreeable to live there.

The real question, however, has not yet been posed. It is whether a large fraction of the population would find it reasonable to live one hundred or two hundred stories in the air. There is the dread of heights. Would that tiny pit of suicide, planted like the small seed of murder in civilized man, flower prematurely into breakdown, terror and dread? Would it demand too much of a tenant to stare down each morning on a flight of 2,000 feet? Or would it prove a deliverance for some? Would the juvenile delinquent festering in the violence of his monotonous corridors diminish in his desire for brutality if he lived high in the air and found the intensity of his inexpressible vision matched by the intensity of the space through a fall?

That question returns us to the perspective of twentieth-century man. Caught between our desire to cling to the earth and to explore the stars, it is not impossible that a new life lived half a mile in the air, with streets in the clouds and chasms beyond each railing could prove nonetheless more intimate and more personal to us than the present congestions of the housing-project city. For that future man would be returned some individuality from his habitation. His apartment in the sky would be not so very different in its internal details from the apartments of his neighbors, no more than one apartment is varied from another in Washington Square Village. But his situation would now be different from any other. His windows would look out on a view of massive constructions and airy bridges, of huge vaults and fine intricacies. The complexity of our culture could be captured again by the imagination of the architect:

our buildings could begin to look a little less like armored tanks and more like clipper ships. Would we also then feel the dignity of sailors on a four-master at sea? Living so high, thrust into space, might we be returned to that mixture of awe and elation, of dignity and self-respect and a hint of dread, that sense of zest which a man must have known working his way out along a yardarm in a stiff breeze at sea? Would the fatal monotony of mass culture dissolve a hint before the quiet swaying of a great and vertical city?

b) A Statement for *Architectural Forum*

The essence of totalitarianism is that it beheads. It beheads individuality, variety, dissent, extreme possibility, romantic faith; it blinds vision, deadens instinct; it obliterates the past. It makes factories look like college campuses or mental hospitals, where once factories had the specific beauty of revealing their huge and sometimes brutal function. It makes the new buildings on college campuses look like factories. It depresses the average American with the unconscious recognition that he is installed in a gelatin of totalitarian environment which is bound to deaden his most individual efforts. This new architecture, this totalitarian architecture, destroys the past. There is no trace of the forms which lived in the centuries before us, none of their arrogance, their privilege, their aspiration, their canniness, their creations, their vulgarities. We are left with less and less sense of the lives of men and women who came before us. So we are less able to judge the psychotic values of the present: overkill, fallout shelters, and adjurations . . . to drink a glass of milk each day. . . .

People who admire the new architecture find it of value because it obliterates the past. They are sufficiently totalitarian to wish to avoid the consequences of the past. Which of course is not to say that they see themselves as totalitarian. The totalitarian passion is an unconscious one. Which liberal, fighting for bigger housing and additional cubic feet of air space in elementary schools, does not see himself as a benefactor? Can he comprehend that the somewhat clammy pleasure he obtains from looking at the completion of the new school—that architectural horror!—is a reflection of a buried and ugly pleasure, a totalitarian glee that the Gothic knots and Romanesque oppressions which entered his psyche through the schoolhouses of his youth have now been excised? But those architectural wounds, those forms from his childhood, not only shamed him and scored him, but marked upon him as well a wound from culture itself—its buried message of the cruelty and horror which were rooted in the majesties of the past. Now the flat surfaces, blank ornamentation, and pastel colors of the new schoolhouses will maroon his children in an endless hallway of the present. A school is an *arena* to a child. Let it look like what it should be, mysterious, even gladiatorial, rather than look like a reception center for war brides. The totalitarian impulse not only washes away distinctions but looks for a style in buildings, in clothing, and in the ornamentations of tools, appliances, and daily objects which will diminish one's sense of function and reduce one's sense of reality by reducing such emotions as awe, dread, beauty, pity, terror, calm, horror, and harmony. By dislocating us from the most powerful emotions of reality, totalitarianism leaves us further isolated in the empty landscapes of psychosis, precisely that inner landscape of void and dread which we flee by turning to totalitarian styles of life. The totalitarian liberal looks for new schools and more desks; the real liberal looks for more difficult books to force upon the curriculum. A good school can survive in a converted cow barn.

Yes, the people who admire the new architecture are looking to eject into their environment and landscape the same deadness and monotony life has put into them. A vast deadness and a huge monotony, a nausea without spasm, has been part of the profit of American life in the last fifteen years—we will pay in the next fifteen as this living death is disgorged into the buildings our totalitarian managers will manage to erect for us.

Our commodities are swollen in price by false, needless and useless labor. Modern architecture is the child of this fact. It works with a currency which (measured in terms of the skilled and/or useful labor going into a building) is worth half the real value of nineteenth-century money. The mechanical advances in construction hardly begin to make up for the wastes of advertising, public relations, building union covenants, city grafts, land costs, and the anemia of a dollar diminished by armaments and taxes. In this context the formulas of modern architecture have triumphed, and her bastards —those new office skyscrapers—proliferate everywhere: one suspects the best reason is that modern architecture offers a pretext to a large real-estate operator to stick up a skyscraper at a fraction of the money it should cost, so helps him to conceal the criminal fact that we are being given a stricken building, a denuded, aseptic, unfinished work, stripped of ornament, origins, prejudices, not even a peaked roof or spire to engage the heavens.

It is too cheap to separate Mafia architects with their Mussolini Modern (concrete dormitories on junior-college campuses) from serious modern architects. No, I think Le Corbusier and Wright and all the particular giants of the Bauhaus are the true villains; the Mafia architects are their proper sons; modern architecture at its best is even more anomalous than at its worst, for it tends to excite the Faustian and empty appetites of the architect's ego rather than reveal an artist's vision of our collective desire for shelter which is pleasurable, substantial, intricate, intimate, delicate, detailed, foibled, rich in gargoyle, guignol, false closet, secret stair, witch's hearth, attic, grandeur, kitsch, a world of buildings as diverse as the need within the eye. Beware: the ultimate promise of modern architecture is collective sightlessness for the species.

POLITICS AND
THE ENGLISH LANGUAGE

George Orwell

Most people who bother with the matter at all would admit that the English language is in a bad way, but it is generally assumed that we cannot by conscious action do anything about it. Our civilization is decadent and our language—so the argument runs—must inevitably share in the general collapse. It follows that any struggle against the abuse of language is a sentimental archaism, like preferring candles to electric light or hansom cabs to aeroplanes. Underneath this lies the half-conscious belief that language is a natural growth and not an instrument which we shape for our own purposes.

Now, it is clear that the decline of a language must ultimately have political and economic causes: it is not due simply to the bad influence of this or that individual writer. But an effect can become a cause, reinforcing the original cause and producing the same effect in an intensified form, and so on indefinitely. A man may take to drink because he feels himself to be a failure, and then fail all the more completely because he drinks. It is rather the same thing that is happening to the English language. It becomes ugly and inaccurate because our thoughts are foolish, but the slovenliness of our language makes it easier for us to have foolish thoughts. The point is

POLITICS AND THE ENGLISH LANGUAGE: From *Shooting an Elephant and Other Essays*, copyright, 1945, 1946, 1949, 1950 by Sonia Brownell Orwell. Reprinted by permission of Harcourt, Brace & World, Inc. and Secker & Warburg.

that the process is reversible. Modern English, especially written English, is full of bad habits which spread by imitation and which can be avoided if one is willing to take the necessary trouble. If one gets rid of these habits one can think more clearly, and to think clearly is a necessary first step towards political regeneration: so that the fight against bad English is not frivolous and is not the exclusive concern of professional writers. I will come back to this presently, and I hope that by that time the meaning of what I have said here will have become clearer. Meanwhile, here are five specimens of the English language as it is now habitually written.

These five passages have not been picked out because they are especially bad—I could have quoted far worse if I had chosen—but because they illustrate various of the mental vices from which we now suffer. They are a little below the average, but are fairly representative samples. I number them so that I can refer back to them when necessary:

(1) I am not, indeed, sure whether it is not true to say that the Milton who once seemed not unlike a seventeenth-century Shelley had not become, out of an experience ever more bitter in each year, more alien [*sic*] to the founder of that Jesuit sect which nothing could induce him to tolerate.

Professor Harold Laski
(Essay in *Freedom of Expression*)

(2) Above all, we cannot play ducks and drakes with a native battery of idioms which prescribes such egregious collocations of vocables as the Basic *put up with* for *tolerate* or *put at a loss* for *bewilder*.

Professor Lancelot Hogben (*Interglossa*)

(3) On the one side we have the free personality: by definition it is not neurotic, for it has neither conflict nor dream. Its desires, such as they are, are transparent, for they are just what institutional approval keeps in the forefront of consciousness; another institutional pattern would alter their number and intensity; there is little in them that is natural, irreducible, or culturally dangerous. But *on the other side*, the social bond itself is nothing but the mutual reflection of these self-secure integrities. Recall the definition of love. Is not this the very picture of a small academic? Where is there a place in this hall of mirrors for either personality or fraternity?

Essay on psychology in *Politics* (New York)

(4) All the "best people" from the gentlemen's clubs, and all the frantic fascist captains, united in common hatred of Socialism and bestial horror of the rising tide of the mass revolutionary movement, have turned to acts of provocation, to foul incendiarism, to medieval

legends of poisoned wells, to legalize their own destruction of proletarian organizations, and rouse the agitated petty-bourgeoisie to
chauvinistic fervor on behalf of the fight against the revolutionary
way out of the crisis.

Communist pamphlet

(5) If a new spirit *is* to be infused into this old country, there is one
thorny and contentious reform which must be tackled, and that is
the humanization and galvanization of the B.B.C. Timidity here will
bespeak canker and atrophy of the soul. The heart of Britain may
be sound and of strong beat, for instance, but the British lion's roar
at present is like that of Bottom in Shakespeare's *Midsummer Night's
Dream*—as gentle as any sucking dove. A virile new Britain cannot
continue indefinitely to be traduced in the eyes, or rather ears, of
the world by the effete languors of Langham Place, brazenly mas-
querading as "standard English." When the Voice of Britain is
heard at nine o'clock, better far and infinitely less ludicrous to hear
aitches honestly dropped than the present priggish, inflated, in-
hibited, school-ma'amish arch braying of blameless bashful mewing
maidens!

Letter in *Tribune*

Each of these passages has faults of its own, but, quite apart from
avoidable ugliness, two qualities are common to all of them. The
first is staleness of imagery; the other is lack of precision. The writer
either has a meaning and cannot express it, or he inadvertently says
something else, or he is almost indifferent as to whether his words
mean anything or not. This mixture of vagueness and sheer incom-
petence is the most marked characteristic of modern English prose,
and especially of any kind of political writing. As soon as certain
topics are raised, the concrete melts into the abstract and no one
seems able to think of turns of speech that are not hackneyed: prose
consists less and less of *words* chosen for the sake of their meaning,
and more and more of *phrases* tacked together like the sections of a
prefabricated hen-house. I list below, with notes and examples,
various of the tricks by means of which the work of prose-construc-
tion is habitually dodged:

Dying metaphors. A newly invented metaphor assists thought by
evoking a visual image, while on the other hand a metaphor which
is technically "dead" (e.g. *iron resolution*) has in effect reverted to
being an ordinary word and can generally be used without loss of
vividness. But in between these two classes there is a huge dump of
worn-out metaphors which have lost all evocative power and are
merely used because they save people the trouble of inventing

phrases for themselves. Examples are: *Ring the changes on, take up the cudgels for, toe the line, ride roughshod over, stand shoulder to shoulder with, play into the hands of, no axe to grind, grist to the mill, fishing in troubled waters, on the order of the day, Achilles' heel, swan song, hotbed.* Many of these are used without knowledge of their meaning (what is a "rift," for instance?), and incompatible metaphors are frequently mixed, a sure sign that the writer is not interested in what he is saying. Some metaphors now current have been twisted out of their original meaning without those who use them even being aware of the fact. For example, *toe the line* is sometimes written *tow the line*. Another example is *the hammer and the anvil*, now always used with the implication that the anvil gets the worst of it. In real life it is always the anvil that breaks the hammer, never the other way about: a writer who stopped to think what he was saying would be aware of this, and would avoid perverting the original phrase.

Operators or *verbal false limbs*. These save the trouble of picking out appropriate verbs and nouns, and at the same time pad each sentence with extra syllables which give it an appearance of symmetry. Characteristic phrases are *render inoperative, militate against, make contact with, be subjected to, give rise to, give grounds for, have the effect of, play a leading part (role) in, make itself felt, take effect, exhibit a tendency to, serve the purpose of*, etc., etc. The keynote is the elimination of simple verbs. Instead of being a single word, such as *break, stop, spoil, mend, kill*, a verb becomes a *phrase*, made up of a noun or adjective tacked on to some general-purposes verb such as *prove, serve, form, play, render*. In addition, the passive voice is wherever possible used in preference to the active, and noun constructions are used instead of gerunds (*by examination of* instead of *by examining*). The range of verbs is further cut down by means of the *-ize* and *de-* formations, and the banal statements are given an appearance of profundity by means of the *not un-* formation. Simple conjunctions and prepositions are replaced by such phrases as *with respect to, having regard to, the fact that, by dint of, in view of, in the interests of, on the hypothesis that*; and the ends of sentences are saved from anticlimax by such resounding common-places as *greatly to be desired, cannot be left out of account, a development to be expected in the near future, deserving of serious consideration, brought to a satisfactory conclusion*, and so on and so forth.

Pretentious diction. Words like *phenomenon, element, individual* (as noun), *objective, categorical, effective, virtual, basic, primary, promote, constitute, exhibit, exploit, utilize, eliminate, liquidate,* are used to dress up simple statements and give an air of scientific impartiality to biased judgments. Adjectives like *epoch-making, epic, historic, unforgettable, triumphant, age-old, inevitable, inexorable, veritable,* are used to dignify the sordid processes of international politics, while writing that aims at glorifying war usually takes on an archaic color, its characteristic words being: *realm, throne, chariot, mailed fist, trident, sword, shield, buckler, banner, jackboot, clarion.* Foreign words and expressions such as *cul de sac, ancien régime, deus ex machina, mutatis mutandis, status quo, gleichschaltung, weltanschauung,* are used to give an air of culture and elegance. Except for the useful abbreviations *i.e., e.g.,* and *etc.,* there is no real need for any of the hundreds of foreign phrases now current in English. Bad writers, and especially scientific, political and sociological writers, are nearly always haunted by the notion that Latin or Greek words like *expedite, ameliorate, predict, extraneous, deracinated, clandestine, subaqueous* and hundreds of others constantly gain ground from their Anglo-Saxon opposite numbers.[1] The jargon peculiar to Marxist writing (*hyena, hangman, cannibal, petty bourgeois, these gentry, lacquey, flunkey, mad dog, White Guard,* etc.) consists largely of words and phrases translated from Russian, German or French; but the normal way of coining a new word is to use a Latin or Greek root with the appropriate affix and, where necessary, the size formation. It is often easier to make up words of this kind (*deregionalize, impermissible, extramarital, nonfragmentary* and so forth) than to think up the English words that will cover one's meaning. The result, in general, is an increase in slovenliness and vagueness.

Meaningless words. In certain kinds of writing, particularly in art criticism and literary criticism, it is normal to come across long passages which are almost completely lacking in meaning.[2] Words like *romantic, plastic, values, human, dead, sentimental, natural,*

[1] An interesting illustration of this is the way in which the English flower names which were in use till very recently are being ousted by Greek ones, *snapdragon* becoming *antirrhinum, forget-me-not* becoming *myosotis,* etc. It is hard to see any practical reason for this change of fashion: it is probably due to an instinctive turning-away from the more homely word and a vague feeling that the Greek word is scientific.

[2] Example: "Comfort's catholicity of perception and image, strangely Whitmanesque in range, almost the exact opposite in aesthetic compulsion, continues to evoke that trembling atmospheric accumulative hinting at a cruel, an inexorably serene timelessness. . . . Wrey Gardiner scores by aiming at simple bull's-eyes with precision. Only they are not so simple, and through this contented sadness runs more than the surface bitter-sweet of resignation." (Poetry Quarterly)

vitality, as used in art criticism, are strictly meaningless, in the sense that they not only do not point to any discoverable object, but are hardly ever expected to do so by the reader. When one critic writes, "The outstanding feature of Mr. X's work is its living quality," while another writes, "The immediately striking thing about Mr. X's work is its peculiar deadness," the reader accepts this as a simple difference of opinion. If words like *black* and *white* were involved, instead of the jargon words *dead* and *living*, he would see at once that language was being used in an improper way. Many political words are similarly abused. The word *Fascism* has now no meaning except in so far as it signifies "something not desirable." The words *democracy, socialism, freedom, patriotic, realistic, justice*, have each of them several different meanings which cannot be reconciled with one another. In the case of a word like *democracy*, not only is there no agreed definition, but the attempt to make one is resisted from all sides. It is almost universally felt that when we call a country democratic we are praising it: consequently the defenders of every kind of régime claim that it is a democracy, and fear that they might have to stop using the word if it were tied down to any one meaning. Words of this kind are often used in a consciously dishonest way. That is, the person who uses them has his own private definition, but allows his hearer to think he means something quite different. Statements like *Marshal Pétain was a true patriot, The Soviet Press is the freest in the world, The Catholic Church is opposed to persecution*, are almost always made with intent to deceive. Other words used in variable meanings, in most cases more or less dishonestly, are: *class, totalitarian, science, progressive, reactionary, bourgeois, equality*.

Now that I have made this catalogue of swindles and perversions, let me give another example of the kind of writing that they lead to. This time it must of its nature be an imaginary one. I am going to translate a passage of good English into modern English of the worst sort. Here is a well-known verse from *Ecclesiastes:*

"I returned and saw under the sun, that the race is not to the swift, nor the battle to the strong, neither yet bread to the wise, nor yet riches to men of understanding, nor yet favour to men of skill; but time and chance happeneth to them all."

Here it is in modern English:

"Objective consideration of contemporary phenomena compels the conclusion that success or failure in competitive activities exhibits no tendency to be commensurate with innate capacity, but that a considerable element of the unpredictable must invariably be taken into account."

This is a parody, but not a very gross one. Exhibit (3), above, for instance, contains several patches of the same kind of English. It will be seen that I have not made a full translation. The beginning and ending of the sentence follow the original meaning fairly closely, but in the middle the concrete illustrations—race, battle, bread—dissolve into the vague phrase "success or failure in competitive activities." This had to be so, because no modern writer of the kind I am discussing—no one capable of using phrases like "objective consideration of contemporary phenomena"—would ever tabulate his thoughts in that precise and detailed way. The whole tendency of modern prose is away from concreteness. Now analyse these two sentences a little more closely. The first contains forty-nine words but only sixty syllables, and all its words are those of everyday life. The second contains thirty-eight words of ninety syllables: eighteen of its words are from Latin roots, and one from Greek. The first sentence contains six vivid images, and only one phrase ("time and chance") that could be called vague. The second contains not a single fresh, arresting phrase, and in spite of its ninety syllables it gives only a shortened version of the meaning contained in the first. Yet without a doubt it is the second kind of sentence that is gaining ground in modern English. I do not want to exaggerate. This kind of writing is not yet universal, and outcrops of simplicity will occur here and there in the worst-written page. Still, if you or I were told to write a few lines on the uncertainty of human fortunes, we should probably come much nearer to my imaginary sentence than to the one from *Ecclesiastes*.

As I have tried to show, modern writing at its worst does not consist in picking out words for the sake of their meaning and inventing images in order to make the meaning clearer. It consists in gumming together long strips of words which have already been set in order by someone else, and making the results presentable by sheer humbug. The attraction of this way of writing is that it is easy. It is easier—even quicker, once you have the habit—to say *In my opinion it is not an unjustifiable assumption that* than to say *I think*. If you use ready-made phrases, you not only don't have to hunt about for words; you also don't have to bother with the rhythms of your sentences, since these phrases are generally so arranged as to be more or less euphonious. When you are composing in a hurry—when you are dictating to a stenographer, for instance, or making a public speech—it is natural to fall into a pretentious, Latinized style. Tags like *a consideration which we should do well to bear in mind* or *a conclusion to which all of us would readily assent* will save many a sentence from coming down with a bump. By using stale metaphors, similes and idioms, you save much mental effort, at the cost of leaving your meaning vague, not only for your reader but for yourself. This is the significance of mixed metaphors. The sole aim of a metaphor is to call up a visual image. When these images clash— as in *The Fascist octopus has sung its swan song, the jackboot is thrown into the melting pot*—it can be taken as certain that the writer is not seeing a mental image of the objects he is naming; in other words he is not really thinking. Look again at the examples I gave at the beginning of this essay. Professor Laski (1) uses five negatives in fifty-three words. One of these is superfluous, making nonsense of the whole passage, and in addition there is the slip *alien* for akin, making further nonsense, and several avoidable pieces of clumsiness which increase the general vagueness. Professor Hogben (2) plays ducks and drakes with a battery which is able to write prescriptions, and, while disapproving of the everyday phrase *put up with*, is unwilling to look *egregious* up in the dictionary and see what it means; (3), if one takes an uncharitable attitude towards it, is simply meaningless: probably one could work out its intended meaning by reading the whole of the article in which it occurs. In (4), the writer knows more or less what he wants to say, but an accumulation of stale phrases chokes him like tea leaves blocking a sink. In (5), words and meaning have almost parted company. People who write in this manner usually have a general emotional meaning—they dislike one thing and want to express solidarity with another—but they are not interested in the detail of what they are saying. A scrupulous writer, in every sentence that he writes, will ask himself at least four questions, thus: What am I trying to say? What words will express it? What image or idiom will make it clearer? Is this image fresh enough to have an effect? And he will probably ask himself two more: Could I put it more shortly? Have I said anything that is avoidably ugly? But you are not obliged to go to all this trouble. You can shirk it by simply throwing your mind open and letting the ready-made phrases come crowding in. They will construct your sentences for you—even think your thoughts for you, to a certain extent—and at need they will perform the important service of partially concealing your meaning even from yourself. It is at this point that the special connection between politics and the debasement of language becomes clear.

In our time it is broadly true that political writing is bad writing. Where it is not true, it will generally be found that the writer is some kind of rebel, expressing his private opinions and not a "party line." Orthodoxy, of whatever color, seems to demand a lifeless, imitative style. The political dialects to be found in pamphlets, leading articles, manifestos, White Papers and the speeches of under-secretaries do, of course, vary from party to party, but they are all alike in that one almost never finds in them a fresh, vivid, home-made turn of speech. When one watches some tired hack on the platform mechanically repeating the familiar phrases—*bestial atrocities, iron heel, bloodstained tyranny, free peoples of the world, stand shoulder to shoulder*—one often has a curious feeling that one is not watching a live human being but some kind of dummy: a feeling which suddenly becomes stronger at moments when the light catches the speaker's spectacles and turns them into blank discs which seem to have no eyes behind them. And this is not altogether fanciful. A speaker who uses that kind of phraseology has gone some distance towards turning himself into a machine. The appropriate noises are coming out of his larynx, but his brain is not involved as it would be if he were choosing his words for himself. If the speech he is making is one that he is accustomed to make over and over again, he may be almost unconscious of what he is saying, as one is when one utters the responses in church. And this reduced state of consciousness, if not indispensable, is at any rate favorable to political conformity.

In our time, political speech and writing are largely the defence of the indefensible. Things like the continuance of British rule in India, the Russian purges and deportations, the dropping of the atom bombs on Japan, can indeed be defended, but only by arguments which are too brutal for most people to face, and which do not square with the professed aims of political parties. Thus political language has to consist largely of euphemism, question-begging and sheer cloudy vagueness. Defenceless villages are bombarded from the air, the inhabitants driven out into the countryside, the cattle machine-gunned, the huts set on fire with incendiary bullets: this is called *pacification*. Millions of peasants are robbed of their farms and sent trudging along the roads with no more than they can carry: this is called *transfer of population* or *rectification of frontiers*. People are imprisoned for years without trial, or shot in the back of the neck or sent to die of scurvy in Arctic lumber camps: this is called *elimination of unreliable elements*. Such phraseology is needed if one wants to name things without calling up mental pictures of them. Consider for instance some comfortable English professor defending Russian totalitarianism. He cannot say outright, "I believe in killing off your opponents when you can get good results by doing so." Probably, therefore, he will say something like this:

"While freely conceding that the Soviet régime exhibits certain features which the humanitarian may be inclined to deplore, we must, I think, agree that a certain curtailment of the right to political opposition is an unavoidable concomitant of transitional periods, and that the rigors which the Russian people have been called upon to undergo have been amply justified in the sphere of concrete achievement."

The inflated style is itself a kind of euphemism. A mass of Latin words falls upon the facts like soft snow, blurring the outlines and covering up all the details. The great enemy of clear language is insincerity. When there is a gap between one's real and one's declared aims, one turns as it were instinctively to long words and exhausted idioms, like a cuttlefish squirting out ink. In our age there is no such thing as "keeping out of politics." All issues are political issues, and politics itself is a mass of lies, evasions, folly, hatred and schizophrenia. When the general atmosphere is bad, language must suffer. I should expect to find—this is a guess which I have not sufficient knowledge to verify—that the German, Russian and Italian languages have all deteriorated in the last ten or fifteen years, as a result of dictatorship.

But if thought corrupts language, language can also corrupt thought. A bad usage can spread by tradition and imitation, even among people who should and do know better. The debased language that I have been discussing is in some ways very convenient. Phrases like *a not unjustifiable assumption, leaves much to be desired, would serve no good purpose, a consideration which we should do well to bear in mind*, are a continuous temptation, a packet of aspirins always at one's elbow. Look back through this essay, and for certain you will find that I have again and again committed the very faults I am protesting against. By this morning's post I have received a pamphlet dealing with conditions in Germany. The author tells me that he "felt impelled" to write it. I open it at random, and here is almost the first sentence that I see: "[The Allies] have an opportunity not only of achieving a radical transformation of Germany's social and political structure in such a way as to avoid a nationalistic reaction in Germany itself, but at the same time of laying the foundations of a co-operative and unified Europe." You see, he "feels impelled" to write—feels, presumably, that he has something new to say—and yet his words, like cavalry horses answering the bugle, group themselves automatically into the familiar dreary pattern. This invasion of one's mind by ready-made phrases (*lay the foundations, achieve a radical transformation*) can only be prevented if one is constantly on guard against them, and every such phrase anaesthetizes a portion of one's brain.

I said earlier that the decadence of our language is probably curable. Those who deny this would argue, if they produced an argument at all, that language merely reflects existing social conditions, and that we cannot influence its development by any direct tinkering with words and constructions. So far as the general tone or spirit of a language goes, this may be true, but it is not true in detail. Silly words and expressions have often disappeared, not through any evolutionary process but owing to the conscious action of a minority. Two recent examples were *explore every avenue* and *leave no stone unturned*, which were killed by the jeers of a few journalists. There is a long list of flyblown metaphors which could similarly be got rid of if enough people would interest themselves in the job; and it should also be possible to laugh the *not un-* formation out of existence,[3] to reduce the amount of Latin and Greek in the average sentence, to drive out foreign phrases and strayed scientific words, and, in general, to make pretentiousness unfashionable. But all these are minor points. The defence of the English language implies more than this, and perhaps it is best to start by saying what it does *not* imply.

To begin with it has nothing to do with archaism, with the salvaging of obsolete words and turns of speech, or with the setting up of a "standard English" which must never be departed from. On the contrary, it is especially concerned with the scrapping of every word or idiom which has outworn its usefulness. It has nothing to do with correct grammar and syntax, which are of no importance so long as one makes one's meaning clear, or with the avoidance of Americanisms, or with having what is called a "good prose style." On the other hand it is not concerned with fake simplicity and the attempt to make written English colloquial. Nor does it even imply in every case preferring the Saxon word to the Latin one, though it does imply using the fewest and shortest words that will cover one's meaning. What is above all needed is to let the meaning choose the word, and not the other way about. In prose, the worst thing one can do with words is to surrender to them. When you think of a concrete object, you think wordlessly, and then, if you want to describe the thing you have been visualizing you probably hunt about till you find the exact words that seem to fit it. When you think of something abstract you are more inclined to use words from the start, and unless you make a conscious effort to prevent it, the existing dialect will come rushing in and do the job for you, at the expense of blurring or even changing your meaning. Probably it is better to put off using words as long as possible and get one's mean-

[3] One can cure oneself of the *not un-* formation by memorizing this sentence: *A not unblack dog was chasing a not unsmall rabbit across a not ungreen field.*

ing as clear as one can through pictures or sensations. Afterwards one can choose—not simply *accept*—the phrases that will best cover the meaning, and then switch round and decide what impression one's words are likely to make on another person. This last effort of the mind cuts out all stale or mixed images, all prefabricated phrases, needless repetitions, and humbug and vagueness generally. But one can often be in doubt about the effect of a word or a phrase, and one needs rules that one can rely on when instinct fails. I think the following rules will cover most cases:

(i)   Never use a metaphor, simile or other figure of speech which you are used to seeing in print.

(ii) Never use a long word where a short one will do.

(iii) If it is possible to cut a word out, always cut it out.

(iv) Never use the passive where you can use the active.

(v)   Never use a foreign phrase, a scientific word or a jargon word if you can think of an everyday English equivalent.

(vi) Break any of these rules sooner than say anything outright barbarous.

These rules sound elementary, and so they are, but they demand a deep change of attitude in anyone who has grown used to writing in the style now fashionable. One could keep all of them and still write bad English, but one could not write the kind of stuff that I quoted in those five specimens at the beginning of this article.

I have not here been considering the literary use of language, but merely language as an instrument for expressing and not for concealing or preventing thought. Stuart Chase and others have come near to claiming that all abstract words are meaningless, and have used this as a pretext for advocating a kind of political quietism. Since you don't know what Fascism is, how can you struggle against Fascism? One need not swallow such absurdities as this, but one ought to recognize that the present political chaos is connected with the decay of language, and that one can probably bring about some improvement by starting at the verbal end. If you simplify your English, you are freed from the worst follies of orthodoxy. You cannot speak any of the necessary dialects, and when you make a stupid remark its stupidity will be obvious, even to yourself. Political language—and with variations this is true of all political parties, from Conservatives to Anarchists—is designed to make lies sound truthful and murder respectable, and to give an appearance of solidity to pure wind. One cannot change this all in a moment, but one can at least change one's own habits, and from time to time one can even, if one jeers loudly enough, send some worn-out and useless phrase—some *jackboot, Achilles' heel, hotbed, melting pot, acid test, veritable inferno* or other lump of verbal refuse—into the dustbin where it belongs.

THE DARLINGS AT
THE TOP OF THE STAIRS

James Thurber

Childhood used to end with the discovery that there is no Santa Claus. Nowadays, it too often ends when the child gets his first adult, the way Hemingway got his first rhino, with the difference that the rhino was charging Hemingway, whereas the adult is usually running from the child. This has brought about a change in the folklore and mythology of the American home, and of the homes of other off-spring-beleaguered countries. The dark at the top of the stairs once shrouded imaginary bears that lay in wait for tiny tots, but now parents, grandparents, and other grown relatives are afraid there may be a little darling lurking in the shadows, with blackjack, golf club, or .32-caliber automatic.

The worried psychologists, sociologists, anthropologists, and other ologists, who jump at the sound of every backfire or slammed door, have called our present jeopardy a "child-centered culture." Every seven seconds a baby is born in the United States, which means that we produce, every two hours, approximately five companies of infantry. I would say this amounts to a child-overwhelmed culture, but I am one of those who do not intend to surrender meekly and unconditionally. There must be a bright side to this menacing state of civilization, and if somebody will snap on his flashlight, we'll take a look around for it.

More has been written about the child than about any other age of man, and it is perhaps fortunate that the literature is now so extensive a child would have become twenty-one before its parents could get through half the books on how to bring it up. The trouble with the "child expert" is that he is so often a dedicated, or desiccated, expository writer and lecturer, and the tiny creative talents he attempts to cope with are beyond him. Margaret Mead, the American

THE DARLINGS AT THE TOP OF THE STAIRS: Copyright © 1960 James Thurber. From *Lanterns and Lances*, published by Harper and Row.

anthropologist, is an exception, for she realizes the dangers inherent in twisting infantile creativity into the patterns of adult propriety, politeness, and conformity. Let us glance at a few brief examples of creative literature in the very young, for which they should have been encouraged, not admonished.

The small girl critic who wrote, "This book tells me more about penguins than I wanted to know," has a technique of clarity and directness that might well be studied by the so-called mature critics of England and the United States, whose tendency, in dealing with books about penguins or anything else, is to write long autobiographical rambles.

Then there was the little American girl who was asked by her teacher to write a short story about her family. She managed it in a single true and provocative sentence: "Last night my daddy didn't come home at all." I told this to a five-year-old moppet I know and asked her if she could do as well, and she said, "Yes," and she did. Her short story, in its entirety, went like this: "My daddy doesn't take anything with him when he goes away except a nightie and whiskey."

I am known to parents as a disruptive force, if not indeed a naughty influence, upon my small colleagues in the field of imaginative writing. When Sally, aged four, told me, "I want to be a ghost," her mother said quickly, "No, you don't," and I said, "Yes, she does. Let her be a ghost. Maybe she will become another W. E. Henley, who wrote, 'And the world's a ghost that gleams, flickers, vanishes away.'"

"Who is W. E. Henley?" the child's mother asked uneasily.

"Wilhelmina Ernestine Henley," I explained. "A poet who became a ghost."

Her mother said she didn't want Sally to become a poet or a ghost, but a good wife and mother.

Finally, there was Lisa, aged five, whose mother asked her to thank my wife for the peas we had sent them the day before from our garden. "I thought the peas were awful, I wish you and Mrs. Thurber was dead, and I hate trees," said Lisa, thus conjoining in one creative splurge the nursery rhyme about pease porridge cold, the basic plot sense of James M. Cain, and Birnam wood moving upon Dunsinane. Lisa and I were the only unhorrified persons in the room when she brought this out. We knew that her desire to get rid of her mother and my wife at one fell swoop was a pure device of creative literature. As I explained to the two doomed ladies later, it is important to let your little daughters and sons kill you off figuratively, because this is a natural infantile urge that cannot safely be channeled into amenity or what Henry James called "the twaddle of graciousness." The child that is scolded or punished for its natural human desire to destroy is likely to turn later to the blackjack, the golf club, or the .32-caliber automatic.

The tiny twaddler of ungraciousness has my blessing, as you can see. You can also see that I am mainly concerned with the incipient, or burgeoning, creativity of the female child. This is because I am more interested in Thurber's theory of Elaine Vital, the female life force, than in Bergson's theory of Elan Vital, the masculine life force, which it seems to me is all he isolated. Elaine Vital, if properly directed—that is, let alone—may become the hope of the future. God knows we have enough women writers (at least one too many, if you ask me), but I believe they are the product of a confined and constrained infantile creativity. Being females, they have turned to the pen and the typewriter, instead of the blackjack, golf club, and .32-caliber automatic.

Boys are perhaps beyond the range of anybody's sure understanding, at least when they are between the ages of eighteen months and ninety years. They have got us into the human quandary, dilemma, plight, predicament, pickle, mess, pretty pass, and kettle of fish in which we now find ourselves. Little boys are much too much for me at my age, for it is they who have taken over the American home, physically. They are in charge of running everything, usually into the ground.

Most American parents will not answer the telephone when it rings, but will let a little boy do it. Telephone operators, I have been informed, now frequently say to a mumbling toddler, "Is there anyone older than you in the house?" Many of the tradespeople and artisans I deal with, or try to, in my part of Connecticut, go in for this form of evasionism. A small male child will pick up the receiver and burble into the transmitter. In this way urgency, or even crisis, is met with baby talk, or prattle tattle. The fact that my plumbing has let go or a ceiling is falling down is reduced, in this new system of non-communication, to a tiny, halting, almost inaudible recital of what happened to a teddy bear, or why cereal is not good with sliced bananas and should be thrown at Daddy. The tradesman or artisan and his wife are spared the knowledge of a larger disaster at the expense of the nerves and mental balance of the caller. I shall set down here an exasperating personal experience in this area of obfuscation.

"Oo tiss?" a tiny voice demanded when I called the plumber one day.

"This is Tanta Twaus," I said, "and Tanta Twaus won't give you any Twissmas pwesents this Twissmas if you do not put Mommy or Daddy on the other end of this doddam apparatus."

"Appawana?" asked the tiny voice. At this point his mother, like a woman in transport and on her third martini, grabbed up the receiver.

"He said, 'Appomattox,' didn't he?" she cried. "Isn't that wonderful?"

"Madam," I said, chilling the word, "the answer to the question I just put to your son is Waterloo, not Appomattox. The next voice you hear will be that of me, dying in the flood of broken pipes and the rubble of fallen ceilings." And I slammed up the receiver.

Ours is indeed a child-centered culture in the sense that the little boys have got me squarely centered in their gun sights. I shall continue to urge on the little girls who hate trees, are indifferent to penguins, envy Banquo, wish Mother were with the angels, and can read Daddy like a book. What you are going to do, I don't know, but I advise you to keep glancing over your shoulder, and look out for the darlings at the top of the stairs.

A GREAT DREAM COME TRUE

Edmund Wilson

The Empire State Building was the largest building in the world. The Radio City Music Hall in New York City is the largest theater in the world. It contains 6,200 seats, has a stage 144 feet wide and 80 feet deep, and cost $7,000,000. The Music Hall and its fellow, the RKO Roxy Theater, represented for Samuel L. Rothafel "the fulfillment of the aspirations of a lifetime, a great dream come true." He had already had a notable failure with one monster amusement palace; but, applying to the Rockefellers, under the sponsorship of Mr. Owen D. Young, that large-visioned electrical magnate, he was able to persuade these capitalists to back him in a second attempt on an even more tremendous scale. One of the features of the original Roxy's had been a bust of Napoleon in the lobby.

And in less than two years' time, over 11,000 tons of steel, over 9,600 tons of brick, had been assembled into two gigantic theaters

---

A GREAT DREAM COME TRUE: From *The American Earthquake*. Reprinted by permission of the author.

and a limestone-and-aluminum skyscraper, which makes against the pale New York sky what seems a sheer shaft of packed sand.

Outside, a long aluminum-gray strip winks "Radio City" vertically in rose-red neon letters. The lobby is paved with mats in subdued colors, brown and gray, and from the ceiling shine round light-reflectors with black-blobbed bulbs in the centers, like the eyes of enormous Mickey Mice.

Inside, the Grand Foyer has a majesty which might be described as imperial if it were not entirely meaningless. Against walls of henna-red, with wainscots of dried-blood-red marble, rise mirror-lengths, framed in long gray curtains and with cylindrical lusters embedded in them, to the height of the highest mezzanine; but if one looks up past the chandeliers—two immense cylinder-shaped crystal tassels—one finds that the distant ceiling, a reddish cartridge-copper and studded with unpunctured cartridge-tops, contracts the vertiginous hall to the shape of a straight tin canteen. The doors that swing into the auditorium are bossed with bronze plaques by Paul Manship, on which, interposing the Orient between Roxy and his vaudeville art, he has managed to reduce the idea of a song-and-dance team, a trained-seal act, a wild-animal act, etc., to his conventionalized smoothness and roundness. And what has become of the still-lifes of Picasso, Léger, and Braque?—they lie like autumn leaves underfoot, their banjos and guitars, their broken surfaces, uniformly brown and gray now, trodden into the pattern of the carpet, which stretches away and away. It extends up a giant staircase, which mounts to a greenish-and-brownish mural: "the upward march of mankind," in dim unconvincing figures and pale decorative colors.

The Grand Lounge installed in the basement is suggestive of a cave of mystery at some amusement park. Large bright gray diamonds in the ceiling are made to shed a sort of indoor twilight on dim gray diamonds on the floor. Diamond-shaped pillars, black and polished, reflect the lounge as a maze of lozenges. On a background of pale crinkled curtains, zigzagged with zebra-stripes, a number of big round frameless mirrors take the pillars as polished black streaks. A dancer by Zorach, dull silver, a giantess with legs like thick lead pipes and a rounded wad of hair like a lead sinker, kneels stiffly and stiff-neckedly turns her head.

The auditorium itself—from the point of view of comfort, quite perfect—rather gives one the impression of being inside a telescopic drinking-cup. Under magnificent looped-up portières—revealed by another curtain that opens and closes like a camera shutter and needs thirteen electric motors to work it—and to the music of a gigantic orchestra that rises on an elevator, a veritable grandstandful of girls, in green and red Indian headdresses and equipped with tambourines and fans, sing *My Old Kentucky Home, Dixie* and other beloved Southern melodies, with a vast heart-shaped lace valentine for background.

In the center sits poor old DeWolf Hopper keeping time with one foot. It is about the only thing he can do. You feel melancholy as you see him and Weber and Fields, ineffective in the enormous theater, abjectly delivering lines about the greatness of Rockefeller Center. First—as these remind you—there was Weber and Fields, a show that people visited like a household; then there were the "extravaganzas," the equivalent of English pantomimes, with favorite funny men and fairy-tale stories—*Bluebeard, The Wizard of Oz, Babes in Toyland,* etc.—usually framed among the blue and green peacocks of the pre-Ziegfield New Amsterdam Theater; then, later, there were the Hippodrome shows, which, though too big for personalities—with the exception of the great Spanish clown Marceline—though lacking in human interest, had something of the excitement of a circus; then there were the Ziegfield Follies, which, framed richly by their gold proscenium, caught the speed, the intensity, the savagery, the luxury, the dazzle of the city. And now there is the Radio City Music Hall, the most elaborate theater ever built—a theater not merely too huge for personality, story, intensity, but actually too big for a show.

The performance with which the Music Hall opened scarcely survived even the first night. On such a stage, the frame, although gorgeous, is so far beyond and away from the actor that it can no longer focus interest on him: he might as well be trying to hold an audience in the grand concourse of the Pennsylvania Station. Even the girls cannot make much impression except by appearing in quantity and executing "precision" dances that suggest setting-up exercises. One can almost believe them controlled by a photo-electric cell. The comedians and the singers have actually been partly electrified: though their faces may go for nothing, their voices have been swollen by loud-speakers—fifty—till they devour the whole house. And they also talk into microphones for the benefit of radio audiences—with an effect rather disconcerting on the audience in the theater who have paid. The theater is, thus, no longer really a theater, but rather a source of canalized entertainment; the performance is no longer for you, but something that is also directed at thousands of scattered old ladies sitting around in mortgaged farmhouses, at thousands of stocking-footed men reading the paper in Statler hotels.

As for the program, there was a tabloid version of *Carmen,* which resembled one of those fifteen-minute film prologues but which in this case had the added demerit of not leading up to a film. And, at one point, an army of toe-dancers burst out of surprise entrances in the audience, grouped itself as a great white wedding cake, and enacted the death of a Long Island swan farm on a slowly revolving turntable. A serious German dancer, whose inclusion seems to have been due—like the works by Manship and Zorach—to Roxy's imperial desire to have a little of the best of everything—this unfortunate German dancer had apparently missed fire so badly in the first two or three performances with a ballet called *The Angel of Death* that he was provided with a humorous announcer who gave a kidding account of the scenario and caused some to think it was meant to be funny.

Nor was the spectacle confined to the stage. It was contrived that the immense auditorium itself should change color, with every new number, like the inside of a chameleon watermelon. This was supposed to represent "a stylized sunset, an idea conceived by Roxy while standing on a ship's deck at dawn." The half-circle of the stage is the sun, and the watermelon stripes are rays, which run through a gamut of lavender on green, red on green, red on red, etc. There are no less than two hundred spotlights, each capable of forty changes. Two strong-lunged cathedral organs play *Leave the Dishes in the Sink*.

And Roxy himself, the Sun King, has quarters befitting his rank. He has had installed, above the Music Hall, an apartment of which the equipment and furnishings—charged to the Rockefellers as part of the opening expenses—cost $250,000. There is a dining room nineteen feet high, with a separate solid silver service for each of the three meals, and there is a dining staff which includes a chef, a pastry cook, a headwaiter and two other waiters. These are supposed to be in constant readiness to serve up, at short notice, a dinner for as many as thirty people. The pots and pans in the kitchen alone cost $2,200.

But Roxy was unable to do the honors. Though the Rockefellers, Owen D. Young, Will Hays and Nicholas Murray Butler all loyally attended his openings, the auspices were already ominous. Roxy himself had fallen ill, and, the night of the second opening, was removed from the theater on a stretcher. It was decided that the Radio City Music Hall, though a flop on an unheard-of scale, was unmistakably, irretrievably a flop, and that it would have to be turned into a cinema.

When Roxy had got well enough to be interviewed, he was invited to make a statement on the present depression. "All you can do," he said, "is spread your feet a little wider and stand it. Don't ever sell this country short. We'll all be proud of this country some day. Proud of America like an Englishman is proud of England after he has gone to see *Cavalcade!*"

I remember him as I saw him once some fifteen years ago, with his little round head and straight talk, in a discussion with other men of the movies. I remember how his energy and assurance seemed to contrast with the qualities of the rest, and I regret that he should have been encouraged to make such a fool of himself. There are people who have never recovered from the fantastic ambitions and imaginings engendered by the boom of the twenties.

Apparently the only person who has been pleased by the opening of the Music Hall is a veteran financier who was at one time roughly handled by Rockefeller. "Think of that son of a bitch Rockefeller," he is said to have exclaimed with jubilation, "losing $100,000 a week!"

1934

1957. Radio City Music Hall has prospered as a movie theater and makes use of its stage facilities with an elaborate spectacle that precedes the film.

CLEAN FUN AT RIVERHEAD

Tom Wolfe

The inspiration for the demolition derby came to Lawrence Mendelsohn one night in 1958 when he was nothing but a spare-ribbed twenty-eight-year-old stock-car driver halfway through his 10th lap around the Islip, L.I., Speedway and taking a curve too wide. A lubberly young man with a Chicago boxcar haircut came up on the inside in a 1949 Ford and caromed him 12 rows up into the grandstand, but Lawrence Mendelsohn and his entire car did not hit one spectator.

"That was what got me," he said, "I remember I was hanging upside down from my seat belt like a side of Jersey bacon and wondering why no one was sitting where I hit. 'Lousy promotion,' I said to myself.

"Not only that, but everybody who *was* in the stands forgot

CLEAN FUN AT RIVERHEAD: Reprinted with the permission of Farrar, Straus & Giroux, Inc. From *The Kandy-Kolored Tangerine Flake Streamline Baby* by Tom Wolfe. Copyright © 1963 by the New York Herald Tribune Inc.

about the race and came running over to look at me gift-wrapped upside down in a fresh pile of junk."

At that moment occurred the transformation of Lawrence Mendelsohn, racing driver, into Lawrence Mendelsohn, promoter, and, a few transactions later, owner of the Islip Speedway, where he kept seeing more of this same underside of stock car racing that everyone in the industry avoids putting into words. Namely, that for every purist who comes to see the fine points of the race, such as who is going to win, there are probably five waiting for the wrecks to which stock car racing is so gloriously prone.

The pack will be going into a curve when suddenly two cars, three cars, four cars tangle, spinning and splattering all over each other and the retaining walls, upside down, right side up, inside out and in pieces, with the seams bursting open and discs, rods, wires and gasoline spewing out and yards of sheet metal shearing off like Reynolds Wrap and crumpling into the most baroque shapes, after which an ash-blue smoke starts seeping up from the ruins and a thrill begins to spread over the stands like Newburg sauce.

So why put up with the monotony between crashes?

Such, in brief, is the early history of what is culturally the most important sport ever originated in the United States, a sport that ranks with the gladiatorial games of Rome as a piece of national symbolism. Lawrence Mendelsohn had a vision of an automobile sport that would be all crashes. Not two cars, not three cars, not four cars, but 100 cars would be out in an arena doing nothing but smashing each other into shrapnel. The car that outrammed and out-dodged all the rest, the last car that could still move amid the smoking heap, would take the prize money.

So at 8:15 at night at the Riverhead Raceway, just west of Riverhead, L.I., on Route 25, amid the quaint tranquility of the duck and turkey farm flatlands of eastern Long Island, Lawrence Mendelsohn stood up on the back of a flat truck in his red neon warmup jacket and lectured his 100 drivers on the rules and niceties of the new game, the "demolition derby." And so at 8:30 the first 25 cars moved out onto the raceway's quarter-mile stock car track. There was not enough room for 100 cars to mangle each other. Lawrence Mendelsohn's dream would require four heats. Now the 25 cars were placed at intervals all about the circumference of the track, making flatulent revving noises, all headed not around the track but toward a point in the center of the infield.

Then the entire crowd, about 4,000, started chanting a countdown, "Ten, nine, eight, seven, six, five, four, three, two," but it was impossible to hear the rest, because right after "two" half the crowd went into a strange whinnying wail. The starter's flag went up, and the 25 cars took off, roaring into second gear with no mufflers, all headed toward that same point in the center of the infield, converging nose on nose.

The effect was exactly what one expects that many simultaneous crashes to produce: the unmistakable tympany of automobiles colliding and cheap-gauge sheet metal buckling; front ends folding together at the same cockeyed angles police photographs of nighttime wreck scenes capture so well on grainy paper; smoke pouring from under the hoods and hanging over the infield like a howitzer cloud; a few of the surviving cars lurching eccentrically on bent axles. At last, after four heats, there were only two cars moving through the junk, a 1953 Chrysler and a 1958 Cadillac. In the Chrysler a small fascia of muscles named Spider Ligon, who smoked a cigar while he drove, had the Cadillac cornered up against a guard rail in front of the main grandstand. He dispatched it by swinging around and backing full throttle through the left side of its grille and radiator.

By now the crowd was quite beside itself. Spectators broke through a gate in the retaining screen. Some rushed to Spider Ligon's car, hoisted him to their shoulders and marched off the field, howling. Others clambered over the stricken cars of the defeated, enjoying the details of their ruin, and howling. The good, full cry of triumph and annihilation rose from Riverhead Raceway, and the demolition derby was over.

That was the 154th demolition derby in two years. Since Lawrence Mendelsohn staged the first one at Islip Speedway in 1961, they have been held throughout the United States at the rate of one every five days, resulting in the destruction of about 15,000 cars. The figures alone indicate a gluttonous appetite for the sport. Sports writers, of course, have managed to ignore demolition derbies even more successfully than they have ignored stock car racing and drag racing. All in all, the new automobile sports have shown that the sports pages, which on the surface appear to hum with life and earthiness, are at bottom pillars of gentility. This drag racing and demolition derbies and things, well, there are too many kids in it with sideburns, tight Levis and winkle-picker boots.

Yet the demolition derbies keep growing on word-of-mouth publicity. The "nationals" were held last month at Langhorne, Pa., with 50 cars in the finals, and demolition derby fans everywhere know that Don McTavish, of Dover, Mass., is the new world's champion. About 1,250,000 spectators have come to the 154 contests held so far. More than 75 per cent of the derbies have drawn full houses.

The nature of their appeal is clear enough. Since the onset of the Christian era, i.e., since about 500 A.D., no game has come along to fill the gap left by the abolition of the purest of all sports, gladiatorial combat. As late as 300 A.D. these bloody duels, usually between men but sometimes between women and dwarfs, were enormously popular not only in Rome but throughout the Roman Empire. Since then no game, not even boxing, has successfully acted out the underlying motifs of most sport, that is, aggression and destruction.

Boxing, of course, is an aggressive sport, but one contestant has actually destroyed the other in a relatively small percentage of matches. Other games are progressively more sublimated forms of sport. Often, as in the case of football, they are encrusted with oddments of passive theology and metaphysics to the effect that the real purpose of the game is to foster character, teamwork, stamina, physical fitness and the ability to "give-and-take."

But not even those wonderful clergymen who pray in behalf of Congress, expressway ribbon-cuttings, urban renewal projects and testimonial dinners for ethnic aldermen would pray for a demolition derby. The demolition derby is, pure and simple, a form of gladiatorial combat for our times.

As hand-to-hand combat has gradually disappeared from our civilization, even in wartime, and competition has become more and more sophisticated and abstract, Americans have turned to the automobile to satisfy their love of direct aggression. The mild-mannered man who turns into a bear behind the wheel of a car—i.e., who finds in the power of the automobile a vehicle for the release of his inhibitions—is part of American folklore. Among teen-agers the automobile has become the symbol, and in part the physical means, of triumph over family and community restrictions. Seventy-five per cent of all car thefts in the United States are by teen-agers out for "joy rides."

The symbolic meaning of the automobile tones down but by no means vanishes in adulthood. Police traffic investigators have long been convinced that far more accidents are purposeful crashes by belligerent drivers than they could ever prove. One of the heroes of the era was the Middle Eastern diplomat who rammed a magazine writer's car from behind in the Kalorama embassy district of Washington two years ago. When the American bellowed out the window at him, he backed up and smashed his car again. When the fellow leaped out of his car to pick a fight, he backed up and smashed his car a third time, then drove off. He was recalled home for having "gone native."

The unabashed, undisguised, quite purposeful sense of destruction of the demolition derby is its unique contribution. The aggression, the battering, the ruination are there to be enjoyed. The crowd at a demolition derby seldom gasps and often laughs. It enjoys the same full-throated participation as Romans at the Colosseum. After each trial or heat at a demolition derby, two drivers go into the finals. One is the driver whose car was still going at the end. The other is the driver the crowd selects from among the 24 vanquished on the basis of his courage, showmanship or simply the awesomeness of his crashes. The numbers of the cars are read over loudspeakers, and the crowd chooses one with its cheers. By the same token, the crowd may force a driver out of competition if he appears cowardly or merely cunning. This is the sort of driver who drifts around the edge of the battle avoiding crashes with the hope that the other cars will eliminate one another. The umpire waves a yellow flag at him and he must crash into someone within 30 seconds or run the risk of being booed off the field in dishonor and disgrace.

The frank relish of the crowd is nothing, however, compared to the kick the contestants get out of the game. It costs a man an average of $50 to retrieve a car from a junk yard and get it running for a derby. He will only get his money back—$50—for winning a heat. The chance of being smashed up in the madhouse first 30 seconds of a round are so great, even the best of drivers faces long odds in his shot at the $500 first prize. None of that matters to them.

Tommy Fox, who is nineteen, said he entered the demolition derby because, "You know, it's fun. I like it. You know what I mean?" What was fun about it? Tommy Fox had a way of speaking that was much like the early Marlon Brando. Much of what he had to say came from the trapezii, which he rolled quite a bit, and the forehead, which he cocked, and the eyebrows, which he could bring together expressively from time to time. "Well," he said, "you know, like when you hit 'em, and all that. It's fun."

Tommy Fox had a lot of fun in the first heat. Nobody was bashing around quite like he was in his old green Hudson. He did not win, chiefly because he took too many chances, but the crowd voted him into the finals as the best showman.

"I got my brother," said Tommy. "I came in from the side and he didn't even see me."

His brother is Don Fox, thirty-two, who owns the junk yard where they both got their cars. Don likes to hit them, too, only he likes it almost too much. Don drives with such abandon, smashing into the first car he can get a shot at and leaving himself wide open, he does not stand much chance of finishing the first three minutes.

For years now sociologists have been calling upon one another to undertake a serious study of America's "car culture." No small part of it is the way the automobile has, for one very large segment of the population, become the focus of the same sort of quasi-religious dedication as art is currently for another large segment of a higher social order. Tommy Fox is unemployed, Don Fox runs a junk yard, Spider Ligon is a maintenance man for Brookhaven Naval Laboratory, but to categorize them as such is getting no closer to the truth than to have categorized William Faulkner in 1926 as a clerk at Lord & Taylor, although he was.

Tommy Fox, Don Fox and Spider Ligon are acolytes of the car culture, an often esoteric world of arts and sciences that came into its own after World War II and now has believers of two generations. Charlie Turbush, thirty-five, and his son, Buddy, seventeen, were two more contestants, and by no stretch of the imagination can they be characterized as bizarre figures or cultists of the death wish. As for the dangers of driving in a demolition derby, they are quite real by all physical laws. The drivers are protected only by crash helmets, seat belts and the fact that all glass, interior handles, knobs and fixtures have been removed. Yet Lawrence Mendelsohn claims that there have been no serious injuries in 154 demolition derbies and now gets his insurance at a rate below that of stock car racing.

The sport's future may depend in part on word getting around about its relative safety. Already it is beginning to draw contestants here and there from social levels that could give the demolition derby the cachet of respectability. In eastern derbies so far two doctors and three young men of more than passable connections in eastern society have entered under whimsical *noms de combat* and emerged neither scarred nor victorious. Bull fighting had to win the same social combat.

All of which brings to mind that fine afternoon when some high-born Roman women were out in Nero's box at the Colosseum watching this sexy Thracian carve an ugly little Samnite up into prime cuts, and one said, darling, she had an inspiration, and Nero, needless to say, was all for it. Thus began the new vogue of Roman socialites fighting as gladiators themselves, for kicks. By the second century A.D. even the Emperor Commodus was out there with a tiger's head as a helmet hacking away at some poor dazed fall guy. He did a lot for the sport. Arenas sprang up all over the empire like shopping center bowling alleys.

The future of the demolition derby, then, stretches out over the face of America. The sport draws no lines of gender, and post-debs may reach Lawrence Mendelsohn at his office in Deer Park.

A Narrative and Critical Response

STEPHEN CRANE'S OWN STORY

He Tells How the Commodore Was Wrecked
and How He Escaped

FEAR-CRAZED NEGRO NEARLY SWAMPS BOAT

Young Writer Compelled to Work in Stifling Atmosphere
of the Fire Room

BRAVERY OF CAPTAIN MURPHY AND HIGGINS

Tried to Tow Their Companions Who Were on the Raft—
Last Dash for the Shore Through the Surf

JACKSONVILLE, FLA., Jan. 6.—It was the afternoon of New Year's. The Commodore lay at her dock in Jacksonville and negro stevedores processioned steadily toward her with box after box of ammunition and bundle after bundle of rifles. Her hatch, like the mouth of a monster, engulfed them. It might have been the feeding time of some legendary creature of the sea. It was in broad daylight and the crowd of gleeful Cubans on the pier did not forbear to sing the strange patriotic ballads of their island.

Everything was perfectly open. The Commodore was cleared with a cargo of arms and munition for Cuba. There was none of that extreme modesty about the proceeding which had marked previous departures of the famous tug. She loaded up as placidly as if she were going to carry oranges to New York, instead of Remingtons to Cuba. Down the river, furthermore, the revenue cutter Boutwell, the old isosceles triangle that protects United States interests in the St. John's, lay at anchor, with no sign of excitement aboard her.

392

EXCHANGING FAREWELLS

On the decks of the Commodore there were exchanges of farewells in two languages. Many of the men who were to sail upon her had many intimates in the old Southern town, and we who had left our friends in the remote North received our first touch of melancholy on witnessing these strenuous and earnest goodbys.

It seems, however, that there was more difficulty at the custom house. The officers of the ship and the Cuban leaders were detained there until a mournful twilight settled upon the St. John's, and through a heavy fog the lights of Jacksonville blinked dimly. Then at last the Commodore swung clear of the dock, amid a tumult of goodbys. As she turned her bow toward the distant sea the Cubans ashore cheered and cheered. In response the Commodore gave three long blasts of her whistle, which even to this time impressed me with their sadness. Somehow, they sounded as wails.

Then at last we began to feel like filibusters. I don't suppose that the most stolid brain could contrive to believe that there is not a mere trifle of danger in filibustering, and so as we watched the lights of Jacksonville swing past us and heard the regular thump, thump, thump of the engines we did considerable reflecting.

But I am sure that there were no hifalutin emotions visible upon any of the faces which fronted the speeding shore. In fact, from cook's boy to captain, we were all enveloped in a gentle satisfaction and cheerfulness. But less than two miles from Jacksonville, this atrocious fog caused the pilot to ram the bow of the Commodore hard upon the mud and in this ignominious position we were compelled to stay until daybreak.

HELP FROM THE BOUTWELL

It was to all of us more than a physical calamity. We were now no longer filibusters. We were men on a ship stuck in the mud. A certain mental somersault was made once more necessary.

But word had been sent to Jacksonville to the captain of the revenue cutter Boutwell, and Captain Kilgore turned out promptly and generously fired up his old triangle, and came at full speed to our assistance. She dragged us out of the mud, and again we headed for the mouth of the river. The revenue cutter pounded along a half mile astern of us, to make sure that we did not take on board at some place along the river men for the Cuban army.

This was the early morning of New Year's Day, and the fine

golden southern sunlight fell full upon the river. It flashed over the ancient Boutwell, until her white sides gleamed like pearl, and her rigging was spun into little threads of gold.

Cheers greeted the old Commodore from passing ship and from the shore. It was a cheerful, almost merry, beginning to our voyage. At Mayport, however, we changed our river pilot for a man who could take her to open sea, and again the Commodore was beached. The Boutwell was fussing around us in her venerable way, and, upon seeing our predicament, she came again to assist us, but this time, with engines reversed, the Commodore dragged herself away from the grip of the sand and again headed for the open sea.

The captain of the revenue cutter grew curious. He hailed the Commodore: "Are you fellows going to sea to-day?"

Captain Murphy of the Commodore called back: "Yes, sir."

And then as the whistle of the Commodore saluted him, Captain Kilgore doffed his cap and said: "Well, gentlemen, I hope you have a pleasant cruise," and this was our last word from shore.

When the Commodore came to enormous rollers that flee over the bar a certain light-headedness departed from the ship's company.

SLEEP IMPOSSIBLE

As darkness came upon the waters, the Commodore was a broad, flaming path of blue and silver phosphorescence, and as her stout bow lunged at the great black waves she threw flashing, roaring cascades to either side. And all that was to be heard was the rhythmical and mighty pounding of the engines. Being an inexperienced filibuster, the writer had undergone considerable mental excitement since the starting of the ship, and in consequence he had not been to sleep and so I went to the first mate's bunk to indulge myself in all the physical delights of holding one's-self in bed. Every time the ship lurched I expected to be fired through a bulkhead, and it was neither amusing nor instructive to see in the dim light a certain accursed valise aiming itself at the top of my stomach with every lurch of the vessel.

THE COOK IS HOPEFUL

The cook was asleep on a bench in the galley. He is of a portly and noble exterior, and by means of a checker board he had himself wedged on this bench in such a manner the motion of the ship would be unable to dislodge him. He woke as I entered the galley and delivered himself of some dolorous sentiments: "God," he said in the course of his observations, "I don't feel right about this ship, some-

how. It strikes me that something is going to happen to us. I don't
know what it is, but the old ship is going to get it in the neck, I
think."

"Well, how about the men on board of her?" said I. "Are any of
us going to get out, prophet?"

"Yes," said the cook. "Sometimes I have these damned feelings
come over me, and they are always right, and it seems to me, somehow, that you and I will both get and meet again somewhere, down at
Coney Island, perhaps, or some place like that."

ONE MAN HAS ENOUGH

Finding it impossible to sleep, I went back to the pilot house. An
old seaman, Tom Smith, from Charleston, was then at the wheel. In the
darkness I could not see Tom's face, except at those times when he
leaned forward to scan the compass and the dim light from the box
came upon his weatherbeaten features.

"Well, Tom," said I, "how do you like filibustering?"

He said "I think I am about through with it. I've been in a number
of these expeditions and the pay is good, but I think if I ever get back
safe this time I will cut it."

I sat down in the corner of the pilot house and almost went to sleep.
In the meantime the captain came on duty and he was standing near
me when the chief engineer rushed up the stairs and cried hurriedly
to the captain that there was something wrong in the engine room.
He and the captain departed swiftly.

I was drowsing there in my corner when the captain returned, and,
going to the door of the little room directly back of the pilothouse,
he cried to the Cuban leader:

"Say, can't you those fellows to work. I can't talk their language
and I can't get them started. Come on and get them going."

HELPS IN THE FIREROOM

The Cuban leader turned to me and said: "Go help in the fireroom.
They are going to bail with buckets."

The engine room, by the way, represented a scene at this time
taken from the middle kitchen of hades. In the first place, it was in-
sufferably warm, and the lights burned faintly in a way to cause
mystic and grewsome shadows. There was a quantity of soapish
sea water swirling and sweeping and swishing among machinery that
roared and banged and clattered and steamed, and, in the second
place, it was a devil of a ways down below.

Here I first came to know a certain young oiler named Billy Higgins. He was sloshing around this inferno filling buckets with water and passing them to a chain of men that extended up the ship's side. Afterward we got orders to change our point of attack on water and to operate through a little door on the windward side of the ship that led into the engine room.

NO PANIC ON BOARD

During this time there was much talk of pumps out of order and many other statements of a mechanical kind, which I did not altogether comprehend but understood to mean that there was a general and sudden ruin in the engine room.

There was no particular agitation at this time, and even later there was never a panic on board the Commodore. The party of men who worked with Higgins and me at this time were all Cubans, and we were under the direction of the Cuban leaders. Presently we were ordered again to the afterhold, and there was some hesitation about going into the abominable fireroom again, but Higgins dashed down the companionway with a bucket.

LOWERING BOATS

The heat and hard work in the fireroom affected me and I was obliged to come on deck again. Going forward, I heard as I went talk of lowering the boats. Near the corner of the galley the mate was talking with a man.

"Why don't you send up a rocket?" said this unknown man. And the mate replied: "What the hell do we want to send up a rocket for? The ship is all right."

Returning with a little rubber and cloth overcoat, I saw the first boat about to be lowered. A certain man was the first person in this first boat, and they were handing him in a valise about as large as a hotel. I had not entirely recovered from astonishment and pleasure in witnessing this noble deed when I saw another valise go to him.

HUMAN HOG APPEARS

This valise was not perhaps so large as a hotel, but it was a big valise anyhow. Afterward there went to him something which looked to me like an overcoat.

Seeing the chief engineer leaning out of his little window, I remarked to him:

"What do you think of that blank, blank, blank?"

"Oh, he's a bird," said the old chief.

It was now that was heard the order to get away the lifeboat, which was stowed on top of the deckhouse. The deckhouse was a mighty slippery place, and with each roll of the ship, the men there thought themselves likely to take headers into the deadly black sea.

Higgins was on top of the deckhouse, and, with the first mate and two colored stokers, we wrestled with that boat, which, I am willing to swear, weighed as much as a Broadway cable car. She might have been spiked to the deck. We could have pushed a little brick school-house along a corduroy road as easily as we could have moved this boat. But the first mate got a tackle to her from a leeward davit, and on the deck below the captain corralled enough men to make an impression upon the boat.

We were ordered to cease hauling then, and in this lull the cook of the ship came to me and said: "What are you going to do?"

I told him of my plans, and he said:

"Well, my God, that's what I am going to do."

A WHISTLE OF DESPAIR

Now the whistle of the Commodore had been turned loose, and if there ever was a voice of despair and death, it was in the voice of this whistle. It had gained a new tone. It was as if its throat was already choked by the water, and this cry on the sea at night, with a wind blowing the spray over the ship, and the waves roaring over the bow, and swirling white along the decks, was to each of us probably a song of man's end.

It was now that the first mate showed a sign of losing his grip. To us who were trying in all stages of competence and experience to launch the lifeboat he raged in all terms of fiery satire and hammer-like abuse. But the boat moved at last and swung down toward the water.

Afterward, when I went aft, I saw the captain standing, with his arm in a sling, holding on to a stay with his one good hand and directing the launching of the boat. He gave me a five-gallon jug of water to hold, and asked me what I was going to do. I told me what I thought was about the proper thing, and he told me then that the cook had the same idea, and ordered me to go forward and be ready to launch the ten-foot dingy.

IN THE TEN-FOOT DINGY

I remember well that he turned then to swear at a colored stoker who was prowling around, done up in life preservers until he looked like a feather bed. I went forward with my five-gallon jug of water, and when the captain came we launched the dingy, and they put me over the side to fend her off from the ship with an oar.

They handed me down the water jug, and then the cook came into the boat, and we sat there in the darkness, wondering why, by all our hopes of future happiness, the captain was so long in coming over to the side and ordering us away from the doomed ship.

The captain was waiting for the other boat to go. Finally he hailed in the darkness: "Are you all right, Mr. Graines?"

The first mate answered: "All right, sir."

"Shove off, then," cried the captain.

The captain was just about to swing over the rail when a dark form came forward and a voice said: "Captain, I go with you."

The captain answered: "Yes, Billy; get in."

HIGGINS LAST TO LEAVE SHIP

It was Billy Higgins, the oiler. Billy dropped into the boat and a moment later the captain followed, bringing with him an end of about forty yards of lead line. The other end was attached to the rail of the ship.

As we swung back to leeward the captain said: "Boys, we will stay right near the ship till she goes down."

This cheerful information, of course, filled us all with glee. The line kept us headed properly into the wind, and as we rode over the monstrous waves we saw upon each rise the swaying lights of the dying Commodore.

When came the gray shade of dawn, the form of the Commodore grew slowly clear to us as our little ten-foot boat rose over each swell. She was floating with such an air of buoyancy that we laughed when we had time, and said "What a gag it would be on those fellows if she didn't sink at all."

But later we saw men aboard of her, and later still they began to hail us.

HELPING THEIR MATES

I had forgot to mention that previously we had loosened the end of the lead line and dropped much further to leeward. The men on board were a mystery to us, of course, as we had seen all the boats leave the ship. We rowed back to the ship, but did not approach too near, because we were four men in a ten-foot boat, and we knew that the touch of a hand on our gunwale would assuredly swamp us.

The first mate cried out from the ship that the third boat had foundered alongside. He cried that they had made rafts, and wished us to tow them.

The captain said, "All right."

Their rafts were floating astern. "Jump in!" cried the captain, but there was a singular and most harrowing hesitation. There were five white men and two negroes. This scene in the gray light of morning impressed one as would a view into some place where ghosts move slowly. These seven men on the stern of the sinking Commodore were silent. Save the words of the mate to the captain there was no talk. Here was death, but here also was a most singular and indefinable kind of fortitude.

Four men, I remember, clambered over the railing and stood there watching the cold, steely sheen of the sweeping waves.

"Jump," cried the captain again.

The old chief engineer first obeyed the order. He landed on the outside raft and the captain told him how to grip the raft and he obeyed as promptly and as docilely as a scholar in riding school.

THE MATE'S MAD PLUNGE

A stoker followed him, and then the first mate threw his hands over his head and plunged into the sea. He had no life belt and for my part, even when he did this horrible thing, I somehow felt that I could see in the expression of his hands, and in the very toss of his head, as he leaped thus to death, that it was rage, rage, rage unspeakable that was in his heart at the time.

And then I saw Tom Smith, the man who was going to quit filibustering after this expedition, jump to a raft and turn his face toward us. On board the Commodore three men strode, still in silence and with their faces turned toward us. One man had his arms folded and was leaning against the deckhouse. His feet were crossed, so that the toe of his left foot pointed downward. There they stood gazing at us, and neither from the deck nor from the rafts was a voice raised. Still was there this silence.

TRIED TO TOW THE RAFTS

The colored stoker on the first raft threw us a line and we began to tow. Of course, we perfectly understood the absolute impossibility of any such thing; our dingy was within six inches of the water's edge, there was an enormous sea running, and I knew that under the circumstances a tugboat would have no light task in moving these rafts.

But we tried it, and would have continued to try it indefinitely, but that something critical came to pass. I was at an oar and so faced the rafts. The cook controlled the line. Suddenly the boat began to go backward and then we saw this negro on the first raft pulling on the line hand over hand and drawing us to him.

He had turned into a demon. He was wild—wild as a tiger. He was crouched on this raft and ready to spring. Every muscle of him seemed to be turned into an elastic spring. His eyes were almost white. His face was the face of a lost man reaching upward, and we knew that the weight of his hand on our gunwale doomed us.

THE COMMODORE SINKS

The cook let go of the line. We rowed around to see if we could not get a line from the chief engineer, and all this time, mind you, there were no shrieks, no groans, but silence, silence and silence, and then the Commodore sank.

She lurched to windward, then swung afar back, righted and dove into the sea, and the rafts were suddenly swallowed by this frightful maw of the ocean. And then by the men on the ten-foot dingy were words said that were still not words—something far beyond words.

The lighthouse of Mosquito Inlet stuck up above the horizon like the point of a pin. We turned our dingy toward the shore.

The history of life in an open boat for thirty hours would no doubt be instructive for the young, but none is to be told here and now. For my part I would prefer to tell the story at once, because from it would shine the splendid manhood of Captain Edward Murphy and of William Higgins, the oiler, but let it suffice at this time to say that when we were swamped in the surf and making the best of our way toward the shore the captain gave orders amid the wildness of the breakers as clearly as if he had been on the quarter deck of a battleship.

John Kitchell of Daytona came running down the beach, and as he ran the air was filled with clothes. If he had pulled a single lever and undressed, even as the fire horses harness, he could not seem to me to have stripped with more speed. He dashed into the water and dragged the cook. Then he went after the captain, but the captain sent him to me, and then it was that he saw Billy Higgins lying with his forehead on sand that was clear of the water, and he was dead.

Stephen Crane

THE OPEN BOAT

Stephen Crane

None of them knew the colour of the sky. Their eyes glanced level, and were fastened upon the waves that swept toward them. These waves were of the hue of slate, save for the tops, which were of foaming white, and all of the men knew the colours of the sea. The horizon narrowed and widened, and dipped and rose, and at all times its edge was jagged with waves that seemed thrust up in points like rocks.

Many a man ought to have a bathtub larger than the boat which here rode upon the sea. These waves were most wrongfully and barbarously abrupt and tall, and each froth-top was a problem in small-boat navigation.

The cook squatted in the bottom, and looked with both eyes at the six inches of gunwale which separated him from the ocean. His sleeves were rolled over his fat forearms, and the two flaps of his unbuttoned vest dangled as he bent to bail out the boat. Often he said, "Gawd! that was a narrow clip." As he remarked it he invariably gazed eastward over the broken sea.

The oiler, steering with one of the two oars in the boat, sometimes raised himself suddenly to keep clear of water that swirled in over the stern. It was a thin little oar, and it seemed often ready to snap.

The correspondent, pulling at the other oar, watched the waves and wondered why he was there.

The injured captain, lying in the bow, was at this time buried in that profound dejection and indifference which comes, temporarily at least, to even the bravest and most enduring when, willy-nilly, the firm fails, the army loses, the ship goes down. The mind of the master of a vessel is rooted deep in the timbers of her, though he command for a day or a decade; and this captain had on him the stern impression of a scene in the greys of dawn of seven turned faces, and later a stump of a topmast with a white ball on it, that slashed to and fro at the waves, went low and lower, and down. Thereafter there was something strange in his voice. Although steady, it was deep with mourning, and of a quality beyond oration or tears.

"Keep 'er a little more south, Billie," said he.

"A little more south, sir," said the oiler in the stern.

A seat in this boat was not unlike a seat upon a bucking broncho, and by the same token a broncho is not much smaller. The craft pranced and reared and plunged like an animal. As each wave came, and she rose for it, she seemed like a horse making at a fence outrageously high. The manner of her scramble over these walls of water is a mystic thing, and, moreover, at the top of them were ordinarily these problems in white water, the foam racing down from the summit of each wave requiring a new leap, and a leap from the air. Then, after scornfully bumping a crest, she would slide and race and splash down a long incline, and arrive bobbing and nodding in front of the next menace.

A singular disadvantage of the sea lies in the fact that after successfully surmounting one wave you discover that there is another behind it just as important and just as nervously anxious to do something effective in the way of swamping boats. In a ten-foot dinghy one can get an idea of the resources of the sea in the line of waves that is not probable to the average experience which is never at sea in a dinghy. As each slaty wall of water approached, it shut all else from the view of the men in the boat, and it was not difficult to imagine that this particular wave was the final outburst of the ocean, the last effort of the grim water. There was a terrible grace in the move of the waves, and they came in silence, save for the snarling of the crests.

In the wan light the faces of the men must have been grey. Their eyes must have glinted in strange ways as they gazed steadily astern. Viewed from a balcony, the whole thing would doubtless have been weirdly picturesque. But then men in the boat had no time to see it, and if they had had leisure, there were other things to occupy their minds. The sun swung steadily up the sky, and they knew it was broad day because the colour of the sea changed from slate to emerald green streaked with amber lights, and the foam was like tumbling snow. The process of the breaking day was unknown to them. They were aware only of this effect upon the colour of the waves that rolled toward them.

In disjointed sentences the cook and the correspondent argued as to the difference between a life-saving station and a house of refuge. The cook had said: "There's a house of refuge just north of the Mosquito Inlet Light, and as soon as they see us they'll come off in their boat and pick us up."

"As soon as who see us?" said the correspondent.

"The crew," said the cook.

"Houses of refuge don't have crews," said the correspondent. "As I understand them, they are only places where clothes and grub are stored for the benefit of shipwrecked people. They don't carry crews."

"Oh, yes, they do," said the cook.

"No, they don't," said the correspondent.

"Well, we're not there yet, anyhow," said the oiler, in the stern.

"Well," said the cook, "perhaps it's not a house of refuge that I'm thinking of as being near Mosquito Inlet Light; perhaps it's a life-saving station."

"We're not there yet," said the oiler in the stern.

2

As the boat bounced from the top of each wave the wind tore through the hair of the hatless men, and as the craft plopped her stern down again the spray slashed past them. The crest of each of these waves was a hill, from the top of which the men surveyed for a moment a broad tumultuous expanse, shining and wind-riven. It was probably splendid, it was probably glorious, this play of the free sea, wild with lights of emerald and white and amber.

"Bully good thing it's an on-shore wind," said the cook. "If not, where would we be? Wouldn't have a show."

"That's right," said the correspondent.

The busy oiler nodded his assent.

Then the captain, in the bow, chuckled in a way that expressed humour, contempt, tragedy, all in one. "Do you think we've got much of a show now, boys?" said he.

Whereupon the three were silent, save for a trifle of hemming and hawing. To express any particular optimism at this time they felt to be childish and stupid, but they all doubtless possessed this sense of the situation in their minds. A young man thinks doggedly at such times. On the other hand, the ethics of their condition was decidedly against any open suggestion of hopelessness. So they were silent.

"Oh, well," said the captain, soothing his children, "we'll get ashore all right."

But there was that in his tone which made them think; so the oiler quoth, "Yes! if this wind holds."

The cook was bailing. "Yes! if we don't catch hell in the surf."

Canton-flannel gulls flew near and far. Sometimes they sat down on the sea, near patches of brown seaweed that rolled over the waves with a movement like carpets on a line in a gale. The birds sat comfortably in groups, and they were envied by some in the dinghy, for the wrath of the sea was no more to them than it was to a covey of prairie chickens a thousand miles inland. Often they came very close and stared at the men with black bead-like eyes. At these times they were uncanny and sinister in their unblinking scrutiny, and the men hooted angrily at them, telling them to be gone. One came, and evidently decided to alight on the top of the captain's head. The bird flew parallel to the boat and did not circle, but made short sidelong jumps in the air in chicken-fashion. His black eyes were wistfully fixed upon the captain's head. "Ugly brute," said the oiler to the bird. "You look as if you were made with a jack-knife." The cook and the correspondent swore darkly at the creature. The captain naturally wished to knock it away with the end of the heavy painter, but he did not dare do it, because anything resembling an emphatic gesture would have capsized this freighted boat; and so, with his open hand, the captain gently and carefully waved the gull away. After it had been discouraged from the pursuit the captain breathed easier on account of his hair, and others breathed easier because the bird struck their minds at this time as being somehow gruesome and ominous.

In the meantime the oiler and the correspondent rowed. And also they rowed. They sat together in the same seat, and each rowed an oar. Then the oiler took both oars; then the correspondent took both oars; then the oiler; then the correspondent. They rowed and they rowed. The very ticklish part of the business was when the time came for the reclining one in the stern to take his turn at the oars. By the very last star of truth, it is easier to steal eggs from under a hen than it was to change seats in the dinghy. First the man in the stern slid his hand along the thwart and moved with care, as if he were of Sèvres. Then the man in the rowing-seat slid his hand along the other thwart. It was all done with the most extraordinary care. As the two sidled past each other, the whole party kept watchful eyes on the coming wave, and the captain cried: "Look out, now! Steady, there!"

The brown mats of seaweed that appeared from time to time were like islands, bits of earth. They were travelling, apparently, neither one way nor the other. They were, to all intents, stationary. They informed the men in the boat that it was making progress slowly toward the land.

The captain, rearing cautiously in the bow after the dinghy soared on a great swell, said that he had seen the lighthouse at Mosquito Inlet. Presently the cook remarked that he had seen it. The correspondent was at the oars then, and for some reason he too wished to look at the lighthouse; but his back was toward the far shore, and the waves were important, and for some time he could not seize an opportunity to turn his head. But at last there came a wave more gentle than the others, and when at the crest of it he swiftly scoured the western horizon.

"See it?" said the captain.

"No," said the correspondent, slowly; "I didn't see anything."

"Look again," said the captain. He pointed. "It's exactly in that direction."

At the top of another wave the correspondent did as he was bid, and this time his eyes chanced on a small, still thing on the edge of the swaying horizon. It was precisely like the point of a pin. It took an anxious eye to find a lighthouse so tiny.

"Think we'll make it, Captain?"

"If this wind holds and the boat don't swamp, we can't do much else," said the captain.

The little boat, lifted by each towering sea and splashed viciously by the crests, made progress that in the absence of seaweed was not apparent to those in her. She seemed just a wee thing wallowing, miraculously top up, at the mercy of five oceans. Occasionally a great spread of water, like white flames, swarmed into her.

"Bail her, cook," said the captain, serenely.

"All right, Captain," said the cheerful cook.

3

It would be difficult to describe the subtle brotherhood of men that was here established on the seas. No one said that it was so. No one mentioned it. But it dwelt in the boat, and each man felt it warm him. They were a captain, an oiler, a cook, and a correspondent, and they were friends—friends in a more curiously iron-bound degree than may be common. The hurt captain, lying against the water-jar in the bow, spoke always in a low voice and calmly; but he could never command a more ready and swiftly obedient crew than the motley three of the dinghy. It was more than a mere recognition of what was best for the common safety. There was surely in it a quality that was personal and heart-felt. And after this devotion to the commander of the boat, there was this comradeship, that the correspondent, for instance, who had been taught to be cynical of men, knew even at the time was the best experience of his life. But no one said that it was so. No one mentioned it.

"I wish we had a sail," remarked the captain. "We might try my overcoat on the end of an oar, and give you two boys a chance to rest." So the cook and the correspondent held the mast and spread wide the overcoat; the oiler steered; and the little boat made good way with her new rig. Sometimes the oiler had to scull sharply to keep a sea from breaking into the boat, but otherwise sailing was a success.

Meanwhile the lighthouse had been growing slowly larger. It had now almost assumed colour, and appeared like a little grey shadow on the sky. The man at the oars could not be prevented from turning his head rather often to try for a glimpse of this little grey shadow.

At last, from the top of each wave, the men in the tossing boat could see land. Even as the lighthouse was an upright shadow on the sky, this land seemed but a long black shadow on the sea. It certainly was thinner than paper. "We must be about opposite New Smyrna," said the cook, who had coasted this shore often in schooners. "Captain, by the way, I believe they abandoned that life-saving station there about a year ago."

"Did they?" said the captain.

The wind slowly died away. The cook and the correspondent were not now obliged to slave in order to hold high the oar. But the waves continued their old impetuous swooping at the dinghy, and the little craft, no longer under way, struggled woundily over them. The oiler or the correspondent took the oars again.

Shipwrecks are apropos of nothing. If men could only train for them and have them occur when the men had reached pink condition, there would be less drowning at sea. Of the four in the dinghy none had slept any time worth mentioning for two days and two nights previous to embarking in the dinghy, and in the excitement of clambering about the deck of a foundering ship they had also forgotten to eat heartily.

For these reasons, and for others, neither the oiler nor the correspondent was fond of rowing at this time. The correspondent wondered ingenuously how in the name of all that was sane could there be people who thought it amusing to row a boat. It was not an amusement; it was a diabolical punishment, and even a genius of mental aberrations could never conclude that it was anything but a horror to the muscles and a crime against the back. He mentioned to the boat in general how the amusement of rowing struck him, and the weary-faced oiler smiled in full sympathy. Previously to the foundering, by the way, the oiler had worked a double watch in the engine-room of the ship.

"Take her easy now, boys," said the captain. "Don't spend yourselves. If we have to run a surf you'll need all your strength, because we'll sure have to swim for it. Take your time."

Slowly the land arose from the sea. From a black line it became a line of black and a line of white—trees and sand. Finally the captain said that he could make out a house on the shore. "That's the house of refuge, sure," said the cook. "They'll see us before long, and come out after us."

The distant lighthouse reared high. "The keeper ought to be able to make us out now, if he's looking through a glass," said the captain. "He'll notify the life-saving people."

"None of those other boats could have got ashore to give word of this wreck," said the oiler, in a low voice, "else the life-boat would be out hunting us."

Slowly and beautifully the land loomed out of the sea. The wind came again. It had veered from the north-east to the south-east. Finally a new sound struck the ears of the men in the boat. It was the low thunder of the surf on the shore. "We'll never be able to make the lighthouse now," said the captain. "Swing her head a little more north, Billie."

"A little more north, sir," said the oiler.

Whereupon the little boat turned her nose once more down the wind, and all but the oarsman watched the shore grow. Under the influence of this expansion doubt and direful apprehension were leaving the minds of the men. The management of the boat was still most absorbing, but it could not prevent a quiet cheerfulness. In an hour, perhaps, they would be ashore.

Their backbones had become thoroughly used to balancing in the boat, and they now rode this wild colt of a dinghy like circus men. The correspondent thought that he had been drenched to the skin, but happening to feel in the top pocket of his coat, he found therein eight cigars. Four of them were soaked with sea-water; four were perfectly scatheless. After a search, somebody produced three dry matches; and thereupon the four waifs rode impudently in their little boat and, with an assurance of an impending rescue shining in their eyes, puffed at the big cigars, and judged well and ill of all men. Everybody took a drink of water.

4

"Cook," remarked the captain, "there don't seem to be any signs of life about your house of refuge."

"No," replied the cook. "Funny they don't see us!"

A broad stretch of lowly coast lay before the eyes of the men. It was of low dunes topped with dark vegetation. The roar of the surf was plain, and sometimes they could see the white lip of a wave as it spun up the beach. A tiny house was blocked out black upon the sky. Southward, the slim lighthouse lifted its little grey length.

Tide, wind, and waves were swinging the dinghy northward. "Funny they don't see us," said the men.

The surf's roar was here dulled, but its tone was nevertheless thunderous and mighty. As the boat swam over the great rollers the men sat listening to this roar. "We'll swamp sure," said everybody.

It is fair to say here that there was not a life-saving station within twenty miles in either direction; but the men did not know this fact, and in consequence they made dark and opprobrious remarks concerning the eyesight of the nation's life-savers. Four scowling men sat in the dinghy and surpassed records in the invention of epithets.

"Funny they don't see us."

The light-heartedness of a former time had completely faded. To their sharpened minds it was easy to conjure pictures of all kinds of incompetency and blindness and, indeed, cowardice. There was the shore of the populous land, and it was bitter and bitter to them that from it came no sign.

"Well," said the captain, ultimately, "I suppose we'll have to make a try for ourselves. If we stay out here too long, we'll none of us have strength left to swim after the boat swamps."

And so the oiler, who was at the oars, turned the boat straight for the shore. There was a sudden tightening of muscles. There was some thinking.

"If we don't all get ashore," said the captain—"if we don't all get ashore, I suppose you fellows know where to send news of my finish?"

They then briefly exchanged some addresses and admonitions. As for the reflections of the men, there was a great deal of rage in them. Perchance they might be formulated thus: "If I am going to be drowned—if I am going to be drowned—if I am going to be drowned, why, in the name of the seven mad gods who rule the sea, was I allowed to come thus far and contemplate sand and trees? Was I brought here merely to have my nose dragged away as I was about to nibble the sacred cheese of life? It is preposterous. If this old ninny-woman, Fate, cannot do better than this, she should be deprived of the management of men's fortunes. She is an old hen who knows not her intention. If she has decided to drown me, why did she not do it in the beginning and save me all this trouble? The whole affair is absurd.—But no; she cannot mean to drown me. She dare not drown me. She cannot drown me. Not after all this work." Afterward the man might have had an impulse to shake his fist at the clouds. "Just you drown me, now, and then hear what I call you!"

The billows that came at this time were more formidable. They seemed always just about to break and roll over the little boat in a turmoil of foam. There was a preparatory and long growl in the speech of them. No mind unused to the sea would have concluded that the dinghy could ascend these sheer heights in time. The shore was still afar. The oiler was a wily surfman. "Boys," he said swiftly, "she won't live three minutes more, and we're too far out to swim. Shall I take her to sea again, Captain?"

"Yes; go ahead!" said the captain.

This oiler, by a series of quick miracles and fast and steady oarsmanship, turned the boat in the middle of the surf and took her safely to sea again.

There was a considerable silence as the boat bumped over the furrowed sea to deeper water. Then somebody in gloom spoke: "Well, anyhow, they must have seen us from the shore by now."

The gulls went in slanting flight up the wind toward the grey, desolate east. A squall, marked by dingy clounds and clouds brick-red, like smoke from a burning building, appeared from the southeast.

"What do you think of those life-saving people? Ain't they peaches?"

"Funny they haven't seen us."

"Maybe they think we're out here for sport! Maybe they think we're fishin'. Maybe they think we're damned fools."

It was a long afternoon. A changed tide tried to force them southward, but wind and wave said northward. Far ahead, where coastline, sea, and sky formed their mighty angle, there were little dots which seemed to indicate a city on the shore.

"St. Augustine?"

The captain shook his head. "Too near Mosquito Inlet."

And the oiler rowed, and then the correspondent rowed; then the oiler rowed. It was a weary business. The human back can become the seat of more aches and pains than are registered in books for the composite anatomy of a regiment. It is a limited area, but it can become the theatre of innumerable muscular conflicts, tangles, wrenches, knots, and other comforts.

"Did you ever like to row, Billie?" asked the correspondent.

"No," said the oiler; "hang it!"

When one exchanged the rowing-seat for a place in the bottom of the boat, he suffered a bodily depression that caused him to be careless of everything save an obligation to wiggle one finger. There was cold sea-water swashing to and fro in the boat, and he lay in it. His head, pillowed on a thwart, was within an inch of the swirl of a wave-crest, and sometimes a particularly obstreperous sea came inboard and drenched him once more. But these matters did not annoy him. It is almost certain that if the boat had capsized he would have tumbled comfortably out upon the ocean as if he felt sure that it was a great soft mattress.

"Look! There's a man on the shore!"

"Where?"

"There! See 'im? See 'im?"

"Yes, sure! He's walking along."

"Now he's stopped. Look! He's facing us!"

"He's waving at us!"

"So he is! By thunder!"

"Ah, now we're all right! Now we're all right! There'll be a boat out here for us in half an hour."

"He's going on. He's running. He's going up to that house there."

The remote beach seemed lower than the sea, and it required a searching glance to discern the little black figure. The captain saw a floating stick, and they rowed to it. A bath towel was by some weird chance in the boat, and, tying this on the stick, the captain waved it. The oarsman did not dare turn his head, so he was obliged to ask questions.

"What's he doing now?"

"He's standing still again. He's looking, I think.—There he goes again—toward the house.—Now he's stopped again."

"Is he waving at us?"

"No, not now; he was, though."

"Look! There comes another man!"

"He's running."

"Look at him go, would you!"

"Why, he's on a bicycle. Now he's met the other man. They're both waving at us. Look!"

"There comes something up the beach."

"What the devil is that thing?"

"Why, it looks like a boat."

"Why, certainly, it's a boat."

"No; it's on wheels."

"Yes, so it is. Well, that must be the life-boat. They drag them along shore on a wagon."

"That's the life-boat, sure."

"No, by God, it's—it's an omnibus."

"I tell you it's a life-boat."

"It is not! It's an omnibus. I can see it plain. See? One of these big hotel omnibuses."

"By thunder, you're right. It's an omnibus, sure as fate. What do you suppose they are doing with an omnibus? Maybe they are going around collecting the life-crew, hey?"

"That's it, likely. Look! There's a fellow waving a little black flag. He's standing on the steps of the omnibus. There come those other two fellows. Now they're all talking together. Look at the fellow with the flag. Maybe he ain't waving it!"

"That ain't a flag, is it? That's his coat. Why, certainly, that's his coat."

"So it is; it's his coat. He's taken it off and is waving it around his head. But would you look at him swing it!"

"Oh, say, there isn't any life-saving station there. That's just a winter-resort hotel omnibus that has brought over some of the boarders to see us drown."

"What's that idiot with the coat mean? What's he signalling, anyhow?"

"It looks as if he were trying to tell us to go north. There must be a life-saving station up there."

"No; he thinks we're fishing. Just giving us a merry hand. See? Ah, there, Willie!"

"Well, I wish I could make something out of those signals. What do you suppose he means?"

"He don't mean anything; he's just playing."

"Well, if he'd just signal us to try the surf again, or to go to sea and wait, or go north, or go south, or go to hell, there would be some reason in it. But look at him! He just stands there and keeps his coat revolving like a wheel. The ass!"

"There come more people."

"Now there's quite a mob. Look! Isn't that a boat?"

"Where? Oh, I see where you mean. No, that's no boat."

"That fellow is still waving his coat."

"He must think we like to see him do that. Why don't he quit it? It don't mean anything."

"I don't know. I thing he is trying to make us go north. It must be that there's a life-saving station there somewhere."

"Say, he ain't tired yet. Look at 'im wave!"

"Wonder how long he can keep that up. He's been revolving his coat ever since he caught sight of us. He's an idiot. Why aren't they getting men to bring a boat out? A fishing-boat—one of those big yawls—could come out here all right. Why don't he do something?"

"Oh, it's all right now."

"They'll have a boat out here for us in less than no time, now that they've seen us."

A faint yellow tone came into the sky over the low land. The shadows on the sea slowly deepened. The wind bore coldness with it, and the men began to shiver.

"Holy smoke!" said one, allowing his voice to express his impious mood, "if we keep on monkeying out here! If we've got to flounder out here all night!"

"Oh, we'll never have to stay here all night! Don't you worry.

They've seen us now, and it won't be long before they'll come chasing out after us."

The shore grew dusky. The man waving a coat blended gradually into this gloom, and it swallowed in the same manner the omnibus and the group of people. The spray, when it dashed uproariously over the side, made the voyagers shrink and swear like men who were being branded.

"I'd like to catch the chump who waved the coat. I feel like socking him one, just for luck."

"Why? What did he do?"

"Oh, nothing, but then he seemed so damned cheerful."

In the meantime the oiler rowed, and then the correspondent rowed, and then the oiler rowed. Grey-faced and bowed forward, they mechanically, turn by turn, plied the leaden oars. The form of the lighthouse had vanished from the southern horizon, but finally a pale star appeared, just lifting from the sea. The streaked saffron in the west passed before the all-merging darkness, and the sea to the east was black. The land had vanished, and was expressed only by the low and drear thunder of the surf.

"If I am going to be drowned—if I am going to be drowned—if I am going to be drowned, why, in the name of the seven mad gods who rule the sea, was I allowed to come thus far and contemplate sand and trees? Was I brought here merely to have my nose dragged away as I was about to nibble the sacred cheese of life?"

The patient captain, drooped over the water-jar, was sometimes obliged to speak to the oarsman.

"Keep her head up! Keep her head up!"

"Keep her head up, sir." The voices were weary and low.

This was surely a quiet evening. All save the oarsman lay heavily and listlessly in the boat's bottom. As for him, his eyes were just capable of noting the tall black waves that swept forward in a most sinister silence, save for an occasional subdued growl of a crest.

The cook's head was on a thwart, and he looked without interest at the water under his nose. He was deep in other scenes. Finally he spoke. "Billie," he murmured, dreamfully, "what kind of pie do you like best?"

5

"Pie!" said the oiler and the correspondent, agitatedly. "Don't talk about those things, blast you!"

"Well," said the cook, "I was just thinking about ham sandwiches, and—"

A night on the sea in an open boat is a long night. As darkness settled finally, the shine of the light, lifting from the sea in the south, changed to full gold. On the northern horizon a new light appeared, a small bluish gleam on the edge of the waters. These two lights were the furniture of the world. Otherwise there was nothing but waves.

Two men huddled in the stern, and distances were so magnificent in the dinghy that the rower was enabled to keep his feet partly warm by thrusting them under his companions. Their legs indeed extended far under the rowing-seat until they touched the feet of the captain forward. Sometimes, despite the efforts of the tired oarsman, a wave came piling into the boat, an icy wave of the night, and the chilling water soaked them anew. They would twist their bodies for a moment and groan, and sleep the dead sleep once more, while the water in the boat gurgled about them as the craft rocked.

The plan of the oiler and the correspondent was for one to row until he lost the ability, and then arouse the other from his sea-water couch in the bottom of the boat.

The oiler plied the oars until his head drooped forward and the overpowering sleep blinded him; and he rowed yet afterward. Then he touched a man in the bottom of the boat, and called his name. "Will you spell me for a little while?" he said meekly.

"Sure, Billie," said the correspondent, awaking and dragging himself to a sitting position. They exchanged places carefully, and the oiler, cuddling down in the sea-water at the cook's side, seemed to go to sleep instantly.

The particular violence of the sea had ceased. The waves came without snarling. The obligation of the man at the oars was to keep the boat headed so that the tilt of the rollers would not capsize her, and to preserve her from filling when the crests rushed past. The black waves were silent and hard to be seen in the darkness. Often one was almost upon the boat before the oarsman was aware.

In a low voice the correspondent addressed the captain. He was not sure that the captain was awake, although this iron man seemed to be always awake. "Captain, shall I keep her making for that light north, sir?"

The same steady voice answered him. "Yes. Keep it about two points off the port bow."

The cook had tied a life-belt around himself in order to get even the warmth which this clumsy cork contrivance could donate, and he seemed almost stove-like when a rower, whose teeth invariably chattered wildly as soon as he ceased his labour, dropped down to sleep.

The correspondent, as he rowed, looked down at the two men

sleeping underfoot. The cook's arm was around the oiler's shoulders, and, with their fragmentary clothing and haggard faces, they were the babes of the sea—a grotesque rendering of the old babes in the wood.

Later he must have grown stupid at his work, for suddenly there was a growling of water, and a crest came with a roar and a swash into the boat, and it was a wonder that it did not set the cook afloat in his life-belt. The cook continued to sleep, but the oiler sat up, blinking his eyes and shaking with the new cold.

"Oh, I'm awful sorry, Billie," said the correspondent, contritely.

"That's all right, old boy," said the oiler, and lay down again and was asleep.

Presently it seemed that even the captain dozed, and the correspondent thought that he was the one man afloat on all the ocean. The wind had a voice as it came over the waves, and it was sadder than the end.

There was a long, loud swishing astern of the boat, and a gleaming trail of phosphorescence, like blue flame, was furrowed on the black waters. It might have been made by a monstrous knife.

Then there came a stillness, while the correspondent breathed with open mouth and looked at the sea.

Suddenly there was another swish and another long flash of bluish light, and this time it was alongside the boat, and might almost have been reached with an oar. The correspondent saw an enormous fin speed like a shadow through the water, hurling the crystalline spray and leaving the long glowing trail.

The correspondent looked over his shoulder at the captain. His face was hidden, and he seemed to be asleep. He looked at the babes of the sea. They certainly were asleep. So, being bereft of sympathy, he leaned a little way to one side and swore softly into the sea.

But the thing did not then leave the vicinity of the boat. Ahead or astern, on one side or the other, at intervals long or short, fled the long sparkling streak, and there was to be heard the *whirroo* of the dark fin. The speed and power of the thing was greatly to be admired. It cut the water like a gigantic and keen projectile.

The presence of this biding thing did not affect the man with the same horror that it would if he had been a picnicker. He simply looked at the sea dully and swore in an undertone.

Nevertheless, it is true that he did not wish to be alone with the thing. He wished one of his companions to awake by chance and keep him company with it. But the captain hung motionless over the water-jar, and the oiler and the cook in the bottom of the boat were plunged in slumber.

6

"If I am going to be drowned—if I am going to be drowned—if I am going to be drowned, why, in the name of the seven mad gods who rule the sea, was I allowed to come thus far and contemplate sand and trees?"

During this dismal night, it may be remarked that a man would conclude that it was really the intention of the seven mad gods to drown him, despite the abominable injustice of it. For it was certainly an abominable injustice to drown a man who had worked so hard, so hard. The man felt it would be a crime most unnatural. Other people had drowned at sea since galleys swarmed with painted sails, but still—

When it occurs to a man that nature does not regard him as important, and that she feels she would not maim the universe by disposing of him, he at first wishes to throw bricks at the temple, and he hates deeply the fact that there are no bricks and no temples. Any visible expression of nature would surely be pelleted with his jeers.

Then, if there be no tangible thing to hoot, he feels, perhaps, the desire to confront a personification and indulge in pleas, bowed to one knee, and with hands supplicant, saying, "Yes, but I love myself."

A high cold star on a winter's night is the word he feels that she says to him. Thereafter he knows the pathos of his situation.

The men in the dinghy had not discussed these matters, but each had, no doubt, reflected upon them in silence and according to his mind. There was seldom any expression upon their faces save the general one of complete weariness. Speech was devoted to the business of the boat.

To chime the notes of his emotion, a verse mysteriously entered the correspondent's head. He had even forgotten that he had forgotten this verse, but it suddenly was in his mind.

A soldier of the Legion lay dying in Algiers;
There was lack of woman's nursing, there was dearth of woman's tears;
But a comrade stood beside him, and he took that comrade's hand,
And he said, "I never more shall see my own, my native land."

In his childhood the correspondent had been made acquainted with the fact that a soldier of the Legion lay dying in Algiers, but he had never regarded it as important. Myriads of his school-fellows had informed him of the soldier's plight, but the dinning had naturally ended by making him perfectly indifferent. He had never considered it his affair that a soldier of the Legion lay dying in

Algiers, nor had it appeared to him as a matter for sorrow. It was less to him than the breaking of a pencil's point.

Now, however, it quaintly came to him as a human, living thing. It was no longer merely a picture of a few throes in the breast of a poet, meanwhile drinking tea and warming his feet at the grate; it was an actuality—stern, mournful, and fine.

The correspondent plainly saw the soldier. He lay on the sand with his feet out straight and still. While his pale left hand was upon his chest in an attempt to thwart the going of his life, the blood came between his fingers. In the Far Algerian distance, a city of low square forms was set against a sky that was faint with the last sunset hues. The correspondent, plying the oars and dreaming of the slow and slower movements of the lips of the soldier, was moved by a profound and perfectly impersonal comprehension. He was sorry for the soldier of the Legion who lay dying in Algiers.

The thing which had followed the boat and waited had evidently grown bored at the delay. There was no longer to be heard the slash of the cut-water, and there was no longer the flame of the long trail. The light in the north still glimmered, but it was apparently no nearer to the boat. Sometimes the boom of the surf rang in the correspondent's ears, and he turned the craft seaward then and rowed harder. Southward, some one had evidently built a watch-fire on the beach. It was too low and too far to be seen, but it made a shimmering, roseate reflection upon the bluff in back of it, and this could be discerned from the boat. The wind came stronger, and sometimes a wave suddenly raged out like a mountain cat, and there was to be seen the sheen and sparkle of a broken crest.

The captain, in the bow, moved on his water-jar and sat erect. "Pretty long night," he observed to the correspondent. He looked at the shore. "Those life-saving people take their time."

"Did you see that shark playing around?"

"Yes, I saw him. He was a big fellow, all right."

"Wish I had known you were awake."

Later the correspondent spoke into the bottom of the boat. "Billie!" There was a slow and gradual disentanglement. "Billie, will you spell me?"

"Sure," said the oiler.

As soon as the correspondent touched the cold, comfortable seawater in the bottom of the boat and had huddled close to the cook's life-belt he was deep in sleep, despite the fact that his teeth played all the popular airs. This sleep was so good to him that it was but a moment before he heard a voice call his name in a tone that demonstrated the last stages of exhaustion. "Will you spell me?"

"Sure, Billie."

The light in the north had mysteriously vanished, but the correspondent took his course from the wide-awake captain.

Later in the night they took the boat farther out to sea, and the captain directed the cook to take one oar at the stern and keep the boat facing the seas. He was to call out if he should hear the thunder of the surf. This plan enabled the oiler and the correspondent to get respite together. "We'll give those boys a chance to get into shape again," said the captain. They curled down and, after a few preliminary chatterings and trembles, slept once more the dead sleep. Neither knew they had bequeathed to the cook the company of another shark, or perhaps the same shark.

As the boat caroused on the waves, spray occasionally bumped over the side and gave them a fresh soaking, but this had no power to break their repose. The ominous slash of the wind and the water affected them as it would have affected mummies.

"Boys," said the cook, with the notes of every reluctance in his voice, "she's drifted in pretty close. I guess one of you had better take her to sea again." The correspondent, aroused, heard the crash of the toppled crests.

As he was rowing, the captain gave him some whiskey-and-water, and this steadied the chills out of him. "If I ever get ashore and anybody shows me even a photograph of an oar—"

At last there was a short conversation.

"Billie!—Billie, will you spell me?"

"Sure," said the oiler.

7

When the correspondent again opened his eyes, the sea and the sky were each of the grey hue of the dawning. Later, carmine and gold was painted upon the waters. The morning appeared finally, in its splendour, with a sky of pure blue, and the sunlight flamed on the tips of the waves.

On the distant dunes were set many little black cottages, and a tall white windmill reared above them. No man, nor dog, nor bicycle appeared on the beach. The cottages might have formed a deserted village.

The voyagers scanned the shore. A conference was held in the boat. "Well," said the captain, "if no help is coming, we might better try a run through the surf right away. If we stay out here much longer we will be too weak to do anything for ourselves at all." The others silently acquiesced in this reasoning. The boat was headed for the beach. The correspondent wondered if none ever ascended the tall wind-tower, and if then they never looked seaward. This tower was a giant, standing with its back to the plight of the ants. It represented in a degree, to the correspondent, the serenity of nature amid the struggles of the individual—nature in the wind and nature in the vision of men. She dod not seem cruel to him then, nor beneficent, nor treacherous, nor wise. But she was indifferent, flatly indifferent. It is, perhaps, plausible that a man in this situation, impressed with the unconcern of the universe, should see the innumerable flaws of his life, and have them taste wickedly in his mind, and wish for another chance. A distinction between right and wrong seems absurdly clear to him, then, in this new ignorance of the grave-edge, and he understands that if he were given another opportunity he would mend his conduct and his words, and be better and brighter during an introduction or at a tea.

"Now, boys," said the captain, "she is going to swamp sure. All we can do is to work her in as far as possible, and then when she swamps, pile out and scramble for the beach. Keep cool now, and don't jump until she swamps sure."

The oiler took the oars. Over his shoulders he scanned the surf. "Captain," he said, "I think I'd better bring her about and keep her head-on to the seas and back her in."

"All right, Billie," said the captain. "Back her in." The oiler swung the boat then, and, seated in the stern, the cook and the correspondent were obliged to look over their shoulders to contemplate the lonely and indifferent shore.

The monstrous inshore rollers heaved the boat high until the men were again enabled to see the white sheets of water scudding up the slanted beach. "We won't get in very close," said the captain. Each time a man could wrest his attention from the rollers, he turned his glance toward the shore, and in the expression of the eyes during this contemplation there was a singular quality. The correspondent, observing the others, knew that they were not afraid, but the full meaning of their glances was shrouded.

As for himself, he was too tired to grapple fundamentally with the fact. He tried to coerce his mind into thinking of it, but the mind was dominated at this time by the muscles, and the muscles said they did not care. It merely occurred to him that if he should drown it would be a shame.

There were no hurried words, no pallor, no plain agitation. The men simply looked at the shore. "Now, remember to get well clear of the boat when you jump," said the captain.

Seaward the crest of a roller suddenly fell with a thunderous crash, and the long white comber came roaring down the boat.

"Steady now," said the captain. The men were silent. They turned their eyes from the shore to the comber and waited. The boat slid up the incline, leaped at the furious top, bounced over it, and swung down the long back of the wave. Some water had been shipped, and the cook bailed it out.

But the next crest crashed also. The tumbling, boiling flood of white water caught the boat and whirled it almost perpendicular. Water swarmed in from all sides. The correspondent had his hands on the gunwale at this time, and when the water entered at that place he swiftly withdrew his fingers, as if he objected to wetting them.

The little boat, drunken with this weight of water, reeled and snuggled deeper into the sea.

"Bail her out, cook! Bail her out!" said the captain.

"All right, Captain," said the cook.

"Now, boys, the next one will do for us sure," said the oiler. "Mind to jump clear of the boat."

The third wave moved forward, huge, furious, implacable. It fairly swallowed the dinghy, and almost simultaneously the men tumbled into the sea. A piece of life-belt had lain in the bottom of the boat, and as the correspondent went overboard he held this to his chest with his left hand.

The January water was icy, and he reflected immediately that it was colder than he had expected to find it off the coast of Florida. This appeared to his dazed mind as a fact important enough to be noted at the time. The coldness of the water was sad; it was tragic. This fact was somehow mixed and confused with his opinion of his own situation, so that it seemed almost a proper reason for tears. The water was cold.

When he came to the surface he was conscious of little but the noisy water. Afterward he saw his companions in the sea. The oiler was ahead in the race. He was swimming strongly and rapidly. Off to the correspondent's left, the cook's great white and corked back bulged out of the water; and in the rear the captain was hanging with his one good hand to the keel of the overturned dinghy.

There is a certain immovable quality to a shore, and the correspondent wondered at it amid the confusion of the sea.

It seemed also very attractive; but the correspondent knew that it was a long journey, and he paddled leisurely. The piece of life-preserver lay under him, and sometimes he whirled down the incline of a wave as if he were on a hand-sled.

But finally he arrived at a place in the sea where travel was beset with difficulty. He did not pause swimming to inquire what manner of current had caught him, but there his progress ceased. The shore was set before him like a bit of scenery on a stage, and he looked at it and understood with his eyes each detail of it.

As the cook passed, much farther to the left, the captain was calling to him, "Turn over on your back, cook! Turn over on your back and use the oar."

"All right, sir." The cook turned on his back, and, paddling with an oar, went ahead as if he were a canoe.

Presently the boat also passed to the left of the correspondent, with the captain clinging with one hand to the keel. He would have appeared like a man raising himself to look over a board fence if it were not for the extraordinary gymnastics of the boat. The correspondent marvelled that the captain could still hold to it.

They passed on nearer to shore—the oiler, the cook, the captain—and following them went the water-jar, bouncing gaily over the seas.

The correspondent remained in the grip of this strange new enemy—a current. The shore, with its white slope of sand and its green bluff topped with little silent cottages, was spread like a picture before him. It was very near to him then, but he was impressed as one who, in a gallery, looks at a scene from Brittany or Algiers.

He thought: "I am going to drown? Can it be possible? Can it be possible? Can it be possible?" Perhaps an individual must consider his own death to be the final phenomenon of nature.

But later a wave perhaps whirled him out of this small deadly current, for he found suddenly that he could again make progress toward the shore. Later still he was aware that the captain, clinging with one hand to the keel of the dinghy, has his face turned away from the shore and toward him, and was calling his name. "Come to the boat! Come to the boat!"

In his struggle to reach the captain and the boat, he reflected that when one gets properly wearied drowning must really be a comfortable arrangement—a cessation of hostilities accompanied by a large degree of relief; and he was glad of it, for the main thing in his mind for some moments had been horror of the temporary agony. He did not wish to be hurt.

Presently he saw a man running along the shore. He was undressing with most remarkable speed. Coat, trousers, shirt, everything flew magically off him.

"Come to the boat!" called the captain.

"All right, Captain," As the correspondent paddled, he saw the captain let himself down to bottom and leave the boat. Then the correspondent performed his one little marvel of the voyage. A large wave caught him and flung him with ease and supreme speed completely over the boat and far beyond it. It struck him even then as an event in gymnastics and a true miracle of the sea. An overturned boat in the surf is not a plaything to a swimming man.

The correspondent arrived in water that reached only to his waist, but his condition did not enable him to stand for more than a moment. Each wave knocked him into a heap, and the undertow pulled at him.

Then he saw the man who had been running and undressing, and undressing and running, come bounding into the water. He dragged ashore the cook, and then waded toward the captain; but the captain waved him away and sent him to the correspondent. He was naked— naked as a tree in winter; but a halo was about his head, and he shone like a saint. He gave a strong pull, and a long drag, and a bully heave at the correspondent's hand. The correspondent, schooled in the minor formulæ, said, "Thanks, old man." But suddenly the man cried, "What's that?" He pointed a swift finger. The correspondent said, "Go."

In the shallows, face downward, lay the oiler. His forehead touched sand that was periodically, between each wave, clear of the sea.

The correspondent did not know all that transpired afterward. When he achieved safe ground he fell, striking the sand with each particular part of his body. It was as if he had dropped from a roof, but the thud was grateful to him.

It seems that instantly the beach was populated with men with blankets, clothes, and flasks, and women with coffee-pots and all the remedies sacred to their minds. The welcome of the land to the men from the sea was warm and generous; but a still and dripping shape was carried slowly up the beach, and the land's welcome for it could only be the different and sinister hospitality of the grave.

When it came night, the white waves paced to and fro in the moonlight, and the wind brought the sound of the great sea's voice to the men on the shore, and they felt that they could then be interpreters.

THE ESSENTIALS OF LIFE:
"THE OPEN BOAT"
AS EXISTENTIALIST FICTION

Peter Buitenhuis

Stephen Crane's "The Open Boat" is not a naturalistic story, although it has often been labelled as such.[1] The protagonist, in the interpretation of his own experience in the boat, transcends the limits of naturalistic philosophy and makes the kind of affirmation that has become familiar to us from the work of Albert Camus and other existentialist writers. No story of Crane more profoundly embodies within its structure, style, and symbolism the meaning of experience. Several critics have examined these techniques, but they have done so without fully relating them to the story's meaning.[2] It is the intention of this essay to show how Crane brings his protagonist to the realization of the absurdity of the experience and thence to his realization of the human condition.

A good deal of the criticism of "The Open Boat" has gone astray in assuming that the story is more autobiographical than fictional.[3]

[1] A good example is Richard P. Adams's study "Naturalistic Fiction: 'The Open Boat,'" *Tulane Studies in English*, IV (1954), 137–46. He concludes that the story, although it combines contradictory elements into a "synthesis of great power and beauty," exposes the "weakness of naturalism as a philosophy and a way of life."

[2] The most thorough studies are by John Berryman in *Stephen Crane*, American Men of Letters Series (New York 1950), pp. 277–93; R. W. Stallman in the introduction to his edition *Stephen Crane: Stories and Tales* (New York, Vintage Books, 1955), pp. xv–xxxii, and notes to the story, pp. 209–14; and Stanley B. Greenfield, "The Unmistakable Stephen Crane," *PMLA*, LXXIII (Dec. 1958), 562–72. Berryman's work is the starting point for most recent discussions of Crane, while Stallman has made the first intensive study of the text. Greenfield, in his recent article, criticized Stallman for "distortions" in his reading. He commented on the "richness" of the story, but ignored some of its elements. I believe also that he has overemphasized the role of fate in "The Open Boat."

[3] A recent example of the biographical interpretation is Cyrus Day's "Stephen Crane and the Ten-foot Dinghy," *Boston University Studies in English*, III (Winter, 1957), 193–213. Mr. Day has discovered a number of facts about the actual sinking and the actual dinghy voyage from contemporary records. He points out the discrepancy between the facts and the voyage in the dinghy as

THE ESSENTIALS OF LIFE: "THE OPEN BOAT" AS EXISTENTIALIST FICTION: *Modern Fiction Studies* © 1959 by Purdue Foundation, Lafayette, Indiana.

It was certainly based on immediate personal experience, but even the subtitle confessing as much—"A Tale intended to be after the Fact"—is ambiguous. The whole account of the ill-fated filibustering expedition, of which the escape in the dinghy is only a part, was told by Crane in a newspaper story for the *New York Press*. This has been reprinted by R. W. Stallman in his Vintage edition of Crane's work. Almost all of the newspaper account is taken up with the departure, voyage, and sinking of the ship. But it seems that Crane is deliberately saving up the dinghy episode for artistic treatment when he writes near the end of the account: "The history of life in an open boat for thirty hours would no doubt be instructive for the young, but none is to be told here and now." [4] He must have seen at once that the episode, though only inferior material for journalism, would provide him with an excellent situation for the development of his favorite fictional theme.

"The Open Boat," like *The Red Badge of Courage*, is the story of an initiation. Unlike Henry Fleming, however, the correspondent, the protagonist of "The Open Boat," is no stripling. He is represented as an experienced, cynical, somewhat dogmatic individual. His initiation is not into manhood, as is Fleming's, but into a new attitude towards nature and his fellow-men. Crane's remark that the story would be instructive for the young betrays a didactic intention that he did not entirely overcome. His considerable success in doing so is the result of the way in which he portrays the attitudes which the protagonist takes towards the experience and towards himself.

These are attitudes which occur frequently in Crane's work. John Berryman first pointed them out in his book on Crane in the American Men of Letters Series. He noted that Crane often combines the traits found in the traditional opponents in classic Greek comedy, *Alazon*, the impostor, and *Eiron*, the ironical man, into one character. The impostor, trying to be more than he is, is invariably routed by the ironical man, who affects to be a fool. "As comedy," Berryman writes, "his work is a continual examination of pretension—an attempt to cast overboard, as it were, impediments to our salvation." Under the stress which always appears in Crane's fiction, the impostor side of the character is constantly being unmasked by the ironical side. "A Crane creation, or character," Berryman states, "normally

---

portrayed in "The Open Boat," and concludes on this basis that the story "as a work of fiction must be reappraised." The essay only makes plain, however, that the story is even less "factual" than has been previously thought. Mr. Day does, on the other hand, usefully point out some howlers in Crane's seamanship.

[4] Stallman, p. 265.

is *pretentious* and *scared*—the human condition; fitted by the second for pathos, by the first for irony." [5]

This statement exactly describes the situation of the correspondent in "The Open Boat." Moreover it gives a clue to the central conception of the story, a conception responsible for its peculiar effectiveness. The correspondent's conflicting attitudes are part of a whole series of conflicts and paradoxes that are reflected in the story's rhetoric and symbolism and provide it with its structure.

From the outset it is obvious that the correspondent and his three companions are at the mercy of nature, which appears savagely hostile to them. Their helplessness is captured by the correspondent's image of his companions as "babes of the sea—a grotesque rendering of the old babes in the wood." The tiny dinghy can be swamped at any moment by the "barbarously abrupt and tall" waves. On the other hand, they are, even at the beginning of the journey, only a few miles off-shore. This is to be no heroic odyssey of endurance. We know soon enough that they have a good chance of getting safely to shore in a relatively short time.

The structure of the story depends on the fluctuating moods of pretension (optimism, assurance) and fear (pessimism, despair) that the correspondent, the cook, and the oiler feel in the course of the journey. The captain, after an initial plunge into apathy, soon demonstrates a stoic serenity that acts as a silent commentary on the emotions of the others. Early in the story, as the men debate their chances of survival, his chuckle breaks through their talk. It comprehends the whole of the experience, expressing "humour, contempt, tragedy, all in one." He is the still center of the story's conflicts. By exploring the fluctuating moods of the others, Crane not only gives form to the story, he is also able to suggest the slow drag of time.

The story is divided into seven parts. The first sets the scene, stresses the selfish concerns of each of the four characters, and briefly defines their individual natures. At the end of the first part there is a conversation (strikingly similar in style to Hemingway's dialogue) in which the cook shows his facile optimism, the correspondent his cynical assurance, and the oiler his common sense. The captain remains silent.

> The cook had said: "There's a house of refuge just north of the Mosquito Inlet Light, and as soon as they see us they'll come off in their boat and pick us up."
> "As soon as who sees us?" said the correspondent.
> "The crew," said the cook.

[5] Berryman, pp. 278–80.

"Houses of refuge don't have crews," said the correspondent. "As I understand them they are only places where clothes and grub are stored for the benefit of shipwrecked people. They don't carry crews."

"Oh, yes, they do," said the cook.

"No, they don't," said the correspondent.

"Well, we're not there yet, anyhow," said the oiler, in the stern.

In the following four parts the men's moods fluctuate between the cheerfulness they feel on sighting the lighthouse to their despair on finding out that they cannot get through the surf to land before night falls. In the fifth and sixth they are shown to go beyond pretension and fear as they work and sleep their way stolidly through the night. The seventh part opens with the splendor of dawn and ends with three of them swimming ashore and the fourth drowning.

To accord with this framework of shifting moods, Crane used several contrasting strands of rhetoric in the story. A good deal of the narrative, like the dialogue, is written in a realistically colloquial, casual, and straightforward style. Other parts are written in a brilliantly "poetic" and rhythmic manner. Still other parts are written so awkwardly and flabbily as to seem like parody; for example, "In a ten-foot dinghy one can get an idea of the resources of the sea in the line of waves that is not probable to the average experience which is never at sea in a dinghy." It could be said that these and similar shoddy sentences merely show Crane's carelessness. Yet this explanation seems inadequate after taking account of the craftsmanship lavished on the story as a whole. Could it be that Crane is deliberately using a kind of immature "adventure-yarn" style in order to parody the pretentiousness of his own story and also the *genre* in which it appears to fall? Even if parody is not intended, such flat prose stands in vivid contrast to the "inspired audacity of epithet," to use Conrad's phrase,[6] of, for example, "the terrible grace in the move of the waves," "the ominous slash of the wind," and "the *whirroo* of a dark fin." Too much of this audacity would cloy. By using prosy idioms, Crane punctures the pretension that the poetic idiom tends to inflate.

The shifting strains of rhetoric reflect the different attitudes that are taken towards the experience. Unfortunately, instead of confining these attitudes to a single character, the protagonist, Crane shifts at times to the points of view of the oiler, the cook, and the captain as well. He was probably trying to emphasize through this device that the experience was deeply shared by the four men, a

[6] Introduction by Joseph Conrad to Thomas Beer's *Stephen Crane* (New York, 1924), p. 13.

point essential to the story's conclusion. However, in attributing to the four not only similar emotions but also similar formulations about the nature of existence, he presumes too much on the reader's willing suspension of disbelief. Crane also unnecessarily seeks to make his point by using the omniscient point of view. Near the beginning of the story, for example, he writes: "Viewed from a balcony, the whole thing would doubtless have been weirdly picturesque. But the men in the boat had no time to see it, and if they had had leisure, there were other things to occupy their minds."

Seen from a balcony, the four men obviously represent a microcosm of life on a waste of waters. The destructive power of the sea is not only continuously insisted upon but also symbolized from the beginning in various ways: by the "somehow gruesome and ominous" seagull that follows them and by the shark that cuts the water around them like a "projectile." At the same time, symbolic images remind the men that they are making their way towards their native element. They pass floating "brown mats of seaweed," which appear to be like "islands, bits of earth." In an ironic domestic simile, Crane compares the seaweed patches to "carpets on a line in a gale." The men can tell from the receding seaweed that they are moving landwards. A little later this progress is made more obvious as they sight a lighthouse on the shore which grows steadily larger.

Their only solid link with the land is the dinghy. This is appropriately compared at first to a "bathtub," then to a "bucking broncho" which rises to the waves "like a horse making at a fence outrageously high." This absurd use of the pathetic fallacy is justified here, for the gallant boat is emotionally identified with life itself. The sea is animistically pictured as the boat's natural enemy, "the mountain cat." It "growls," it "snarls," it "rages" and "rushes" at the boat, finally catching it near the shore and whirling it almost perpendicular before swamping it.

From the outset the attention of the men is riveted on the colors of the threatening sea, which are grey and white. Grey is the sign of desolation and despair, and is often reflected on their faces. White is used to signify the destructive power of the sea. Like hell itself, it seems capable of torment by both fire and ice. Water swarms "like white flames" into the boat. At the same time it feels icy and looks like "tumbling snow." This comparison is comically transformed, however, near the end of the story. As the correspondent is swimming to the shore hanging on to a piece of life-preserver, he sometimes whirls "down the incline of a wave as if he were on a handsled." Black and red are also used as omens of disaster to the men.

Yet their hopes are sustained during the night by someone lighting a watchfire on the beach. It makes a "roseate reflection" against the black. At dawn "carmine and gold" is painted on the waters, and sunlight flames "on the tips of the waves."

This is conventional color symbolism. Yet the quality of the experience is insisted on by the ambiguity of the colors. Land itself, when first sighted, is nothing but "a long black shadow on the sea." Later on, when it appears more distinct, it is "a line of black and a line of white—trees and sand." The land is not only the element of safety but also the dangerous ledge on which the white waves break. As the correspondent swims in the water, the white slope of the shore and its "green bluff topped with little silent cottages" mocks him by its indifferent proximity. The sea, destructive as it is, at one time beckons the correspondent like "a great soft mattress," and when he sleeps in the water at the bottom of the boat he finds it not only cold but also comfortable. The land, even though it finally generously welcomes the men, also extends to the oiler "the different and sinister hospitality of the grave."

The irony of the situation is emphasized by numerous incidents. The hopes of the men in the boat are mocked by their discovery that those whom they see on shore seem to think that they are out on a fishing trip. A hotel omnibus—first thought to be a lifeboat on wheels —comes down full of holiday-makers to see the endangered men as if to an excursion. Even the situation in the boat itself has its comic elements. Although the task of rowing seems like "diabolic punishment," the corerspondent gets a smile from the others when he tells them how the amusement of rowing strikes him. When, exhausted, the oarsman drops down to rest after his trick at the oars, his teeth "play all the popular airs." The cook "dreamfully" asks his hungry companions what kind of pie they would like.

The greatest irony of the story is seen when the men approach the shore only to discover that the dinghy would be swamped if they proceeded through the surf. The decide to remain off-shore all night. Crane formulates the thoughts of the men into a kind of choral lament which is repeated three times in the story: "If I am going to be drowned—if I am going to be drowned—if I am going to be drowned, why, in the name of the seven mad gods who rule the sea, was I allowed to come thus far and contemplate sand and trees?" The correspondent wonders if he has been brought here merely to have his nose dragged away as he is about to "nibble the sacred cheese of life." "If this old ninny-woman, Fate, cannot do better than this," he thinks, "she should be deprived of the management of men's fortunes. . . . If she has decided to drown me, why did she not do it in the beginning and save me all this trouble? The whole affair is absurd." Facing a universe that plays such unjust and incomprehensible tricks on the individual, he rebels, like one of Camus' heroes.[7]

The absurdity of the situation returns again and again to the correspondent's mind throughout the long night. He contemplates the probability that nature, regarding him as a creature of no importance, is about to do away with him. He feels a desire to throw bricks at the temple, but since there are no bricks and no temple, he then feels a desire to confront a personification as a supplicant and at least proclaim the reality of his own existence by saying, "Yes, but I love myself."

Then a few lines of verse mysteriously enter his head:

A soldier of the Legion lay dying in Algiers;
There was lack of woman's nursing, there was dearth of woman's tears;
But a comrade stood beside him, and he took that comrade's hand,
And he said, "I never more shall see my own, my native land."

These lines, discreetly edited, are from a sentimental poem called "Bingen," written by the Victorian poetess Caroline, Lady Norton.[8] For the first time the correspondent appreciates the "actuality" of the poem, originally learnt in childhood. He is moved by a profound and impersonal comprehension. The plight of the soldier, he sees, is his own too. In a sympathy which, however, is expressed in the form of a parody, "he was sorry for the soldier of the Legion who lay dying in Algiers."

As dawn breaks, the men see a white windmill on the shore. To the correspondent it is a symbol of nature, but of nature which is neither cruel nor beneficent, merely "indifferent." Paradoxically, instead of giving in to a similar indifference and yielding to fatalism, the cor-

[7] Both the Introduction and Part One of Albert Camus' *The Rebel* (New York, Vintage Books, 1958) are remarkably germane to the intellectual processes of the correspondent in this part of the story.

[8] The first stanza of the poem runs as follows:

A soldier of the Legion lay dying in Algiers,
There was lack of woman's nursing, there was dearth of woman's tears;
But a comrade stood beside him, while his life-blood ebb'd away,
And bent, with pitying glances, to hear what he might say.
The dying soldier falter'd, as he took that comrade's hand,
And he said, "I never more shall see my own, my native land;
Take a message, and a token, to some distant friends of mine,
For I was born at Bingen,—at Bingen on the Rhine."

From *The Undying One & Other Poems* (New York, 1854), p. 226.

respondent makes the affirmation of the absurd man.[9] He recalls the innumerable flaws in his own life and wishes for another chance. The distinction between right and wrong "seems absurdly clear to him . . . in this new ignorance of the grave-edge." Now he sees the futility of self-love alone, since in order to get ashore he is dependent upon the assistance of his companions, as they are dependent on him. Having recognized his responsibility to them, he once more wishes for another opportunity "to mend his conduct and his words. . . ." To avoid sounding too pretentious, however, he characteristically concludes the sentence "and be better and brighter during an introduction or at a tea."

Immediately after this, the boat enters the surf. The correspondent knows that his companions are not afraid, although the full meaning of their glances is shrouded. The comradeship that has been established during the voyage is now to meet the final test. Four individuals have fully realized the meaning of what Crane earlier in the story called "the subtle brotherhood of men."

The boat fills up; the men jump and attempt to struggle ashore. With mutual assistance and the aid of a man who strips and dashes into the water shining "like a saint" three of them land. By an unlucky chance, the oiler, whose quiet competence has been insisted on throughout the tale, dies. As the night wind brings the voice of the great sea to the survivors, "they felt that they could then be interpreters." Their hardships, the arbitrary death of the oiler, and their success in getting ashore through united effort have initiated them into the ways of nature and the plight of men; and now they feel they know something that can be of value to other men.

The story itself is the interpretation of the experience to the reader. Crane has taken pains to make it not only particular but also universal in its application. At the beginning of the tale, for example, as the captain lies injured in the bow, he is "buried in that profound dejection and indifference which comes, temporarily at least, to even the bravest and most enduring when, willy-nilly, the firm fails, the army loses, the ship goes down." In the course of the journey, however, he rapidly regains his perspective and serenely sustains his role as captain of his three-man crew.

[9] Camus writes: "At that subtle moment when man glances backward over his life, Sisyphus returning toward his rock, in that slight pivoting he contemplates that series of unrelated actions which becomes his fate, created by him, combined under his memory's eye and soon sealed by his death. Thus, convinced of the wholly human origin of all that is human, a blind man eager to see, who knows that the night has no end, he is still on the go. . . . This universe henceforth without a master seems to him neither sterile nor futile" (*The Myth of Sisyphus and Other Essays* [New York, Vintage Books, 1959], p. 91).

Similarly the correspondent, by enduring this experience, which is the most bitter but at the same time "the best experience of his life," as comic as it is tragic, comes face to face with the absurd nature of existence. When he concludes that nature is not hostile but merely indifferent, he is ready to realize existentially the responsibilities of being a man. Conrad was right when he said that the story "by the deep and simple humanity of presentation seems somehow to illustrate the essentials of life itself, like a symbolic tale." [10] The correspondent's ultimate recognition is that "in the ignorance of the grave-edge" every man is in the same boat, which is not much more substantial than a ten-foot open dinghy on a rough sea.

[10] Beer, p. 13.

STYLE AND MEANING IN STEPHEN CRANE: "THE OPEN BOAT"

James B. Colvert

As a stylist, Stephen Crane puzzled some of his contemporaries. One critic, reviewing *The Red Badge of Courage* in 1900, identified him as one of the worst offenders of a new school of writers who, "in their effort to be vivid and striking, have allowed themselves to be carried away into extremes. The straining after effect and the extravagant use of onomatopoeticism here become so evident as to be uncouth." [1]

Another reviewer, writing in the *Literary Digest*, offered a parody:

> Nothing is easier. The method is simple. It presents no difficulties. It is distinct. It appeals to many. It is new. Therefore it pleases. For a time. But not permanently. Men of intelligence yawn. The trick is too readily seen through. It is like an infant's reader: My cat is called Tom. Do you like cats? No, I like dogs. I like both cats and dogs.[2]

Critics of a later generation were not so much concerned with Crane's eccentricities of style. One reason, perhaps, is that readers in

[1] *The Literary Digest*, XX (Feb. 10, 1900), 182.
[2] Jane H. Findlater, "The New Art of Description in Fiction," *The National Review* (Jan., 1900); quoted in *The Literary Digest*, XX (Feb. 10, 1900), 182.

STYLE AND MEANING IN STEPHEN CRANE: "THE OPEN BOAT" By James B. Colvert, from *Texas Studies in English*, XXXVII (1958), 34–45. Reprinted by permission of *Texas Studies in English* and the author.

the 'twenties, accustomed to the experiments of the imagists and symbolists, no longer expected writing to adhere to the prose norm of the 1890's, a compromise between the nineteenth-century grand style and the plain style of the literary realists. A more important reason is that academic criticism by this time had already firmly attached to Crane's writing a literary label which encouraged the critic to ignore, largely, the question of style. He was a Naturalist. And since the Naturalist—particulary one of the school of Zola, to which Crane was assumed to belong—is theoretically indifferent to style, critics generally gave their attention to the ethical implications of his "mechanistic" world view, reading in his work a vision of man as a helpless and driven animal at the mercy of all-powerful forces about him. Beyond a few observations about his extraordinary color imagery and his predilection for ironic understatement, critics, especially the academic critics, seldom pursued the question of his language.

Robert Spiller's account of "The Open Boat" in *The Literary History of the United States* excellently summarizes the established attitude. To Spiller, Crane's "masterpiece" is a "simple record of the actual wreck of a filibustering vessel off the coast of Florida," an account which "achieves its effect by understatement." The significant meaning, the meaning which strikes deepest into Crane's world view, Spiller says, is expressed in the revelation that nature is indifferent to man. "This," he remarks, "is [to Crane] the meaning of life, in so far as it has a meaning." [3]

The doctrine of Naturalism is, of course, supremely rational and consequently invites the test of logical coherence and consistency. The important question which the Naturalistic story raises is whether the fictional statement squares in all its implications with the demands of the doctrine it is supposed to exemplify. Charles Walcutt, who applies this test to Crane, finds this consistency to be the chief proof of his excellence:

> The meaning is always the action; there is no wandering into theory that runs counter to what happens in the action; and nowhere does a character operate as a genuinely free ethical agent in defiance of the author's intentions. Crane's success is a triumph of style: manner and meaning are one. [4]

[3] Robert E. Spiller, "Toward Naturalism in Fiction," in *The Literary History of the United States*, ed. Spiller, Canby, Thorp, *et al.* (New York, 1948), p. 1024.
[4] Charles C. Walcutt, *American Literary Naturalism, A Divided Stream* (University of Minnesota Press, 1956), p. 67.

If the reader is able to ignore the intrusion of "extraneous elements," Walcutt's phrase for certain stylistic features presumably outside the requirements of a pure Naturalistic fiction, then this seems to be a just appraisal of Crane's art. But another critic, reading Crane as a Naturalist and giving close attention to details of style, disagrees. Examining the images and metaphors of "The Open Boat," John W. Schroeder finds that they introduce non-logical elements which tend to contradict the logic of the Naturalistic attitude which he assumes to underlie the story:

> Logically, a vision of Nature's indifference should cancel out the equally powerful vision of Nature as somehow possessed by forces deadly to man. It seems somewhat curious that the same work which contains this clear and definite statement of indifference should also speak of the "wrath" of the ocean, which "growls" at least three times and whose waves rage "like a mountain cat." It is curious, too, that the prospect of drowning in this viciously animated sea should be styled "a cessation of hostilities." [5]

The "logical force" of Crane's reaction to nature as both *hostile* and *indifferent*, Schroeder thinks, "is slight," though he admits that "its poetic force is extreme." But the critic's concern is not with poetic force but with logical contradictions. Committed to his understanding of Crane as a Naturalist, he seems to conclude that "clear and definite statements" of this view should not be confused by contradictions implicit in metaphor and imagery.

The fact that these critics have written on Crane in very recent years suggests how persistent these traditional assumptions about his method and themes really are. Not until after 1950, when a revival of interest in Crane began to place him in a new critical light, was the standard approach to his writing challenged. Robert W. Stallman, who has been largely responsible for this revival, has shifted the focus of attention away from Crane's Naturalism to his style, which this critic finds not at all extraneous to Crane's art, but on the contrary the most significant aspect of it. "A great stylist," Stallman writes, "Crane puts language to poetic uses, which is to use it reflexively and symbolically. *The works that employ this reflexive and symbolic language constitute what is permanent of Crane.*" [6] Applying the techniques of formal analysis, Stallman discovers Crane's fiction to be mythic, ritualistic, symbolical, and allegorical:

[5] John W. Schroeder, "Stephen Crane Embattled," *University of Kansas City Review*, XVII (Winter, 1950), 127.

[6] Robert W. Stallman, "Introduction," *Stephen Crane: An Omnibus* (New York, Knopf, 1952; London, Heinemann, 1954), p. xlv.

Crane's language is the language of symbol and paradox: the wafer-like sun in *The Red Badge*; or in *The Open Boat* the paradox of "cold, comfortable sea-water," an image that calls to mind the poetry of Yeats, with its fusion of contradictory emotions. This single image evokes the sensation of the whole experience of the men in the dinghy.[7]

To Stallman, clearly, Crane's stories are for the consideration of practical criticism, long prose-poems; in those very elements which the "Naturalist" critics ignore or find so unaccountable, he discovers new dimensions of meaning.

Stallman's reading has been vigorously disputed by Philip Rahv, who finds it, like so much recent criticism of fiction, vitiated by a "wholesale disgorgement of shibboleths lifted from contemporary poetry criticism" with all its biases toward symbolism, allegory, paradox, and irony.[8] Protesting against a critical system derived from a widespread "superstition of the word," Rahv argues that "a novel and a lyric poem are not to be equated as works of verbal art because the relation in them between theme and composition is quite different." [9] Normally, he says,

> . . . the language of the novel does not possess the autonomous value that it has in poetry. It only intermittently lends itself to that verbal play characteristic of poetic speech, a play which uncovers the phonic texture of the word while at the same time releasing its semantic potential.[10]

And though he grants that "there is such a thing . . . as a purely formal prose, in which the elements of style and composition dominate . . ." he seems to regard this kind of "art-prose" as decadent and somewhat outside the healthy norm of fiction as a genre distinct from poetry. He condemns Stallman's approach to Crane on the grounds that it falsely identifies "style as the essential activity of imaginative prose . . . and confuses the intensive speech proper to poetry with the more openly communicative, functional, and extensive language proper to prose." [11]

I am not concerned here with the significance of this argument for the theory of style in fiction. But it does seem to be a timely warning for the practical critic, for certainly, as Rahv says, we need to

[7] *Ibid.*
[8] Philip Rahv, "Fiction and the Criticism of Fiction," *The Kenyon Review,* XVIII (Spring, 1956), 282.
[9] *Ibid.*, 291–292.
[10] *Ibid.*, 293
[11] *Ibid.*, 280.

make clearer distinctions between the forms of the poem and of the story—even, I would add, of the symbolist story, to which the concepts of modern poetry criticism would seem most applicable. Stallman's failure to make this distinction sometimes leads him, I think, into error. His reading of *The Red Badge*, for example, as a Christian allegory insists that the symbols and images in the novel function in the same way that they seem to function in the more highly organized language of poetry; clearly, as Stallman says, there is crucifixion imagery in the famous passage describing Jim Conklin's death, but to say also that "the key to the symbolism of the whole [novel is] the religious symbolism that radiates outwards from Jim Conklin" is to press for an allegorical meaning which the structure of the novel cannot express. What bearing does the religious symbolism associated with Conklin's death have upon the subsequent moral development of Henry Fleming? So far as we are told, Conklin entres Henry's thoughts only once more, when the youth, rejoining his regiment, suddenly remembers and relates almost casually the news of Conklin's death (Chapter Fourteen). And in the end, when Henry takes stock of his experience and comes to some conclusions about the meaning of all the events of his life as a soldier, it is not the image of Conklin's death, but the image of the deserted tattered man which occupies the central place in his thoughts.

Still, Stallman's approach to Crane is much more meaningful than the one suggested by Rahv, who insists that the language of fiction is properly nothing more than a "kind of transparent envelope or medium through which we watch the action." This, it seems to me, is doubtful. Action in fiction exists only in the language, not apart from it; if the language is changed the character and meaning of the action is changed. For it would appear that language in even the most "objective" fictional style embodies attitudes and value judgments which must be dealt with as elements in the structure of the story. Rahv's point of view seems to favor, as his remarks about Dostoevsky's style indicate, the notion that an "objective realism" in writing is a possible and desirable aesthetic.

> . . . we are able to recognize Dostoevsky's greatness as a novelist at the same time that we are not in the least impressed by his stylistic powers. He is in fact a most indifferent stylist, but that hardly bothers us in reading him, for once we are caught up by the moving current of mock-reality in his narratives we cease noticing the words as such. . . .[12]

It is just this bias, as I have tried to show, which underlies the attitudes of Cranes contemporaries, which vitiated Crane criticism for

[12] *Ibid.*, 295.

over fifty years and which still stands behind the kind of assertions made in Gordon Haight's recent comparison of Crane's "decadent impressionism" to De Forest's "true realism":

> Everything that Crane sees looks like something else; De Forest describes things are they are. He never sees a wood as a chapel, boughs as a door, and pine needles as a carpet, nor do his corpses remind one of the exhibits in Madame Taussaud's chamber of horrors. Crane's hero sees tents spring up "like strange plants. Camp fires, like red, peculiar blossoms, dotted the night." To De Forest, who sees them from the inside, tents are canvas usually rotten enough to let the rain through, and campfires are lit for warmth. That is the difference between a somewhat decadent impressionism and true realism.[13]

But this is merely an objection to style predominantly metaphorical and indirect. What these images might mean, how they might be significantly relevant to Crane's aesthetic or to his world view are questions which the method altogether discourages. Rahv's plea for a reading of *The Red Badge* that will tell us that "the novel is actually 'about' what it seems to be, war and its impact on human beings moved by pride, bravado, fear, anxiety and sudden panic," seems implicitly to demand a similar approach.

But Crane cannot rightly be read in this way. His method, unlike that of the realists, is metaphorical, imagistic, and symbolic. The burden of meaning in his fiction is carried in large part by image, metaphor, recurring motifs, contrasts in tone and mood, and other suggestive devices—in other words, by style. Consider, for example, the stylistic indirection of the writing in the first chapter of "The Open Boat." The poetically heightened opening sentence ("None of them knew the color of the sky") sets the dramatic tone of the passage, suggests the condition of mental stress of the men in the boat, and establishes the point of view to be developed—the point of view of the men totally absorbed in the experience of the rushing waves. The diction and regularized rhythm of the second sentence ("Their eyes glanced level and were fastened upon the waves that swept toward them") sustains the poetic heightening (chiefly in the phrase "glanced level"), fixes more firmly the point of view, and enforces the image of the men's fearful concentration on the threatening sea. The comparatively irregular third sentence is nearer to the rhythmic norm of prose ("These waves were of the hue of slate, save for the tops, which were of foaming white"), but toward the end it is again regularized ("and all of the men knew the colors of the sea") into

---

[13] Gordon S. Haight, "Introduction," *Miss Ravenel's Conversion*, by J. W. De Forest (New York, 1955), p. xvi.

a rhetorical and rhythmical balance with the first sentence ("None of them knew the color of the sky"). Coming in the middle of the paragraph, this gives the paragraph something of the balance and design of a stanza of poetry, a subtle commitment carried out in the deliberate onomatopoeia of the last sentence, which imitates the movement of the waves in the first half and suggests in the buzzing, sibilant sounds and broken rhythms of the last part the cruel threat of the imagined rocks:

> The horizon narrowed and widened
> and dipped and rose,
> and at all times its edge was jagged with waves
> that seemed thrust up in points like rocks.

Obviously the language here is not so highly organized rhythmically as the more or less tightly metered language of poetry, but if this analysis is acceptable it should suggest that Crane's style is more consciously poetic than the prose "norm" which Rahv seems to have in mind. Crane does in this sense put language to poetic uses, and it would seem that the techniques of poetry analysis, used with discretion and with regard for the more expansive and more explicitly dramatic structure of his fiction, are valid and necessary if we are to grasp the full meaning and significance of his writing. And to get at his meaning—to search out not only the structure of his art but also the nature of the world view which it expresses—is to remove from his best writing the stigma of a naive and ingenuous philosophical naturalism and find in it, as Edward Garnett did years ago, something of the "perfect fusion of [the] forces of passion and irony [which] creates Crane's spiritual background and raises his work, at its finest, into the higher zone of man's tragic conflict with the universe." [14]

No reader could find this meaning in his work without taking style into account, for it is in style that this meaning exists in Crane's fiction. To read, for instance, the image of nature's wrath in "The Open Boat" into the author's world view is to fall into the error which leads Schroeder to conclude that contradictory visions of the sea as both hostile and indifferent are proof of Crane's confused "Naturalism." But it is important to understand that these different visions of nature are aspects of Crane's perception of irreconcilable contradictions in reality. To the men, whose vision is concentrated with such fierce intensity upon the rolling sea, an intensity suggested in their exquisite perception of the violent contrast between the slate-

[14] Edward Garnett, "Stephen Crane and His Work," in *Friday Nights* (New York, 1922), p. 213–214.

colored waves and their crests of boiling white and suggested further in their vivid sense of the shifting, swelling motion of the sea—to these men, then, the hostile appearance of the waves *is*, at this moment, their absolute reality. "As each slaty wall of water approached, it shut all else from the view of the men in the boat, and it was difficult to imagine that this particular wave was the final outburst of the ocean, the last effort of the grim water." But from the point of view of the narrator (and the reader), whose sense of the situation is not affected by an imprisoning wall of jagged waves, their reality might well be something else. "Viewed from a balcony," the narrator states later on, "the whole thing would, doubtless, have been weirdly picturesque. But the men in the boat had not time to see it. . . ."

This ironic contrast suggests a theme so central to Crane's consciousness that it can be taken as almost a definition of his world view, the vision of life governed by his profound sense of the consequences of our faulty perceptions of reality. The grand subject of his fiction is man's struggle to bring into some sort of meaningful order the confusions and contradictions of experience. His heroes, burdened with a perceptual machinery which renders them incapable of reconciling all the apparently disparate elements in their experience, stand uncertain and defenseless in a flux of imperfectly comprehended events. One of Crane's letters shows, I think, his sense of the meaning of this limitation of consciousness:

> I understand that a man is born into the world with his own pair of eyes, and he is not at all responsible for his quality of personal honesty. To keep close to this personal honesty is my supreme ambition.
> There is a sublime egotism in talking of honesty. I, however, do not say that I am honest. I merely say that I am as nearly honest as a weak mental machinery will allow. This aim in life struck me as being the only thing worth while. A man is sure to fail at it, but there is something in the failure.[15]

Crane's heroes rarely have such a clear insight into their own limitations for seeing the world clearly and truly. More often they are compelled to maintain in the their private worlds the images of themselves which their fallible consciousness demands. They must be the darlings of the gods, the central facts of creation, the aspiring masters of nature and themselves. Bound in darkness, they must be children of light—or what they think is light.

When we speak of Crane's ironical style we refer properly to the

[15] Stallman, *op. cit.*, p. 680.

general relation between this attitude and the verbal forms which express it, not merely to the fact that his writing is normally couched in the language of ironic understatement. "Irony," Kierkegaard observes, "is an existential determination and nothing is more ridiculous than to suppose that it consists in the use of a certain phraseology, or when an author congratulates himself upon succeeding in expressing himself ironically. Whoever has irony has it all day long, not bound to any specific form, because it is the infinite within him." [16]

But our question is how irony in this sense is expressed in the structure and style of Crane's writing, and for a characteristic example we may return to the opening section of "The Open Boat," where two apparently contradictory ideas about the reality of the sea are set up not only in direct, openly communicative statement, but also—and more significantly—in the images of space, color, and motion and in the rhythm, balance, and tone of the sentences. I have mentioned how the image of the waves as threatening, pointed rocks suggests to the men that nature is hostile and how the contrary idea is introduced in the narrator's statement that the scene, "viewed from a balcony," might be merely picturesque. But before the narrator intrudes to state it openly and discursively, the idea is evoked by stylistic indirection. The tone and direction of reference of the first sentence of the second paragraph ("Many a man ought to have a bathtub larger than the boat which here rode upon the sea") seems to express not so much an opinion of the narrator as a self-conscious protest from the sailors who, overwhelmed by the pathos of their situation, cry out against the injustice of their plight. Although there are ironic overtones in the conditional *ought* and in the the implicit contrast of the domestic bathtub with the nearly swamped boat, still the main expressive force of the sentence is nonironical because the cry can be taken as a just and accurate expression of the genuine pathos of their situation. But the ethical reproach expressed in the sentence which immediately follows ("These waves were most wrongfully and barbarously abrupt and tall") must be taken ironically: to a detached observer ocean waves are neither right nor wrong, barbarous nor civilized. Clearly another attitude is admissible; the sea is perhaps weirdly picturesque or, as the correspondent comes finally to believe, merely indifferent.

But only admissible, not necessarily true; nature is only *perhaps* indifferent or picturesque. The reservations are important, indeed, the

[16] Soren Kierkegaard, *Kierkegaard's Concluding Unscientific Postscript*, trans. by David Senson and Walter Lowrie (Princeton University Press, 1941), p. 449.

very essence of the ironic view; for the ironical man, though detached from the world of contradictions he perceives, does not pass final judgments upon them. "In fact," as Andrew Wright says,

> "the ironist is deeply concerned with both aspects of the contradictions he perceives; and this concern leads to an ambivalence of attitudes to one side and to the other—to both at once. Searching the orchards of human experience he finds the bittersweet apple of confusing appearance and ambiguous essence—and he becomes a man of the divided, the ironic, vision.
> This has led some to feel that "the basic feature of every irony is a contrast between a reality and an appearance." But the matter is not so simple: the ironist is not sure which is and which merely seems.[17]

The ambivalence of attitude of the true ironist bears greatly upon the structure and meaning of "The Open Boat," for in his handling of point of view and imagery, Crane always implicitly allows for errors of perception—his own as well as the men's. Though nature appears at different times in different guises, sometimes cruel, wrathful, deadly to man; sometimes wildly beautiful, picturesque; and sometimes merely indifferent—still none of these aspects, the detached narrator knows, necessarily excludes the others. The language always allows for perceptual error. To the men the waves only *"seemed* thrust up in points like rocks." Seen from a balcony the sea would *doubtless* have been picturesque. It was *probably* splendid, it was *probably* glorious. It merely *occurs* to a man that nature does not regard him as important, and the "high cold star" is the word the correspondent *feels* that nature says to him. Sometimes, as we have seen, the narrator seems to be *in* the boat, seeing and feeling as intensely as the men, sharing sympathetically their conclusions about the meaning of their plight; at other times he seems to be observing their situation from afar, seeing it then critically, dispassionately, or even mockingly.

Consider how the tension between these conflicting points of view is basic to the ironic effect of the argument between the cook and the correspondent about the difference between a life-saving station and a house of refuge. The cook's assertion that they will be rescued by the life-saving crew is like a proposition in a formal debate, challenged after a brief question and answer by the correspondent's formal counter-assertion. The futile impasse is moderated by the oiler's "Well, we're not there yet," and then the cook, unwilling to

[17] Andrew H. Wright, "Irony and Fiction," *The Journal of Aesthetics and Art Criticism*, XII (Sept., 1953), 113.

abandon his hopeful position, again asserts his conviction that they will finally be rescued by a crew from the shore. The passage ends with the skeptical oiler's repeated "We're not there yet." The formal design of this colloquy, with its balance and contrast of assertion and counter-assertion and the refrain-like interpolations of the oiler, gives to the men's speculations a tone of ironic presumption. The effect is powerfully reinforced when the narrator later states almost casually:"It is fair to say here that there was not a life-saving station within twenty miles in either direction; but the men did not know this fact, and in consequence they made dark and opprobrious remarks concerning the eyesight of the nation's life-savers."

Ironic tension is also sustained in the leitmotifs which refer to various contradictory aspects of nature. To the men, the sea gulls seem at one point to be allies of the hostile sea, for "the wrath of the sea was no more to them than it was to a covey of prairie chickens a thousand miles inland." Against the malice—if indeed it is malice—of the gull which attacks the captain's head, the men are almost helpless. The captain waves it "gently and carefully" away with the heavy painter just as the oiler gingerly and skillfully navigates the hostile sea with a "thin little oar . . . [which] seemed often ready to snap." When the gulls came close "and stared at the men with black beadlike eyes," they then seemed "uncanny and sinister" and "struck their minds at this time as being somehow gruesome and ominous." But only at this time, for later, when the birds are seen going in "slanting flight up the wind toward the gray desolate east," they seem less a symbol of an ineffable, perhaps demoniac malice, than a remote and beautiful design in nature.

The shark, the unnamable "thing" whose "enormous fin" cuts "like a shadow through the water" is to the corerspondent both admirable and horrifying. Subjectively, it is, like the gulls, a symbol of nature's inscrutable malice; still, in his despair and exhaustion, the correspondent can also see the shark objectively. It does not affect him with "the same horror that it would if he had been a picnicker," and at the same time that he looks dully into the sea and swears in an undertone, he can reflect that "the speed and power of the thing was to be greatly admired." But later the image of this terrible "thing" seems to the narrator to suggest indifference rather than hostility. "The thing which had followed the boat and waited had evidently grown bored at the delay. There was no longer to be heard the slash of the cutwater, and there was no longer the flame of the long trail."

In the end the correspondent to whom the "high cold star" and the wind-tower are the correlatives of nature's indifference, concludes that it is just this which is the significant reality of his experience:

> This tower was a giant, standing with its back to the plight of the ants. It represented in a degree, to the correspondent, the serenity of nature amid the struggles of the individual—nature in the wind, and nature in the vision of men. She did not seem cruel to him then, nor beneficent, nor treacherous, nor wise. But she was indifferent, flatly indifferent.

The passage is always read as an expression of not only the correspondent's conclusion, but of Crane's as well, as if at this point in the story the ironic contradictions are resolved in a final statement of the author's naturalistic world view. Daniel Hoffman, commenting on the meaning of the oiler's death, makes the point that the correspondent at the end of the story is still under Crane's ironic inspection, the evidence being according to Hoffman the fact that the correspondent sees not the oiler as the men's true sacrificial savior, but the "haloed and saintlike" vacationer who rushed into the surf to rescue the foundering men. The whole question of the theme of sacrificial death in Crane is, I think, debatable,[18] but Hoffman's feeling that Crane's irony extends beyond the correspondent's final conviction about the relation of man to nature is crucially significant. "The truth of the correspondent's interpretation," Mr. Hoffman says in reference to this failure of consciousness, "lies not in his last impressions but in the manner in which he recreates the entire experience in the readers imagination." [19]

The correspondent's passionate conviction that his experience has led him to the final truth, however deeply moving, is after all only a passionate conviction. The ironic overtones of other convictions, held at other times just as passionately, echo contradictions. It is suggestive that the story closes on an image of the sea as romantically and mysteriously beautiful:

> When it came night, the white waves paced to and fro in the moonlight, and the wind brought the sound of the great sea's voice to the men on shore, and they felt they could then be interpreters.

Who can say in what various ways the survivors interpret their experience or what one way could be understood to exclude the others? In the reverberating ironies of the last word, charged with the cumulative meanings evoked in the poetic indirections of Crane's style, the final meaning of the men's experience escapes at last into mystery.

---

[18] A heroic sacrifice would seem to involve a conscious choice on the part of the one who offers himself for immolation. The oiler's death, like Jim Conklin's in *The Red Badge*, is a matter not of choice but of fate.

[19] Daniel G. Hoffman, *The Poetry of Stephen Crane* (Columbia University Press, 1957), p. 278.

INDEX OF CRITICAL TOPICS

AUTHOR-TITLE INDEX

21-100

A 9
B 0
C 1
D 2
E 3
F 4
G 5
H 6
I 7
J 8